Chinese American Literature without Borders

King-Kok Cheung 張敬珏

Chinese American Literature without Borders

Gender, Genre, and Form

King-Kok Cheung
Department of English
University of California, Los Angeles
Los Angeles, California, USA

ISBN 978-1-349-68701-5   ISBN 978-1-137-44177-5 (eBook)
DOI 10.1057/978-1-137-44177-5

Library of Congress Control Number: 2016960011

© The Editor(s) (if applicable) and The Author(s) 2016
This work is subject to copyright. All rights are solely and exclusively licensed by the Publisher, whether the whole or part of the material is concerned, specifically the rights of translation, reprinting, reuse of illustrations, recitation, broadcasting, reproduction on microfilms or in any other physical way, and transmission or information storage and retrieval, electronic adaptation, computer software, or by similar or dissimilar methodology now known or hereafter developed.
The use of general descriptive names, registered names, trademarks, service marks, etc. in this publication does not imply, even in the absence of a specific statement, that such names are exempt from the relevant protective laws and regulations and therefore free for general use.
The publisher, the authors and the editors are safe to assume that the advice and information in this book are believed to be true and accurate at the date of publication. Neither the publisher nor the authors or the editors give a warranty, express or implied, with respect to the material contained herein or for any errors or omissions that may have been made. The publisher remains neutral with regard to jurisdictional claims in published maps and institutional affiliations.

Cover image © Richard Wong / Alamy Stock Photo
Cover design by Samantha Johnson

Printed on acid-free paper

This Palgrave Macmillan imprint is published by Springer Nature
The registered company is Nature America Inc
The registered company address is: 1 New York Plaza, New York, NY 10004, U.S.A.

FOR Gerard Maré AND Antony Cheung Maré 马念东

Acknowledgments

This book is made possible by individuals and opportunities on both sides of the Pacific.

The University of California, Los Angeles (UCLA) is a dreamland for any scholar engaged in Asian American literary studies. The English Department and the Asian American Studies Center have provided the most lasting support for my work. I want to thank David Schaberg, dean of Humanities; Lowell Gallagher, chair of the English Department; David Yoo, director of the Asian American Studies Center; and the late Don Nakanishi, former director of the Center, for their moral and material support. Ali Behdad, while chair of the English Department, promoted the research of his colleagues unstintingly; his question prompting the linkage of comparative literature and American studies opens this study, which also constitutes a modest answer. Students, colleagues, and students-turned-colleagues have sustained my excitement in the field through the decades. I have been buoyed by intellectual exchanges with Victor Bascara, Keith Camacho, Denise Cruz, Helen Deutsch, Cindy Fan, Khanh Ho, Tamara Ho, Grace Kyungwon Hong, Lynn Itagaki, Susan Koshy, Brenda Kwon, Joyce Lee, Kenneth Lincoln, Jinqi Ling, Purnima Mankekar, Valerie Matsumoto, Harryette Mullen, Michael Murashige, Christina Nagao, Brian Niiya, Thu-hong Nguyen-Vo, Michael North, Mark Seltzer, Jenny Sharpe, Shu-mei Shih, Erin Suzuki, Tooktook Thongthiraj, James Tong, Stan Yogi, and Min Zhou. Special thanks to Dominika Ferens, Robert Ji-Song Ku, James Kyung-Jin Lee, Julia H. Lee, Rachel C. Lee, and Margaret Rhee for their inspiration and for alerting me to the most recent scholarship.

Three colleagues—Richard Yarborough, Karen Rowe, and Valerie Smith—offered support and encouragement when I needed it most (at a time when others spelled doom at my plunge into an emerging field) and served as my role models as educators committed to ethnic studies and gender studies, in word and in deed. Thanks to Jeanette Gilkison, my lifeline to UCLA has remained untrammeled despite several forays abroad; her heartwarming electronic missives make me feel at home wherever I am.

My intellectual journey has been enriched by two years, as a Fulbright scholar and a Lingnan fellow, respectively, at Hong Kong University (HKU); three visits to the Institute of European and American Studies, Academia Sinica, Taipei; a semester as a visiting professor at Beijing Foreign Studies University; almost three years as a University of California Education Abroad Program (UCEAP) faculty director in Beijing; two years as a UCEAP faculty director in Shanghai; and three successive summers as a visiting professor at the international summer school at Renmin University. The chapters on gender are informed by the works of HKU colleagues Staci Ford, Kam Louie, and Gina Marchetti. I also benefited from the scrupulous scholarship of Wenching Ho, Yu-cheng Lee, and Te-hsing Shan from Academia Sinica. Many colleagues in mainland China have been tireless in advancing Comparative literature and American studies. I thank Cheng Aimin, Diao Keli, Guo Yingjian, Li Guicang, Liu Kuilan, Luo Xuanmin, Pu Ruoqian, Wang Hui, Wang Ning, Zhao Baisheng, Zhu Ping, and the late Wu Bing for inviting me to speak at conferences that planted the seeds for several chapters, and for providing delectable food for thought and for the palate. I also thank Joan Chiung-huei Chang, Chen Guangchen, Ding Yuan, Huang Qinghua, Li Hanping, Pu Ruoqian, Shan Te-hsing, Wu Shuang, Xu Shuangru, and Zhang Hongyun for translating some of my conference presentations into Chinese.

Ha Jin, David Wong Louie, Ruthanne Lum McCunn, and Shawn Wong, no less piquant in person than in the yarns they spin, shared with me precious inside tips about their works. Gish Jen sent me an advance copy of her *Tiger Writing*, which illuminates the concept of interdependence with great panache and which turns into the cornerstone of my chapter on life-writing. Russell Leong not only gave me the necessary nudge to launch this book but also remained at hand to bounce off titles and scan chapters in Los Angeles, New York, Beijing, and Shanghai. Marilyn Chin, alias Fox Poet Immortal, performed the incredible feat—apparently tantamount to moving heaven and earth—of cajoling her publisher to remove the time limit from the permissions agreement so I can reprint "Get Rid of the X" ad infinitum. Thank you, Goddess.

I am grateful beyond measure to three research assistants cum ideal captive readers, who have tended my manuscript far beyond the call of duty. Hannah Nahm located countless texts I needed for my research and spirited them cybernetically across the ocean; she also read several chapters attentively and offered unmatched intuitive responses. Robert Kyriakos Smith proffered penetrating insights into a number of texts as well as improved the syntax and diction of many a sentence. David Martinez lent his professional expertise to give the book a much-needed once-over. I cherish their scintillating intellectual camaraderie as much as their conscientious research assistance, which is funded by two generous grants from the UCLA Academic Senate as well as a grant from the UCLA Asian American Studies Center. I thank Jay Jin for his word-processing wizardry in helping me "embed" endnotes in the manuscript in accordance with the publisher's specifications.

Desmund Wu used his legal expertise to ensure that my text has not crossed the line vis-à-vis sexuality; Jeff Spielberg savagely nixed all the academic jargon in the introduction. I alone am responsible for any off-color expressions and jawbreakers that remain.

Palgrave Macmillan has presented me with an efficient team. I am beholden to Brigitte Shull for soliciting the still inchoate manuscript (with twice as many chapters as the present volume); to Paloma Yannakakis for her forbearance when deadlines were missed, and for her prompt response as soon as the manuscript was received; to Ryan Jenkins for importuning me to come up with a book cover until I sighted a photo of Liu Fang Yuan, the Chinese garden in the Huntington Library, a perfect trope for something "Wholly formed in China, yet forming another America" (a line from Russell Leong's "Bie You Dong Tian," analyzed in Chap. 8). I thank S. Mary Shiny and Asma Azeezullah for handling the production. I treasure immensely the external reviewer's magnanimous comments and constructive suggestions.

My extended family on three continents has made me feel intercontinental intimacies, viscerally. My dear, yet obstinately gratis, tai chi gurus—Lu Renan, Wang Jun, and Ivy Liu Hao—kept me going by teaching me how to harvest the requisite *qi*. To them my lifelong gratitude.

Gerard Maré imposed the discipline I sorely needed in the final laps while offering affectionate diversion and abiding companionship. In leaving for college, Antony Cheung Maré enabled Mom to brood undistracted (except for pangs of love in his absence) in an empty nest, and inquired via email within a week whether the book was finished. To my spouse and son this work is dedicated.

Thanks to the following for permissions to reprint two poems by Marilyn Chin and two poems by Russell Leong; illustrations of Liu Fang Yuan and of the marble with Xu's poem; and portions of my earlier articles and book chapters:

"Get Rid of the X," from RHAPSODY IN PLAIN YELLOW by Marilyn Chin. Copyright © 2002 by Marilyn Chin. Reprinted by permission of Marilyn Chin, W. W. Norton & Company, Inc., and the Sandra Dijkstra Literary Agency (in Chap. 9).

"Song of the Sad Guitar" from *The Phoenix Gone, The Terrace Empty* by Marilyn Chin (Minneapolis: Milkweed Editions, 1994). Copyright © 1994 by the author. Reprinted with permission from Milkweed Editions (in Chap. 9). www.milkweed.org

"*Bie You Dong Tian*: Another World Lies Beyond" *Amerasia Journal* 37.1 (2011): 41–42. © 2008, Russell C. Leong. Reprinted with the permission of the author (in Chap. 9).

"Your *Tongzhi* Body" from *Asian Americans: The Movement and the Moment*, ed. Steven G. Louie and Glenn K. Omatsu (Los Angeles: UCLA Asian American Studies Center Press, 2001), 234–235. © 2001, Russell C. Leong. Reprinted with the permission of the author (in Chap. 9).

Photo of Liu Fang Yuan, the Chinese garden at the Huntington Library (in Chap. 9) © 2009, Mary Uyematsu Kao.

Photos of the marble featuring Xu Zhimo's poem in King's College, Cambridge University (in Chap. 4), by KC Lee, 2015.

"The Woman Warrior versus The Chinaman Pacific: Must a Chinese American Critic Choose between Feminism and Heroism?" *Conflicts in Feminism*, ed. Marianne Hirsch and Evelyn Fox Keller (New York: Routledge, 1990), 234–251 (in Chap. 2).

"Art, Spirituality, and the Ethic of Care: Alternative Masculinities in Chinese American Literature," in *Masculinity Studies & Feminist Theory*, ed. Judith Kegan Gardiner (Copyright © 2002 Columbia University Press, 2002), 261–289 (in Chap. 5). Portions reprinted with permission of the publisher.

"Chinese and Chinese American Life-Writing," *Cambridge Journal of China Studies* 10.2 (2015): 1–20 (in Chap. 6).

"'Theorizing in Narrative Form': Premonitions of Orientalism and 'Racist Love' in Bing Xin's 'The Photograph,'" *Transnational Literature* 5.1 (Nov. 2012): 1–17 (in Chap. 7).

"The Chinese American Writer as Migrant: Ha Jin's Restive Manifesto," *Amerasia Journal* 38.2 (2012): 2–12 (in Chap. 8).

"Environment for 'A Free Life,'" *Asian American Literature and the Environment*, ed. Lorna Fitzsimmons, Youngsuk Chae, and Bella Adams (New York: Routledge, 2015), 189–208 (in Chap. 8).

"Slanted Allusions: Bilingual Poetics and Transnational Politics in Marilyn Chin and Russell Leong," *positions: asia critique* 21.1 (2014): 237–262 (in Chap. 9).

Los Angeles, California; Shanghai, China   King-Kok Cheung

Contents

1 Introduction   1

Part I   Gender   27

2 (S)wordswoman versus (S)wordsman: Maxine Hong Kingston and Frank Chin   29

3 Manhood Besieged: Gus Lee and David Wong Louie   67

4 Masculine Mystique: Xu Zhimo 徐志摩, Younghill Kang, Pang-Mei Natasha Chang, and Anchee Min   101

5 Art, Spirituality, and *Ren* or the Ethics of Care: Shawn Wong, Li-Young Lee, and Russell C. Leong   141

Part II Genre and Form	171
6 In(ter)dependence in Chinese/American Life-Writing: Liang Qichao 梁启超, Hu Shi 胡适, Shen Congwen 沈从文, Maxine Hong Kingston, William Poy Lee, and Ruthanne Lum McCunn	173
7 Theorizing in Narrative Form: Bing Xin 冰心	201
8 (Im)migrant Writing, Moving Homelands: Ha Jin 哈金	229
9 Slanted Allusions: Marilyn Chin and Russell C. Leong	263
Coda	295
Index	299

List of Figures

Fig. 4.1 Marble inscribed with excerpt of Xu Zhimo's "A Second Farewell to Cambridge" 《再别康桥》 110
Fig. 4.2 Plaque describing the inscription on the marble 110
Fig. 9.1 Liu Fang Yuan 流芳园, the Chinese Garden at the Huntington Library (Photo by Mary Kao) 284
Fig. 9.2 *Di lü ting* 涤虑亭 Pavilion for Washing Away Thoughts, Liu Fang Yuan, the Huntington Library 288

CHAPTER 1

Introduction

"What Can American Studies and Comparative Literature Learn from Each Other?" asked Ali Behdad (2014) in his eponymous article in which he recommends coupling comparative literature's "multinational and multilingual approach" with American studies' "nonbelletristic interdisciplinarity" (613). In bridging the two disciplines through an intercultural and bilingual approach to Chinese American writing, this book follows Behdad's recommendation and answers the call for American studies to become newly transnational. It looks to and from both the United States and China to reveal the multiple engagements of American-born and Sinophone writers. This venture would have been unthinkable, if not roundly censured, in Asian American literary circles in the 1970s and 1980s, when American nativity and Anglophone writing were key to the formation of the field. I seek to expand its scope while maintaining, albeit pluralizing, the original goal of self-definition as self-definitions. I advance a critical strategy that spans languages and national cultures to illuminate the writers' hyphenated consciousness and bicultural aesthetics. Part I examines gender refashioning, especially "remasculinization" (to borrow Viet Thanh Nguyen's word), in light of the Chinese dyadic ideal of *wen-wu* 文武 (literary arts and martial arts). Part II dissects the formal experiments of selected writers, who interweave hybrid poetics with two-pronged critiques of the world.

Common to all the chapters is a fresh look at both American and Chinese mores through an intercultural analysis. Earlier phases of Asian American studies tended to concentrate on anti-Asian sentiment in North America and to downplay troubling Asian legacies, including discrimination against women, laborers, ethnic and sexual minorities; even the stereotype of the "Asian American minority" is not so different from a Chinese model child or citizen whose cardinal virtue traditionally is obedience. Rather than privileging identity politics, "de-nationalized" inquiry, or postmodernist poetics, I demonstrate that local and diasporic poetics and politics are far from incompatible. The writers I examine provide a reflexive lens through which audiences on both sides of the Pacific are beckoned to look homeward and to view the "other" afresh. They draw on transnational resources to devise forms that expose local and global predicaments and open up new vistas in American and Chinese literature.

In approaching their works I have also blurred several lines: as a "gender-bender" in masculinity studies since the 1990s, but less self-consciously so today with the evolution of women's studies into gender studies; and as an Asian Americanist making forays into transpacific comparative literature, heeding recent summons to track stateside works of art through other continents and to delve into the interstices between comparative literature and American studies. By stretching across linguistic and cultural bounds, I seek to decenter the European American heritage and work toward a bilateral literary analysis.

The "borders" in my title refer to those of gender, ethnicity, and nation; of genre, languages, and disciplines; of poetics and politics; of centers and margins. Back in 1997, I stated in the introduction to *An Interethnic Companion to Asian American Literature* that without the initial naming, institutionalization, and contestation over this body of work, the multitudinous strains now being heard might have remained mute; that perhaps the most important reason to retain the designation is not the presence of any cultural or thematic unity but rather the continuing benefit of amplifying marginalized voices, however dissimilar ("Re-viewing" 26). Since its inception, the field has proved a welcoming venue for productive experimentation by both writers and scholars. Therefore, I adhere to the historic labels "Asian American literature" and "Chinese American literature" (instead of using the longer "Asian American and Pacific Islander literature" or the shorter "Third literature"), but with the qualifier "without borders" that simultaneously undermines any barriers, that allows for as many tributaries and confluences as possible.

My study also attends to the inextricability of form and content through historically informed (hence "nonbelletristic") close reading. Because of an enduring, albeit attenuating, tendency in the literary establishment, and even in ethnic communities, to view creative writing by people of color as ethnography or social history, paying attention to its formal invention is a first step toward overcoming these biases. Literature speaks, especially the unspeakable, through myriad aesthetic measures. To combat invisibility and exclusion, many Asian American writers deploy what Michel de Certeau calls "tactic," which he defines as "an art of the weak" and as "a form of *legerdemain*," using Sun Tzu's *The Art of War* as a key example (Certeau 37, xx). Shortly after World War II, Hisaye Yamamoto published a tale in *Partisan Review* that indicts the Japanese American internment in the guise of a breezy "legend" about a seemingly deranged ballet dancer; a scrupulous close reading of this text is required to unravel its layers of sociopolitical meanings.[1] Oblique critique similarly abounds in the Chinese American archive, though the target is no longer confined to white racism, but is extended to Asian and Asian American ethnocentrism, and other forms of suppression. Every one of us, to use Stanley Fish's term in a different context, can be "surprised by sin"; the enemy or oppressor can start to look remarkably like ourselves.

Unlike most of the transnational and interdisciplinary enterprises surveyed in the following section on theoretical crosscurrents, which telescope geopolitical connections and contradictions, I zero in on literary convergences and divergences between Chinese America and China. Yet this comparative project, like the literature perused, also has unmistakable (if at times elliptical) geopolitical repercussions. In line with de Certeau's formulation and with what I argued in *Articulate Silences*, it is no less important to plot literary ambushes and guerilla actions than to challenge structures of domination head-on, in a world where equal right to speak or freedom of expression still cannot be taken for granted. Literature matters, both inside and outside the charmed circles of academia, because it is sometimes the only vehicle by which dissenting voices can be heard effectively, if at all. Dorothy J. Wang, who observes that overtly political poetry does not sit well with the literary establishment, notes how Marilyn Chin's "pervasive use of irony" has allowed her to gain canonical recognition notwithstanding her otherwise in-your-face politics against "racism, sexism, and imperialism" (D. Wang 115). The deployment of "slanted allusions," on which I elaborate in the last chapter, is yet another "tactic" whereby M. Chin can have her impudent say in high poetry societies and gobble up praise in two continents and languages too.[2]

Like literature, languages matter, especially in introducing alternative norms and in providing a forum for counternarratives. Some Chinese concepts, such as *wen* 文 ("pattern," "writing," "culture," "humanities," "the arts"), *ren* 仁 ("both 'human-kindness' and 'humankind-ness'") (Levenson and Schurmann 42), and even *wu* 武 ("martial arts") have no simple English equivalents, because they carry with them very different values (and therefore valences) in traditional China than in North America. *Wen* and *ren* are, for *men*, two of the highest ideals in Confucian culture, and yet they wane in masculine significance and wax in feminine association in the United States. *Wu*, by contrast, has ossified into one of the most prominent stateside stereotypes of Chinese males—as kung fu fighters. Moving across languages, therefore, can open our eyes to alternative ways of seeing, being, and becoming. Even more urgently, linguistic code-switching can create an asylum in another tongue. Shuttling between languages and cultures, even transposing languages and cultures (e.g. writing about China in English), can sometimes be the only way for a writer to be heard. By adopting an interlingual and bidirectional interpretive strategy, my study amplifies voices muffled on either shore. I tune in to traditional Chinese norms to examine Chinese American gender reconstruction; I monitor international resonance and dissonance by extending Asian Americanist critique to Asia.

In so doing, I try also to disabuse mainstream literary scholars in America and China of an ingrained prejudice against Asian American literature that it somehow falls short of the literary canons East and West. Before the civil rights movement, hardly any writer of Asian descent was on the American literary radar. As probably the first major publication to include Asian American writers, the *Heath Anthology of American Literature*, edited by Paul Lauter et al. and first published in 1990, was revolutionary. Since then, Asian American writers have been present in most American literature compendiums, but they are still absent from many American literature courses and in Asian Studies altogether. Even more reluctant to embrace these writers are academics in the Chinese literary establishment (both English and Chinese departments). In 2000, during an editorial meeting in Hong Kong over the possibility of publishing a version of the *Heath Anthology* in Asia, the most adamant opponents to including more Asian American texts were scholars from China.[3] In the face of such dual relegation, this book magnifies the variegated tapestry of Chinese American writing to find it at the vanguard of iridescent world literature. Instead of gauging it *against* Eastern and Western literary heritages, I demonstrate how it revivifies both. Many of the writers discussed are able to cross-pollinate two cultures, loosening deep-rooted assumptions and grafting new semantics and forms to each, thereby melding centers and margins.

THEORETICAL CROSSCURRENTS

The new millennium has witnessed a transnational turn in American studies, strongly endorsed by Shelley Fisher Fishkin in her 2004 Presidential Address to the American Studies Association: "The United States is and has always been a transnational crossroads of cultures.... American studies is increasingly doing justice to the transnational crossroads" (Fishkin 43). Wai-Chee Dimock, who bemoans that "for too long American literature has been seen as a world apart," makes up for this lack in *Through Other Continents* by ranging over the terrains of world literature in her examination of canonical writers (Dimock 2). Lisa Lowe, echoing Dimock's title in *The Intimacies of Four Continents*, documents the interrelatedness "between the emergence of European liberalism, settler colonialism in the Americas, the transatlantic African slave trade, and the East Indies and China trades in the late eighteenth and early nineteenth centuries"; Lowe submits that the social inequities of our time are a legacy of the triages involving blacks and Asians in the name of European and Anglo-American liberalism (Lowe, *Intimacies* 1, 3).

Nowhere are these pleas for intercontinental inquiries more pertinent than in ethnic studies. What Dimock says of American literature in general roundly applies to Asian American writing: "Rather than being a discrete entity, it is better seen as a crisscrossing set of pathways ... binding America to the rest of the world" (Dimock 3). It is quite impossible to survey Asian American studies outside an international frame. The watershed historical events in the field, such as the Asian Exclusion Act, the Japanese American internment, the ambiguous national status of early Filipino immigrants, the Korean conflict, and the Vietnam War tie the field to other countries in Asia geographically, politically, culturally, and linguistically. Most of the earliest works by Chinese, Japanese, Korean, and Vietnamese immigrants are written in Asian languages, and there is also a growing body of literary works by new immigrants scripted in other tongues. Frederick Buell, in *National Culture and the New Global System*, singles out Asian American literature to show the impact of globalization, listing the following as "circumstantial factors" for his choice: the rapid growth of its literary tradition; its interface with new immigration; and its ties to the world marketplace—"the Pacific Rim" (Buell 177). In fact, as Lowe indicates, Asia was already very much a player, though an upstaged one, in the global theater back in the late eighteenth century.

Asian American literary history has largely followed the trajectory of American studies. Its foremost critical paradigms may be distilled in three catchphrases: "Claiming America," "Claiming Diaspora," and "Reclaiming the Hyphen."[4] The first phase, from the 1970s to the 1980s, was characterized by the rise of cultural nationalism and feminism, the desire to define a collective body of work distinct from its mainstream Chinese and American counterparts, and concern with social justice. There was intense critical discomfort revolving around gender trouble, Orientalism, and white reception. In the influential introduction to *Aiiieeeee! An Anthology of Asian American Writing* (1974), editors Frank Chin, Jeffery Paul Chan, Lawson Fusao Inada, and Shawn Wong decried the notion of a "dual personality" and regarded American nativity (with minor exception) and Anglophone works as crucial to what they considered to be "Asian American sensibility." They resented the dominant culture's tendency to regard American-born Asians as outlanders and to expect "some strange continuity between the great high culture of a China that hasn't existed for five hundred years and the American-born Asian" (xxiv). Their stress on American indigeneity grew out of the frustration, shared by many American citizens of Asian extraction, of being treated as perpetual foreigners. Writing by Asian Americans during this period, as noted by Elaine H. Kim (author of the groundbreaking *Asian American Literature: An Introduction to the Writings and Their Social Context*), coalesced around the theme of "claiming an American, as opposed to Asian, identity" (Kim, "Defining" 88). This imperative accounted for the purposeful omission of the hyphen in most Asian American self-references. "We ought to leave out the hyphen in 'Chinese-American,'" Maxine Hong Kingston declared in relation to her second book *China Men*. "Without the hyphen, 'Chinese' is an adjective and 'American' a noun; a Chinese American is a type of American" (Kingston 60).

Gender crosscuts race and ethnicity from the outset. The editors of *Aiiieeeee!* considered racial "emasculation" to be among the most damaging legacies of the American media: "Good or bad, the stereotypical Asian is nothing as a man ... devoid of all the traditionally masculine qualities of originality, daring, physical courage, and creativity" (xxx). They saw this affront as bound up with "the lack of a recognized style of Asian-American manhood" (Chin, Chan, and Inada xxxviii). Outraged by Hollywood's representation of Asians as either sinister or subservient, they resolved to contrive a virile ethnopoetics, a commitment made good 17 years later in *The Big Aiiieeeee!* (1991). In this sequel, the editors (Frank Chin in particular) took great pains to unearth an Asian heroic tradition comprising selected Chinese and Japanese epics; they contended that "authentic" Asian American writing must hark back to these famous tales. These editors, so instrumental in promulgating Asian American writing, have subsequently vilified much of it by dismissing as "fake" just about every work that has become a national best seller—Kingston's *The Woman Warrior*, David Henry Hwang's *M. Butterfly*, and Amy Tan's *Joy Luck Club*. The authors who protested most trenchantly against the white establishment for the silencing of "Fifty Years of Our Whole Voice" (title of the *Aiiieeeee!* Introduction) also issued the most exclusive criteria for Asian American literature.

These spokes*men* seemed oblivious to their own biases in conceiving a male, straight, and American-born Asian American subject, and in preferring the misogynist attributes imposed on other men of color to those "effeminate" ones imputed to Asian men. Feminist critics and scholars were quick to call them out for their masculinist responses to racist representation. The dissension came to a head over the publication of *The Woman Warrior* (1976), the first Asian American work to receive national acclaim. Frank Chin lambasted the book and accused Kingston of falsifying Chinese myths and catering to white audiences. Ink was spilled and spurted for almost a decade in the ensuing pen wars between Kingston and her defenders on the one side and F. Chin and his supporters on the other. The identity politics at the time, while uplifting and empowering, also played out the paradox noted by Ann Anlin Cheng in Ralph Ellison's *Invisible Man*, that "'community' embodies its inverse—exclusion," that the "discourse of identity fosters division and dis-identification as well" (Cheng 60).

Where competing claims of cultural nationalism and feminism marked the 1980s, the 1990s was fraught with division over the primary nexus of the field, whether it should go diasporic or remain vigilant about its American stakes. The diasporic turn was spearheaded by Lisa Lowe's influential essay "Heterogeneity, Hybridity, Multiplicity" (1991) and exemplified by David Palumbo Liu's *Asian/American: Historical Crossings of a Racial Frontier* (1999), which traces the widespread interpenetration of "Asia" and "America." This "second phase" of Asian American studies, Kent A. Ono observes, extended the contours of the early nationalist period and its social mission to groups neglected previously (Ono 1).

These changes were occasioned in part by shifting demography. Following the 1965 Immigration and Nationality Act, which abolished quotas favoring applicants from northwestern European nations, the number of Asian immigrants has risen sharply, unfixing the earlier categories.[5] Critics such as Oscar Campomanes (1992), R. Radhakrishnan (1994), Susan Koshy (1996), and Shirley Geok-lin Lim (1997) challenged the idea of a unifying Asian American identity, seeing it as replicating erstwhile white nativist calls for a shared American identity; like Lowe, they underlined the need to factor in "heterogeneity," "exile," and "diaspora" in unpacking Asian American literature.

Not everyone was comfortable with the morphing of a coalitional national identity into a diffused subjectivity. Sau-ling Cynthia Wong, author of the seminal *Reading Asian American Literature: From Necessity to Extravagance*, sounded a note of alarm about the mutation from a domestic to a diasporic perspective in her landmark 1995 essay "Denationalization Reconsidered" (12). While recognizing that changes in global capital and migration have resulted in a growing permeability between "Asian" and "Asian American," and that the domestic and the diasporic stances are not irreconcilable, she upheld the continual political need to establish the Asian *American* presence (Wong, "Denationalization" 5, 16). David Leiwei Li was even more vehement in sustaining the centrality of race and nation, in "retaining 'Asian' as a racial description and 'American' as a national signifier" so as to confront the uneven historical opposition between citizens and aliens, as well as "the contemporary contradiction between the legal assurance of equal rights and the cultural rearticulation of national competence" (Li, *Imagining* 202, 203).[6]

Yet a homeward view must also take in what Rachel C. Lee calls "tyrannies within the household" (R.C. Lee, *Americas* 140)—domestic matters that paradoxically train our eyes across the ocean. The deference toward authority, civic and filial piety, preference for male offspring, the rejection of gays and lesbians, not to mention discrimination against the racial and ethnic other, are by no means habits acquired after landing in America. A transpacific exploration can deepen the critical insights generated by Asian American literary studies, which in turn can echo afield. If there remains one attribute of Asian American literature that still holds through all the internal convulsion, it is its enduring salience as social text, a textual world contiguous with the one we inhabit, like the Globe Theatre of Shakespeare that put the world on stage. As such, this literature can also serve as a mirror on another shore. I would go so far as to posit that this social text could only be fully legible in both national and transnational contexts.

To range across national divides, the field must admit a polyglot archive and an eclectic hermeneutics, as promulgated in "A Third literature" (outlined here in conjunction with the third phase of "Reclaiming the Hyphen"). In 2012, the University of California, Los Angeles (UCLA) Asian American Studies Center published a special issue of *Amerasia Journal* (38.2) titled "Towards a Third Literature: Chinese Writing in the Americas," coedited by Evelyn Hu-DeHart (Brown University), Wang Ning (Tsinghua University, Beijing), and Russell C. Leong (former editor of *Amerasia Journal*, UCLA). This issue broadens Chinese American literary terrain to include writers who compose in their native or second tongues, including Chinese, Spanish, and English. In the introductory essay, Leong and Hu-Dehart redefine Chinese American writing beyond the existing limits by breaking down linguistic as well as national barriers ("Forging"). Leong later explains that the new term derives from Teshome Gabriel's writing on "Third Cinema," which foregrounds a decolonized, post-1950s Third World perspective (Leong, "Third" 111), and which also dovetails with the subversive intent of most ethnic writing. The same cannot be said about Wang Ning's contention—that Third literature should be viewed as part of "cultural China" (*wenhua zhongguo*文化中国), as synonymous with "International Chinese Literature" (N. Wang, "(Re)Considering" xii)—a perspective that risks replicating the cultural imperialism of Chinese past and present.

Furthermore, a China-centric approach might sit ill with the growing number of thoroughly bilingual Chinese emigrant (some even dual national) writers in the United States, including Kenneth Pai Hsien Yung, Ha Jin (who is profiled in this issue on Third literature), Yiyun Li, Anchee Min, Qiu Xiaolong, and Yan Geling. Using Yan's work as an example, Pin-Chia Feng makes a compelling case for enfolding into the field contemporary fiction written in Chinese but set in the United States (Feng). Belinda Kong, in a chiasmic move, plumps for writers who, in part to skirt censorship, use English to write about China. These writers, Kong pleads, deserve a special hearing: "Asian-American Studies would appear stubbornly doctrinaire and exclusive if it clings to claiming America as the absolute yardstick for inclusion" (Kong 145). Kong proposes a "return to the hyphen" and a "bilateral hermeneutics" in reading this cluster of texts, so as to highlight "forms of sovereign biopower in the world today" (Kong 136, 155).

While Kong veers to the left of the hyphen, Shu-mei Shih and Eleanor Ty wish to do away with national markers altogether, with

Shih substituting "Sinophone" for "Chinese American" and with Ty replacing "Asian American" with "Asian Global." In her introduction to *Sinophone Studies*, Shih argues that indiscriminate use of the term "Chinese" presumes "cultural dependence on, if not political loyalty to, China" (Shih 6). Unlike Shih, I see a significant difference between the noun "China" and the adjective "Chinese": where the noun designates the nation, the adjective denotes a spectrum of ethnicities (admittedly Han-centric traditionally) and cultural artifacts; hence my continual use of the adjective, reserving the term "Sinophone" for works written originally in Chinese. Eleanor Ty, in *Unfastened*, recommends the term "Asian Global" to reference narratives that "arise out of and are contingent on globalization" (Ty 133). But this term does not connote the sense of marginality that still pervades much of the literature in the field, including the works discussed in her book (and mine).

"Reclaiming the Hyphen" or "Third literature" has gone further than the second phase of "Claiming Diaspora" in advancing a hemispheric, transpacific, and especially multilingual approach. Both the neo-East-West and the North-South transactions involve linguistic shuttling. Other languages can inspire alternative lines of vision commensurate with newly "unfastened" identities. Kenneth Pai, Ha Jin, and Yan Geling are publishing in both Chinese and English, about both China and the United States. Even Jhumpa Lahiri, one of the best-known Asian American writers, has switched to Italian with *In altre parole* (2015). Rather than redounding to the credit of any one nation, the newly multilingual field can bring complementary sets of questions to bear. For the "phases" of Asian American literary studies are neither discrete nor teleological; each has quickened the field and contributed to its prismatic configuration. As Stephen Hong Sohn, Paul Lai, and Donald C. Goellnicht have observed, Asian American literature can be approached from disparate analytical angles, accommodating heterogeneous "critical practices and definitional boundaries" (Sohn, Lai and Goellnicht 8). I use "phase" in this section to refer to the period when a particular paradigm gained currency, but all these modes still prevail. Instead of replacing one model or one set of questions with another, we can, if you will, attack both sides of the hyphen concurrently.

Effacing Boundaries

Chinese American Literature without Borders attempts to maintain the original mandate of the field and to expand its reach, thereby connecting local and transpacific politics and poetics. As a veteran player in this field, I have communed with divergent camps. This book engages with the foregoing theoretical crosscurrents, but privileging neither America nor China as a case of cultural exceptionalism. Originally composed at different historical junctures, the chapters in Part I intervene in the debates over gender that raged during the 1980s and 1990s, reflecting the tensions among feminists, between feminists and cultural nationalists, and between gay and straight Asian Americans. I reexamine these earlier disagreements because the issues broached then, such as "emasculation," the association of masculinity with physicality, the heightened objectification of Asian women, and homophobia, speak to us still. Furthermore, these topics provide a tangible example of transpacific relevance. According to a 2016 piece by Javier C. Hernandez in the *New York Times* (6 Feb), Chinese educators, too, fret about producing "effeminate boys," about how to "make boys men"; pupils are asked to "sign petitions pledging to act like 'real men.'" Why the sudden need to "salvage masculinity in schools"? Out of a concern for the preponderance of female teachers in the classroom, who allegedly are incapable of instilling valor, among other desirable qualities, in young fellows (Hernandez). This Chinese policy reveals diehard codes of gender and the enmeshment of manly cult and female welfare.

If we think that the United States is beyond such antiquated codes, we must think again. In an even more recent piece in the *New York Times* (29 March 2016), op-ed columnist David Brooks laments the resurgence of a new "Order of Trumps" (Brooks). Brook is alluding to a conflict during the Civil War, when Colonel Robert McAllister's remonstration against debauchery ignited a fiery opposition by the line officers in his regiment who formed an organization, called the Independent Order of Trumps, which championed "boozing and whoring, cursing and card-playing." Adducing Lorien Foote's observation that these rival camps represent two different ideals of masculinity, namely chivalry versus physical domination, Brooks observes that our contemporary masculine ideal, in which a man treats a woman with respect and as an equal, has now sparked a backlash that he dubs the current "Independent Order of Trumps." Brooks does not mince words when he accuses Donald Trump for embracing "unvarnished misogyny," wherein women are "the vixens, sirens and monsters" who should be "surrounded with taboos and purgation rituals." Because a female body for Trump reflects male status, he does not scruple to "emasculate a rival man" by insulting or conquering his woman, nor to tell struggling men that they are at least "better than women, Mexicans, and Muslims," thereby conjoining white and male privileges (Brooks). That such regressive notions of masculinity could carry the day in the twenty-first century should provoke consternation. By lobbying for gender parity, I hope to do my part in deflating Trumpism.[7]

But I have encroached on the men's arena by interrogating the literary revamping of Asian American masculinity since the 1980s. Complementing and inverting David Henry Hwang's quip in *M. Butterfly*, spoken by Song Liling, the female impersonator, that "only a man knows how a woman is supposed to act" (63), I take the liberty to hold forth on masculine ideals. The reasons for my crossover endeavor are fourfold. First, as often "feminized" subjects in the United States, Asian American men rightly fall under the purview of feminist discourse. Second, many traits that are looked askance as "effeminate" in the West are considered winsomely masculine in traditional Chinese culture; overseas benchmarks can vitiate hegemonic masculinity. Third, a feminist lens can deflect recursive patriarchal reconstructions. Finally, in calling forth an alternative masculine ideal from Chinese culture, I also unveil a corresponding feminine model that belies the stereotypes of China dolls and dragon ladies in American popular culture. By collating Chinese and American gender norms and tuning in to bicultural aesthetics, I trace how the writers tap their ancestral and adoptive cultures for artistic inspiration, all the time questioning the mores of both societies.

The four chapters in Part I foster an alliance between feminist and masculinity studies. I introduce the Chinese *wen-wu* dyad (nicely explicated by Kam Louie) to offset the overemphasis of the *wu* hero or martial artist in American and Chinese popular cultures; the figure of Chinese poet Xu Zhimo 徐志摩 to epitomize the *wen* ideal and revive a matching feminine ideal; Mei Lanfang 梅兰芳 and Ren Jianhui 任剑辉 (Peking opera and Cantonese opera luminaries and female and male impersonators, respectively) to drive home the performativity of gender; the Confucian teaching of *ren* 仁—a key component of *wen* 文—to untether the ethic of care from its putative feminine sphere.

The age-old association of *wen* (the humanities in general but literary productions in particular) with moral character accounts in part for the premium many Far Eastern Asian countries—cultures steeped in Confucianism—put on education traditionally. Today, the *wen* ideal can easily strike one as elitist, as a privilege accessible to those who can afford an "Ivy League" education or as a prerequisite to a cushy profession. Traditionally, *wen* is tied above all to self-cultivation and ethical development, as captured in the saying *wenyizaidao* 文以载道: "literature as a vehicle of moral instruction" (L.O.-f. Lee 249) or "keeping the truth through literature" (X. Xu 19). Learning is the path to being a *junzi* 君子—a person of probity, but not necessarily a rich or powerful one. The two most important ingredients in the *junzi* culture, according to Joseph R. Levenson and Franz Schurmann, were "*li* ('ritual,' or 'decorum'...) and *jen* [*ren*]" (42).⁸ Notwithstanding the sexism of Confucius, who brazenly classified women as *xiaoren* 小人 (the opposite of *junzi*), his injunctions about *ren* and about the potential of *wen* in shaping character are worth recuperating. May Fourth intellectuals, according to Leo Lee, still believed strongly in their moral responsibility toward society, and in the function of literature "to sway and change social mores, to cleanse China of old values and habits and to bring in new ones from the West" (L.O.-f. Lee 251). Asian American literature too can be deployed to sway and change both American and Chinese mores, to overcome benighted values and habits in both nations, and to usher in progressive ones from the four seas.

Chapter 2 interweaves the gender debates involving Kingston and Frank Chin with the duo's pyrotechnics on the page. It correlates the historical debasement of Asian men in the United States with the traditional subjugation of women in China and cautions against boosting manhood by subscribing to patriarchal conventions of masculinity. It then analyzes how both Kingston and F. Chin retool Chinese classics to create a usable past relevant to their concerns as Chinese American female and male, respectively. By invoking the Chinese heroic tradition to voice their gender and cultural nationalist concerns, the twain launch a transpacific literary tradition that straddles the twinned ideal of *wen-wu*—writing and fighting.

Chapter 3 shows the eclipse of *wen* by *wu* in the New World. The male protagonists in Gus Lee's *China Boy* and David Wong Louie's *Pangs of Love* have internalized American gender codes that impugn Asian American virility, thereby deeming themselves as not quite *real men* and trying to "pass" as black or white. Lee's China boy aspires to be a black youngster by learning how to fight, putting aside his Chinese calligraphy (*wen*) for boxing (*wu*); D.W. Louie's protagonists, whose manhood is constantly slighted despite their literary sophistication, try in vain to impersonate whites, literally or vicariously. The chapter concludes by sighting viable models such as *wenren* 文人 (men of letters) and *renren* 仁人—caring men(tors).

Chapter 4 delineates the masculine ideal of *wenren* or poet-scholar, as promulgated in traditional Chinese drama and as exemplified by Xu Zhimo, a Chinese poet who appears in three Asian American works (as well as in Pearl Buck's writing). Xu, who won the hearts of women and men of diverse nationalities in real life, is depicted as a charismatic idealist in Younghill Kang's *East Goes West*; as a bicultural literary vanguard adored by both British and Chinese intellectuals in Pang-mei Natasha Chang's *Bound Feet and Western Dress*; and as Pearl Buck's soul mate and lover in Anchee Min's *Pearl of China*. His allure can be ascribed to his cultural hybridity, romantic spirit, intellectual generosity, and the uncanny ability to draw together a literary community. Nicknamed "the Chinese Shelley," Xu is also a forerunner of today's diasporic writers, heralding the intercultural innovations made possible by moving comfortably across geographical, linguistic, and cultural borders. This chapter also introduces a roster of brilliant women of letters, to whom Xu is irresistibly attracted.

Chapter 5 uncovers alternative masculinities in works that valorize artistic accomplishment, spiritual pursuit, and *ren* 仁, or the ethic of care. (I juxtapose the Confucian precept with the feminist ethic not to make hairsplitting distinctions but to show that the capacity for caring is in fact gender-neutral.) Shawn Wong, Li-Young Lee, and Russell C. Leong counter the "emasculation" of Asian men without falling into the trap of purveying domineering or self-denigrating counterexamples. Wong's *American Knees* features a seductive lover whose eloquence and wit is reminiscent of Chinese poet-scholars. Lee's *Winged Seeds* portrays a spellbinding Christian pastor who ministers tirelessly to the needy. Leong's "Phoenix Eyes" sketches gay men who practice mutual caring in the shadow of AIDS and in the light of Buddhism. These works also reveal how perceptions of masculinity fluctuate with geographical location and with the racial makeup of the dominant culture.

Part II applies an intertextual hermeneutics to Chinese American writing to chart the convergences and divergences of Chinese and Chinese American writing and to accentuate formal innovations. Instead of pitting a "national" paradigm against a "diasporic" schema, I show that a transnational approach to Asian American literature does not entail disavowal of stateside hegemony. The edgy evocation of Chinese classics can cast aspersions on both sides of the hyphen; mining linguistic margins can engender singular poetics; and works published in China and insights derived from postcolonial and Asian American studies can resonate abroad. I also call for different optics in assessing hyphenated writers, including non-native English speakers. Rather than asking whether these writers are as good as canonical American and Chinese writers, or as eloquent as native speakers, I spotlight what they bring to the English and Chinese language—how they revolutionize conventional genre and forms, and enrich the world literary heritage.

Chapter 6 shows how three Chinese American writers introduce plural voices—intergenerational, interracial, synchronic, or diachronic—into life-writing, thereby transforming a *self*-centered genre into a convivial rendezvous. It takes exception to Frank Chin's postulations that autobiography is a Western genre and that autobiographical Chinese American works reek of Christian confession (F. Chin, "Autobiography"). My comparison of three Sinophone and three Anglophone works uses F. Chin's remarks as a point of entry to mine an indigenous Chinese (auto)biographical tradition, probe transpacific similarities and differences, and offer a transnational perspective on the controversial leverage of Chinese material in Chinese American writing. I trace the commonalities to the inculcation of an interdependent self and the disparities to changing attitudes toward authorities. Unlike the Sinophone authors, the Chinese American authors do not scruple to disclose family secrets and flout genre boundaries. Bicultural literacy can obviate cultural misreading, allay critical qualms caused by the politics of representation, and heighten textual polyphony.

Chapter 7 studies "The Photograph" (1934) by Bing Xin 冰心, a Chinese writer during the May Fourth Movement. This story anticipates ideas later articulated by postcolonialist and Asian American critics and fleshes out Barbara Christian's assertion that literature can perform the work of theory. The Chinese narrative furnishes a dual critique of American Orientalism and Chinese patriarchal familism (especially filial gratitude and implicit obedience) and contributes to ongoing debates about the viability of a culturalist upbringing for adoptees from Asia. It interweaves three strands of Orientalism—missionary denigration of the Chinese as inferior heathens, the American construct of the Asian as the demure model minority, and Chinese complicity in enacting the stereotype. Susan Sontag's observation that photography is often made to serve possessive colonialist ends is inverted by the eponymous photograph, through which the master's tool is used to deconstruct the master's predatory vision. Bing Xin, who is herself subject to gendered reception, illuminates mechanisms of gender and race in China that parallel stateside patterns. This chapter broadens Asian American literary studies by adjoining it with Sinophone literature, comparative literature, and postcolonialist theory.

Chapter 8 decodes the double-voice in Ha Jin's *The Writer as Migrant* (*Migrant*) and *A Free Life* (*AFL*) as well as uses the collection of essays to shed light on the novel. *Migrant*, a scholarly commentary on bilingual English writers, coincides with a covert apologia; *AFL*, ostensibly an immigrant tale, also figures as metafiction about a linguistic voyage, wherein the author turns lexical displacement into creative possibility by recasting both the Chinese and the American pastoral. Jin's marshaling of Chinese and American tropes, I submit, deliberately detaches the expressions from their national moorings, a figurative move in keeping with the idea of freedom in the novel, which is as much about writing in an open climate as breathing clean air, transitioning to a second language as finding a new home. The themes explored in *Migrant*—social role of a writer, limits and opportunities associated with an adoptive language, relation between the state and the individual, and the shifting contours of homeland—are brought to life in the novel. Through mapping the correspondences between ecological and moral landscapes, geographical and linguistic crossings, and pastoral and existential solitude, this chapter expands ecological concerns to encompass political climate, and envisages other Asian American sensibilities.

Chapter 9 demonstrates how Marilyn Chin and Russell C. Leong juggle with Chinese allusions to defy transpacific social disparities. Disagreeing both with scholars who consider Chinese references in Asian American writing inescapably Orientalist and with critics who advocate a wholesale reclamation of an Asian tradition, I monitor how the two poets contest gender and class discrimination by maneuvering tropes from different cultures. M. Chin turns a Tang poem into a feminist parable in "Get Rid of the X"; she remakes traditional sites of female confinement (strewn across both Chinese and American literature) into a creative room of one's own in "Song of the Sad Guitar." Leong spins a homophobic slur into a term of compassion and solidarity in "Your *Tongzhi* Body"; in "*Bie You Dong Tian*," a proverb designed to extol the picturesque landscape of the Huntington Library's Chinese garden is used concomitantly to disinter its subterranean skeletons and to disclose transpacific exploitation of migrant laborers. Like Kingston and F. Chin, M. Chin and Leong reenact the *wen-wu* dyad—fighting through writing.

These last four chapters align literary texts with genre reformation, postcolonialist theory, environment studies, and tactics of "translation," respectively. The chapter on life-writing shows how the interdependent subject-formation undergirding the Sinophone and Chinese American texts transforms Western (auto)biography into multivoiced narratives. The chapter on Bing Xin reveals how postcolonialist theory is embedded in the Chinese tale, which connects the manifestations of Orientalism in China and the United States, and contrasts the plight of the racialized other bilaterally. The chapter on Ha Jin catches glimpses of the author through the palimpsest of his treatise and novel, both of which connect physical and linguistic uprooting, (im)migrant dwelling and the house of fiction. The last chapter shows how the Chinese allusions in M. Chin and Leong have a way of slanting nationalist or patriarchal ideologies, playing havoc with both sides of the hyphen.

To put in a capsule, Part I presents alternative masculinities; Part II teases out alternative forms of (auto)biography, theory, metafiction, pastoral, ecocriticism, and translation. But the gender concerns and literary strategies in the two sections decidedly overlap. Though featured in Part I, Frank Chin, Maxine Hong Kingston, David Wong Louie, Li-young Lee, and Shawn Wong are all formidable wordsmiths. Though placed in Part II, Bing Xin, Marilyn Chin, William Poy Lee, Ruthanne Lum McCunn, and Russell C. Leong insistently grapple with gender and sexuality; their texts spell out different ways of being Chinese (American) and female, being straight and gay, with M. Chin and Leong even entertaining androgynous bodies. Focusing mainly on writers of Chinese descent (with the exception of Korean American writer Younghill Kang), I show how familiarity with Chinese cultural productions can enhance our appreciation of Asian American writing, defamiliarize traditional Chinese assumptions and American norms, and build an intercultural literary heritage. Just as knowledge of Chinese language and literature can deepen our understanding of Chinese American writing, critical paradigms developed in American ethnic studies can travel overseas.

This book shows that Asian Americans can still "claim America"—assert and manifest the historical and cultural presence of Asians in North America—*and* maintain affiliation with another polity. Individuals may feel braced by an ethnic American identity, by a diasporic identity, or by both, but the field can stand to gain from these divergent perspectives. Most, if not all, of the writers discussed in this book—be they Sinophone writers (Bing Xin, Hu Shi, Liang Qichao, Shen Congwen, and Xu Zhimo), immigrants who write in English (Marilyn Chin, Ha Jin, Li-Young Li, Ruthanne Lum McCunn, and Anchee Min), or American-born who allude to their mother tongue (Pang-Mei Natasha Chang, Frank Chin, Maxine Hong Kingston, Russell C. Leong, William Poy Lee, Gus Lee, David Wong Louie, and Shawn Wong)—speak to the simultaneous claiming and disclaiming of both China and the United States. A hyphenated consciousness has enabled some writers to withstand a racist and patriarchal definition of national identity. An exilic or diasporic identity has spurred others to dispute the exclusiveness of state or cultural nationalism. Furthermore, by opening up the field to other languages, we can discover cognate sensibilities across nations. While I home in on the linkages between Chinese and Chinese American culture and literature, analogous strategies can be used to examine literary works by different Asian and Pacific groups, surmounting additional boundaries.[9]

Beyond Orientalism

Speaking of "limits" in the field, Colleen Lye wrote in 2008 that "Asian American culture is still understood as a reaction-formation to American racism"; she urged Asian Americanists to move "beyond Orientalism" so as to exceed its critique (Lye 454). I would like to offer a dual response to Lye's thoughtful intervention. On the one hand, Orientalism remains alive and too well. (To be convinced, one only has to watch the 2014 Netflix television drama series *Marco Polo*, in which naked Asian damsels prance in every episode.) As Hamid Dabashi, Ali Behdad, and Juliet Williams contend, scholars need to continue to take on anti-Orientalist critiques and pay attention to its new incarnations, often produced by Asians themselves (Dabashi, Behdad, and Williams, "Neo-Orientalism").

On the other hand, comparativist approaches to Asian American writing, whether counterposing Asian Americans and other racial minorities, or setting side-by-side gender and racial asymmetries in Asia and in the United States, provide one way of moving beyond a dualistic methodology. Looking at the representations of diverse ethnic groups in American literature illuminates the persistent triangulation of race in our society, while extending the field to offshore writing encourages reflexive critique beyond national borders. As noted by Wu Bing, founder of the Chinese American Literature Research Center at Beijing Foreign Studies University, Chinese American writing can function as "*fansiwenxue*反思文学," namely, "introspection literature" for Chinese readers (Wu, "Concerning" 105; "Reading" 20), perhaps even as transgressive introspection. Its formal impact reverberates as well. In my chapter on life-writing, I turn around F. Chin's objection to Asian American autobiography as a derivative Western Christian genre by showing how Chinese American writers have infused this most subjective "Western" genre with intersubjectivity, thereby stretching life-writing to accommodate the interdependent self that is a part of their cultural inheritance and enlarging the American literary heritage. Instead of reaction-formation, Asian American literary studies can diversify the mainstream.

Because the very impetus of this field is self-definition, one reason why literary critics are slow to negotiate the intersection of Asian American and comparative literature is the understandable fear of reinforcing Orientalism and of muddling the distinction between Asian and Asian American writing. Tracing the poetry of Marilyn Chin and Russell Leong to China does not make them less American, any more than Dimock's tracing of Emerson and Thoreau to other continents makes the canonical writers any less American. But the time has also come for the field to overcome the misgivings, prevalent in the "Claiming America" phase, about writers from China who allegedly "write about Chinese America as foreigners" authenticating "the concept of the dual personality" and who are, therefore, unable to "communicate the Chinese-American sensibility" (Chin, Chan, and Inada xxxviii). *Chinese American Literature without Borders* displays an array of Chinese American sensibility and various shades of self-definition, including duality—both its gains in "double consciousness" and its pain of dividedness. My chapter on Ha Jin shows how it is possible for a writer to teeter on the hyphen creatively, to claim America as a new homeland while infusing into English, even revisiting, the Chinese mother tongue as a linguistic homeland. Thoroughly bilingual writers like Jin also bring up another reason for the dearth of research on transpacific influence: the lack of students and scholars in North America versed in at least one Asian language. Globalizing Asian American literary studies entails not only multicultural but also multilingual literacy. The growing enrollment of American students in Asia and of Asian students in America and the increase of bilingual scholars in worldwide academia should allow us to uncover Orientalism in its many guises and various geographic manifestations, as well as to move beyond Orientalism.

The author of *Orientalism* never perceives "reaction-formation" as an end in itself. Rather, Edward Said has always advocated manifold perceptions similar to those of exiles: "Most people are principally aware of one culture, one setting, one home; exiles are aware of at least two, and this plurality of vision gives rise to an awareness of simultaneous dimensions, an awareness that ... is *contrapuntal*." He adds, "There is a unique pleasure in this sort of apprehension, especially if the exile is conscious of other contrapuntal juxtapositions that diminish orthodox judgment and elevate appreciative sympathy" (Said, *Exile* 148). Asian American literary studies—with its multiple channels, kinship networks, forms of attachment, and linguistic polyphony—is a perfect venue for a host of contrapuntal possibilities.

That does not presage that the field will dissolve in endless proliferation. In *Mappings* Susan Stanford Friedman voiced her belief that "the time has come ... to reinvent a singular feminism that incorporates myriad and often conflicting cultural and political formations in a global context" (4). I entertain a similar hope for Asian American literary studies. What Friedman said of feminism applies equally to this field: "The pluralization of feminism has contributed profoundly to the expansion and diversification of feminism," vitally necessary for "the development of a multicultural, international, and transnational feminism"; but its very success has engendered "the need for a new singularization of feminism that assumes difference without reifying or fetishizing it" (Friedman 4). Asian American literary studies has gone through even more intricate ramifications, but it too must not be ensconced in its separate sites; boundaries must be transgressed for dialogues to continue.

To reckon with contradictory stances is not to take refuge in a postmodern protean identity that flits from one location to the next, but to make room for reciprocal critique and multidirectional coalition and empathy. Bestriding these positions may involve painful alienation that renders us ill at ease within our own communities. But assuming such vantage points also makes it possible to discern the mutual enmeshment of nations and to rally around concerns as an ethnic minority while avoiding the pitfalls of chauvinism and separatism that can at times accompany unthinking national and cultural allegiances. The proper role of the American humanist, to quote Said again, "is not to consolidate and affirm one tradition over all others. It is rather to open them all, or as many as possible, to each other, to question each of them for what it has done with the others, to show how in this polyglot country in particular many traditions have interacted" (Said, Humanism 49). It is in this spirit that I hope readers will use the book as a springboard to forge further connections across borders.

Notes

1. This story is analyzed in "Thrice Muted Tale" (Cheung, "Thrice").
2. In addition to being recipient of the PEN Oakland/Josephine Miles Literary Award and five Pushcart Prizes, M. Chin won the 2015 Anisfield-Wolf National Award for *Hard Love Province*. Her selected poems have been translated into Chinese by Li Guicang 李贵苍 and Hu Luping 胡路苹 as 《一抹黄色: Plain Yellow》 (Beijing: Intellectual Property Publishing House, 2016).

3. The objection was grounded in the fear the proposed anthology would not be adopted widely as textbooks if the selections by canonical white writers were shortened to make room for Asian American writers. At Peking University, Asian American literature is seldom taught in the English Department, which also would not recommend students who wish to pursue Chinese American literature in stateside doctoral programs for nationwide scholarships.
4. The first phrase was coined by Maxine Hong Kingston, the second by Jeffrey F. L. Partridge, the third by my variation on Belinda Kong's bid to "return to the hyphen" (Kingston 60; Partridge; Kong 143).
5. Asian American literary studies currently comprises works by Americans of Bangladeshi, Burmese, Cambodian, Chinese, Filipino, Hawaiian, Hmong, Japanese, Korean, Indian, Indonesian, Laotian, Nepali, Pakistani, Sri Lankan, Tamil, Thai, Vietnamese, and mixed-race descent, as well as diverse Pacific Islanders.
6. Yet Li himself, after editing a monumental four-volume reference work on Asian American literature (Li, *AAL*), seems to have vaulted into the left of the hyphen, for his latest book is exclusively on Chinese capitalism and cinema (Li, *Economy*).
7. Another *New York Times* piece dated 4 April 2016 similarly observes that "despite the emergence of the metrosexual and an increase in stay-at-home dads, tough-guy stereotypes die hard" and that "some colleges are waking up to the fact that men may need to be *taught* to think beyond their own stereotypes" (Reiner).
8. The concept of *li* is criticized by Xu Zhimo as vague yet constraining in "Art and Life" (Z. Xu 172).
9. I note briefly in Chapter 4 that Korean American writer Younghill Kang and Chinese poet Xu Zhimo (who figures as Hsu Tsimou in Kang's *East Goes West*) seem closer kindred spirits than between Kang and any Asian American writer, or between Xu and any Chinese writer. I also observe in Chapter 7 that Bing Xin and Sui Sin Far share a similar "Asian American sensibility."

Works Cited

Behdad, Ali, and Juliet Williams. "Neo-Orientalism." In *Globalizing American Studies*. Ed. Brian T. Edwards and Dilip Parameshwar Gaonkar. Chicago: University of Chicago Press, 2010. 283–299.

Behdad, Ali. "What can American Studies and Comparative Literature Learn from Each Other?" *American Literary History* 24.3 (2012): 608–617.

Brooks, David. "The Sexual Politics of 2016." *New York Times*, 29 March 2016: A25.

Buell, Frederick. *National Culture and the New Global System*. Baltimore, MD: John Hopkins University Press, 1994.
Campomanes, Oscar V. "Filipinos in the United States and Their Literature of Exile." In *Reading the Literature of Asian America*. Ed. Shirley Geok-lin Lim and Amy Ling. Philadelphia: Temple University Press, 1992. 49–78.
Certeau, Michel de. *The Practice of Everyday Life*. Trans. Steven Rendall. Berkeley: University of California Press, 1984.
Cheng, Anne Anlin. "The Melancholy of Race." *Kenyon Review* 19.1 (1997): 49–61.
Cheung, King-Kok. *Articulate Silences: Hisaye Yamamoto, Maxine Hong Kingston, Joy Kogawa*. New York: Cornell University Press, 1993.
———. "Re-viewing Asian American Literary Studies." In *An Interethnic Companion to Asian American Literature*. Ed. King-Kok Cheung. Cambridge: Cambridge University Press, 1997. 1–36.
———. "Thrice Muted Tale: Interplay of Art and Politics in Hisaye Yamamoto's 'The Legend of Miss Sasagawara.'" *MELUS* 17.3 (1991–1992): 109–125.
Chin, Frank. "Come All Ye Asian American Writers of the Real and the Fake." In *The Big Aiiieeeee! An Anthology of Asian American Writers*. Ed. Jeffery Paul Chan, et al. New York: New American Library-Meridian, 1991. 1–92.
———. "This Is Not An Autobiography." *Genre* 18.2 (1985): 109–130.
Chin, Frank, et al. *Aiiieeeee! An Anthology of Asian-American Writers*. Washington, DC: Howard University Press, 1974/1983.
Chin, Marilyn 陈美玲.《一抹黄色: Plain Yellow》. Trans. Guicang Li 李贵苍 and Luping Hu 胡路莘. Beijing: Intellectual Property Publishing House, 2016.
Cruz, Denise. *Transpacific Femininities: The Making of the Modern Filipina*. Durham: Duke University Press, 2012.
Dabashi, Hamid. "Native Informers and the Making of the American Empire." *Al-Ahram Weekly* 1 June 2006. <http://www.campus-watch.org/article/id/2802> (accessed 12 December 2014).
Diaz, Vincente M. "To 'P' or Not to 'P'?: Marking the Territory Between Pacific Islander and Asian American Studies." *Journal of Asian American Studies* 7.3 (2004): 183–208.
Dimock, Wai-Chee. *Through Other Continents: American Literature across Deep Time*. Princeton: Princeton University Press, 2006.
Eng, David L. *Racial Castration: Managing Masculinity in Asian America*. Durham: Duke University Press, 2001.
Feng, Pin-chia. "Re-Mapping Asian American Literature: The Case of Fu Sang." *American Studies International* 38.1 (2000): 61–70.
Fishkin, Shelley Fisher. "Crossroads of Cultures: The Transnational Turn in American Studies—Presidential Address to the American Studies Association, November 12, 2004." *American Quarterly* 57.1 (2005): 17–57.
Foote, Lorien. *The Gentlemen and the Roughs: Violence, Honor, and Manhood in the Union Army*. New York: NYU Press, 2011, 2013.

Friedman, Susan Stanford. *Mappings: Feminism and the Cultural Geographies of Encounter*. Princeton: Princeton University Press, 1998.
Hernandez, Javier C. "Wanted in China: More Male Teachers, to Make Boys Men." *New York Times*, 6 February 2016.
Ho, Tamara. *Romancing Human Rights: Gender, Intimacy, and Power between Burma and the West*. Honolulu: University of Hawai'i Press, 2015.
Huang, Yunte. *Transpacific Displacement: Intertextual Travel in Twentieth Century American Literature*. Berkeley: University of California Press, 2002.
Jin, Wen. *Pluralist Universalism: An Asian Americanist Critique of U.S. and Chinese Multiculturalisms*. Columbus: Ohio State University Press, 2012.
Kim, Elaine H. *Asian American Literature: An Introduction to the Writings and Their Social Context*. Philadelphia: Temple University Press, 1982.
———. "Defining Asian Amerian Realities through Literature." *Cultural Critique* 6 (1987): 87–111.
Kingston, Maxine Hong. "Cultural Mis-readings by American Reviewers." In *Asian and Western Writers in Dialogue: New Cultural Identities*. Ed. Guy Amirthanayagam. London: Macmillan, 1982. 55–65.
Kong, Belinda. "Theorizing the Hyphen's Afterlife in Post-Tiananmen Asian America." *MFS Modern Fiction Studies* (2010): 136–159.
Koshy, Susan. "The Fiction of Asian American Literature." *Yale Journal of Criticism* 9 (1996): 315–346.
Lee, Leo Ou-fan. *The Romantic Generation of Modern Chinese Writers*. Cambridge: Harvard University Press, 1973.
Lee, Rachel C. *The Americas of Asian American Literature: Gendered Fictions of Nation and Transnation*. Princeton: Princeton University Press, 1999.
———, ed. *Routledge Companion to Asian American and Pacific Islander Literature*. New York: Routledge, 2014.
Leong, Russell C. "A Third Literature of the Americas: With Evelyn Hu-DeHart, Kathleen Lopez, Maan Lin, Yibing Huang & Wen Jin." *CUNY Forum: Asian American/Asian Studies* 1.1 (2013–2014): 111–115.
Leong, Russell C., and Evelyn Hu-DeHart. "Forging a Third Chinese Literature of the Americas." *Amerasia Journal* 38.2 (2012): vii–xiv.
Levenson, Joseph R., and Franz Schurmann. *China: An Interpretive History*. Berkeley: University of California Press, 1969.
Li, David Leiwei. "(In Lieu of an) Introduction: The Asian American Subject between Liberalism and Neoliberalism." In *Asian American Literature*. Ed. David Leiwei Li. 4 vols. London: Routledge, 2012. Vol. I:1–29.
———. *Economy, Emotion, and Ethics in Chinese Cinema: Globalization on Speed*. New York: Routledge, 2016.
———. *Imagining the Nation: Asian American Literature and Cultural Consent*. Stanford: Stanford University Press, 1998.
———, ed. *Asian American Literature*. 4 vols. New York: Routledge, 2012.

Lim, Shirley Geok-lin. "Immigration and Diaspora." In *An Interethnic Companion to Asian American Literature*. Ed. King-Kok Cheung. Cambridge: Cambridge University Press, 1997. 289–311.

Louie, Kam. *Theorizing Chinese Masculinity: Society and Gender in China*. Cambridge: Cambridge University Press, 2002.

Lowe, Lisa. "Heterogeneity, Hybridity, Multiplicity: Marking Asian American Differences." *Diaspora* 1.1 (1991): 24–44.

———. *The Intimacies of Four Continents*. Durham, NC: Duke University Press, 2015.

Lye, Colleen. "In Dialogue with Asian American Studies and Racial Form." *Representations* 99 (2007): 1–6.

Nguyen, Viet. "The Remasculinization of Chinese America: Race, Violence, and the Novel." *American Literary History* 12.1 (2000): 130–157.

Ono, Kent A. "Retracing an Intellectual Course in Asian American Studies." In *A Companion to Asian American Studies*. Ed. Kent A. Ono. Trans. Companion. Malden: Blackwell Publishing, 2005. 1–14.

Palumbo-Liu, David. *Asian/American: Historical Crossings of a Racial Frontier*. Stanford: Stanford University Press, 1999.

Partridge, Jeffrey F. L. "Claiming Diaspora in Shirley Geok-lin Lim's Joss & Gold." *Asian Diasporas: Cultures, Identities, Representations*. Ed. Robbie B. H. Goh and Shawn Wong. Hong Kong: Hong Kong University Press, 2004. 131–147.

Radhakrishnan, R. "Is the Ethnic 'Authentic' in the Diaspora?" In *The State of Asian America: Activism and Resistance in the 1990s*. Ed. Jr. Karin Aguilar-San Juan. Cambridge: South End Press, 1994. 219–233.

Reiner, Andrew. "Teaching Men to Be Emotionally Honest." *New York Times*, 4 April 2016: ED11.

Said, Edward W. *Humanism and Democratic Criticism*. New York: Columbia University Press, 2004.

———. *Reflections on Exile and Other Essays*. Cambridge: Harvard University Press, 2002.

Shih, Shu-mei. "Introduction: What Is Sinophone Studies?" *Sinophone Studies: A Critical Reader*. Ed. Shu-mei Shih, Chien-hsin Tsai, and Brian Bernards. New York: Columbia University Press, 2013. 1–16.

Sohn, Stephen Hong, Paul Lai, and Donald C. Goellnicht. "Introduction: Theorizing Asian American Fiction." *Modern Fiction Studies* 56.1 (2010): 1–18.

Srikanth, Rajini. *The World Next Door: South Asian American Literature and the Idea of America*. Philadelphia: Temple University Press, 2004.

Ty, Eleanor. *Unfastened: Globality and Asian North American Narratives*. Minneapolis: University of Minnesota Press, 2010.

Wang, Dorothy. *Thinking Its Presence: Form, Race, and Subjectivity in Contemporary Asian American Poetry.* Stanford: Stanford University Press, 2013.

Wang, Ning. "(Re)Considering Chinese American Literature: Toward Rewriting Literary History in a Global Age." *Amerasia Journal* 38.2 (2012): xv–xxii.

Wong, Sau-ling Cynthia. "Denationalization Reconsidered: Asian American Cultural Criticism at a Theoretical Crossroads." *Amerasia* 21.1–2 (1995): 1–27.

———. *Reading Asian American Literature: From Necessity to Extravagance.* Princeton: Princeton University Press, 1993.

Wu, Bing. "Concerning Asian American Literary Studies." *Foreign Literary Criticism* 2 (2008): 15–23.

———. "Reading Chinese American Literature to Learn about America, China, and Chinese America." *Amerasia Journal* 34.2 (2008): 99–108.

Xu, Xinjian. "On Historical View of Multiethnic Literature." *Journal of Cambridge Studies* 4.2 (2009): 15–23.

Xu, Zhimo. ""Art and Life" (1922)." In *Modern Chinese Literary Thought: Writings on Literature, 1893–1945.* Ed. Kirk A. Denton. Stanford: Stanford University Press, 1996. 169–181.

PART I

Gender

CHAPTER 2

(S)wordswoman versus (S)wordsman: Maxine Hong Kingston and Frank Chin

For almost two decades, Asian American literary studies was animated by the ruckus over Maxine Hong Kingston's *The Woman Warrior* (1976), winner of the National Book Critics Circle Award and the first book by an American-born Asian to garner broad popular acclaim. Not everyone in the Asian American community was pleased. Kingston's harshest critic was Frank Chin, a writer, editor, actor, and playwright; *The Chickencoop Chinaman* (1972) and *The Year of the Dragon* (1974) by Chin were the first Chinese American plays performed at the American Place Theatre in New York. This chapter revisits the feud between the two writers and builds on an essay originally published in *Conflicts in Feminism* (1990), which traces the contesting politics of gender as reflected in the literary arena between Chinese American women and men in the 1980s and 1990s (K.-K. Cheung, "The Woman Warrior versus The Chinaman Pacific"). I advocated then what has come to be called "intersectionality" (Crenshaw), pointing out the inextricability of sexism and racism, urging white feminists to pay attention to both gender and race, and trying to steer Asian American men away from sexist and homophobic solutions to racism.

Caught up in the gender quarrel, I gave short shrift to the two antagonists' inauguration of a spirited transpacific literary intercourse. For too long, the innovative deployment of Chinese classics by Kingston and Chin has met with lukewarm, even hostile responses from both Chinese and Asian American scholars for reasons ranging from alleged infidelity to the original sources, anxiety about Orientalist interpretations, unfamiliarity with Asian classics, alleged misrepresentation of the ethnic community, desire to distinguish Asian American literature from Asian literature, and preoccupation with "claiming America."[1] These reasons conflate textual criticism with the critics' desire to divorce Chinese American from Chinese literature, and with anxieties about mainstream reception. In the case of Chin, owing to his intransigent attacks on a roster of Chinese American writers (Kingston, David Henry Hwang, C. Y. Lee, Lin Yutang, Amy Tan, Jade Snow Wong, Yung Wing, to name just a few) and feminist critics (including myself), his polemical reputation has overshadowed his otherwise astute critical insight, his pioneering role in Asian American literary studies, his dissemination of the Asian heroic tradition, and his literary pyrotechnics. Many feminist scholars have deemed Chin's ideas to be too over the top to be worthy of engagement, preferring to leave the self-styled Chinatown cowboy in his own Wild West; other Asian Americanists are indifferent to his painstaking exegesis and literary deployment of Asian classics. It is not too late, however, for me to bury the hatchet and make amends for not having paid sufficient attention to his inventive deployment of source material. In addition to recapitulating the original debate and my position as a Chinese American critic, this chapter gives Chin and Kingston their dues for decentering the European American heritage through integrating Chinese tradition with American culture and literature, thereby ushering in a brave new tradition.

In the late 1980s, I shared the frustrations of many women of color that most mainstream feminists were unfamiliar with the historical and cultural contexts of peoples of color, making dialogue difficult. I maintained that in order to understand friction among feminists, we need to look at women and men concomitantly. Because the problems of race and gender are closely intertwined, we must approach gender issues in Chinese American literary studies from multiple fronts: recognize the historical feminization of Asian American men, address the dialectic between racial stereotypes and cultural nationalist discourse, and dismantle obdurate codes of masculinity and femininity in both Asian and Western cultures. Since a wish for self-empowerment often involves cultural reconstruction, gender and race have played key roles in shaping American literary history. Although an increasing number of people of color and sexual minorities have questioned white male universals, dominant patriarchal norms continue to seduce even those writers and critics who otherwise challenge white male literary historians' monolithic authority. They remain in thrall to such norms, unwittingly upholding the criteria of those whom they assail. Equating silence and passivity or victimization with femininity and conflating masculinity with physicality and martial valor have had an intractable purchase in Chinese American literary circles.

Having entered the field as a bilingual woman of Cantonese descent, I analyze what I take to be the feminist and heroic impulses that have invigorated Chinese American literature but also divided its authors and critics. Structuring my argument around the writing of Kingston, an avowed feminist, and Frank Chin, a vociferous champion of Asian American manhood, I use their literary strategies to address several controversial issues (e.g. Kingston's alleged distortion of Chinese myths and her fusion of fact and fiction) concerning "proper" deployment of the Chinese original. I argue that, notwithstanding Chin's sworn enmity, remarkable artistic affinities exist between the two writers, for both of them redefine gender and heroism by sifting through their ancestral culture, altering details to suit their own need for a "usable past" (to borrow Renato Constantino's term). Chin can afford to be relatively true to the Chinese raw material because it accords with his androcentric agenda, whereas Kingston must recast that material to bring forth a feminist and pacifist subjectivity.

STEREOTYPES AND REVERSE STEREOTYPES

Sexual politics in Chinese America reflect invidious cultural and historical legacies. These issues, which have touched many sensitive nerves, sparked the controversy over Kingston's works. A theme explored in *The Woman Warrior* is the primacy of patrilineage in traditional Chinese culture, the predisposition of many Chinese immigrants of the older generations to favor male over female offspring. This is not to discount the history of inequality and exclusion that Chinese American men have had to confront (Espiritu; Takaki, Nee and Nee; Lowe). Of the early immigrants, 90 percent of whom were male; antimiscegenation laws and laws prohibiting Chinese laborers' wives from entering the United States ghettoized these men into bachelor communities in various Chinatowns and prevented them from fathering a subsequent generation. Furthermore, white historians often chose not to record these early immigrants' contributions to American history, which included building roads, mining gold, cultivating plantations, even fighting in the American Civil War (McCunn). To the American public, Chinamen were noted for performing traditionally "women's work"—as restaurant cooks, laundry workers, domestic helpers, and waiters.

The social and economic oppression described above, together with what Said has identified as the long-standing Orientalist casting of the Asian in the role of the silent and passive Other (Said), provide fodder for the degrading, stereotypical depiction of Asians of both sexes in the American popular imagination (Iwamura; Marchetti; J. Lee; R.G. Lee, "Invention"; J. Chan). Elaine H. Kim notes, for instance, that the popular images of Asian women as submissive and dainty sex objects, as exotic "dream girls of the mysterious East," have given rise to demands for "X-rated films featuring Asian women and the emphasis on [their] bondage in pornographic material"; for "Oriental" bathhouse workers in American cities; and for mail-order marriages and expensive dating services for American men "seeking young Asian brides" (Kim, "BR" 64). Little has changed in the American media since: Every single episode of *Marco Polo*—the 2014 Netflix television drama series—features a harem of naked Asian damsels, one of whom is a femme fatale who can inflict mortal wounds in the nude.

Chinese men in popular culture don't escape such insidious inscriptions either, for they are often depicted as "inferior in both physique and ethics" to white men (Kang 77). Frank Chin describes how the American silver screen has always impugned Chinese American virility:

> The movies were teachers. In no uncertain terms they taught America that we were lovable for being a race of sissies... Unlike the white stereotype of the evil black stud, Indian rapist, Mexican macho, the evil of the evil Dr. Fu Manchu was not sexual, but homosexual... [Charlie Chan] is awkward in a baggy suit and clumsy... The large family of the bovine detective isn't the product of sex, but animal husbandry... *He never gets into violent things.* (Chin, "Confessions" 66; my emphasis)

Chin and Jeffery Paul Chan argue in "Racist Love" that each racial stereotype comes in either an "unacceptable" model that is uncontrollable by whites or an "acceptable" model that is tractable: "There is racist hate and racist love" (Chin and Chan, "RL" 65, 79). While the "masculine" stereotypes of blacks, Indians, and Mexicans are generated by "racist hate," Chin and Chan contend, "racist love" has been lavished on Chinese Americans, "raw material for the 'flock,' pathological sheep for the shepherd.... A race without sinful manhood" (69).

If racist love denies "manhood" to Asian men, it endows Asian women with an excess of "womanhood." Elaine Kim observes that "the characterization of Asian men is a reflection of a white male perspective that defines the white man's virility," and therefore "it is possible for Asian men to be viewed as asexual and the Asian woman as only sexual" (Kim, "BR" 64). The putative gender difference among Asian Americans, exaggerated out of all proportion in the popular imagination, has created intra-racial resentment that persists to this day. For example, a slew of anonymous hate mail has been directed at Asian women dating white men at both University of California, Los Angeles, (UCLA) and University of Southern California (USC) in the last few years (Romero).

The Third World and feminist movements' attempts to counter extant stereotypes could not curb the escalating tensions between women and men in Asian American communities. Many Chinese American men, like Chin and Chan, remained blind to their own patriarchal positions even as they attempted to debunk the dominant culture's distorted representation of Asian males. Their discussion of Charlie Chan and Fu Manchu and their juxtaposition of stock images of Asian men with those of other men of color betray homophobia and preference for stereotypes that link race to predatory violence ("evil black stud, Indian rapist, Mexican macho"). Their sexist bias is all too blatant: "Our nobility [as Asian] is that of an efficient housewife. At our worst we are contemptible because we are womanly, effeminate, devoid of all the traditionally masculine qualities of originality, daring, physical courage, creativity" (68). In deprecating domestic work as "feminine" and slotting laudable attributes under the rubric of masculinity, Chin and Chan further buttressed gender hierarchy.

The thirst for a viable Asian American male model accounted in part for the immense appeal of Bruce Lee and the ascendency of Kung fu heroes. Although the cinematic image of Bruce Lee as a Kung fu master countered the feminine representations of Chinese American men, his role in the only Hollywood film in which he appeared during his lifetime was, in Elaine Kim's view, "less a human being than a fighting machine" (Kim, "PC" 107). Chin seemed to think otherwise: "Bruce Lee could kick anybody he wanted to in China; all he could do in America was to be buried as a foreigner" (Chin, "Kung Fu" 137). While Kim objected to the brutish portrayal of Bruce Lee, Chin hankered after a more pugnacious image. Are women and men, to borrow one of Kim's titles, indeed "such opposite creatures"?[2]

The groundbreaking *Aiiieeeee! An Anthology of Asian-American Writers* (1974) and its sequel, *The Big Aiiieeeee!* (1991), edited by Chin, Chan, Lawson Inada, and Shawn Wong, had an overlapping agenda: remasculinization. In *Aiiieeeee!* the coeditors deplored "the lack of a recognized style of Asian American manhood" (xxxviii). *The Big Aiiieeeee!* issued a corrective, wherein Chin elaborates an Asian heroic tradition, touting specifically the following Chinese and Japanese classics: *Water Margin* (also translated as *Outlaws of the Marsh* and *All Men Are Brothers*), *Romance of the Three Kingdoms* (hereafter *Three Kingdoms*), *Journey to the West* (also translated as *Monkey*), and *Chushingura* (Chin, "Come" 1–92). In venerating Chinese and Japanese epic heroes who are not unlike their Western counterparts—"the champions of man's ambitions," seeking "self-sufficient manhood" (Bowra 14)—Chin's cultural nationalist stance would exclude dissident voices so as to reinstate an Asian patriarchy.

Behind the alternative literary tradition that Chin attempts to construct is heard the patriarchal tenor of both Chinese and American cultures which, ironically, only reproduces the exclusionary practices of the white literary establishment. Opposed to the heroic tradition that Chin has reclaimed is the queer and feminist scholarly reassessment of the Western code of heroism. The traditional values of competitive individualism and martial prowess questioned by feminist scholars (Gilligan; Wolf; King) Chin relishes, citing certain maxims, purported to be from traditional Chinese epics and war manuals, such as "I am the law," "life is war," and affirmations of the "ethic of private revenge" (Chin, "Come" 35–37). Indistinguishable from hegemonic violence is the belligerence implicit in these slogans. As Viet Thanh Nguyen wryly notes: "Although violence throughout American history had been used to emasculate Chinese American men by exploiting their labor and excluding them from American society, young Asian Americans discovered that violence could also be used to *re*masculinize themselves and the historical memory of their immigrant predecessors" (Nguyen 130). Furthermore, because the warrior profile does not conventionally fit women and sexual minorities, they are excluded from Chin's heroic past. In demanding that Asian American writers pass a heroic litmus test for authenticity, Chin and his fellow editors only reappropriate the literary establishment's strategy of censoring minority voices that do not echo white male "universals."

Gender and Genre

The *Aiiieeeee!* editors (and Chin in particular) and feminist critics also have collided over the question of genre. According to Chin, the genre most antithetical to the heroic tradition is autobiography, which he denounces as a form of Christian confession. "The fighter writer uses literary forms as weapons of war, not the expression of ego alone, and ... [not] dandyish expressions of feeling and psychological attitudinizing," he pronounces. "Confession and autobiography celebrate the process of conversion from an object of contempt to an object of acceptance.... It's the quality of submission, not assertion that counts" (Chin, "Autobiography" 112, 130). Chin further insists that autobiography is not an indigenous genre in China, that "the Christian Chinese American autobiography is the only Chinese American literary tradition" (122–124). His pronouncements are multiply skewed. First, Western autobiography is not the sole preserve of Christians. Second, as I demonstrate in Chapter 6, there is a Chinese autobiographical tradition. Third, even if autobiography is much more prevalent in the West, Chinese American writers, as Sau-ling Wong contends, are entitled to appropriate a genre "indigenous to the Chinese in America" (S.-l.C. Wong 256–257). Last but not least, far from being a form of submission, autobiography is often a vehicle of subversion and "self-invention" (Eakin). Floyd Cheung advances, for instance, that in the wake of a "discourse that connected national and individual manliness" (promoted by Theodore Roosevelt at the turn of the twentieth century), Yung Wing uses his autobiography (one specifically panned by Chin) as a testament of individual and collective "manliness" (32; see also Chapter 6).

Chin's aversion to the genre, to be sure, is rooted in the vexed history of Asian American autobiography in relation to the marketplace. Many early Asian American writers had to employ autobiography as a means to be published and read by a mainstream audience, hence the preponderance of Asian American life-writing in English. Writing by Chinese Americans (and arguably by any ethnic American) is susceptible to being read as ethnography, as representative of the author or the author's presumed community, to the degree that getting published and gaining a mainstream readership can mean subjecting oneself to its patronizing gaze and Orientalist expectations, an act Chin decries as Christian confession. Traise Yamamoto notes: "Popular misconceptions and stereotypes and their resultant market forces, U.S. relations with Asia, and immigration histories have significantly shaped the publishing history of Asian American autobiography";

consequently, autobiographical writing from the late nineteenth century through approximately 1940 confirmed "dominant cultural notions of Asian foreignness and exotic customs" (380).

While the refrain of Asian backwardness or quaintness can be heard in many prototypical examples of this genre, some also use it to counter the negative portrayal of Asians in mainstream literature. Both Patricia Chu and Sunn Shelley Wong have shown how Asian American writers of autobiography and bildungsroman use these realist forms to both claim America and question established notions of being American, to both answer a popular demand and highlight their particular experience, as well as address pressing sociopolitical issues (Chu, *Assimilating Asians* 1–26; S.S. Wong 61). Feminist critics who have been some of the most avid exponents of autobiography are concerned less with social context than with interiority, concurring with Paul John Eakin about the genre's self-fashioning potential; they believe that women have always used autobiography to *assert*, however tentatively, their subjectivity (Jelinek; Smith; Stanton; Miller; Benstock).

The publication of *The Woman Warrior* in 1976 triggered an inevitable standoff between Asian American cultural nationalists and feminists (K.-K. Cheung, "WW vs. CP"; Chu, *Assimilating Asians*; Kim, "Opposite"; D.L. Li; R.G. Lee, "Invention"; S.-l.C. Wong; Woo). Mainstream Feminist scholars lavished praise on the book (Rabine; Juhasz; Yalom), but it was censured by a number of Chinese and Chinese American critics. Much of the criticism stems from its initial classification as autobiography (when it is anything but an unembellished, factual account), its alleged misrepresentation of Chinese and Chinese American culture, and reinforcement of the stereotype of Chinese culture as sexist. Jeffery Paul Chan, responding to a positive review by Diane Johnson in the *New York Review of Books*, upbraided Knopf for publishing *The Woman Warrior* as biography rather than fiction and ridiculed the reviewer for her ignorance of Chinese American history and for her indiscriminate praise of the book owing to its "female anger" (J. P. Chan, "Mysterious" 41; D. Johnson). Benjamin Tong called it a "fashionably feminist work written with white acceptance in mind" (Tong, "Critic" 20). Katheryn Fong fretted about "non-Chinese" reading the book as "true accounts of Chinese and Chinese American history" and about its negative portrayal of Chinese men (Fong 67, 68). Chinese scholar Ya-Jie Zhang recalls her finding the book "somewhat twisted" initially, offending her "sense of national pride"; only by viewing the book as "an American story" can she accept Kingston's "distortions of the stories ... sacred in [her] homeland" (Zhang 17, 18).

The negative reactions arose from what I consider as ethnographic fallacy: the assumption that ethnic autobiography is a faithful record of external reality representative of the autobiographer's community. This tendency to read Asian American life narratives as transparent, along with the lack of bicultural literacy in the general reading public and the concern with mainstream perception of Chinese Americans, explains in large part the divided reception of *The Woman Warrior*, which was widely taught not only in literature but also in anthropology classes, as though the book were a window to the ethnic enclave. While many critics praise the memoir for breaking new frontiers in the tradition of American autobiography, the very strategies considered to be innovative, such as combining fact and fantasy and splicing historical and legendary figures, do not sit well with some Asian Americans and scholars from China. Because of the prevalence of ethnological assumptions, the inclusion of unusual practices such as monkey feasts or frenum-cutting in Kingston's memoir has roused consternation among fellow Asian Americans who find such details incendiary, adding fuel to Orientalist perceptions about the barbaric Other (Ma; Zhao, "Orientalism"). Thus, the anxiety was less about its circulation within the ethnic community than about its reception in the non-Asian public.

If, as Susan Stanford Friedman has pointed out, genre is all too often gendered (203–228), then Kingston's infusion of autobiography with fiction is more than a genre concern. As noted above, feminist scholars of autobiography suggest that female autobiographers are more formally concerned with narrating their subjective experience as opposed to objectively recording the chronological record of their lives. *The Woman Warrior* follows this tradition. Because many white readers persisted in apprehending creative expressions by writers of color as auto-ethnography, formal experimentation for the "minority" author in the 1970s was perilous business. Furthermore, in comparison to their response to antiracist texts, the general reading public tends to be more amenable to work that highlights sexism within the ethnic enclave. Though *The Woman Warrior* addresses both sexism and racism, the novel's feminist themes preoccupied white critics while members of the Chinese American community felt betrayed, maligned by one of their own.

Where Kingston insists on shuttling between the world of facts and the world of fantasy, on giving multiple versions of truth as subjectively perceived, her detractors demand genre purity and historical authenticity. Perhaps precisely because Kingston is female, writing amid discouraging realities, she can only forge a viable and expansive identity by rewriting patriarchal myths and envisioning alternative scenarios. Suzanne Juhasz observes that to resolve the outright conflict many women face "between societal possibility and imaginative possibility," Kingston "makes autobiography from fiction, from fantasy, from forms that have conventionally belonged to the novel" (Juhasz 62). Her autobiographical act, far from betokening submission, as Chin would have it, turns the self into a "heroine" and is in a sense an act of "revenge" (a word represented in Chinese by two ideographs which Kingston loosely translates as "report a crime") against both the Chinese and the white cultures that erode her self-esteem. To discredit her for taking artistic liberties is to align with white reviewers who reduce literary works by ethnic authors to sociohistorical documentary. According to James Clifford, even ethnography has been rethought as subjective composition rather than objective record, for "culture is composed of seriously contested codes and representations" and "the poetic and the political are inseparable" (Clifford 2). Kingston herself clarifies: "I am not writing history or sociology but a 'memoir' like Proust" (Kingston, "Mis-Readings" 64).

Gender-Bending

Kingston is accused not only of passing fiction as autobiography but also of doctoring Chinese myths and reinforcing the stereotype of Chinese men as sexist. Frank Chin calls her one of "the yellow agents of yellow extinction and white acceptance and assimilation," and reprimands her for faking tradition, writing from the Christian autobiographical tradition, and telling "the same Cinderella story of rescue from the perverse, the unnatural, and cruel Chinese into the one true universe" (Chin, "Autobiography" 110). In his prefatory essay to *The Big Aiiieeeee!* entitled "Come All Ye Asian American Writers of the Real and the Fake," Chin argues that "myths are, by nature, immutable and unchanging" (Chin, "Come" 29). He is particularly livid over Kingston's rewriting of the tale of Mulan:

> Kingston takes a childhood chant, "The Ballad of Mulan," which is as popular today as "London Bridge Is Falling Down," and rewrites the heroine … to the specs of the stereotype of the Chinese woman as a pathological white supremacist victimized and trapped in a hideous Chinese civilization. The tattoos Kingston gives Fa Mulan, to dramatize cruelty to women, actually belong to the hero Yue Fei. (Chin, "Come" 3)

Chin contends that Kingston gives the woman warrior a prolonged tattoo session to support the racist stereotype about Chinese "misogynistic cruelty" (6). "The Ballad of Mulan" (木兰诗) is reprinted within his essay as though the Chinese poem were the "real" myth that had not gone through revisions (Chin, "Come" 4–6). In fact, "the Fa Mu Lan story… exists in a multitude of Chinese texts differing from each other in purpose as well as detail" (S.-l.C. Wong 271).

To magnify Kingston's alleged fraud by analogy, Chin wrote a satirical parody of *The Woman Warrior*—"The Most Popular Book in China" (1984)—about a French girl growing up in a French hand-laundry in Canton who draws inspiration from her ancestor: "Poor Joan of Arc. Born a son to a family that craved a daughter. They dressed their boy as a girl. They forced him into homosexual relationships with the surrounding court society, while young and naked virgins pranced through the deer park singing Vivaldi" (Chin, "Popular" 8). Chin's "unmanly warrior" is intended to cast aspersions on the historical veracity of *The Woman Warrior* and to place Kingston in the same company as the authors of Fu Manchu and Charlie Chan for confirming "the white fantasy that everything sick and sickening about the white self-image is really Chinese" (Chin, "Popular" 12). If the parody is meant to deride Kingston's "tampering" of the Mulan legend, it misfires and points instead to Kingston's ethnic consciousness and deft adaptation. Kingston is no doubt as familiar with Joan of Arc as with Mulan; that she chooses a Chinese heroine as her inspiration registers her ethnic pride. While Joan's parents in Chin's version are guilty of reverse sexism, the woman warrior's parents inflict pain on a voluntary daughter so as to empower her. Chin's warrior is expressly "unmanly"; his counterpart in *The Woman Warrior* is bravely androgynous.

Kingston's attempt at creating an androgynous heroine accounts for her melding of the Mulan legend and the Yue Fei (hi)story—to my mind an artistic amalgamation rather than a forgery. The narrator never claims that she is retelling the traditional Chinese legend. All she says is that her mother told her children bedtime stories about "swords-women" and taught them "the song of the warrior woman, Fa Mu Lan" (Fa Muk Lan in Cantonese and Hua Mulan in pinyin). Kingston warns the reader from the outset that she cannot tell Chinese traditions from movies, nor her mother's stories from dreams: "I couldn't tell where the stories left off and the dreams began, [the mother's] voice the voice of the heroines in my sleep" (Kingston, WW 6, 19). This confusion gives the author the poetic license to mingle fact and fiction and to forge a bracing Chinese American tradition. Hence when the narrator fancies herself as the warrior in the next paragraph, beginning with a subjunctive ("The call would come from a bird" (20), she is relating not a traditional tale but a dream or fantasy in which she morphs into the legendary warrior.

Within this fantasy, the warrior(s) remain nameless, but the story of Yue Fei, a general in the Song Dynasty, is grafted onto that of Fa Mu Lan. It is the male warrior's back, not the female's, that is tattooed in the Chinese sources. Yue Fei's mother acts as tattooist, inscribing onto her son's back before his departure a motto enjoining him to be loyal to his country. If, as Susan Gubar argues, Kingston's re-gendering of this ordeal literalizes the painful truth of woman as text (251), the author also claims other rights of authorship, like that of re-forming myths and transposing gender. But Kingston does more than adapt Chinese lore to comment on her American present. She refashions an identity that is neither Chinese nor white American but Chinese American. Furthermore, her revision of Chinese legends de-emphasizes the theme of physical prowess. Instead, her myth concerns verbal injuries and textual power. Historically, the four ideographs on Yue Fei's back function as a reminder to be patriotic. In Kingston's fantasy, there are many words, marshaled "in red and black files, like an army," to fortify the warrior (35).

The inscription on the woman warrior's back signifies word magic, not misogyny:

> The swordswoman and I are not so dissimilar... What we have in common are the words at our backs... The reporting is the vengeance—not the beheading, not the gutting, but the words. And I have so many words—"chink" words and "gook" words too—that they do not fit on my skin. (53)

While the dorsal script might mirror the demeaning sexist sayings the narrator has grown up with, she has transformed the aching words into amulets, scars into escutcheon, and humiliation into heroism. Unlike Fa Mu Lan, the narrator-as-warrior avenges herself less by slinging a sword than by spinning words. Instead of excelling in martial arts, she has learned the art of storytelling from the mother who "funneled China" into her ears (89). Brave Orchid's endless tales, which could well have clogged the young daughter's memory, have actually nourished her imagination. From this "mother tongue," she now creates tales that sustain her Chinese American identity. Far from disparaging Chinese culture, as Chin alleges, Kingston's memoir pays deep homage to ancestral, especially maternal, heritage and resounds to the drumbeat of the Asian American movement of the seventies in asserting a distinct ethnic consciousness. Colleen Lye observes: "Rather than representing a blocking figure that the youthful protagonist must leave or destroy ... the mother here is a resource ... not just a residual past to be left behind but a renewable resource for the future" (Lye, "AA" 215). It is therefore especially puzzling that Chin singles out *The Woman Warrior* as instantiating Christian self-contempt when it is arguably one of the first works that breaks away from an earlier Asian American autobiographical tradition, which stresses overcoming ethnic obstacles in order to assimilate into American culture.

In drawing from her Chinese legacy, Kingston must at the same time parry its patriarchal thrust. That her most scathing detractors and the most ardent purveyors of Chinese American "manhood" were one and the same was not coincidental. Chin, like some other Asian American men, felt her exposure of antifemale prejudices in their ethnic communities as a betrayal. But it is undeniable that some American-born daughters continue to suffer the sting of Chinese sexism. Kingston, one of these daughters, evinces a double allegiance: sensitive to the marginality of the men in her ethnic community but resentful of their male chauvinism.

The opening legend of *China Men* conveys these conflicting emotions by bringing out the parallel asymmetry of gender and ethnicity. Kingston borrows and adapts the legend from one of the first feminist novels written by a man, an eighteenth-century Chinese novel entitled *Flowers in the Mirror* (J.-C. Li). In Kingston's version, the male protagonist, Tang Ao, after his capture in the Land of Women, is transformed into an Oriental courtesan (a paramour for Her Highness) via feet binding, ear piercing, facial depilation, and rouging of his cheeks and lips. (Originally, it is

Tang Ao's brother-in-law who is made-over.) Kingston's conclusion reorients this opening tale: "Some scholars say that [the Land of Women] was discovered during the reign of Empress Wu (A.D. 694–705), and some say earlier than that, A.D. 441, and it was in North America" (5). The author's hypothetical relocation of the Land of Women to North America prompts readers to connect Tang Ao's ignominy abroad with the emasculation of Chinamen in the United States. The racial violence that men of Chinese descent have encountered in the New World has a long history, often tied to affronts to their manhood. The cross-dressings involved in the Mulan and the Tang Ao tales have unequal valences. Unlike Mulan's transvestism, Tang Ao's cross-dressing represents a "demotion," Donald Goellnicht observes, for "no one, it seems, wants to fill the 'feminine' gender role" (192).

Kingston's deliberate reversal of masculine and feminine roles foregrounds the construction of gender. Her legend speaks to both the mortification of Chinese men in the New World and the subjugation of women in China and America. Tang Ao's tortures are but the cosmetic routine that Chinese women had performed for men's pleasures for centuries. Following the author of *Flowers in the Mirror*, Kingston's treatment of her male character defamiliarizes the sexual objectification of Chinese women, at once unveiling the racist debasement of Chinese American men and the sexist degradation of Chinese women. As a companion volume to *The Woman Warrior*, *China Men*—notwithstanding its commemoration of the founding fathers of Chinese America—also registers "feminist anger." The author objects as keenly to her ancestral culture's patriarchy as to the racist treatment of her forefathers in their adopted country.

In addition to revealing the consilient suffering of Chinese American men and Chinese women, Kingston, like many other women writers of color, connects the men's umbrage at racism with their own misogynist behavior. In one episode, the narrator's immigrant father, a laundryman who seldom opens his mouth except to utter obscenities about women, is cheated by a gypsy and harassed by a white policeman. Upon their departure, the children, the narrator relates, learn to behave themselves so their father would not "turn on" them: "We knew that it was to feed us you had to endure demons and physical labor. You screamed wordless male screams that jolted the house upright" (13). Even as the daughter deplores the father's deafening epithets and brooding silences, she imputes the bad temper to his sense of "emasculation" in a white society. As in the analogous situations of Cholly Breedlove in Toni Morrison's *Bluest Eye*, Grange Copeland in Alice Walker's *Third Life of Grange Copeland*, and Victor Conway in Nina Revoyr's *Southland*, male tyranny erupts hard on the heel of racial violence. These men, who have to put up with white abuse, reassert their power by venting their anger at those who are even more powerless—the women and children in their families.

China Men issues a tacit call for mutual empathy between Chinese American men and women. In an interview with Kay Bonetti, Kingston likens herself to Tang Ao. Where Tang Ao enters the Land of Women and feels what it means to be of the other gender, so Kingston enters the realm of men and becomes "the kind of woman that loves men, and … can tell their stories without judging them" (Bonetti 36; see also Jardine & Smith). In addition, the author may be spurring her male readers to think as women, to discern correspondences between their plight and women's plight. If Asian men have been emasculated in America, they should be able to commiserate with women who have long been denied male privileges.

Heroism, Real and Fake

Given the representation of Asian American men in American public discourse as either absent, "unmanly," or villainous, it is no wonder that the coeditors of *Aiiieeeee!* and *The Big Aiiieeeee!* set out to redefine Asian American masculinity. The deprivation of history, language, and a literary heritage, according to *Aiiieeeee!*, results in this crisis in masculinity. *The Big Aiiieeeee!* prescribes, as antidote to Asian American emasculation, an "Asian heroic tradition," embodied by the martial heroes of Chinese and Japanese epics who are, presumably, worthy of emulation by Asian Americans.

But we cannot reconstruct Chinese American literary history without mutual empathy between all genders and all sexualities. I am divided about the Asian (American) heroic tradition that Chin attempts to enshrine. The herculean feat for which Chin has not received his due, but one I welcome, is his effort to introduce Asian classics to a wider readership. His reclamation of Chinese and Japanese epics has won him disapproval from some, such as filmmaker Frank Abe and Zhao Wenshu, a Chinese scholar, who would prefer to separate Asian from Asian American literature (*What's Wrong*; Zhao, "Orientalism"). But I appreciate Chin's critique of, and response to, American Eurocentric education, a topic I revisit in Chapter 6. Chin, who considers himself a lone champion of the "Chinaman" tradition in the United States because of the lack of Chinese cultural literacy among Americans, bemoans the fact that while he was "fluent" in the Western literary tradition, his former English professors at Berkeley knew pathetically little about Asian classics (Chin, "Autobiography" 118). Decades after Chin first sought redress for his grievance, the cultural asymmetry persists. Few American undergraduates have heard of the Chinese and Japanese epics that Chin adduces, but Shakespeare, and even the Bible, is part of the curriculum for most college students in China. The pluralistic vision that an increasing number of Asian American writers have advanced requires greater familiarity with the Eastern heritage. Particularly, a critic cannot abstract the phony from the authentic without a thorough knowledge of the source material.

However, I cannot embrace the gender ideology of the Asian heroic tradition by which Chin and the other editors of *The Big Aiiieeeee!* arbitrate between "the real and the fake":

> We describe the real, from its sources in the Asian fairy tale and the Confucian heroic tradition, to make the work of these Asian American writers understandable in its own terms. We describe the fake—from its sources in Christian dogma and in Western philosophy, history, and literature—to make it clear why the more popularly known writers ... are not represented here. (xv)

Having previously spoken out against the emasculation of Asian Americans in their introduction to *Aiiieeeee!*, the editors wish to show further that Chinese and Japanese Americans have a heroic—which is to say militant— heritage. Their promulgation of this tradition appears inseparable from their earlier attempt to overhaul "effeminate" representations and to erect Asian American manhood. In this light, the special appeal held by the war heroes for the editors comes to be rather obvious. Take Guan Yu/Kwan Kung (AD 160–221) in *Three Kingdoms*: loud, passionate, and vengeful, this deified patron of "fighters and writers" is antithetical in every way to the image of the quiet, passive, and submissive Oriental. Chin and his coeditors no doubt use the icon of this imposing hero to contravene pervasive assumptions about Chinese American docility.

For the American public to acknowledge the Robin Hoods and John Waynes of Chinese culture requires, of course, their acquaintance with the pantheon of Chinese folk heroes. But the masculinist orientation of the heroic tradition as expounded by Chin—who sees loyalty, revenge, and individual honor as its overriding ethos—gives me pause. If white media have chosen to highlight the nonthreatening characteristics of Asians, Chin is equally tendentious in playing up bellicose icons. When machismo is glorified to refute effeminate stereotypes, patriarchal terms and assumptions prevail.

Chin's contention is that the "use of the heroic tradition in Chinese literature as the source of Chinese American moral, ethical and esthetic universals is not literary rhetoric and smartass cute tricks ... but a simple history" (Chin, "Autobiography" 127). But the history that Chin describes is but a *his*tory. The Asian heroic tradition demands reevaluation to delineate its strengths and weaknesses. I do not dispute the tradition's emotional appeal and the intellectual excitement it stimulates. Characters such as Zhou Yu and Zhuge Liang in *Three Kingdoms* share Odysseus's strategic brilliance; the fraternal bond that three brothers—Liu Bei, Guan Yu (Kwan Kung), Zhang Fei (Cheung Fei)—swear to each other is reminiscent of Achilles's relationship to Patroclus. But just as all humankind does not find its spokesperson in Homer, something that encompasses "Asian Universals" is not to be found in an Asian heroic canon composed exclusively by men.

The editors' revival of an alternative literary history to shore up Asian American masculinity deserves sympathy; exalting loyalty, honor, wisdom, courage, and resistance is laudable. But I cannot countenance the resuscitation of manly codes that endorse violence. For all their avowed intent to retrieve an Asian American legacy, the frontier myth of conquest in the American West, wherein Asian immigrants first settled, appears to have infected the editors' discourse. Chin's preference for the bad guys rather than the heroes in the Chinatown movies he grew up with instigates his search for John Wayne's Chinese doppelganger: "The bad guy, a man invincible in individual combat, goes down under the gang swords of a hero, who's stepped out into life to learn ... that the individual needs friends. The balls the Chinese movie celebrated in Chinatown was [sic] gang balls and didn't really clash with John Wayne" (Chin, "Confessions" 66). Chin is, if you will, looking for a John Wayne vis-à-vis in a Chinese hero. His valorization of individualism and independence over teamwork or interdependence—which he dismisses as gang spirit but which is indeed inculcated in much of East Asia—betrays his thorough absorption of American mores.[3]

Chin takes upon himself to bring out "ballsy individuality" in Chinese classics. "Come All Ye Asian American Writers of the Real and the Fake," his 92-page manifesto in *The Big Aiiieeeee!*, puts forward a Chinese ethos that at once contradicts Orientalist perceptions of Chinese culture and aligns Chinese with white masculinity. He distills the following essence from *The Analects* by Confucius: "We are born to fight to maintain our personal integrity. All art is martial art. Writing is fighting... Living is fighting. Life is war" (35). Confucius most likely would have been shocked to hear his teaching summarized as the "ethic of private revenge [and] the ethic of popular revenge against the corrupt state" (34–35). Such a worldview is less reflective of the Sage—famous and notorious for his abiding respect for hierarchy—than of the American "national character" which, according to Richard Slotkin, embraces "the myth of regeneration through violence" (Slotkin 5). James Baldwin puts it more cuttingly: "In the United States, violence and heroism have been made synonymous except when it comes to blacks" (Baldwin 72). And when it comes to Asians, one might add. Chin's drive to counter Orientalist constructions thus produces an equally partial interpretation of Chinese culture; his selective invocation of Chinese mores echoes European American ideologies of masculinity, and his cultural nationalist gesture is marred by an apparent counterinvestment in patriarchal formula.

While I am no Sinologist, I grew up in Hong Kong reading many of the Chinese heroic epics, along with works of less heroic modes—found in works as diverse as Cao Xueqin's *Dream of the Red Chamber*, Tao Qian's pastoral poems, Qu Yuan's elegiac *Li Sao*《离骚》, writings by Lao Zi and Zhuang Zi, and Pu Songling's *Liaozhai Zhiyi*《聊斋志异》. I cannot concur with Chin's finger-pointing at Christianity for the submissive and "unheroic" traits that have been assigned to Chinese Americans. And I disagree with Benjamin R. Tong's contention that Confucian ethics were of little concern for early Chinese immigrants, the majority of whom were Cantonese peasants; that traits such as meekness and acquiescence to authority are only putatively Chinese, in that these behaviors were but part of the immigrants' arsenal for use in their fight against white racism ("Ghetto"). Though the early immigrants' folk culture is not to be confused with the highbrow culture of the Chinese literati, mainstream Chinese thought permeates the Cantonese folk imagination that synthesizes both the heroic ethos and Buddhism, Taoism, and Confucianism, which does advocate self-restraint and obedience to parental and state authority. Relegating the compliant traits of Chinese Americans to

Christianity or to white racism alone is to discount the complexity and the rich contradictions of Cantonese culture.

The Chinese heroic tradition itself is multivalent. More than martial glory or individual power, it values benevolence and peace. We need to only read the *Three Kingdoms* closely to see that behind the senseless deaths it tabulates and the ravages of war it recounts, there lies a longing for peace and unification that the division of the "three kingdoms" makes impossible. Even *The Art of War* recommends diplomacy over violence: "To subdue the enemy without fighting is the acme of skill" (77). In the prototype for Kingston's woman warrior, the "Ballad of Mulan," the denunciation of war is even more pronounced. According to the ballad, filial piety motivates the heroine to join the army. Because she is taking the place of her aged father, Mulan must assume male disguise. The poem hardly mentions her martial prowess. It describes, instead, a bleak battlefield and a lonely daughter. Understated lines such as "generals dead after hundreds of battles/warriors home after ten years" (my translation) enumerate the heavy cost and long duration of war. Thus the ballad contains a pacifist subtext, much in the way that the *Iliad* conceals an antiwar message beneath heraldic trappings (King 50ff). The Chinese heroic tradition is therefore richer and more nuanced than Chin, intent on finding models of truculence, would allow.

Unfortunately, the ability to perform ferocious acts implied in the concepts of warrior and epic hero is often bruited as manly courage, and men who have been historically subjugated are all the more tempted to adopt a jingoistic stance to signal their testosterone (see Chapter 3). bell hooks notes that many black men in the sixties worshipped men who exploited and brutalized women (87–117). Harryette Mullen, commenting on the Black Arts Movement of the 1960s and 1970s, which was primarily concerned with "defining and empowering blackness," observes: "several poets associated with this movement defined blackness specifically in ways that celebrated young militant black male heterosexuals [but] alienated other elements of the African American communities they ostensibly hoped to organize and empower" (Mullen 69). Toni Cade Bambara cautions against "equating black liberation with black men gaining access to male privilege" and offers an alternative to patriarchal prescriptions for manhood: "Perhaps we need to let go of all notions of manhood and femininity and concentrate on Blackhood… It perhaps takes less heart to pick up the gun than to face the task of creating a new identity … perhaps an androgynous self" (Bambara 103).

Trying to affirm an ethnic heritage while undermining its patriarchal authority, Kingston has taken pains to fashion androgynous selves in *The Woman Warrior* and *China Men*. Coming from a culture that places a high value on familial and communal solidarity, she has found it difficult to rally to the feminist cause without feeling divided or without being accused of betrayal. Because she feels that identification with Asian men at times inhibits her feminist impulse, she publishes *The Woman Warrior* and *China Men* separately (though they were conceived and written together as an "interlocking story"), lest the men's stories "undercut the feminist viewpoint." "I care about men ... as much as I care about women," she relates. "Given the present state of affairs, perhaps men's and women's experiences have to be dealt with separately for now, until more auspicious times are with us" (Kim, *Context* 209).

Redefinition of Heroism

Louis Althusser warns that hegemonic interests are secured when a dominated class takes in as common sense a dominant system of ideology (Althusser 174–183). Chinese American men who use the heroic dispensation to promote yellow power risk remaking themselves in the image of their oppressors—albeit in Asian panoply. Precisely because the racist treatment of Asians has taken the peculiar form of sexism—insofar as the indignities suffered by men of Chinese descent are analogous to those traditionally suffered by women—they must refrain from seeking masculinist solutions to racism. To do otherwise reinforces not only patriarchy but also cultural imperialism.

Asian Americans may eschew hegemonic ideals for alternative ontologies. Both Kingston and Chin have recuperated the Asian heroic tradition while redefining heroism as verbal prowess. *The Woman Warrior*'s recreated swordswoman draws power from the tattooed words on her back and from her martial training in equal measure. The interleaving of Chinese legends into her American memoir is a testament to Kingston's bicultural defiance: she is against male domination in *both* Chinese and American cultures. This is not to say that her transformed heroine, who wields power only under the (dis)guise of male armor, spells no trouble. The simile she tacitly valorizes—"fighting like a man"—serves rather than subverts sexist ideals.

Kingston, in fact, demurs from being identified with the swordswoman: "I don't really like warriors, [or] war as a way of solving things" (Bonetti

36–37). The Mulan wannabe's physical combat is incidental to the memoir. It is the battle against female silence and invisibility that *The Woman Warrior* wages. Writing is a heroic act of self-expression for the narrator, who is forbidden by her mother to tell a secret, unable to read aloud in English while first attending American school, and later fired for opening her mouth against racism. At the end of the book, her tutelary genius has changed from Mulan to T'sai Yen (蔡琰)—a female poet renowned for her intercultural cantos. Kingston's combination of the Yue Fei and Mulan legends in the narrator's childhood fantasy is thus fully integral to the structural design of the memoir, one that accentuates the potency of words at every step, from childhood struggle with silence to emergence as writer.

Kingston again recasts Chinese classics and renews her commitment to pacifism in *Tripmaster Monkey* (1989), her first novel. Her recurrent allusions to the Chinese heroic tradition, albeit filtered through a feminist lens, anticipate *The Big Aiiieeeee!*. Frank Chin is instantly recognizable in the novel's protagonist, Wittman Ah Sing—"a Chinese playwright, idealistic and enraged over racism, with the persona of an angry young man who can be exasperating—especially in his sexism—but is fundamentally decent" (Chu, "Tripmaster" 117). Like Chin, Wittman loves the Chinese epics *Three Kingdoms* and *Journey to the West*. Wittman, also known as the American Monkey (after the Monkey King in *Journey to the West*), even directs a marathon show inspired by *Three Kingdoms*. At the end of the performance, Wittman has a Damascene moment:

> He had made up his mind: he will not go to … any war. He had staged the War of the Three Kingdoms as heroically as he could, which made him start to understand: The three brothers and Cho Cho were masters of the war; they had worked out strategies and justifications for war so brilliantly that their policies and their tactics are used today, even by governments with nuclear-powered weapons. And they *lost*… Studying the mightiest war epic of all time, Wittman changed—beeen!—into a pacifist. (Kingston, *TM* 348)

The seemingly easy transformation of Wittman—a not so uncanny double of Chin—is achieved through Kingston's sleight of hand, whereby the pacifist author shows that it is possible to relish the ingenious strategies of the ancient Chinese warriors without embracing, wholesale, the heroic code that motivates their behavior and without endorsing proclivity to violence as machismo.

Chin's *Donald Duk* (1991) likewise relates the Asian heroic tradition to Chinese American lives. Many of the tenets set forth in *Aiiieeeee!* and *The Big Aiiieeeee!* are fleshed out in this bildungsroman, which Viet Nguyen rightly sees as a "project of *re*masculation" (Nguyen 142). The eponymous teenage protagonist has been taught in school that the Chinese are passive and nonassertive, "helpless against the relentless victimization by aggressive, highly competitive Americans" (Chin, *DD* 2). He later overcomes his racial self-contempt by learning about the Chinese epics and his predecessors' history in America. As one of the few early works by Asian Americans that contain sympathetic father figures, the novel also addresses a concern first articulated in *Aiiieeeee!*: "the failure of Asian American manhood to express itself in its simplest form: fathers and sons" (xlvi). King Duk, Donald's father, and Uncle Donald Duk are unusually patient and cogent in teaching Donald about his Chinese legacy. King Duk initiates the project of building 108 paper airplanes for the Chinese New Year to commemorate the 108 outlaws in *Water Margin*. When Donald mischievously burns one named after Lee Kuey (李逵), Uncle Donald Duk gives him a lesson that piques his curiosity about the fabled outlaws and his own ancestors: "Your Chinese name is not Duk, but Lee. Lee, just like Lee Kuey" (23). This passing reference to names is one of the many textual details that provokes Donald, who feels mortified by his cartoonish name, to learn more about the Chinese classic and Chinese American history.

Chin skillfully splices the mythical and historical narratives throughout the novel. The heroes in *Water Margin* are mostly righteous men victimized by a corrupt regime; they become rebels with prices on their heads and live separately as a fraternity away from society. Similarly, because of the 1882 Chinese Exclusion Act, many early immigrants entered the United States as "outlaws"—illegally, by forging immigration documents (hence Donald's fake surname). The strategies by which these early immigrants defied racist American legislation were not unlike those adopted against Chinese officialdom by the 108 outlaws. Furthermore, like the legendary fugitives, the immigrants—ghettoized in various Chinatowns—were likewise segregated from mainstream society. For Chin, who has set out to revamp Asian American manhood, *Water Margin* provides a resonant source. By highlighting the affinity between the intrepid outlaws and the Chinese forefathers in America, he represents those abused "Chinamen" who built the transpacific railroad as dauntless pioneers.

The epic also presents Chin with Chinese characters that match well with European American worthies. According to Uncle Donald Duk, the

Chinese brothers' hideout, Liang Shan (梁山), is similar to Sherwood Forest: "All the good guys who want better government are badmouthed by the guys in charge, and they go outlaw… Just like Robin Hood. But in the Chinese book, there are 108 Robin Hoods" (22). As Wang Xiaoxue points out, Chin subverts "History" with "history" in reclaiming the history of the transcontinental railroad (Wang 118). Its elision by the dominant culture is poignantly encapsulated in Kingston's *China Men*, in which the narrator describes how Ah Goong (grandfather) labors under inhuman conditions in building the railroad, but is nowhere to be found in the celebratory pictures that commemorate the completion of the feat: "While the demons posed for photographs, the China Men dispersed… The Driving Out had begun. Ah Goong does not appear in railroad photographs" (*CM* 145). Just as Kingston's imaginative rendering of the lives of her male ancestors must be read in the context of such historical erasure, so Chin's dreamlike conflation of the railroad builders and the heroes of *Water Margin* are intended to raise these builders from oblivion to heroic stature.

Yet Chin is rather partial in his representation of the Chinese rebels, who seem far more savage than Robin Hood and the Merry Men. Of the 108 colorful outlaws who appear in the Chinese classic (some of whom are quite civil, even chivalrous), Lee Kuey—one of the most brutish and obstreperous—soars to greatest prominence in *Donald Duk*. Uncle Donald Duk tells his nephew that this character "gets mad very easily," "loves to fight and kill people," and after a battle "his body is covered with layers of other peoples' [sic] drying blood" (22, 23). Since the teen has been told that he and Lee Kuey share the same last name, the implication seems to be that this virtual ancestor should inspire young Donald with awe, though the only similarity between bloodthirsty Lee Kuey and fainthearted Donald is their want of good judgment. Another figure extolled in *Donald Duk* is Kwan Kung (关公), whom King Duk describes as "the most powerful character" (67). Power here figures again as the ability to kill: "One look into your Kwan Kung eyes and he's dead" (67). Although the book effectively explodes the myth of the passive and submissive Oriental, it conflates animal savagery and lethal fury with virility and fortitude.

Thankfully, the novel also offers alternative glimpses of heroism. Kwan Kung, the God of War whom King Duk impersonates skillfully, is also the God of Literature. King Duk only exhibits a "killer's sense of individuality" when he plays Lord Kwan. As the chef who invites and cooks for an entire opera troupe of 300 people and distributes rice to every household in Chinatown during the lunar new year, he epitomizes the bounty of Soong Gong (宋江), one of the most respected heroes in the epic. More importantly, like Brave Orchid, the narrator's mother in *The Woman Warrior*, King Duk is a phenomenal storyteller, matching the epic hero's literary penchant. Instilling ethnic pride in his son by gainsaying dominant perceptions of the Chinese and enacting the heroic tales, King Duk is instrumental in transforming Donald from being ashamed to being proud of his ethnic heritage. Through a dream sequence in which Donald finds himself working on the railroad with his immigrant forebears under foreman Kwan—a dream replica that fuses Kwan Kung and King Duk—Donald learns both Chinese classics and Chinese American history, which reveals that his own ancestors not only built the railroad but also staged a strike demanding equal pay. In elucidating Chinese customs and in teaching Donald that "Chinatown is America" (Chin, *DD* 90), King Duk plays the role of a cultural transmitter, a role often reserved for strong mothers in Asian American literature. Donald is inspired thereby to stand up for justice and truth. He provides an alibi for a man falsely accused of murder; he and his pal Arnold Azalea openly challenge and rectify the skewed representations of Asians in their American classroom. Their joint effort in disputing stock Chinese images presented in the classroom and in standing up for a falsely convicted criminal exemplifies valor that is life-affirming rather than life-threatening.

Chin, like Kingston in *The Woman Warrior*, has transformed traditional Chinese fighters into Chinese Americans jousting with words rather than with swords. For the *Aiiieeeee!* editors, a culturally distinctive language is the sine qua non of manhood: "Language coheres the people into a community… a man in any culture speaks for himself. Without a language of his own, he no longer is a man" (xlviii). Hence recovering a literary tradition and ethnopoetics of one's own is also a way to remasculate, to borrow Viet Nguyen's term. Given the importance the editors attach to language, it is particularly fitting that swordsmanship is transformed into wordsmanship in both *The Woman Warrior* and *Donald Duk*. Regrettably, such verbal power does not extend to any woman in Chin's novel. The mother and daughters in *Donald Duk*, all of whom endorse assimilation into the European American culture, are little more than caricatures: "they fall into sitcom patter, removed from the challenges of life and cocooned in two-dimensional inanity" (Samarth 92). Chin gamely unburies a heroic past of his Chinese American ancestors, and represents several male figures as viable paternal models, but descends into sexist typecasting in his portrayal of women. To unmask oppression in its manifold guises, to reclaim cultural traditions without getting bogged down in the mire of patriarchal constraints, to chart new topographies for manliness and womanliness entail genuine heroism.

MULTICULTURAL LITERACY

When this essay was first conceived over two decades ago, I cautioned against being complicit with the gender ideologies of both the dominant and ethnic cultures and reiterated Teresa de Lauretis's injunction to work toward notions of gender and ethnicity that are nonhierarchical, nonbinary, and nonprescriptive, that can embrace contradictions rather than perpetuate divisions (246; De Lauretis 11). Since then, important theoretical paradigms that intersect gender, race, class, and sexuality have increased exponentially, and many Asian Americanists have proceeded to dismantle not just white but also male and straight supremacy. Despite the considerable strides toward intersectionality, however, multicultural and multilingual literacy has not fallen in step beyond tokenized inclusion of texts by people of color. As I mentioned at the outset, the earlier concern among Asian Americans to "claim America" and the gender trouble revolving around Kingston and Chin have eclipsed the transnational reach of both writers and their brave refashioning of Chinese classics. Kingston and Chin are rare among American-born writers in being not only conversant with Chinese and Western canons but also adept at welding the two and retooling them for Chinese America. This final section demonstrates how greater familiarity with Chinese lore can better reveal the two writers' intercultural innovation and unsettle heteronormative assumptions in both Asia and the United States.

The sword slingers and word slingers that figure prominently in both *The Woman Warrior* and *Donald Duk* embody the dual masculine ideal of *wen-wu* 文武—the cultivated man and the martial man—in traditional Chinese culture. Kam Louie has expatiated on these two different (and at times composite) models: "The Chinese tradition of macho hero represented in terms such as *yingxiong* (outstanding male) and *haohan* (good fellow) is counterbalanced by a softer, cerebral male tradition—the *caizi* (the talented scholar) and the *wenren* (the cultured man)." "The cerebral male model tends to dominate that of the macho, brawny male," he adds (Louie 8). The title of this chapter uses "sword" and "word" implicitly as metonyms for the *wen-wu* dyad (which will be explored further in the next two chapters). Several layers of irony emerge when this age-old dyad is examined in relation to Chinese America and the texts at hand. First, whereas men in China are conventionally admired for their literary talent and/or martial strength, Chinese American men are often stereotyped as devoid of both. Second, whereas the Chinese yardstick for masculinity has placed brain over brawn, Chinese American male writers who take it upon themselves to remasculinize Asians have stressed brawn over brain in accordance with the metrics of American popular culture, notwithstanding the fact that as writers they would be better off resuscitating the *wen* ideal. Third, both *wen* and *wu*, Kam Louie contends, have been male prerogatives traditionally: "The public corporealisation of *wen* and *wu* necessarily occurred in the male sex. Donning male attire therefore usually precedes the women's temporary forays into the male arena."[4] Louie rests his case on Mulan, who "dressed as a man for over ten years during her military forays" and who appears "*even more* feminine and conventional" upon returning to her female role than she did before assuming male guise (Louie 12).

To highlight the novelty of Chin's and Kingston's literary enterprise and the value of Chinese literacy in mediating between the real and the fake, allow me to return yet once more to the uproar over *The Woman Warrior* and to Chin's reconfiguration of Kwan Kung. Fuming over the female warrior's dorsal tattoo, Chin condemns Kingston, as well as David Henry Hwang and Amy Tan, as "the first writers of any race, and certainly the first writers of Asian ancestry to so boldly fake the best-known works from the most universally known body of Asian literature" (Chin, "Come" 3). But other writers have been able to revise ancient tales for literary purposes without incurring critical ire. John Milton got away with demonizing Homeric gods as fallen angels in *Paradise Lost*, and Christa Wolf with ascribing to Achilles a different sexual orientation in *Cassandra*. Kingston herself retells the tale of Robinson Crusoe as a Chinese story and transforms a story from Ovid's *Metamorphoses* into a Hawaiian legend, more or less with impunity (K.-K. Cheung, "Talk-Story"). If "The Ballad of Mulan" were, as Chin claims, known to every Chinese since childhood, then only non-Chinese readers would mistake the fake for the real. Had Kingston's audience been as familiar with "The Ballad of Mulan" as with Western lore, Chinese American critics would have focused on her architectonics rather than on cultural authenticity.

A writer should not be held responsible for a reader's ignorance. If we ask Asian Americans to write with a wary eye against possible misappropriation by non-Asians or against possible offense to "Asian American manhood," we end up implicitly sustaining racial and sexual hierarchies. But much more can be done to forestall cultural misreading and to promote bicultural literacy. For all the advances in curricular reform to foster diversity, the European American heritage still predominates. S.C. Wong observes that among Kingston's detractors, "The ignorance of white readers seems to be taken for granted as immutable. . . . The possibility that the less unregenerate readers may learn to read the allusion in *The Woman Warrior*, just as generations of minority readers have learned to read the Eurocentric canon, is never once raised" (S.-l.C. Wong 260). Wong unveils the unequal demands on European American readers and on assorted ethnic others. While American students of all stripes are expected to do the homework required to understand the allusions in T.S. Eliot's *The Waste Land* and even James Joyce's *Finnegans Wake*, it seems too much to expect non-Asian readers to fathom the Chinese allusions in *The Woman Warrior* or *Tripmaster Monkey*. Yet a truly multicultural education cannot be secured without expanding the Anglo-American heritage and drawing upon cultural inheritances from around the world.

While I take exception to Chin's fixation on heroic manhood, I wish his plea for greater Asian cultural literacy had not fallen on deaf ears. Before one can judge whether Kingston, and Chin for that matter, use Chinese material irresponsibly, ingeniously, or subversively, whether their revisions amount to "distortion" of Chinese legends or innovative adaptation, one must have a firm grasp of the original sources. In light of Kam Louie's argument that the "*wen* and *wu* realms are the public preserve of men" (12), Kingston's arrogation of sword and word to her imaginary woman warrior through superimposing the story of Yue Fei onto that of Mulan is all the more transgressive, appropriating as it does male privileges for women. Chin's allegation that the dorsal inscription is a form of criminalization (like the branding of Jewish people during World War II) actually betrays a lack of cultural literacy. Chinese scholar Zhao Wenshu remarks: "For Chinese people, the act of inscription always means a source of empowerment and inspiration... Kingston actually understands what she is doing better than Frank Chin when she understands the tattooing as a source of strength" (Zhao, "Frank Chin" 159).

What about Chin's seemingly definitive account of Kwan Kung? Dorothy Ritsuko McDonald observes that Chin finds in Kwan Kung the masculine ideal and the bold individualism sought by his protagonists in *The Chickencoop Chinaman* and *The Year of the Dragon* (McDonald xxv). In Chin's own words, Kwan was "the god of war to soldiers ... the god of literature to fighters who soldier with words, and the god patron protector of actors and anyone who plays him on stage" (McDonald xxvi). This figure is definitely the "most glorified and worshipped" of all characters in Chinese literature and popular culture: "[His] canonization as the essential embodiment of *wu* both perpetuated and reflected his accumulating popularity among ordinary people" (Louie 26). Often decked out in both a warrior's garb and a scholar's robe, Guan Yu holds quadruple appeal to Chin as a writer, playwright, actor, and champion of militant manhood. Guan as a patron of actors strikes a particularly resonant chord in Chin the playwright: "the Kwan blood from my mother meant I was chosen to write theater like making war, throwing everything away and get even" (McDonald xxv).

Chin sees his Cantonese immigrant forebear as the avatar of the god of war: "EVERY CANTONESE IS A WHOLE UNTO HIMSELF AS A PLANET and trusts no other living thing" (McDonald xxvi). He has tailored the Chinese lord to his American experience "to counter the effeminate, Christianized Charlie Chan image of the post-1925 era" by enshrining anew the God of War, "whose strength of mind and body, individuality and loyalty, capacity for revenge, and essential aloneness are reminiscent of the rugged Western hero of American myth" (McDonald xxviii). In his eagerness to highlight Kwan's fierce individualism and credentials as a completely "self-made man," however, Chin goes so far as to fabricate the Chinese hero's childhood in the very essay in which he insists that myths are immutable:

> Kwan Kung ... was an abused child who, betrayed by his parents, ran away from home without a farewell, never giving them another thought. Still, he is the exemplar of the universal man, a physically and morally self-sufficient soldier. (Chin, "Come" 39)

Such a childhood seems to have been fashioned ex nihilo by Chin. Zhao concludes: "Frank Chin's interpretation of Guan Yu as an abused child betrayed by his parents is neither validated by the orthodox Chinese history book ... nor supported by the historical novel... Guan Yu's life story begins with his fleeing from his hometown as an outlaw" (Zhao, "Frank Chin" 157–158). It is perplexing, to say the least, that the critic who faulted Kingston for insinuating, through a dream episode, about Chinese parents' cruelty in tattooing a daughter should go out of his way to drum up parental abuse, inflicted on his favorite hero no less, in an expository essay. Surely Chin's Kwang Kung is no less "fake" and no more "real" than Kingston's Fa Mu Lan.

As in his emphasis on aggressive and militant manhood, Chin is more invested in finding Chinese attributes that correspond to American national values than in uncovering alternative ways of being. His stress on individualism bespeaks his quest for Chinese equivalents rather than for different masculine codes. Hence he draws the following lesson from one of the most famous episodes in *Three Kingdoms*—the Peach Orchard Oath taken by the three sworn brothers, Liu Bei, Zhang Fei, and Guan Yu: "It encouraged an aggressive self-reliance and trust nobody, watch out killer's sense of individuality that reached a peak in China with the Cantonese … grew roots in California and sprouted a Kwan Kung happy race of people" (McDonald xxvii).

I beg to differ. The fraternal bond sealed in the Peach Orchard emblematizes not so much rugged individualism, and even less "trust nobody" mentality, but rather unfaltering comradeship. The emphasis on teamwork or brotherhood, which I consider to be the hallmark of the Chinese heroic tradition, distinguishes *Journey to the West*, *Three Kingdoms*, and *Water Margin* from Homer's *Iliad* and *Odyssey*, in which Achilles, Hector, and Odysseus stand out as lone heroes. Furthermore, the teamwork featured goes hand in hand with individualist bravura; far from suggesting herd instinct or what Chin disparages as "gang balls" in Chinatown martial arts movies, the Chinese heroic teams are made up of shining characters, each with distinctive fortes and foibles, though their loyalty to one another is no less defining than their personal achievements.

The Peach Orchard Oath is a threesome pledge of staunch friendship; the three sworn brothers' agreement to die on the same day goes even further than a marriage vow in sealing a lifelong commitment and evincing mutual trust. What makes Guan Yu such a revered hero in China is not so much his individuality and even his military prowess but his being "a symbol of loyalty and guardianship that inspired an ethic of trust and obligation which could substitute for kinship" (Duara 782; R. G. Lee, "Guan Gong" 32). Loyalty, guardianship, and virtual kinship all imply person-to-person obligation and sustenance, in line with the Confucian concept of *ren* (仁), which I posit in Chapter 5 to be the masculine equivalent of the feminine "ethics of care" expounded by American feminists. Chin's inference of "trust no one" individuality from the Peach Orchard Oath is entirely of his own making. Robert G. Lee's assessment seems right on: "Frank Chin's valorization of Guan Gong ... is at once heroic and authoritarian. In searching for authenticity in the reconstruction of the epic tradition, the discontinuity and contradictions of historical experience are covered over... Chin's 'authentic Chinaman history' can finally only come from speaking through and not with Guan Gong" (R. G. Lee, "Guan Gong" 38).

Chin not only recreates Kwan Kung in his own image but also wrests from his revered icon the authority to be the gatekeeper of Asian American literature and literary history. He fails to decipher what Lee calls the "double-voiced" sign of Guan Gong, which allows for "a revisioning of Chinese American history as a carnival with many resistant voices" (38). Far from being "immutable" as a mythical image, the figure of Guan Yu has been reshaped and reinterpreted in every age. Kam Louie's chapter on Guan Yu in *Theorising Chinese Masculinity*, for example, underscores yet another mode of masculinity that can have ramifications in homophobic China. While *Three Kingdoms* diverges sharply from the European chivalric tradition, in which heterosexual love is often the most important inspiration for heroic deeds, that does not mean, Louie reminds us, that the Chinese heroes are "asexual": "The failure to recognize the sexuality inherent in *wu* lies partly in the dominance of a reading that regarded sexuality as being fundamentally hetero-erotic." Reading against the grain of orthodox interpretation, and "from a perspective where bisexuality is taken as the norm and where homo-eroticism is privileged over the hetero," Louie indicates that Liu Bei, Cao Cao, and Zhuge Liang all sleep with other men regularly, though Kwan alone "serves" only one man—his big brother Liu Bei. At the same time, Louie is quick to acknowledge the sexual antagonism toward women in this homosocial world, wherein heroes harbor "a subconscious hatred of women as their worst enemy" (Louie 23, 24, 29). Still, his reading of *Three Kingdoms* upends a number of homophobic Chinese and Western assumptions: namely, that there is no indigenous homosexuality in China, that homosexuality is a foreign import, and that gay men are "pansies" (more on this in Chapters 5 and 9). In implying that the male warriors, including the three sworn brothers, are often "in bed" with one another, Louie undermines the stereotype of bisexuals and gays as unmanly. The idea that the three heroic brothers may be as homoerotic as Fu Manchu (and that both Zhang Fei and Guan Yu sulk after Liu Bei spends a night with Zhu Geliang) would surely rattle

Chin. Nevertheless, a judicious reclaiming of the Chinese heroic tradition ought to point out its patriarchal pitfalls and detect alternative modes of masculinity.

Chin has articulated vehemently the erasure of Chinese presence in US history and literature. One of the most moving moments in *Donald Duk* occurs in the dream sequence about building the transcontinental railroad. At its completion, the Chinese laborers put their names onto the final railroad tie that marks the junction between the Central Pacific and Union Pacific. But the white owners removed the tie and shunted off the Chinese, eliminating any trace of them from this key historical enterprise. This moment effectively highlights the importance of fighting to keep one's history: "history is war... You gotta keep the history yourself or lose it forever" (Chin, *DD* 123). However, while Chin brings out both the physical and epistemological violence of white European Americans in occluding Chinese immigrant laborers, he disavows similar exclusion in Chinese classics such as *Outlaws of the Marsh* and *Three Kingdoms*, where women are often written out of *his*tory. Alert to the absence of masculine Chinese images in American popular culture, he is oblivious to the near absence of women in his beloved classics.

Both Kingston and Chin have drawn heavily from the Chinese heroic tradition in their respective reconstructions of gender. In part because this predominantly patriarchal tradition is compatible with Chin's intent to remasculate Asian Americans, he does not need to depart radically from the Chinese material, except in his idiosyncratic selection, embellishment, and interpretation of the original texts. In insisting on preserving an authentic history, he has underwritten the historical subordination and marginalization of women, and merely substitutes white patriarchy with Chinese (American) patriarchy. In contrast, Kingston, by virtue of her feminist and pacifist leanings, cannot simply transplant Chinese material without some deliberate modifications. What Chin characterizes as her falsification of Chinese texts is prompted by her determination to reform these texts for subversive ends. Although she alludes to literary material from both China and Euro-America, she breaks away from the patriarchal hold of both worlds in order to contest gender and racial inequality. Be that as it may, the pacifist ethos emphasized by Kingston, as opposed to the bellicose ones promulgated by Chin, is truer to the spirit of the original Chinese heroic texts. Both Kingston and Chin are likely to go down in Asian American literary history as heroic wordsmiths who have amalgamated Chinese and Anglo-American material into an original panoply that reflects the struggle of women and men in the New World. In the battleground for Chinese American subjectivity, however, Chin and his cohort must venture beyond the martial brotherhood of the Peach Orchard Oath to make room for (s)wordsmen and (s)wordswomen of various sexual persuasions. Or go the way of Cho Cho and the three brothers: "The clanging and banging fooled us, but now we know—they lost."

NOTES

1. There are some happy exceptions: Shu-mei Shih examines the use of Chinese folktales in Kingston's *China Men*; Fang Hong and Patricia P. Chu examine the use of heroic epics in *Tripmaster Monkey* (Shih; Chu, "Tripmaster"; Fang)
2. For a nuanced analysis of the representation of Bruce Lee, see *Asian Americans and the Media* by Kent A. Ono and Vincent N. Pham (76–78).
3. See Chapter 6 and Gish Jen's *Tiger Writing* for an elaboration of the Chinese interdependent ethos.
4. In Chapter 4, I take issue with K. Louie's assertion that *wen* is the exclusive province of men traditionally.

WORKS CITED

Althusser, Louis Pierre. *Lenin and Philosophy and Other Essays.* Trans. Ben Brewster. New York: Monthly Review Press, 1971.

Asians in America. *Asians in America.* 3 February 2014. <http://www.asiansinamerica.org/news/is-crime-against-asian-americans-going-up-or-down/> (accessed 30 December 2014).

Baldwin, James. *The Fire Next Time.* New York: Vintage, 1962.

Bambara, Toni Cade. "On the Issue of Roles." *The Black Woman: An Anthology.* Ed. Toni Cade Bambara. York: Mentor-NAL, 1970. 101–110.

Benstock, Shari, ed. *The Private Self: Theory and Practice of Women's Autobiographical Writings.* Chapel Hill: University of North Carolina Press, 1988.

Bonetti, Kay. "An Interview with Maxine Hong Kingston [1986]." *Conversations with Maxine Hong Kingston.* Ed. Paul Skenazy and Tera Martin. Jackson: University Press of Mississippi, 1998. 33–46.

Bowra, C. M. *Heroic Poetry.* London: Macmillan, 1952.

Butler, Judith. *Senses of the Subject.* New York: Fordham University Press, 2015.

Chan, Jeffery Paul. "The Mysterious West." *New York Review of Books*, 28 April 1977: 41.

Chan, Jeffery Paul, Frank Chin, Lawson Fusao Inada, Shawn Wong, eds. *The Big Aiiieeeee! An Anthology of Asian American Writers*. New York: New American Library-Meridian, 1991.
———. "Introduction." *The Big Aiiieeeee! An Anthology of Chinese American and Japanese American Literature*. Ed. Jeffery Paul Chan, et al. New York: New American Library-Meridian, 1991. xi–xvi.
Chan, Justin. *Where Are All the Asian Americans in Hollywood?* 20 August 2014. <http://www.complex.com/pop-culture/2014/08/asian-americans-in-hollywood> (accessed 20 August 2014).
Cheung, Floyd. "Early Chinese American Autobiography: Reconsidering the Works of Yan Phou Lee and Yung Wing." *Recovered Legacies: Authority and Identity in Early Asian American Literature*. Ed. Keith Lawrence and Floyd Cheung. Philadelphia: Temple University Press, 2005. 24–40.
Cheung, King-Kok, and Stan Yogi, eds. *Asian American Literature: An Annotated Bibliography*. New York: Modern Language Association, 1988.
Cheung, King-Kok. "'Don't Tell': Imposed Silences in *The Color Purple* and *The Woman Warrior*." *PMLA* (1988): 162–174.
———. "Talk-Story: Counter-Memory in Maxine Hong Kingston's *China Men*." *Tamkang Review: A Quarterly of Comparative Studies Between Chinese and Foreign Literatures* 24.1 (1993): 21–37.
———. "The Woman Warrior versus The Chinaman Pacific: Must a Chinese American Critic Choose between Feminism and Heroism?" *Conflicts in Feminism*. Ed. Marianne Hirsch and Evelyn Fox Keller. New York: Routledge, 1990. 234–251.
Chin, Frank, and Jeffery Paul Chan. "Racist Love." *Seeing Through Shuck*. Ed. Richard Kostelanetz. New York: Ballantine, 1972. 65–79.
Chin, Frank. "Come All Ye Asian American Writers of the Real and the Fake." *The Big Aiiieeeee! An Anthology of Asian American Writers*. Ed. Jeffery Paul Chan, et al. New York: New American Library-Meridian, 1991. 1–92.
———. "Confessions of the Chinatown Cowboy." *Bulletin of Concerned Asian Scholars* 4.3 (1972): 58–70.
———. *Donald Duk*. Minneapolis: Coffee House Press, 1991c.
———. "'Kung Fu' Is Unfair to Chinese." *New York Times*, 24 March 1974a: 137.
———. *The Chinaman Pacific & Frisco R. R. Co*. Minneapolis: Coffee House Press, 1988.
———. "The Most Popular Book in China." *Quilt* 4 (1984): 6–12.
———. "This Is Not An Autobiography." *Genre* 18.2 (1985): 109–130.
Chin, Frank, Jeffery Paul Chan, Lawson Fusao Inada, and Shawn Hsu Wong, eds. *Aiiieeeee! An Anthology of Asian-American Writers*. Washington: Howard University Press, 1974/1983.
Chu, Patricia P. *Assimilating Asians: Gendered Strategies of Authorship in Asian America*. Durham: Duke University Press, 2000.

———. "*Tripmaster Monkey*, Frank Chin, and the Chinese Heroic Tradition." *American Quarterly* 53.3 (1997): 117–139.
Clifford, Jamese. "Introduction: Partial Truths." *Writing Culture: The Poetics and Politics of Ethnography*. Ed. James Clifford and George Marcus. Berkeley: University of California Press, 1986. 1–26.
Crenshaw, Kimberlé. "Demarginalizing the Intersection of Race and Sex: A Black Feminist Critique of Antidiscrimination Doctrine, Feminist Theory and Antiracist Politics." *University of Chicago Legal Forum* (1989): 139–167.
De Lauretis, Teresa. *Technologies of Gender: Essays on Theory, Film, and Fiction*. Bloomington: Indiana University Press, 1987.
Duara, Prasenjit. "Superscribing Symbols: The Myth of Guandi, Chinese God of War." *Journal of Asian Studies* 47.4 (1988): 778–795.
Eakin, Paul John. *Fictions in Autobiography: Studies in the Art of Self-Invention*. Princeton: Princeton University Press, 1985.
Eng, David L., and Alice Y. Hom, eds. *Q & A: Queer in Asian America*. Philadelphia: Temple University Press, 1998.
Enke, Anne, ed. *Transfeminist Perspectives in and beyond Transgender and Gender Studies*. Philadelphia: Temple University Press, 2012.
Espiritu, Yen Le. "All Men Are Not Created Equal: Asian men in U.S. History." *Men's Lives*. Ed. Michael S. Kimmel and Michael A. Messner. 4th ed. Boston: Allyn & Bacon, 1997. 35–44.
Fang, Hong [方红]. *The Ethnic Trickster in Maxine Hong Kingston's Tripmaster Monkey: His Fake Book*. Hong Kong: Hong Kong University Press, 2003.
Fong, Katheryn M. "An Open Letter/Review." *Bulletin for Concerned Asian Scholars* 9.4: 67–69. 9.4 (1977): 67–69.
Friedman, Susan Stanford. "Gender and Genre Anxiety: Elizabeth Barrett Browning and H.D. as Epic Poets." *Tulsa Studies in Women's Literature* 5.2 (1986): 203–228.
Gilligan, Carol. *In a Different Voice: Psychological Theory and Women's Development*. Cambridge: Harvard University Press, 1982.
Goellnicht, Donald C. "Tang Ao in America: Male Subject Positions in China Men." *Reading the Literatures of Asian America*. Ed. Shirley Geok-lin Lim and Amy Ling. Philadelphia: Temple University Press, 1992. 191–212.
Goodman, Lizbeth. *Gender and Literature*. New York: Routledge, 1996.
Gubar, Susan. "'The Blank Page' and the Issues of Female Creativity." *Critical Inquiry* 8 (1981): 243–263.
hooks, bell. *Ain't I a Woman? Black Women and Feminism*. Boston: South End Press, 1982.
Iwamura, Jane Naomi. *Virtual Orientalism: Asian Religions and American Popular Culture*. New York: Oxford University Press, 2011.
Jardine, Alice, and Paul Smith, eds. *Men in Feminism*. New York: Methuen, 1987.

Jelinek, Estelle, ed. *Women's Autobiography: Essays in Criticism*. Bloomington: Indiana University Press, 1980.

Jen, Gish. *Tiger Writing: Art, Culture, and the Interdependent Self*. Cambridge: Harvard University Press, 2012.

Jill, Nelson. "An Interview with Ishmael Reed The Return of the Nigger Breakers: A Ghetto Reading and Writing Rat Responds to His Critics." *Counterpunch*, 18 May 2010.

Johnson, Barbara. *The Feminist Difference: Literature, Psychoanalysis, Race, and Gender*. Cambridge: Harvard University Press, 2000.

Johnson, Diane. "'Ghosts': Rev. of *The Woman Warrior* by Maxine Hong Kingston." *New York Review of Books*, 3 February 1977: 19+.

Juhasz, Suzanne. "Towards a Theory of Form in Feminist Autobiography: Kate Millet's *Fear of Flying* and *Sita*; Maxine Hong Kingston's *The Woman Warrior*." *International Journal of Women's Studies* 2.1 [1979]: 62. 2.1 (1979): 62–75.

Kang, Laura Hyun Yi. *Compositional Subjects: Enfiguring Asian/American Women*. Durham: Duke University Press, 2002.

Kim, Elaine H. *Asian American Literature: An Introduction to the Writings and Their Social Context*. Philadelphia: Temple University Press, 1982.

——. "Asian American Writers: A Bibliographical Review." *American Studies International* 22.2 (1984b): 41–78.

——. "Asian Americans and American Popular Culture." *Dictionary of Asian American History*. Ed. Hyung-Chan Kim. New York: Greenwood Press, 1986. 99–114.

——. "'Such Opposite Creatures': Men and Women in Asian American Literature." *Michigan Quarterly Review* 29.1 (1990): 68–93.

King, Katherine Callen. *Achilles: Paradigms of the War Hero from Homer to the Middle Ages*. Berkeley: University of California Press, 1991.

Kingston, Maxine Hong. *China Men*. New York: Vintage, 1980.

——. "Cultural Mis-readings by American Reviewers." *Asian and Western Writers in Dialogue: New Cultural Identities*. Ed. Guy Amirthanayagam. London: Macmillan, 1982. 55–65.

——. "San Francisco's Chinatown: A View from the Other Side of Arnold Genthe's Camera." *American Heritage* 30.1 (1978): 35–47.

——. *The Woman Warrior: Memoirs of a Girlhood among Ghosts*. New York: Vintage International, 1976, 1989a.

——. *Tripmaster Monkey: His Fake Book*. New York: Knopf, 1989b.

Lauter, Paul. "Race and Gender in the Shaping of the American Literary Canon: A Case Study from the Twenties" *Feminist Criticism and Social Change: Sex, Class and Race in Literature and Culture*. Ed. Judith Newton and Deborah Rosenfelt. New York: Methuen, 1985. 19–44.

Lee, Josephine. *Performing Asian America: Race and Ethnicity on the Contemporary Stage*. Philadelphia: Temple University Press, 1998.

Lee, Robert G. "In Search of the Historical Guan Gong." *Asian America* 1 (1992): 28–43.

——. "*The Woman Warrior* as an Intervention in Asian American Historiography." *Approaches to Teaching Maxine Hong Kingston's The Woman Warrior*. Ed. Shirley Geok-lin Lim. New York: MLA, 1991. 52–63.

Li, David Leiwei. "Can Maxine Hong Kingston Speak? The Contingency of *The Woman Warrior*." *Asian American Literature*. Ed. David Leiwei Li. 4 vols. New York: Routledge, 2012. II: 213–233.

Li, Ju-Chen. *Flowers in the Mirror*. 《镜花缘》. Ed. Tai-Yi Lin. Trans. Tai-Yi Lin. London: Peter Owen, 1965.

Li, Wenxin. "Review of Sau-ling Cynthia Wong's *Maxine Hong Kingston's The Woman Warrior: A Casebook*." *Rocky Mountain Review* (2000): n.p.

Louie, Kam. *Theorizing Chinese Masculinity: Society and Gender in China*. Cambridge: Cambridge University Press, 2002.

Lowe, Lisa. *Immigrant Acts: On Asian American Cultural Poetics*. Durham: Duke University Press, 1996.Lye, Colleen. "Asian American 1960s." *The Routledge Companion to Asian American and Pacific Islander Literature*. Ed. Rachel C. Lee. New York: Routledge, 2014. 213–223.

——. "Introduction: In Dialogue with Asian American Studies and Racial Form." *Representations* 99 (2007): 1–6.

Lye, Colleen. "Asian American 1960s." *The Routledge Companion to Asian American and Pacific Islander Literature*. Ed. Rachel C. Lee. New York: Routledge, 2014. 213–223.

Ma, Sheng-Mei. *Deathly Embrace: Orientalism and Asian American Identity*. Minneapolis: University of Minnesota Press, 2000.

Marchetti, Gina. *Romance and the "Yellow Peril": Race, Sex, and Discursive Strategies in Hollywood Fiction*. Berkeley: University of California Press, 1993.

McCunn, Ruthanne Lum. *Chinese Yankee*. San Francisco: Design Enterprises of San Francisco, 2014.

McDonald, Dorothy Ritsuko. "Introduction." *The Chickencoop Chinaman and The Year of the Dragon: Two Plays by Frank Chin*. Ed. Frank Chin. Seattle: University of Washington Press, 1981. ix–xxix.

Jardine, Alice, and Paul Smith, eds. *Men in Feminism*. New York: Methuen, 1987.

Miller, Nancy K. *Getting Personal: Feminist Occasions and Other Autobiographical Acts*. New York: Routledge, 1991.

Mullen, Harryette. *The Cracks Between What We Are and What We Are Supposed to Be*. Tuscaloosa: University of Alabama Press, 2012.

Nee, Victor G., and Brett De Bary Nee. *Longtime Californ': A Documentary Study of an American Chinatown 1973*. New York: Pantheon, 1981.

Nguyen, Viet. "The Remasculinization of Chinese America: Race, Violence, and the Novel." *American Literary History* 12.1 (2000): 130–157.

Ono, Kent A., and Vincent N. Pham. *Asian Americans and the Media*. Cambridge: Polity Press, 2009.

Rabine, Leslie W. "No Lost Paradise: Social Gender and Symbolic Gender in the Writings of Maxine Hong Kingston." *Signs: Journal of Women in Culture and Society* 12 (1987): 471–492.

Reed, Ishmael. "Complaint." *New York Review of Books* 21 October 1982. <http://www.nybooks.com/articles/archives/1982/oct/21/complaint/> (accessed 4 January 2015).

Renato, Constantino. "Notes on Historical Writing for the Third World." *Journal of Contemporary Asia* 10.3 (1980): 233–240.

Romero, Dennis. "Racist, Anti-Asian Flier Rocks UCLA, USC Campuses." *L.A. Weekly* 11 February 2014. <http://www.laweekly.com/news/racist-anti-asian-flier-rocks-ucla-usc-campuses-4431258> (accessed 25 February 2015).

Said, Edward. *Orientalism*. New York: Vintage, 1979.

Samarth, Manini. "Affirmations: Speaking the Self into Being." *Parnassus: Poetry in Review* 17.1 (1992): 88–101.

Schenck, Celeste. "All of a Piece: Women's Poetry and Autobiography." *Life/Lines: Theorizing Women's Autobiography*. Ed. Bella Brodzki and Celeste Schenck. Ithaca: Cornell University Press, 1988.

Shih, Shu-mei. "Exile and Intertextuality in Maxine Hong Kingston's *China Men*." *The Literature of Emigration and Exile*. Ed. James Whitlark and Wendell Aycock. Lubbock: Texas Tech University Press, 1992. 65–77.

Slotkin, Richard. *Regeneration through Violence: The Mythology of the American Frontier, 1600–1860*. Middleton: Wesleyan University Press, 1973.

Smith, Sidonie, and Julia Watson. *Reading Autobiography: A Guide for Interpreting Life Narratives, Second Edition*. 2nd ed. Minneapolis: University of Minnesota Press, 2010.

Smith, Sidonie. *A Poetics of Women's Autobiography: Marginality and the Fictions of Self-Representation*. Bloomington: Indiana University Press, 1987.

Stanton, Donna. *The Female Autograph*. New York: New York Literary Forum, 1984.

Takaki, Ronald. *Strangers from a Different Shore: A History of Asian Americans*. Boston: Little, Brown, 1989.

Tong, Benjamin R. "Critic of Admirer Sees Dumb Racist." *San Francisco Journal*, 11 May 1977: 20.

——. "The Ghetto of the Mind." *Amerasia* 1.3 (1971): 1–31.

Wang, Xiaoxue. "A New Historicist Analysis of the Rewriting of Chinese American History in *Donald Duk*." *Cross-Cultural Communications* 10.2 (2014): 118–124.

What's Wrong with Frank Chin? By Curtis Choy and Jean Lau. Dir. Curtis Choy. Chonk Moonhunter Productions, 2005.

Wolf, Christa. *Cassandra: A Novel and Four Essays*. Trans. Jan van Heurck. New York: Farrar, 1984.

Wong, Nellie. "*The Woman Warrior*." *Bridge* (1978): 46–48.

Wong, Sau-ling Cynthia. "Autobiography as Guided Chinatown Tour? Maxine Hong Kingston's *The Woman Warrior* and the Chinese-American Autobiographical Controversy." *Lives, Multicultural Autobiography: American*. Ed. James Robert Payne. Knoxville: U of Tennessee P, 1992. 248–279.

Wong, Shelley Sunn. "Unnaming the Same: Theresa Hak Kyung Cha's *DICTEE*." *Feminist Measures: Soundings in Poetry and Theory*. Ed. Lynn Keller and Miller Christianne. Ann Arbor: University of Michigan Press, 1994. 43–68.

Woo, Deborah. "Maxine Hong Kingston: The Ethnic Writer and the Burden of Dual Authenticity." *Amerasia* 16.1 (1990): 173–200.

Yalom, Marilyn. "*The Woman Warrior* as Postmodern Autobiography." *Approaches to Teaching Kingston's The Woman Warrior*. Ed. Shirley Geok-lin Lim. New York: Modern Language Association, 1991. 108–115.

Yamamoto, Traise. "Asian American Autobiography/Memoir." *The Routledge Companion to Asian American and Pacific Islander Literature*. Ed. Rachel C. Lee. New York: Routledge, 2014. 379–391.

Zhang, Ya-Jie. "A Chinese Woman's Response to Maxine Hong Kingston's *The Woman Warrior*." *The Woman Warrior: A Casebook*. Ed. Sau-ling Cynthia Wong. New York: Oxford University Press, 1999. 17–21.

Zhao, Wenshu. "Why Does Frank Chin Insist on the Authenticity of His Chinese Culture?-A Belated Response to Frank Chin from a "Distractor"." 《跨国语境下的美洲华裔文学与文化研究》. Ed. Aimin Cheng and Wenshu Zhao. Nanjing: Nanjing University Press, 2011. 151–169.

Zhao, Wenshu. "Why Is There Orientalism in Chinese American Literature?" *Global Perspectives on Asian American Literature*. Ed. Guiyou Huang and Wu Bing. Beijing: Foreign Language Teaching and Research Press, 2008. 239–258.

CHAPTER 3

Manhood Besieged: Gus Lee and David Wong Louie

Pacifist strains in Chinese literature are no less prevalent than the battle hymns promulgated in *The Big Aiiieeeee!*. Nowhere is this dialogism more conspicuous than in the realm of masculinity. Kam Louie has provided an exhaustive study of the two complementary codes "central to all discussions of Chinese masculinity": *wen* 文 (literally "literature"), the province of *wenren*, that is, cultured men or men of letters; and *wu* 武 (literally "martial arts"), the domain of fighters and warriors (K. Louie 6). While Chinese culture places greater premium on *wen* than on *wu* historically, *wu*—on account of its affinity with the American national character, notably the frontier hero—tends to overshadow *wen* in Chinese American culture and fiction. This chapter elaborates on the *wen-wu* dyad and demonstrates how *wen* flounders and falters in the process of assimilation in Gus Lee's *China Boy* and in David Wong Louie's *Pangs of Love*. Lee's protagonist, groomed to be a *wenren* by his Chinese mother and tutor, must give up the pen for the fist to survive in a rough San Francisco neighborhood. Louie's protagonists, many of whom are *wenren* par excellence according to traditional Chinese yardsticks, constantly find themselves falling short of hegemonic masculinity in the enduring American geocultural context. Whereas Lee's young narrator aspires to become a black man, Louie's male speakers thirst after white images of manhood.

When I first dallied with masculinity studies, there was little sustained scholarship on traditional Chinese masculine ideals; hence I based my arguments largely on my own cultural background. There has since been burgeoning scholarship in this arena, such as Xueping Zhong's *Masculinity Besieged* (2000), Kam Louie's *Theorizing Chinese Masculinity* (2002), and Geng Song's *The Fragile Scholar* (2004), in addition to James Liu's somewhat dated *The Chinese Knight-Errant* (1967) (Zhong; K. Louie; Song; Liu). Kam Louie persuasively traces the evolution of *wen-wu* from ancient times to the present, noting that "the cerebral male model tends to dominate that of the macho, brawny male" and that the *wenren* (cultured men) have been depicted as "desirable and attractive" throughout Chinese history (K. Louie 8–9). He submits that the application of Western criteria of masculinity to the Chinese case is inappropriate, only leading to the conclusion that Chinese men are not quite "real men" (K. Louie 20). Hence, the *wen-wu* paradigm generated from within the Asian context, wherein "a scholar is considered to be no less masculine than a soldier," is a particularly effective corrective (K. Louie 11). Although Kam Louie ably unpacks the *wen-wu* dyad and maps their manifestations through time in Chinese literature and culture, Asian American literary studies falls outside his purview. I have already shown in Chapter 2 how the dyad applies to Chinese American literature. This chapter illustrates the onslaughts on, and transmutation of, *wen* under the pressure of American assimilation, while the following two chapters explore its alluring variations.

What rights and motives have I as a female critic to deliberate on manhood? That men of different cultures have for centuries prescribed feminine ideals suffices as a quick rejoinder.[1] More seriously, in the Asian American (as in the African American and Chican@) cultural domain, there has been an apparent split between feminism and cultural nationalism, and between women and men. Feminists intent on exposing Asian sexism have been attacked by cultural nationalists who complain that female writers reinforce denigrating stereotypes about Asian males; the effort of some male writers to reconstruct Asian American masculinity and instill cultural pride by reviving an "Asian heroic tradition" has also caused consternation among women and sexual minorities. In the previous chapter, I highlighted Kingston's dual impulse to dismantle Chinese patriarchy and redress the invisibility of Asian American men. The rest of Part I explores alternative expressions of masculinity so as to obviate further the opposition between Asian American women and men, and between heteronormative and alternative gender manifestations. Just as Kingston in *China Men* and *Tripmaster Monkey* attempts to identify with her male protagonists, critics too can cross over.

It may seem retrogressive, however, to reinvoke the notion of masculinity at a time when scholars in ethnic and gender studies are repeatedly stressing the arbitrariness of gender construction and the radical indeterminacy of categories such as sex and race. Yet no amount of academic theorizing can readily undo an egregious history of gender representation, and the fact that gender is constructed does not alter the reality of how it operates within the culture and shapes it. To this day, masculinity and power—both physical and political—still figure in conjunction. White men who have always enjoyed masculine perquisites may well be able to afford to ignore gender expectations, but men of color in pursuit of equality may nevertheless aspire to play roles that have been associated with dominance.

The idea that the Chinese were biologically inferior or diseased was widely circulated during the Chinese Exclusion era. The rhetorical nullification of Chinese manhood took place as early as 1902, in a brochure published by the American Federation of Labor (AFL), rooting for continuing Chinese exclusion. It states that the presence of the Chinese in America was a matter of "Meat vs. Rice, American Manhood vs. Asiatic Coolieism"; that "an advancement with an incubus like the Chinese is like the growth of a child with a malignant tumor upon his back. At the time of manhood death comes of the malignity" (American Federation of Labor 5, see also; K. S. Wong 8, 35n; E. Lee). This same brochure contains an illustration captioned "The American Gulliver and Chinese Lilliputians," with the American Gulliver "resembling Abraham Lincoln ... being shackled to the floor by hordes of tiny Chinese, complete with queues and buckteeth ... tethering 'Gulliver' to the floor with bands and spikes" (K. S. Wong 8). As the AFL brochure makes plain, legislative enactments against Asians were often fueled by negative media representation, which has not been fully redressed to this day.

DESEXUALIZATION OF ASIAN (AMERICAN) MEN IN THE POPULAR MEDIA

For all the advances in gender and ethnic studies challenging traditional notions of manhood and womanhood and unsettling stereotypes about peoples of color, as social beings we continue to be shaped by sexually and racially coded characteristics. David L. Eng observes that both mainstream and minority subjects "remain invested in the normative identification, stereotypes, and fantasies that maintain the dominant social order" (Eng 4). Judith Butler, in refining her theory of performativity, insists that the social construction of identity is far from free: "The 'performative' dimension of construction is precisely the forced reiteration of norms... Performativity is neither free play nor theatrical self-presentation; nor can it be simply equated with performance" (Butler 94–95). But performativity can be governed by the stereotypical roles assigned to a particular group, for there has been a discernible connection between theatrical and cinematic performance and performativity for people of color in the United States. After all, the limited social representations they see of themselves in cultural media—both "high" and "low" brow art—can warp their formation of identity. Chinese American men, and Asian American men in general, who are seldom allowed by the popular media to *perform* "masculine" roles, are sometimes self-driven to rehearse gender norms. Constraint in this instance is not only "that which sets a limit to performativity" but also "that which impels and sustains performativity" (Butler 95). It is necessary to examine the anxieties and aspirations behind these repetitive performances before we can go beyond gender binarism and sidestep dominant scripts for masculinity and femininity.[2]

The interlocking of gender and race has often been evident in the media representation of Asian Americans. Gina Marchetti describes how Hollywood maintains racial and ethnic hierarchies through gendering and how images of ethnicity and race always conjure up images of masculinity and femininity: "Thus, fantasies of threatening Asian men, emasculated eunuchs, alluring Asian 'dragon ladies,' and submissive female slaves all work to rationalize white, male domination" (Marchetti 288, 289). Elaine H. Kim similarly notes: "Asian men have been coded as having no sexuality, while Asian women have nothing else... Both exist to define the white man's virility" (69). In the bitter words of the *Aiiieeeee!* cohort, "The white stereotype of the acceptable and unacceptable Asian is utterly without manhood. Good or bad, the stereotypical Asian is nothing as a man" (xxx). Most recently, Nguyen Tan Hoang, in *A View from the Bottom: Asian American Masculinity and Sexual Representation*, intervenes in the widespread assumption in gay Western male subculture that Asian men possess a propensity for the bottom position in gay sex, because they are "less masculine than men of other races." Nguyen then launches a critique of heteronormative narratives of Asian masculinity while simultaneously embracing Asian "bottomhood" in its capacity to produce sexual pleasure, so as to "flesh out the racial-sexual-gender assumptions" behind these widespread representations (x). Proposing an alternative Asian American model that is non-patriarchal, anti-sexist, and anti-racist may risk further effeminizing heterosexual Asian men (Chan, *Chinese* 11), but coalition with other marginalized groups is an important tactic in dismantling racism alongside heteronormativity (Cheung, "M&M" 191; J. Chan 11; T. H. Nguyen 5).

Despite the new cultural awareness in the wake of the civil rights movement, and despite the increasing variety of roles Hollywood has granted Asian women, little has changed in popular portrayal of Asian males. Writing in 2014, Justin Chan observes: "the number of lead roles offered to Asian Americans has dwindled over the years" since the time Japanese American actor James Shigeta landed a groundbreaking role in 1959 as a detective in the crime drama *The Crimson Kimono* and Bruce Lee almost single-handedly redefined that image as Kato in the 1966 TV series *The Green Hornet*.[3] "The subsequent decades following Shigeta's and Lee's success saw few [Asian Americans], if any, play lead or supporting roles" (J. Chan). In an op-ed piece for the *New York Times* (April 22, 2016), Keith Chow observes that "a majority of roles that are offered to Asian Americans are limited to stereotypes that wouldn't look out of place in an '80s John Hughes comedy" (K. Chow A19). Blockbuster films with attractive Chinese (American) male images (e.g. *In the Mood for Love*; *Happy Together*; *Crouching Tiger, Hidden Dragon*; *The Wedding Banquet*), whether straight or gay, have been directed by Hong Kong or Taiwanese directors such as Ang Lee and Wong Kar-wai; they are not Hollywood productions.

The only enduring "positive" Asian male image made in America is the Bruce Lee figure; the box office success of *Dragon* (a movie based on his life) and the popularity of action movies from Hong Kong—notably those directed by John Woo and Jackie Chan—attest to the continual appeal of that profile. The larger society may enjoy these movies simply as Oriental variations on Hollywood gore and mayhem, but for many Asian Americans these films provide images of Asian heroism not previously encountered in American popular culture. The fetishization of the Kung fu fighter in American cinema may have in part triggered the Chinese American literary revival of the Asian heroic tradition discussed in the last chapter. One cannot overestimate the magnetic attraction these heroic figures have for Asian Americans who seldom see themselves in leading roles in the white media. Because these movies are also eagerly consumed by non-Asians, Asian Americans (who must still grapple with racial slurs and hate crimes outside the cinema) can derive a sense of vicarious acceptance as the larger audience roots for the on-screen Asian fighters. Like some of the martial heroes exalted in *The Big Aiieeeee!*, these fighters on the silver screen only fortify the association of manhood with violence. Though *wen* takes precedence over *wu* in traditional Chinese culture, the *wu* icon has been the only one available to Asian Americans, and the fiction of Gus

Lee and David Wong Louie must be placed within the backstory of such stereotypical representations of Asian men in American popular culture.

Wu's Ascendancy over *Wen* in Gus Lee's *China Boy*

In the ABC sitcom *Fresh Off the Boat*, which premiered February 4, 2015 and is based on Eddie Huang's memoir with the same title (Huang), we see the same association of manhood with machismo. Commenting on his upbringing in Orlando, Florida, Huang states: "If you weren't fighting you were a nerd and a victim" (Yang). Huang's experience is not unlike that of the protagonist in *China Boy* (1991), which Gus Lee admits to be a thinly veiled autobiography. It describes the tribulations and eventual triumph of Kai, a seven-year-old boy who must negotiate between the pacifist teaching of his immigrant mother and the street violence in the Panhandle (at the time a predominantly black district) in San Francisco, not to mention the abusive behavior of his Irish American stepmother. Kai strains to "become an accepted black male youth in the 1950s ... an objective all the more difficult because [he] was Chinese" (G. Lee 14).

This difficulty with being Chinese has to do with not just race but also the *wen* ideal, which has been inculcated in Kai by his mother and his Uncle Shim. This ideal has often been venerated over the *wu*, especially during and after the Qing Dynasty:

> Under the Manchu occupation the martial arts were monopolized by the conquerors, and as a reaction the Chinese, and more especially the members of the literary class, began to consider physical exercise as vulgar and athletic prowess as suited only to the 'Ch'ing barbarians'... The ideal lover is described as a delicate, hyper-sensitive youngster with pale face. (Van Gulik 295–296)

Furthermore, as D.C. Lau and Kam Louie point out, *wen* is intimately connected with music: "In his discussions of music and virtue Confucius clearly shows his preference for the non-*wu* path." Citing Lau, Louie adds that "the connection between music and poetry (*wen*) was intimate because although not all music would have words, all poetry could be sung. ... 'Confucius required of music, and by implication, of literature, not only perfect beauty but perfect goodness as well'" (Lau 39; K. Louie 17–18). Not surprisingly, Kai's mother, who wants her son to become a distinguished musician, tries to instill *wen* in Kai from a tender age. After her death, however, Kai is forced to abandon *wen* in favor of *wu*—but in an African American mode.

A reader unaware of the dual (and at times warring) Chinese ideals of *wen* and *wu*, and contradictory Cantonese maxims such as "a superior person moves his mouth but not his hands" (i.e. prefers verbal to physical confrontation) and "he who does not take revenge is not a superior man," would be nonplussed by the antithetical pronouncements about Chinese beliefs in Chin's *Donald Duk* and in Lee's *China Boy*. Donald, the protagonist of the former, is taught by his father and uncle about war and revenge in the Chinese heroic tradition, whereas Kai is taught by his mother to abstain from fighting under all circumstances; war, according to this narrator, violates the essence of "ancient, classical education and the immutable humanistic standards of Chinese society" (4). The difference illuminates the contradictions within Chinese culture and the degree to which subjectivity enters into the remaking of a cultural tradition. Lee Yu-cheng sees Chin's re-visioning of the Chinese American tradition as motivated by a desire to discover a "usable past" that in this case disproves the Orientalist stereotype of the effete Asian (115). Gus Lee's rendition of the Chinese tradition, on the other hand, serves to emphasize the protagonist's difficult struggle to become an all-American boy. Despite such dramatic differences, ultimately *China Boy* also hammers home the need to fight one's way to American manhood. In Viet Nguyen's words, both Chin's and Lee's texts have assumed the tasks of dismantling stereotypes largely "through the assumption of the same violence that was earlier used to subordinate Chinese Americans"; this praxis, whose features are "nationalist, assimilationist, and masculine, becomes a significant method for claiming an American identity that has a long tradition of deploying violence to define itself" (V. Nguyen 130, 140).

In *China Boy*, the Chinese mother (and later Uncle Shim) and the Irish stepmother represent two dichotomous cultures. Between these two poles lies the Chinese father, who has "refused his roots, recognizing in American soldiery the beauty of action... All the knowledge of the teachings of the philosophers means *nothing* against an airplane with guns and a pilot who knows how to kill" (54). However, Kai's father is also the one who has "nominated" Uncle Shim—"a wonderfully elegant, silver-haired man ... that seemed to contain all the wisdom of China"—to be Kai's tutor and to teach him calligraphy (28). Calligraphy literally encrypts *wen* and its masculine power, evident in "the display of *wen* power in steles, scrolls and banners of the calligraphy of society's leaders, particularly the Emperor" (K. Louie 17). Kam Louie cites the famous example of Mao Zedong, who asserts in his poem "The Snow" that "none of the founding emperors of China's great dynasties ... were truly great because ... they lacked the 'literary achievement' and 'artistic grace' so important in a leader among leaders" and whose own brush*man*ship is "featured prominently as the symbolic expression of his control of the (masculine) *wen* power" (K. Louie 17)[4]

This imperative is inculcated in Kai early on. While Kai is still a toddler, Uncle Shim brings him his "first inexpensive rabbit-hair pens, ink tablets and heavy, black glass ink pots, and soft, floppy books filled with empty graph paper, on which to cast the characters of the Chinese tongue" (G. Lee 208). These four items, known as "the four treasures of the *wen* chamber," are indispensable for anyone who wishes to be a *wenren*. Cheryl Alexander Malcolm observes: "Calligraphy comes to symbolize China and altogether different attitudes toward maleness… Comparable to giving an American football to a small boy, giving a Chinese calligraphy set to a boy can be regarded as affirming his nationality and masculinity" (Malcolm 415). Unlike most American boys, Kai has been "kept indoors until the age of seven… Mere speaking and the use of my body in physical games and sports … were unknown arts," but as a *wenren* or cultured person in the making, he "understood calligraphy" (G. Lee 36). Uncle Shim conveys the superiority of *wen* over *wu* when he praises his ward: "He has a scholar's eyes already, built for reading and not for archery… He will be a great friend of books, unenticed by horses and the games of peasant boys" (G. Lee 37). While Uncle Shim's comment may sound snobbish, it underscores the traditional association of education with self-cultivation, with moral character. Only through a course of study can a person become what Confucius, the *wen* icon, considers to be a "superior man." A *wenren* should also be a person of integrity.

But Kai's *wen* trajectory is abruptly derailed. The mother who tells Kai that hurting people will damage his "*yuing chi*, [his] balanced karma" (4) dies when Kai is only six, whereupon he is exposed to the blows of his stepmother Edna and the punches of the Panhandle. Thanks to Colonel Ting, his "Westernized" father, Kai is soon sent to take boxing lessons at the Young Men's Christian Association (YMCA). Edna, Kai's white stepmother, mandates complete American assimilation at the expense of rooting out everything Chinese. Viet Nguyen calls her "the embodiment of a violent America that threatens to forestall [Kai's] manhood" (V. Nguyen 134). Compared by Kai to German Nazis, she tries to crush any vestiges of Chineseness in her stepson, whose very facial expressions and indeed face can trigger slapping. She also burns all of his mother's belongings, including her wedding dress and photos, in an attempt to deprive the stepson of his cherished maternal mementoes. By compelling Kai to stay outdoors except during meal times and bedtime, she exposes him to bloody street fights. If Kai is subdued at home by oppressive whiteness in the person of Edna, he is literally hobbled on the street by a black bully named Big Willie.

By the time Kai is seven, he has fully accepted physical combat as a way of life: "Fighting was the final test of life on the street. It measured a boy's courage and tested the texture of his guts, the promise of his nascent manhood, his worthiness to live and bear friends on poor streets" (90). The novel proper ends in a scene of unmitigated gore. The reader is expected to cheer when Kai finally beats down his vicious opponent on the street, without reflecting on his equally relentless method of revenge or his role in provoking the fight in the first place. This ending recalls a telling simile introduced at the beginning of the book: "Streetfighting was like menstruation for men" (3). The letting of blood by physical assault is thereby sanctioned as a biological passage into puberty.

The book further suggests that for men of color, the demonstration of strength through force has an extra hold beyond the traditional initiation into manhood. The streetfighting takes place in a predominantly black and Hispanic neighborhood. Kai's black buddy Toussaint (Toos) LaRue explains how African Americans come to see physical combat as a privilege: "In ole days, no Negro man kin hit or fight. We belongs to da whites, like hosses... Man fight 'notha man, be damagin white man goods. So he get whipped... [Now] we kin fights, like men" (98). The passage implies that black men who have been demeaned by whites take up the means of the masters with a vengeance. But in making up for past subjugation by being belligerent toward others, they simply remake themselves in the image of their oppressors. Asian American men, in their quest to empower themselves, may likewise be tempted to use the master's tools of violence.

Kai takes Toos's remarks to mean that "fighting [is] a measure of citizenship. Of civilization" (98). Ironic as his interpretation may sound, it is not wide of the mark, for the book leaves us with a sobering reflection that street violence is not so different from institutionalized violence.[5] The narrator informs us that "some who survived [the Panhandle] became cops, but more became crooks... Almost to a man, or boy, the children of the Panhandle became soldiers" (4–5). The interchangeability or affinity of cops, crooks, and soldiers is unsettling. As readers discover in *Honor and Duty*—the sequel to *China Boy*—Kai himself, after his training at the Y and on the street, completes his education in violence by entering West Point, though he eventually rejects its military ethos. If the lurid descriptions of brutal hand-to-hand combat in *China Boy* are meant to parody the process by which boys are inculcated in violence and to shock one into pacifism, the novel also capitalizes on what it seeks to undermine by its graphic rehearsals. In Viet Nguyen's words: "Asian American masculinity Americanized itself in the most ironic fashion, by affirming patriarchy through violence that had previously been directed at Asian Americans en masse... In *China Boy* Lee frames Kai within this mythology of formative violence" (V. Nguyen 138).

In light of Lee's description of Chinese culture as being averse to bloodshed, the bodily injuries that mark the protagonist's progression into American manhood also signify the violence of assimilation and the need to obliterate the mother tongue along with its exaltation of *wen*. Although *wu* also forms a part of the Chinese masculine ideal, none of the Chinese characters, including Kai's parents and Uncle Shim, associate physical aggression with Chinese culture.[6] Hence in the narrator's mind, his two mothers personify the two cultures. "China, like [his] mother, had grown in modern times to distrust men who accomplished things with muscles and swords" (204). America, on the other hand, represents action, including aggressive action, and marrying Edna was his father's "major-league step toward cementing the American assimilation he so desperately sought" (58). The nonviolent teaching of the Chinese mother is presented as an obstacle to Kai's adjustment to American life. "This is America! And *she does not exist!*" cries Edna (85). The Chinese mother must literally be dead for Kai to become a self-made American man under Edna's aegis. In fighting his way to manhood, Kai sets aside the Chinese *wen* ideal to abide by the terms of dominant masculinity. (Unbeknownst to himself, however, Kai remains an obedient son of China insofar as he arrives at the other Chinese masculine touchstone of *wu*, at the crossover model of aggressive manhood.)

Be that as it may, the China boy is the one who has lived to *write* this tale. In putting on paper his struggle with an American rite of passage, Kai has also reclaimed the *wen* ethos of his mother and Uncle Shim. He uses his hands not only to box but also to "report a crime," mostly notably that of his stepmother, who wishes to extinguish Chinese culture through verbal, physical, and psychological violence. Edna, for all her abusive attempts to extinguish Kai's Chineseness, in a sense only transfers the *wen-wu* ideal to him into its New World cognates of writing (in English) and boxing. Try as she may, she cannot expunge the Chinese in the stepson, because the East-West dichotomy of incompatibility is founded on a false logic, but succeeds in heaping upon herself a long list of ethically incriminating records, thanks to Kai's ineradicable *wen* predilection.

There are other glimpses of alternative masculinity in the novel—if we can stop thinking about manhood as embodying the American ideal of rugged individualism or what Michele Wallace calls "superficial masculine characteristics—demonstrable sexuality; physical prowess; the capacity for warlike behavior" (xix–xx). A number of male characters embody what Nel Noddings, following Carol Gilligan, describes as "caring." Although Noddings proclaims caring to be a "feminine approach to ethics," she adds: "there is no reason why men should not embrace it" (2). In Chapter 5, I show how this ethic actually harks back to the Confucius notion of *ren* 仁, which the Sage associates primarily with men. In *China Boy,* this ethic of caring is enacted by men of diverse national origins. Uncle Shim, a bona fide *wenren*, helps Kai to retain against great odds a vestige of Chinese culture and a sense of self-esteem after his mother's death. No less significant are the trainers Kai rubs up against at the Golden Gate YMCA, where he receives boxing lessons for self-defense under surrogate father figures of African American, Italian, Puerto Rican, and Filipino descent, who take the place of Kai's negligent biological father in shepherding their Chinese protégé, much as Toos's mother cares for him maternally, so much so that to Kai "Mrs. La Rue is Chinese. She just didn't *look* it" (108). Hector Pueblo, a Mexican auto mechanic, rescues Kai from a ferocious beating, tends to him in his garage, and alerts Kai's father to his son's plight. Tony Barraza, Kai's Italian American boxing teacher, ensures that the hungry boy is well fed. Barney Lewis, his African American boxing teacher, on discovering that Edna has removed all the photos of Kai's beloved mother from the house, goes out of his way to obtain one for Kai. These surrogate fathers "share their life gifts" with him (147); they nurture and succor him when his own father seems oblivious to his tribulations. But the character Kai most cherishes is his peer Toos who, despite his dubious equation of fighting and manhood, literally extends his hand to Kai when all the other boys are engaged in the ritual of China boy bashing. Kai recalls: "My primary bond to him was for the things he did not do. He did not pound or trap me. He never cut me down. Or laughed with knives in his eyes. Then he opened his heart by explaining things to me, giving me his learning, and taking me into his home" (97). The passage turns around the hegemonic conception of masculinity as (aggressive) activity. Kai is forever drawn to Toos because he refrains from the cocky and blustering acts conventionally associated with boys. Toos also inspires in Kai reciprocal caring: "I had never had a friend before, and I cared for him as few lads have for another" (99).

In a book that centers on male mentoring, it is important to remember that Kai learns about caring as well as fighting from men. If their efficacy as martial or pugilistic instructors is what enables Kai to survive physically, their care is what makes him wish to continue to live. Noddings advances, "When the attitude of the one-caring bespeaks caring, the cared-for glows, grows stronger, and feels ... that something has been added to him" (20). For Kai, who has felt abandoned by his biological mother and abused by his stepmother, and who at one point wished to "evaporat[e]" (290), this something is nothing short of the courage to go on. Caring women such as Kai's sister Janie, Angelina Costello, and Mrs. LaRue are equally important to Kai. But in shifting Noddings's emphasis from feminine to masculine caring, in showing how well the male characters manifest a nurturing behavior traditionally associated with women, I wish to underline precisely how *dis-arming* such behavior is in men, how much it has rubbed off on Kai, and how attainable it is for men of all ethnicities and classes. (I will elaborate on the ethic of care and its affinity with the Confucian notion of *ren* in Chapter 5.)

Deflated *Wenren* in David Wong Louie's *Pangs of Love*

Frederick Buell says of the characters in Asian American literature: "Manipulated by being pulled back and forth between the poles of black and white, and aware of the playacting involved in imitating either model, Asian-Americans couple fear of nullity with an awareness of perpetually inauthentic, heterogeneous role playing" (Buell 187). This comment seems especially apropos to the works by Gus Lee and David Wong Louie. Published in 1991, the same year as *China Boy*, the male protagonists in David Wong Louie's short-story collection *Pangs of Love* could not be more different from Kai. Most of them are American-born and assimilated adults steeped in American culture, exhibiting a high degree of wit, literacy, individuality, and occasionally even sexual bravado. Measured against the Chinese *wen* ideal, these men should pass with flying colors. They are, as David Eng posits, also perfect exemplars of the Asian American model minority. Be that as it may, they often feel hysterical, bereft, unhinged, and forlorn in white America. All of them are involved in interracial romance and living in predominantly white neighborhoods, but they are no less paranoid than *China Boy*'s Kai, full of angst about trespassing, displacement, and extinction.

The title of the collection is cunningly chosen, and not just because the mother in the title story happens to be "Mrs. Pang." David Louie has borrowed the three words from Hamlet's signature soliloquy: "For who would bear the whips and scorns of time / The oppressor's wrong, the proud man's contumely, / *The pangs of despised love*... When he himself might his quietus make / With a bare bodkin?" (3.1.72–78; my emphasis). Just about every male protagonist in this collection suffers from the white man's "contumely" (insult or disdain), and from successive white women's "despised love," so much so that Louie's men, like the Prince of Denmark, think often of extinction, though not by their own hands. And just as the title of the book is borrowed from the English bard, Louie's antihero seems to be haunted by a nagging sense that the English and American media are somehow not his own, but "borrowed robes" (to borrow from Shakespeare again), that the Western panoply of masculinity hangs on him loosely, "like a giant's robe / Upon a dwarfish thief" (*Macbeth* 1.3.115; 5.2.24–25). The sense of troubled masculinity is especially palpable in "One man's hysteria—Real and Imagined—in the Twentieth Century," "The Movers," and the eponymous "Pangs of Love." All three stories betray the protagonists' sexual anxiety, wistful paternity, and a subconscious desire to "pass" as white. While I focus on these three tales of men in distress, similar neuroses also surface in "Birthday," "Bottles of Beaujolais," and "Social Science."

The recurrent themes of displacement, impersonation, and male hysteria in *Pangs of Love* have been noted by both Sau-ling Wong and David Eng. Why do Louie's protagonists constantly feel their manhood affronted when they have assimilated so very well, both culturally and, in most instances, economically? Wong thinks that these speakers face the prospect of "identity extinction" (S.-l. C. Wong 183). Eng, building on Homi Bhabha's theory of mimicry, considers the idea of trespass to be a type of "urtext" for reading Louie's collection, and believes that "emotional segregation from whiteness" contributes to their male hysteria (Eng 106). What Eng describes as male hysteria is also very much tied to what Anne Anlin Cheng calls "Asian American hypochondria," which "plays out anxieties about the prospect of assimilation for Asian American subjects, caught between the assimilationist model (whereby minority cultures are expected to adopt mainstream values or behavioral patterns) and the pluralist model (whereby ethic minority cultures are expected to value and maintain their culture of difference)" (Cheng 69). Where Eng focuses on the continuing legacy of white racism in a supposedly "color-blind" period, Cheng's notion of melancholia reckons with "racism *on the part of the racialized*" as well (Cheng 68). Building on all these astute observations, I add a complementary analysis of "passing," relating it specifically to the protagonists' obsession with masculinity. In addition to facing the prospect of ethnic extinction and being segregated from whiteness, Louie's men have introjected their "not quite, not white" subaltern status and consequently are always trying to "pass" as white, whether literally, symbolically, or imaginatively. The themes of ethnic extinction and trespass are, therefore, inextricable from that of racial passing.

Homi Bhabha describes a colonial subject as a "*subject of a difference that is almost the same, but not quite*" (Bhabha 85). The fact that the *wen* sophistication of Louie's speakers fails to gain them any masculine leverage in the United States is due not only to the relative depreciation of *wen* masculinity in American culture but also to the sense, real or imagined, of being a virtual *wenren* who is "not quite" because "not white." Louie's protagonists differ from Kai in *China Boy* in three important ways, all of which bring to mind a colonial subject. First, despite being highly educated, they are illiterate in Chinese language and culture. Second, they find themselves not so much beleaguered in a world populated by people of color as marooned in white America. Third, their felicity with English and their full acceptance of the dominant culture's standards of beauty, literacy, and masculinity would have made Edna proud. Yet race and ethnicity continues to matter, as a divider between these protagonists and their white compeers. The Chinese American protagonists are constantly subject to the slights and slurs of their white lovers and acquaintances, prompting them to shore up their manhood by synthetic means or to impersonate as someone else.

The phenomenon of passing explains in part why the *wen* achievement of Louie's many sophisticated personas fails to give them any masculine purchase. If one of Kai's obstacles to easy assimilation is his incoherent mix of Chinese, African American, and European American argots, the male speakers in *Pangs of Love* not only speak English trippingly but can also dispense a savory phrase such as "who could translate our squabbles and make them palatable to another tongue?" (122). However, as David Palumbo-Liu observes, "To make the entry into the 'universal' more fraught, even when the minority subject acquires the cultural capital of the Other it may not be enough. In the cultural politics that leverages a racist national subjectivity even as it presumes upon universal value, entrance can be constantly deferred" (Palumbo-Liu 427n6). Nowhere was this truer than in the publishing marketplace. The *Aiiieeeee!* editors note at the publication of that anthology in 1974 that many Asian American writers had been asked to "write under white pseudonyms," that "C. Y. Lee was told a white pseudonym would enhance his chance for publication" (xliii).

Louie was acutely aware of the publishing world's prejudice against Asian American writers. Speaking about his favorite authors such as Kafka, Günter Grass, Céline, and Flannery O'Connor, he observes: "These authors all articulated a certain kind of 'otherness' to me. They spoke of and wrote from a marginalized place... On some unconscious level, this kind of strangeness and oddness tapped into my own sense of difference and alienation" (Hirose 193). He discloses why his earlier stories did not have identifiably Chinese American narrators, why that aspect of his personality went "underground" though in his head he has "always visualized the speaker as someone not unlike [him], going through his various acrobatics" (Hirose 196, 209). "I did that in the belief that the publishing world wasn't interested in hearing stories by folks like me," he confides. "So I thought that, if I could just cheat a little bit, I might be able to get things published" (Hirose 196). Not only was *Pangs of Love* published, but it also received the 1991 *Los Angeles Times* Book Prize for First Fiction and the *Ploughshares* John C. Zacharis First Book Award. Yet Louie still finds himself pigeonholed by white critics: "They don't talk about you as writing beautiful sentences or having a sense of humor because, you know, what Asian has a sense of humor anyway?" he quips. "The mainstream literary world has managed to ghettoize me... I think that translates in some people's minds as African American does still for some people—as something less than, something not as good, something inferior... It's like putting us in the Chinese laundries" (Hirose 199, 200, 201). Louie's protagonists seem to find themselves going through the same "acrobatics" as does the author, variously dodging, scowling at, and colluding with the white gaze. Regardless of their cultural sophistication, these protagonists are never perceived—by the Other and by themselves—as equals.

"One Man's Hysteria—Real and Imagined—in the Twentieth Century"

In most cases, the protagonists' high degree of hegemonic literacy seems inversely proportional to their literacy in their mother tongue. According to the *Aiiieeeee!* editors, "without a language of his own [an Asian American] is not a man" (xlviii). The editors are referring to a distinctive language with ethnic inflection. Could it be that despite (or because of) the fact that Louie's male protagonists speak Standard English eloquently, the people they commingle with (and even they themselves) still feel that they are not speaking a language of their own, that they are simply mouthing the master's tongue? Is it possible that regardless of their verbal mastery they still feel a lack because they have internalized the idea that the Standard English language is somehow not their own, that they are mere interlopers with borrowed tongues? Or are they afraid of becoming unmoored ethnically in the Anglo-Saxon ocean of words?

The answers to all the questions above seem to be "yes" in Louie's "One Man's Hysteria—Real and Imagined—in the Twentieth Century," set in the 1980s during the height of the Cold War, when a nuclear Armageddon seems imminent, at least to the "hysterical" Stephen, the hyper-assimilated narrator. Stephen, a writer who believes that the most important thing to preserve in the event of a nuclear war is poetry, initially comes across as a perfect incarnation/caricature of the Chinese *wenren*, but one who hails exclusively from a European American heritage: "When the bombs fall, I will be ready. Not with fishing nets or Geiger counters or fallout shelters, but with poetry—memorized, metabolized, and ready to recite. Only poetry can save us now" (137). His mastery of the Western, especially metaphysical, poetic canon (Campion, Dickinson, Donne, Drayton, Eliot, Herbert, Hopkins, Dylan Thomas, Vaughan, Yeats, etc.) is nonpareil. Yet he is totally cut off from his Chinese culture and is interested in safeguarding only the Anglophone trove. To this end, he performs a weekly Sunday ritual with Laura, his girlfriend (whom he refers to as "wife … for expediency"): he recites a line or two from a random poem and Laura is expected to identify the poet. Both of them are writers, though Laura seems to have the upper hand: "My wife writes stories and poems, while I, far less versatile but nonetheless supportive of her dual talents, dabble exclusively in prose—short stories, mostly—but I do aspire toward a novel" (140). Despite his Anglophone literacy, however, Stephen feels inferior to his white wife, the "standard bearer," to borrow Chang-rae Lee's appositive for another Caucasian wife, in *Native Speaker*.

True to the narrator's belletristic profession, the story has a contrapuntal structure, alternating between the presumably "real" interaction between Stephen and Laura, his girlfriend, and the "imagined" family in his somewhat autobiographical fiction, in which the couple has a son. (The edges between the "real" and the "imagined" are often blurry, however, running constantly into each other.) It is soon apparent that Stephen is hysterical not just about the prospect of a nuclear apocalypse but also about his manhood, both in his "real" interaction with his girlfriend and in his "imagined" relationship with his fictional wife. Because of the nebulous boundaries, one can easily get lost in the metafictional universe. On the one hand, since "One Man's Hysteria" is fiction, the reader must assume that both of the versions presented are imagined. On the other hand, because the narrator puts so much of his own life into his fiction, despite his emphatic assertion that he is "not an autobiographical writer" (150), the reader may also wonder whether both versions also reflect the author's "real" anxiety to some extent.

In the putative "extratextual" account within the story, Laura is the one who calls the shots. She stands over Stephen's writing, spews criticism, and demands constant revisions, to the extent of removing the character for whom she is the prototype. In bed, she often rebuffs his amorous overtures; against his own memory of her "multi-orgasmic night" when they first made love, Laura reminds him that she has never been "privileged to such delirium," adding pointedly, "my memory is good. I remember our first time. Your pal down there between your legs took the night off" (147). Stephen also imagines "The Love Song of J. Alfred Prufrock" to be her favorite poem, goading the reader to see resemblances between Eliot's feckless persona and the insecure Stephen, who echoes Prufrock in asking, "But do I dare make love?" (148). The white partner finds fault with the narrator in both the "real" and "imagined" versions. Worse, while she can be "turned on" by metaphysical poetry, she is never aroused by the narrator's fiction, let alone his physical presence. In the narrative within the narrative, the imagined speaker fares ill as father as well, scolded by his wife for buying a soda for their son Todd (thus feeding him junk), for teaching him about war, and for causing an accident in which a goldfish dies. The narrator is always trying to appease his caviling white partner in this two-track narrative.

Although the narrator in this story seems ultra-assimilated—by way of his mastery of Western literature, his suburban neighborhood, and his white partner—he is a perfect illustration that "assimilation tenders a promise of ethnic intermixing that draws itself short of the color line" (Cheng 69). Ample hints can be detected between the lines that race is behind the henpecked narrator's hysteria. At one point, Laura tells Stephen: "'my instincts tell me nothing's going to happen too close to where you're sitting now. Radioactivity might be color-blind, but those who control the bombs aren't... They never dropped any atomic bombs on Germany ... and then went ahead and unloaded on Japan.' She claps her hands together, twice, directly over my head. 'Boom!'" (144). If the comment is meant to reassure Stephen that he is safe in a white neighborhood, by clapping her hands directly above him her reassurance boomerangs, reminding him of his physiognomic similarity to the Japanese. If Laura thinks that Stephen is safe in her company, then he is belittled as a mere yellow appendix to her whiteness.

Viet Nguyen, in his aforementioned essay on Gus Lee, has differentiated between "legitimate" and "illegitimate" forms of violence in the United States: "embodied respectively in the regenerative violence that white mythology claims for itself and the degenerative violence that this mythology displaces onto blackness." He notes that in the international context, the seemingly "regenerative heroic practice" may be considered by other nations as "being simply another particular version of a lawless, degenerative struggle for control." But for Americans, that aspect of violence is domestically displaced onto blackness and the ghetto, where it serves as the other of a state-sponsored, legitimate violence" (V. Nguyen 131, 132). Louie's story gives Nguyen's exposition of violence yet another twist. From the international context, Stephen, as a person of Asian ancestry, is on the receiving end of the ostensible "regenerative heroic practice" that legitimizes American offshore wars; from the national context, being the stereotypical model minority, he falls outside the purview of both legitimate and illegitimate forms of violence that inhere in an American definition of manhood. In the American schema, the Chinamen, rather than sporting heroic manhood, are served up as cannon fodder.

Stephen's sense of manhood is further vitiated by the prospect of extinction, which harks back to the history of the thwarted paternity of Chinese immigrants, denied fatherhood on account of exclusion and antimiscegenation laws. It also recalls the AFL brochure cited earlier, "Meat vs. Rice," in which the Chinese are figured as "a malignant tumor on [a child's] back," incurring death "at the time of manhood." At the beginning of the story, Stephen tries in vain to wake Laura by their poetry game "until the baby cried," teasing the reader into thinking that they have a child, only to be disabused in the following paragraph: "Of course, she is not our child" (138). Although the explicit reason given by the narrator for not having children is the state of the world ("With the world the way it is, babies ... aren't a reasonable option for the thinking couple") (138), he does not conceal his paternal longing: "I want a child to bear my name into the future, its bleakness notwithstanding" (149). Stephen's fictional narrator, who does have a son named Todd, is an inept father, at least in the eyes of his querulous wife. Toward the end of the story, Todd has mistaken the red background of Gauguin's "Jacob Wrestling with the Angel" for blood. The father, who has been gazing at Todd's "shiny black hair" (155), now explains: "Red isn't always blood ... just as black isn't always hair" (157). Stephen then muses: "I wonder now what color Todd's blood is. Does it even have color? Is there blood between us, me and this creation of mine?" This "creation" refers at once to Stephen's first person narrator's offspring and metafictionally to Stephen's imagination. The only "bloodline" Stephen could envision is a fictive one and even that one is open to question. When Todd remarks, "Your hair is black too," the father resumes his reverie: "And as red is blood ... then black must be death. Isn't it?" (157). The motifs of genocide, extinction, and masculinity in ruins bleed into one another even in this tale within a tale. The black hair insinuates that even the fictional father cannot beget a "true-blooded" American. This fixation on blood and posterity resonates not only with racial pedigree and the Chinese American historical legacy of enforced bachelorhood but also with Chinese and American patriarchal and patrilineal ideals, which Stephen can fulfill only virtually, in his overwrought brain. The story ends with the narrator jotting down a few prompts for his fiction, including:

You are Stephen
Nancy is Laura
You are Laura too.

These reminders expose a third layer of fictitiousness. Is Laura any more "real" than Nancy, or is she too a figment of Stephen's imagination? Is the real Stephen a bachelor like his immigrant ancestors of yore? Is Stephen "emasculating" himself in declaring that he is "Laura too"?

"THE MOVERS"

The theme of impersonation—whether out of longing or envy—is especially pronounced in "The Movers." The narrator and his white girlfriend, Suzy, have just driven across the state to their new rental unit in the hope of a fresh start. But Suzy, after cataloging "all that was wrong" with the narrator, walks out on him and drives off in their car. Still waiting for the movers to deliver their second-hand furniture, the narrator languishes in the dark on the floor of his new apartment, without heat, electricity, furniture, or lover. To calm himself, he pretends to be "dead, lying in a morgue in China" (122). A teenager named George—apparently a former resident who has recently moved out with his parents—and his girlfriend Phyllis enter the apartment and proceed upstairs to a room designated by the narrator and Suzy earlier as their "bedroom" (124), unaware that the new tenant has already arrived. There are two more "visits" that evening—first by the girl's father and finally by the two tardy movers.

Throughout the story, the narrator is haunted by a deep sense of isolation, which he tries to allay by putting himself by turns in the shoes of George and of George's father. He surreptitiously follows the young couple upstairs and through a keyhole watches them make love: "I saw plenty through my sharpshooter's squint... At once, my intruders looked like a spirited heap of laundry and an exotic form of torture. But ... who could mistake the sounds of the wondrous suction of love?" (124). The narrator longs to be George, an active participant instead of a lonely spectator at a keyhole.

Like Stephen in "One Man's Hysteria," the narrator in "The Movers" also pines for a white woman and a son. When Phyllis's father comes looking for his daughter, the narrator, on an impulse, pretends to be George's dad, saying to the other father: "I can assure you ... your daughter's safe with my boy." He himself is taken aback by those last two words: "I was astonished by my daring, and certain, despite my thirty years, that my voice lacked the easy authority of a parent. Without question, my 'my boy' had just made its maiden voyage from my lips" (125). After Phyllis's father has left, the narrator, who in his fantasy has conflated Suzy and Phyllis, tries to find himself in George: "All I wanted was to see his face, to see myself there as I had seen Suzy in the girl's face" (134). His impulse to assume, alternately, the roles of George's father and of George reveals his desire for the paternal authority and sexual audacity these non-Asian men possess. He registers the voice of Phyllis's father (who's celebrating his anniversary with his wife that evening) as "full, confident, mature" (125). The narrator, on the contrary, both tells himself that his voice lacks a parent's "easy authority" and is told later by a mover that he doesn't "sound like anyone's father" (131).

He even feels one-upped by teenage George. The roles of resident and trespasser, adult and teen, host and guest, are repeatedly inverted. When George and Phyllis enter the house, the narrator is the one who "remained frozen in place; afraid [he] might be discovered" (123), as though he, and not the teen, were the trespasser. George's escapade with Phyllis aggravates the narrator's sense of deprivation and inadequacy: "My heart needed massage; in my stomach a little man was trying to punch his way out" (134). The positions of the 30-year-old speaker and George are again reversed: the older man has become "a little man" nursing (pun intended) his manhood. He tries to regain the upper hand by voicing paternal solicitude: "I asked [George] if he had gloves, a hat, a scarf. I told him zip up tight" (136). But George, rather than adopting the role of a son or even apologizing for his intrusion, tells the narrator upon leaving the house, with remarkable aplomb and speaking like a man: "Thanks for the visit... I think you'll like it here" (136). The ambiguity of the first clause (reminiscent of the first story "Birthday," in which the person knocking at the door is the owner and the Chinese person inside the house making a birthday cake for his "son" is the intruder) brings out the narrator's angst in his new suburban residence.

The wife and son for whom the narrator seeks in vain are trophies sported by straight men in a heteronormative society, where both matrimony and fatherhood are key to the definition of manhood. Hence, the recurrent insinuations that the speaker is gay further "unman" him. One of the movers, after seeing Phyllis's father leave, asks the narrator: "Who's your boyfriend?" Later, when the narrator complains about the damp mattress that is delivered, saying, "This is Jell-O. Would you like to sleep on this?" The mover quips: "Sorry, bub ... you are not my type" (130). Neither mover believes that he is wedded to Suzy, whose signature is needed for the delivery of the furniture. Furthermore, both movers, though they are two hours late in their delivery, persist in insulting the narrator, who tells himself: "if Suzy were here, this guy would be apologizing for their tardiness; he'd be almost too polite" (128). Given that women are more often the ones who are being slighted by men, race is the unspoken part of the equation here: presumably, the movers would be much more deferential to a white woman than to a Chinaman.

"The Movers" highlights the narrator's difficulty in establishing his manhood as a straight lover and as a father. Although one needs not assume that he is Chinese American to appreciate the humor and pathos of this story, the peculiar insecurities that waylay the protagonist clearly recall the predicament of Chinese American men. As Eng notices, even in the legally desegregated society, "Louie's urbane protagonists are still haunted by past historical legacy and the more subtle form of racism in the putatively colorblind society" (Eng 106). The fact that the narrator's furniture is "secondhand" is redolent of a Chinese American man's attempt to purchase, or obtain a purchase on, a rather slippery, handed-down European American masculinity.[7]

"Pangs of Love"

The title story likewise reveals the difficulty experienced by two Chinese American brothers, one straight and the other gay, in living up to hegemonic manhood. The story revolves around the intergenerational tension resulting from both the language barrier between an immigrant Chinese mother and her American-born sons and the pressure of assimilation. To the narrator, his mother—Mrs. Pang—is a stark misfit in US society, being a woman from rural China who does not speak English after 40 years in the United States and for whom being in a car at 80 miles an hour is analogous to "our country's first astronaut, a monkey strapped into the Mercury capsule, all wires and restraints and electricity, shot screaming into outer space" (86). He does not question why he himself is a "linguistic dwarf" (78) when it comes to Chinese language and culture and why he and his brother are far from fully at home in America. The story evinces the two brothers' fraught assimilation—utter removal from their Chinese heritage yet still out of place in the white culture—despite their cultural sophistication and economic success.

Although the brothers are removed from their ancestral culture, they still feel its heteronormative and patrilineal pressure. When the heterosexual narrator is asked by his mother why his gay brother, Billy ("Bagel") has no girlfriends, he becomes tongue-tied. His speechlessness has as much to do with the language barrier as with the concept of homosexuality, which he believes is incomprehensible to his mother, a woman from another time and another culture. Like most traditional Chinese mothers, Mrs. Pang is eager to see her sons married so she can have grandchildren. But she is unlikely to have her wishes fulfilled. One son is gay, while the other seems incapable of forming a conventional family. His white former fiancée, Mandy, has left him for a Japanese lover; he is currently dating Deborah, a "rebound among rebounds," whom he has no intention of marrying (84). The traditional Chinese household is on shaky ground; even heterosexuality does not guarantee progeny.

The subversive potential of this story in decentering the patriarchal family is achieved at the expense of impugning Chinese American manhood, however. The 35-year-old narrator, who works for a corporation that manufactures synthetic flavors and fragrances, and who sees his mother as antiquated and unsophisticated, is himself riddled with insecurity, especially in dealing with Japanese men and white women. While "One Man's Hysteria" draws a racial parallel between Chinese and Japanese and Asians in general as indiscriminate bomb fodder, in this story Japanese men deem themselves superior to their Chinese counterparts. The narrator works under a Japanese boss named Kyoto: "Every time we meet he sizes me up, eyes crawling across my body, and lots of sidelong glances. *Who is this guy?* It's the same going-over I get when I enter a sushi joint, when the chefs ... take my measure, colonizers amused by the native's hunger for their superior culture" (79). The narrator, made acutely aware of his ethnic difference, expresses a combination of resentment at the condescending gaze of the Japanese and discomfiture at being gazed upon as a Chinese American, intimidated by Japan's former conquest of China and brawny economic standing in the 1970s and 1980s.

White women further unhinge his sense of masculinity: "Deborah wants me to move out of my mother's place, says I'm a mama's boy, calls me that even as we make love" (85). Although it is not uncommon in Chinese households for adult sons and daughters to live with their parents, the narrator does not dispute Deborah's Eurocentric bias. His manhood had been called into question earlier by Mandy, who used to make love with him with the aid of a gamy musk perfume, "each drop equal in potency to the glandular secretions of a herd of buck deer" (81). They would use the perfume "whenever Mandy was feeling amorous but needed a jump start" (81), as though the narrator needed to shore up his sex appeal with the synthetic fragrance. Still, he cannot make the relationship last: "Within a year, about the time Sony purchased Columbia Pictures, she fell for someone named Ito, and broke off our engagement" (80). The narrator mentally links Deborah's defection with Japanese ascendancy, suggesting how Asian American lives are still entangled with what transpires in Asia, and how virility is calibrated by a pecuniary metric.

The narrator's masculinity is thus assailed by both Japanese men and white women. These two affronts converge in Mandy's selection of a new lover. Already feeling piqued as Kyoto's "right-hand slave" (84), the narrator must take peculiar umbrage at Mandy's preference for a Japanese. Worse still, her departure coincides with Kyoto's request that the narrator alter the composition of the musk perfume; he infers from this directive that the "manly scent of musk is no longer manly enough" (82), no doubt spoken with a sniff at his own sexuality. Although Mandy simply leaves one Asian man for another, Japanese men, with their imperial past and superior economic present (not to mention their samurai iconography), may come across as more dominating (and sexist) than Chinese and Chinese American men. In the reductive words of Bernardo Bertolucci (on the differences between the Japanese and Chinese members of his film crew for *The Last Emperor*): "The Japanese have this myth of virility.

They are more macho. The Chinese are the opposite, more feminine. A bit passive" (R. Chow 5).[8]

Daunted by the myth of Japanese puissance, and Kyoto's one-upmanship, the narrator seems to share Bertolucci's invidious assumptions. He betrays his sense of being less potent than Mandy's lover when he tries to convey that lover's ethnicity to his mother by pointing at a Japanese wrestler—whom he describes as a "Samurai Warrior"—on television (94). We have been told earlier that the entire Pang family used to watch wrestling on Saturday nights: "It was myth in action. The American Dream in all its muscle-bound splendor played out before our faithful eyes" (94). The linkage of brute force with success runs deep in America (recall the China boy's initiation). The narrator, in equating physical, financial, and imperial power with manhood, short-circuits his own. "Pangs of Love" thus undermines Chinese patriarchy only to reinstate patriarchal norms. It also accentuates the precariousness of Chinese American masculinity, which stands trial before Caucasian women, Japanese men and, as we will see, white and gay men.

Bagel, the narrator's brother, seems out of place in his own beach house in Long Island—a metaphor for upscale white society. Mrs. Pang and the narrator are invited there for the weekend: "Bagel's house is white. Even the oak floors have been bleached white. A stranger [we later learn that his name is Nino] in a white turtleneck and white pleated trousers opens the door. He's very blond, with dazzling teeth" (88). Jamie, Bagel's partner, is "in a white terry-cloth robe" (88). Mack, presumably Nino's partner, is also casually dressed. When Bagel enters "decked out in hound's-tooth slacks, tight turquoise tennis shirt, and black-and-white saddle shoes, Nino exclaims: "God, Billy…you always look so pulled together" (89). The observation implies that Billy, in stark contrast to his partner, who makes himself "at home" in a bathrobe, always takes pains to be properly dressed even in his own house; the fact that his variegated coordinates call attention to themselves suggests that somehow the homeowner sticks out in the ménage à quatre. Unlike the white apparel of Nino, the white robe of Jamie, and the casuals of Mack, all of whom blend in perfectly with the white environs, Bagel, for all his sartorial finesse, still comes across as being someone in borrowed or made-up garb. His effort at being American masculine, by building "bulk" through "pumping iron," likewise backfires: "I feel as if I'm holding a steer," the narrator relates upon embracing his brother (89). Just as greater respect is accorded to a white woman (the subordinate vis-à-vis a white man) than to a Chinese American man in "The Movers," white gay men (the subordinate vis-à-vis straights) are much more ensconced in the white beach house than the Chinese American homeowner. The gay brother is thus triply frozen out: by his homosexuality, which makes him "deviant" vis-à-vis the heteronormative Chinese and American society; by his race, as registered by his visible difference in his white surroundings; and by his class origins. Part of the pang in the story is his implicit shame about his Chinese family, particularly his mother, who is a "wrestling fan" because "no language skills required here" (93); "He doesn't want his friends to know he dropped from the womb of one who loves something as low as wrestling" (97). Despite being fully assimilated culturally and economically, Bagel, as his nickname implies, cannot rid himself of the brown crust that is an indelible sign of his Chinese heritage, nor make up for the emptiness in the core. Eng, building on Bhabha's insights on mimicry, rightly concludes: "The Chinese American brother's attempts to affiliate with this queer world prove to be at the cost of a split subjectivity that denies his racial differences even while it continually exposes it" (Eng 201).

Such exposure is symbolized chromatically when Mrs. Pang accidentally spills soy sauce from a take-out container of roast duck on the white sofa that she has earlier cautioned Bagel against buying because it won't "withstand the dirt" (88). Now the soy sauce "lands on the chair, spotting the off-white fabric. Bagel has a fit: 'I invite you to dinner and you bring dinner'" (89). Then the four residents of the white house join forces to remove the brown stain on the couch: "Within seconds, Nino, Mack, Jamie, and Bagel converge on the stains with sponges, Palmolive dishwashing detergent, paper towels, and a pot of water. An eight-armed upholstery patrol" (89). The word "patrol" evokes policing authority. In Eng's words, "the furniture itself comes to manifest the hysterical symptoms of a thwarted assimilation. This hysterical symptom is ultimately referenced back to Bagel, [who] becomes the agent of his own self-exclusion" (Eng 202). In both "The Movers" and "Pangs of Love," the legal occupants of their own houses are the ones who seem interlopers.

The image of artifice or mimicry that pervades the story is of a piece with the theme of racial passing. "Pangs of Love" opens with the Johnny Carson show, during which Mrs. Pang would laugh along with the on-screen laughter and applause; the two brothers also ape the media icon: both roll their eyes "the way Johnny does" (76, 90). It ends with the narrator distributing a pill that turns everything sweet at the dinner in the beach house (after the uproar caused by the spilt soy sauce). The narrator describes his profession: "We are the soul of hundreds of household products... Our mission is to make the chemical world, an otherwise noxious, foul-tasting, polysyllabic ocean of consumer dread, a cozier place for the deserving noses and tastebuds of America" (76). These artificial fragrances and flavors provide an illusion of (pass for) the real thing, but they cannot ultimately allay the hidden pangs in the family and in the society: the sons' embarrassment and shame regarding their Chinese mother; the mother's forever deferred hopes for grandchildren; the narrator's sense of besieged manhood; Bagel's inability to come out to his mother; and the interracial and generational tensions between Deborah and Mrs. Pang and between the yuppie white gay household and the Chinese family. Like the spray for the homeless to simulate the odor of home, or the pill that turns everything sweet at the end, the synthetic products mask pressing problems of inequality or simply sweep them under the rug, as the ending of the story suggests:

> I pull out from my pocket gold-foil packets the size and shape of condoms. Inside each is a tablet developed at the lab. You dissolve it in your mouth, and it will disguise the sourness of whatever you drink or eat. I pass them to everyone at the table... They will laugh, delighted by the tricks of their tongues. But soon the old bitterness in our mouths will be forgotten, and from this moment on, our words will come out sweet. (98)

As Eng nicely points out, the narrator's chemical concoction symbolizes the "dangerous politesse of a multicultural age" that attempts to "smooth over the racial and (homo)sexual tensions... They are condoms for the mouth, covering a suppressed bitterness that might well characterize the politics of difference into the twenty-first century" (Eng 203). Just like Bagel is passing for straight in his mother's presence, both brothers are also trying to pass as insiders in the white middle-class society, but to no avail.

There is yet another way to relish Louie's gustatory tablet. Robert Ji-Song Ku, in *Dubious Gastronomy: The Cultural Politics of Eating Asian in the USA*, argues that California roll, Chinese takeout, dogmeat, monosodium glutamate, SPAM, and so on are examples of "dubious" comestibles associated with Asian and Asian American foodways. Commonly understood as "bad, ersatz, or corrupt," Ku contends, these foods ("MSG and SPAM are both synonymous with artificiality") are redolent in the American imaginary of Asian Americans, "human analogs of inauthentic cultural products." "Discursively positioned neither as truly 'Asian' nor truly 'American,' they are read as doubly dubious. The Asian presence in the United States is commonly seen as watered down, counterfeit, inauthentic—at least when measured against a largely mythical if not entirely imaginary standard" (8, 9; see also Carruth on food hierarchy).

Read through Ku's astute, if acerbic, postulations, the doubly artificial sweetener dispensed at the end of "Pangs of Love"—manufactured in a Japanese lab but marketed by an edgy Chinese American, and which smacks of imitativeness, spuriousness, and fakery, the very antithesis of whole food—is also "doubly dubious," a synecdoche of the narrator who is forever plagued by a sense of dual inauthenticity, not quite Chinese enough (in both his mother's and the dominant culture's eyes) to speak or understand Chinese, and not quite American enough to grace a Johnny Carson show except as some butt of a joke, as when "Johnny's in a turban the size of a prize pumpkin" (77). If the roast duck from the Chinese takeout—the source of the brown stain on the white sofa—is the epitome of uncool ethnic practice, eliciting an unheard "yuk!" (Kingston writes in *Tripmaster Monkey* that Chinese traveling with such a "fire duck" would pretend "the smell was coming off somebody else's luggage" (Kingston 74)), the unmarked (and therefore presumably white) tablet the narrator "pass[es] ... to everyone" encapsules his sense of inauthenticity as an American. Neither the brown sauce nor the white tablet could ever garnish haute cuisine (Xu 62–93). Even the *wen* sophistication of Louie's punctilious native English speakers of Chinese descent will always be taken by Americans who "look the part" (80) with a grain of salt, as counterfeit. In *The Barbarians Are Coming*, Louie's first novel, culinary imagery reaches rhetorical heights, reflecting the liminal status the protagonist, a Chinese American chef of haute cuisine. Louie seems to have imparted his own edge as writer into the male protagonists of his fiction, whatever their diegetic profession. What Dorothy J. Wang says of poet Marilyn Chin (Louie's fellow MFA at the University of Iowa; discussed in Chapter 9) also applies to Louie: "For a minority poet, demands for proof of cultural and linguistic authenticity weigh as heavily as notions of race and blood" (Wang 119).[9] Louie's protagonists are not unlike their author in being keenly aware of being perceived by mainstream America "as something less than, something not as good, something inferior," consigned to "the Chinese laundries."

Although legislative racism has seemingly been rectified, Asian men are still stigmatized by US popular culture as sexually deviant or deficient (*Fargo, House of Cards*). As Claude Steele has shown in his study of female and African American students in educational testing, those who suffer from "stereotype threat" invariably exhibit anxiety during performance: "Performing in domains where prevailing stereotypes allege one's inferiority ... creates a predicament in which any faltering of performance threatens to confirm the stereotype as self-characteristic. This predicament ... can cause an apprehension and self-consciousness that directly interferes with performance in that situation" (Steele see also Cheng 6–7). Louie's male characters are all too conscious of this threat, albeit in a sexual terrain; they cannot avoid scrutinizing themselves through the lens of the typecasting majority. Michele Wallace argues that African Americans have been systematically deprived of the continuity of their own African culture not only by the oppression of slavery but also by "integration and assimilation," which have "denied them the knowledge of their history of struggle and the memory of their autonomous cultural practices" and caused them to take on white culture and values in regard to sexuality and gender (xix). The same holds true for many Asian Americans. Because racism toward Asians has traditionally been couched in gendered terms, Kai in *China Boy* tries to stack up against American notions of manliness by assuming pugnacious roles, while the protagonists in *Pangs of Love* are discomfited in their attempts to "pass" as their European American counterparts. None of them can disentangle from the prevailing ideology of manhood or escape its hold. To arrive at a model that is not already implicated in US cultural hegemony and racial hierarchy and that is compatible with both the cultural nationalist impulse to reclaim an Asian legacy and the feminist desire to combat machismo, it may be helpful to revive the memory of "autonomous cultural practices"—to resuscitate the *wen* ideal—which, as a code of masculinity, has been sorely underrated in American society. To be sure, the Occidental ideal, too, takes many forms other than those inspired by frontier heroes—including the courtly lover, the knight-errant, the debonair intellectual, and the "Mr. Smith" idealist who goes to Washington. But Asian American men, in order to counter stereotypes, tend to favor the truculent "Western" models.

Am I thus presenting Asian American men with a double bind in criticizing the martial hero while advocating the *wen* model? If they try to emulate the martial hero, they risk valorizing brute force and perpetuating patriarchal mores. If they pattern themselves after the Chinese *wenren*, they risk appearing "unmanly" to Americans steeped in the New World configuration of gender, thereby reinforcing the popular perception of Asian men as effeminate—as befitting the model minority. Yet to live according to the "Western" ideal, to live in acute awareness of the white gaze, Asian American men may constantly find themselves falling short, as do

Louie's male protagonists. It is especially ironic that contemporary Chinese American male writers, who correspond to the traditional *wenren* by race, gender, and profession, should endorse physical violence or express ethnic self-contempt for not having a piece of the American beefcake.[10]

Asian American men can resist one-way adaptation and turn racial stereotype on its head and into a source of inspiration, as T.H. Nguyen has done in his evaluation of bottomhood, by demonstrating that what the dominant culture perceives as "feminine" may in fact be a transgressive expression of masculinity. If African Americans can recodify black as beautiful, Asian Americans, and perhaps non-Asians as well, can learn to see the *wen* allure in men as seductive. My intention is not to substitute one template for another but to furnish counterexamples to the pantheon of martial heroes erected by the editors of *The Big Aiiieeeee!* and to introduce models unfettered by priapic trappings. From both nationalistic and feminist standpoints, a quest for Chinese American manhood should allow us to reclaim an alternative repertoire rather than simply reproduce clones of Western heroes. The next chapter examines a Chinese figure whose linguistic and poetic predilections took by storm both Chinese and English literary societies, and the Chinese and white women and men therein.

Notes

1. All the paragons of womanhood, be they Homer's Penelope and Helen of Troy (as well as her reincarnation in Marlowe's *Dr. Faustus* and Goethe's *Faust*), Ruth in the Old Testament and the Virgin Mary in the New Testament, Shakespeare's Cleopatra or Spenser's Faerie Queene, Samuel Richardson's Pamela and Clarissa, Puccini's Madame Butterfly or her contemporary, Miss Saigon, have been created by men; not to mention those myriad counterparts created by Asian men.
2. While most of my examples are drawn from Chinese American fiction, the challenges faced by Chinese American men in North America are faced by many other Asian men as well, though the stereotypes associated with different national groups can be contradictory. For instance, whereas Chinese men are considered asexual, Filipino men are often made out to be oversexed.
3. As Kent A. Ono and Vincent N. Pham observe, though the image of Bruce Lee challenged the representation of Asian men's physical inferiority and weakness of an earlier era, the portrayal of Asian men as martial artists "became its own kind of controlling image" (Ono and Pham 76).
4. Such an attitude toward calligraphy is obviously an androcentric one: it is still common to hear people say that women's calligraphy never truly

captures the real essence of the art. Women are regarded as lacking the ability to exude the inner strength required to produce powerful character forms. The famous calligraphers of traditional and contemporary China and Taiwan are all men. Calligraphy, because it is part of the display of *wen* power and closely linked to masculinity, lies beyond the grasp of non-men.
5. Viet Thanh Nguyen elaborates on the thin line between criminal violence and institutionalized violence (V. Nguyen). One need only recall the beating of Rodney King in Los Angeles (1991) and the killings of Jonathan Ferrell in North Carolina (2013), Michael Brown in Ferguson, Missouri (2014), and Michael Garner in Staten Island in New York City (2014) to see the continuing blurring of the line.
6. That the hyper-masculine, fighting model of *wu* is already extant in the Chinese tradition attests to the forced dichotomy of East (in this case China) versus the West (the United States). The two national(ist) traditions are not incommensurable. My attempts at crossing borders and boundaries are designed in part to dismantle artifices of supposed infeasibility of comparing literatures written by Chinese Americans, by Chinese nationals writing in their native soil, and Chinese nationals who have become US immigrants. I thank Hannah Nahm for prompting me to make this point.
7. I thank Robert Kyriakos Smith for this suggestion.
8. Early Japanese immigrants were also more fortunate than their Chinese counterparts in that they were allowed to bring their wives and "picture brides" to the United States.
9. The title of Louie's *The Barbarians Are Coming* is in fact taken from Marilyn Chin's poem "The Barbarians Are Coming": http://www.english.illinois.edu/maps/poets/a_f/chin/online.htm
10. On this point, see also S. Wong's critique of the *Asian Pacific Men* calendar ("Subverting Desire"). The masculine ideal privileged by the editors of *The Big Aiiieeeee!* seems more influenced by African American than by Caucasian models. But African American men too have been indoctrinated in white America's ideal of masculinity. I should also add that the Chinese *wenren* found in classics and opera is typically pale and emaciated; he could certainly benefit from some martial training. In fact, yet another kind of Chinese masculine ideal is embodied by someone who is *wen wu shuang quan* 文武双全—accomplished in both the literary and martial arts (K. Louie 16–17).

Works Cited

American Federation of Labor. "Some Reasons for Chinese Exclusion: Meat vs. Rice, American Manhood against Asiatic Coolieism. Which Shall Survive?" Washington, DC: American Federation of Labor, 1902. 3–30.

Bhabha, Homi. *The Location of Culture*. New York: Routledge, 2004.

Buell, Frederick. *National Culture and the New Global System*. Baltimore, MD: John Hopkins University Press, 1994.
Butler, Judith. *Bodies that Matter: On the Discursive Limits of "Sex."* New York: Routledge, 1993.
Carruth, Allison. *Global Appetites: American Power and the Literature of Food*. New York: Cambridge University Press, 2013.
Chan, Jachinson. *Chinese American Masculinities: From Fu Manchu to Bruce Lee*. New York: Routledge, 2001.
Chan, Justin. "Where Are All the Asian Americans in Hollywood?. 20 August 2014. <http://www.complex.com/pop-culture/2014/08/asian-americans-in-hollywood>.
Cheng, Anne Anlin. *The Melancholy of Race: Psychoanalysis, Assimilation, and Hidden Grief*. New York: Oxford University Press, 2001.
Cheung, King-Kok. "Art, Spirituality, and the Ethic of Care: Alternative Masculinities in Chinese American Literature." *Masculinity Studies and Feminist Theory*. Ed. Judith Kegan Gardiner. New York: Columbia University Press, 2002. 261–289.
———. "Of Men and Men: Reconstructing Chinese American Masculinity." *Other Sisterhoods: Literary Theory and U.S. Women of Color*. Ed. Sandra Kumamoto Stanley. Urbana: University of Illinois Press, 1998. 173–199.
Chin, Frank, Jeffery Paul Chan, Lawson Fusao Inada, and Shawn Hsu Wong, eds. *Aiiieeeee! An Anthology of Asian-American Writers*. Washington, DC: Howard University Press, 1974/1983.
Chow, Keith. "Why Hollywood Won't Cast Asian Actors?." *New York Times*, 23 April 2016: A19.
Chow, Rey. *Woman and Chinese Modernity: The Politics of Reading between West and East*. Minneapolis: University of Minnesota Press, 1991.
Eng, David L. *Racial Castration: Managing Masculinity in Asian America*. Durham: Duke University Press, 2001.
Hirose, Stacey Yukari. "David Wong Louie." *Words Matter: Conversations with Asian American Authors*. Ed. King-Kok Cheung. Honolulu: University of Hawai'i Press, 2000. 189–214.
Huang, Eddie. *Fresh Off the Boat: A Memoir*. New York: Spiegel & Grau, 2013.
Kim, Elaine H. "'Such Opposite Creatures': Men and Women in Asian American Literature." *Michigan Quarterly Review* 29.1 (1990): 68–93.
Kingston, Maxine Hong. *Tripmaster Monkey: His Fake Book*. New York: Knopf, 1989.
Ku, Robert Ji-Song. *Dubious Gastronomy: The Cultural Politics of Eating Asian in the USA*. Honolulu: University of Hawai'i Press, 2013.
Lau, D. C. "Introduction." *Confucius: The Analects*. Trans. D. C. Lau. Harmondsworth: Penguin Books, 1979. 9–55.
Lee, Yu-cheng. "Politics of Memory in *Donald Duk*." *Wen-hua shu-hsing yu hua-yi mei-kuo wen-hsueh [Cultural Identity and Chinese American Literature]*. Ed.

Shan Te-hsing and Ho Wen-ching. Taipei: Institute of European and American Studies, Academia Sinica, 1994. 115–132.

Lee, Erika. *The Making of Asian America: A History.* New York: Simon & Schuster, 2015.

Lee, Gus. *China Boy.* New York: Dutton, 1991.

Liu, James J. Y. *The Chinese Knight-Errant.* Chicago: University of Chicago Press, 1967.

Louie, David Wong. *Pangs of Love.* New York: Plume, 1992.

Louie, Kam. *Theorizing Chinese Masculinity: Society and Gender in China.* Cambridge: Cambridge University Press, 2002.

Malcolm, Cheryl Alexander. "Going for the Knockout: Confronting Whiteness in Gus Lee's *China Boy.*" *MELUS* 29.3/4 (2004): 413–426.

Marchetti, Gina. "Ethnicity, the Cinema, and Cultural Studies." *Unspeakable Images: Ethnicity and the American Cinema.* Ed. Lester D. Friedman. Urbana: University of Illinois Press, 1991. 277–307.

Nguyen, Tan Hoang. *A View from the Bottom: Asian American Masculinity and Sexual Representation.* Durham: Duke University Press, 2014.

Nguyen, Viet. "The Remasculinization of Chinese America: Race, Violence, and the Novel." *American Literary History* 12.1 (2000): 130–157.

Noddings, Nel. *Caring: A Feminine Approach to Ethics & Moral Education.* Berkeley: University of California Press, 1984.

Ono, Kent A., and Vincent N. Pham. *Asian Americans and the Media.* Cambridge: Polity Press, 2009.

Palumbo-Liu, David. *Asian American: Historical Crossings of a Racial Frontier.* Stanford: Stanford University Press, 1999.

Slotkin, Richard. *Gunfighter Nation: The Myth of the Frontier in Twentieth-Century America.* New York: Maxwell Macmillan International, 1992.

Song, Geng. *The Fragile Scholar: Power and Masculinity in Chinese Culture.* Hong Kong: Hong Kong University Press, 2004.

Steele, Claude M. "A Threat in the Air: How Stereotypes Shape Intellectual Identity and Performance." *American Psychologist* 52.6 (1997): 613–629.

Tajima, Renee E. "Lotus Blossoms Don't Bleed: Images of Asian Women." *Making Waves: An Anthology of Writings by and about Asian American Women.* Ed. Asian Women United of California. Boston: Beacon, 1989. 308–317.

Van Gulik, R. H. *Sexual Life in Ancient China.* Leiden: E.J. Brill, 1974.

Wallace, Michele. *Black Macho and the Myth of the Superwoman.* London: Verso, 1990.

Wang, Dorothy. *Thinking Its Presence: Form, Race, and Subjectivity in Contemporary Asian American Poetry.* Stanford: Stanford University Press, 2013.

Wong, K. Scott. "Cultural Defenders and Brokers: Chinese Responses to the Anti-Chinese Movement." *Claiming America: Constructing Chinese American*

Identities during the Exclusion Era. Ed. K. Scott Wong and Sucheng Chan. Philadelphia: Temple University Press, 1998. 3–40.

Wong, Sau-ling Cynthia. "Chinese/Asian American Men in the 1990s: Displacement, Impersonation, Paternity, and Extinction in David Wong Louie's *Pangs of Love*." *Privileging Positions: The Sites of Asian American Studies*. Ed. Gary Y. Okihiro, et al. Pullman: Washington State University Press, 181–191.

Xu, Wenying. *Eating Identities: Reading Food in Asian American Literature*. Honolulu: University of Hawai'i Press, 2007.

Yang, Wesley. "Eddie Huang Against the World." 3 February 2015. <http://www.nytimes.com/2015/02/08/magazine/eddie-huang-against-the-world.html?emc=eta1>.

Zhong, Xueping. *Masculinity Besieged? Issues of Modernity and Male Subjectivity in Chinese Literature of the late Twentieth Century*. Durham: Duke University Press, 2000.

CHAPTER 4

Masculine Mystique: Xu Zhimo 徐志摩, Younghill Kang, Pang-Mei Natasha Chang, and Anchee Min

This chapter attempts to capture the masculine allure of *wen*, of cultural and literary endowments, as an alternative model that breaks with patriarchal notions of manliness. I use both Cantonese opera and the poet Xu Zhimo—both as a historical figure and as confected in three Asian American texts—to illustrate this Chinese legacy. Because of the constructionist nature of gender, "the meaning of masculinity is neither transhistorical nor culturally universal, but rather varies from culture to culture and within any culture over time" (Kimmel and Messner xxi). Kam Louie has pointed out that while there is a macho or *wu* tradition in China it is balanced by "a softer, cerebral male tradition—the *caizi* (the talented scholar) and the *wenren* [also spelled *wen-jen*] (the cultured man)"; that "the cerebral male model tends to dominate that of the macho, brawny male" (K. Louie 8). Song Geng, who devotes an entire book, entitled *The Fragile Scholar*, to expatiating this *wen* icon, concurs: "Despite the association with effeminacy this image recalls for today's (Chinese and Western) audience, it embodies all the desirable masculine qualities in the literary discourse of ideal heterosexual love in traditional China" (Geng viii). Examining paradigms generated from within the Asian context instead of

---

An early version of this chapter was delivered as one of the keynote presentations at the joint Renmin University of China and UCLA Conference on American Literature and the Changing World (June 30–July 1, 2012, Beijing). I thank Professor Diao Keli for the tremendous work he had done to make possible this collaboration.

always looking up to European American norms can open up other manly possibilities, for Asian Americans and for all.

The title of this chapter plays on *The Feminine Mystique* (1963) by Betty Friedan, who reveals that men are the ones who create the "feminine mystique," the idea that women find complete fulfillment in their roles as wives and mothers, an assumption that runs afoul of Friedan's empirical evidence. Where Friedan, drawing on Simone de Beauvoir, traces (though unwittingly from a white middle-class woman's point of view) how one becomes a woman, I explore what becomes a man from a Chinese American academic woman's point of view, with attendant cultural, professional, and feminist biases. Though ostensibly about masculinity, the models advanced in this chapter break down the arbitrary distinctions between what is attractive in gay versus straight men, in men versus women. The male poet-scholars showcased in the following pages appeal to men and women of different orientations. Furthermore, they also second a feminine ideal that is completely different from the China dolls, dragon ladies, and female martial artists that populate Hollywood movies. One of the hallmarks of the poet-scholars is their tendency to be swept off their feet by women of letters, and their propensity to treat these women as equals. Curiously enough, this gallant trait is obfuscated, if not openly denied, by male scholars bent on reclaiming the same Chinese masculine model.

Wen, though generally understood to refer to "those genteel, refined qualities that were associated with literary and artistic pursuits of the classical scholars," is not solely the province of the leisure-class but is open to "a broad range of social classes [that] aspired to scholarly attributes" (K. Louie 20). The traditional *wenren* is most popularly equated with male characters of letters in the countless romances known as *caizi-jiaren* 才子佳人 (literally scholar-beauty) stories, featuring talented poet-scholars and women who are stunning in looks and, I would add (and argue anon), in locutions. The power of the softer, more refined intellectual masculine form is a striking counterexample to Western stereotypes of the Kung fu hero and of the asexual Asian nerd. One of the most striking differences between *wen* and *wu* males is their relationship with women: "While romances of scholars and beauties are common themes, indicating a closeness of *wen* to women, the *wu* hero shows his strength and masculinity by resisting the lure of feminine charm. By contrast to the *wu* male's necessary rejection of women, the *wen* male usually more than fulfills his sexual obligations to women" (K. Louie 19).

However, I am not in full accord with Kam Louie, who insists on "the unique maleness of the dichotomy wen-wu": "The wen-wu dichotomy is applied to women only when they have transformed themselves into men. Women cannot otherwise be productively discussed in terms of wen or wu for both these aspects of official social life were explicitly denied women." Wenren (literary or cultivated people), according to Louie, "can only be translated as 'men accomplished in wen' or 'cultured men.' It was assumed that women who achieved excellence in wen were abnormal" (Louie 11, 12). While this argument is valid to a large extent concerning wu, it seems wide of the wen mark. In the scholar-beauty (caizi-jiaren) genre that emerged in the mid-seventeenth century during the Ming and Qing dynasties, and which Louie singles out as the genre featuring cultured men, wen is appreciated as much, if not more, in women as in men. As Keith McMahon points out, "One of the most prominent features of such works is their portrayal of smart, capable, chaste young women who are equal to and in some cases better than their male counterparts in terms of literary talent, moral fiber, and wit." This genre "provides female characters with a power of self-determination and self-invention that exceeds not only normal female roles but male ones as well"; the appearance of such women in fiction may be traced to the emergence of "a small but significant number of their real counterparts in the mid-seventeenth century … active in social and literary spheres normally off-limits to them," and to the "increasing recognition of women's literary and artistic activity in the late Ming and Qing dynasties" (227–228). This emphasis on female wen attainment and equity with men is so refreshingly enlightened that, to my mind, the genre should really be renamed cainü-caizi "talented women and men" rather than "scholar-beauty." The woman competes in the man's world by wielding language dexterously, in speech and in writing, often proving herself his superior. These romantic works support the lovers' freedom to choose their marriage partners themselves, rather than acquiesce to parental arrangement. But intellectual chemistry must precede sexual union. In McMahon's words: "The chaste couple replaces sex with words: poems, letters, and polite conversations. They end up as *Zhiji*, 'intimate companions' or 'knowers-of-each-other's-innermost'"; "the intercourse of the lovers is verbal, modeled on the polite medium of the written word, through which the youths pass the test of marriage by the time-honored means of establishing one's worth—poetic expression" (McMahon 229, 245–246).

Instead of viewing *wen* as a male quality that is never conferred on women, I contend that the ability of the male scholar to appreciate the literary or artistic talents in the lady (and vice versa) explains his sexual appeal, a point highly relevant to the Cantonese opera and the Xu Zhimo example staged in this chapter. While it is true that a small number of *wen* women have to cross-dress as men in order to gain initial recognition, the point is less to reinforce the "exclusivity of male rights implicit in this construct" (Louie 12) than to underline the arbitrariness of a gender distinction that discriminates against women. Furthermore, the scholar-beauty genre often shows that men and women share the same appeal: literary or artistic talent and a concomitant ability to appreciate the same in the beloved; attentiveness and emotional sensitivity; and the determination to be true to oneself and to select a partner who is also a soul mate.

I also disagree with Kam Louie's assertion that the ultimate *wen* objective consists of succeeding in the imperial exams and obtaining an official post, therefore positioning women (and romantic love) as a "distraction" to that end. Citing Yang Bojun, who notes that Confucius directs his followers to "keep women at a respectable distance" (Yang 198; cited in K. Louie 45), Louie observes that in Confucius's estimation women are a class of people who are "considered troublesome and who should be eschewed" (45). Be that as it may, many *wenren* who exalt romantic love and flout official recognition have made their way into Chinese drama and Cantonese opera. Where Louie cites *The Story of Yingying*, *The Story of the West Wing*, and the People's Republic of China (PRC) writer Zhang Xianliang to argue his case about the importance of self-control in men to guard against feminine charms, he disregards quixotic and unstinting embodiments of *wen*, such as Liu Mengmei 柳梦梅, the male protagonist in *The Peony Pavilion*, the most popular play of the Ming Dynasty by famed playwright Tang Xianzu 汤显祖; Liang Shanbo 梁山伯 in *The Butterfly Lovers*, Tang Bohu 唐伯虎 in *The Flirting Scholar*, or the love-crazed poet Xu Zhimo, the centerpiece of this chapter, whose name is known to every native Chinese intellectual of my generation.

Growing up in Hong Kong watching Cantonese opera and film versions of *The Peony Pavilion*, *The Butterfly Lovers*, *The Flirting Scholar*, and many other romantic comedies and tragedies, I was arrested by one of the most irresistible Chinese male images—that of *shusheng* 书生 or *caizi*, that is, poet-scholar. The difference between the two, as far as I can tell, is that a *caizi* is often from an aristocratic class, whereas a *shusheng* is more often from a humble background. I will refer to both as *wenren* or poet-scholars. These masculine figures had a much stronger hold on the popular imagination, at least in Hong Kong, than the examples of elitist *wenren* presented by Kam Louie. The poet-scholar is seductive because of his gentle demeanor, his wit, his refined sensibility, and, above all, his ability to discern and revere a woman of like mind. Unlike the *wenren* in Louie's study, who aspire to be mandarins/state scholar-officials, many of the poet-scholars in Cantonese films pride themselves on being indifferent to wealth and political power; they seek women and men who are their equals in intelligence and integrity.

Chinese opera has also furnished the most concrete, literally theatrical, examples for the performativity of gender.[1] The Peking opera player Mei Lanfang 梅兰芳 (1894–1961) was the reigning female impersonator of all time. His influence was international, inspiring Charlie Chaplin in the USA, Bertolt Brecht in Germany, and Constantin Stanislavski in Russia. The most popular Cantonese opera player, Yam Kim Fai/Ren Jianhui 任剑辉 (1912–1989), aka *ximi-qingren* 戏迷情人 i.e. "the darling of movie fans" (of whom my mother was one), was unquestionably the most admired male impersonator from the 1950s to the 1970s. No less iconic is her partner Pak Suet Sin/Bai Xuexian 白雪仙 (1926–), the prima donna. The duo blazed such a dramaturgical trail that in 1996, Hong Kong University named a building after them—Yam Pak Building or Ren Bai Lou 任白楼—to commemorate their consummate performances as well as their joint efforts in training a troupe among the next generation. When Yam died in November 1989, over a decade after their concurrent retirement, all the florists in Hong Kong were depleted on the day of her funeral. What garnered Yam so many fans was her masculine mien on stage and on screen as a quixotic *wenren* who tries to win the heart of Pak, who invariably plays the role of highly literate, dazzling, if somewhat supercilious beauty; the two captivated audiences and listeners with poetic repartee and musical duets. Their most famous librettos were penned by a highly gifted and poetic scriptwriter Tang Disheng 唐涤生 (1917–1959). Yam's fan base among heterosexual women far exceeded that of her coeval male actors. On stage (s)he exemplified a kind of manhood that radiated literary talent, caring, sensitivity, and lyrical eloquence, redolent of the *wen* ideal explicated by Kam Louie. But unlike most of the *wenren* discussed by Louie, the male roles played by Yam are so overwhelmingly dedicated to their female love interests that they give up worldly fame and fortune and even life for their beloveds. Because Yam and Pak were as inseparable offstage as onstage, most Hong Kongers today assume they must have been lesbians.

The fact that Mei (the female impersonator) and Yam (the male impersonator) had so many fans perhaps attests to David Henry Hwang's ironic observation in *M. Butterfly* (already cited in Chapter 3, but literally here) that "only a man knows how a woman is *supposed* to *act*" (Hwang 63; my emphases). And vice versa: Only a woman knows how a man is supposed to act. Coincidentally, Yam, a woman, played Liu Mengmei, the male scholar in *The Peony Pavilion*, against Pak as Du Liniang 杜丽娘, the beauty of the play; Mei Lanfang, a man, played the exquisite Du Liniang, his most celebrated role, to rave reviews. Yam's and Mei's raging success provides corporeal thespian testimonies to the performativity of gender.

If reviving the image of the martial hero can counteract "effeminate" stereotypes of Asian American men, surely reclaiming the ideal of the poet-scholar will debunk asexual stereotypes. This model belies popular perceptions of Asian men as inarticulate, unromantic, and unimaginative. It further offers a vision of masculinity that is at once sensual and nonaggressive, and a mode of conduct that breaks down the putative dichotomy of gay and straight behavior, of what behooves women and men. If the *wu* ideal aligns with the American frontier code that associates masculinity with physical exploits, the *wen* ideal seems uniquely East Asian or specifically Chinese. (The closest Western equivalent I can think of would be the courtly lovers, who were by definition aristocratic.) I retrieve this image not out of any nostalgic longing for a specific historical type, however. What comes to mind when I think of the poet-scholar is not whether he is actually a poet or a scholar, but the accompanying attributes: attentiveness, courtesy, humor, personal integrity, indifference to material accumulation and political power, and aversion to brute force—qualities that, in my humble opinion, still very much become a man.

For any positive Asian images to take hold in the United States, however, they must first contend with cultural and political hegemony. As documented in the last chapter, the *wen* ideal has gone the way of Gus Lee's China boy, who has to put aside his calligraphy to develop pugnacious skills, and of David Wong Louie's lovelorn protagonists who, notwithstanding their agile minds and belle-lettrist flair, can only measure themselves against beefy *wu* heroes and remain tantalized by interracial matrimony and paternity in white America. In 1993, a Hong Kong movie entitled *Flirting Scholar*, starring Stephen Chow, was shown in a Los Angeles theater. Having seen as a child a movie of the same title based on a well-known poet-scholar of the Ming Dynasty, starring the nonpareil Yam and Pak, I had been pleasantly surprised at first that a film featuring a Chinese *wenren* would finally make its way to California. I was soon disabused. The 1993 film drastically alters the source story, transforming, a la Superman, the traditional scholar into a deadly Kung fu fighter in disguise. The changes undoubtedly heightened the movie's appeal to an American audience. The globalization of the movie industry, instead of fostering greater diversity, can in fact exacerbate cultural myopia. The advent of communism in China also contributed to the eclipse of *wen* by *wu*. As Kam Louie points out, "In the early decades of the PRC, there were very few *wen* models which were congruent with traditional norms ... and attempts to valorize intellectuals in the aftermath of the Cultural Revolution produced nerd-heroes." He continues: "Between 1949 and 1976, the new class analysis positively discouraged any form of individuality that did not manifestly advance the good of the worker-peasant-soldiers, and produced heroes who were anti-intellectual and hence anti-*wen*" (K. Louie 49).

Therefore, we must travel back in time to the 1920s and 1930s to find a *wen* exemplar and to appreciate its spell. Xu Zhimo 徐志摩 (January 15, 1897–November 19, 1931) was verily a romantic figure without borders. He was the beloved of Chinese female talents Zhang Youyi, Phyllis Lin Huiyin, Lu Xiaoman, and Ling Shuhua; American writers Pearl Buck and Agnes Smedley (before she switched her sexual and political allegiance to Lu Xun in the 1930s); dear to Indian poet Rabindranath Tagore, Bloomsbury associates Goldsworthy Lowes Dickinson, Roger Fry, and E.M. Forster; and Chinese luminaries Hu Shi, Liang Qichao, Shen Congwen, and Lin Changmin (father of Lin Huiyin and director of the Chinese Association for the League of Nations).[2] Not surprisingly, Xu also figures prominently in three Asian American works written over 70 years apart: Younghill Kang's *East Goes West: The Making of an Oriental Yankee* (1937), Pang-Mei Natasha Chang's *Bound Feet and Western Dress: A Memoir* (1996), and Anchee Min's *Pearl of China: A Novel* (2010). In all three, he epitomizes masculine glamor, cultural hybridity, and nomadic sensibility. His fabled comeliness, ebullience, and literary sparkle are welcome antidotes to American popular images of Asian (American) men. In using Xu to exemplify alternative masculinity, I extend my earlier argument against reconstructing Chinese American masculinity by subscribing to the Western ideal—a tendency that could aggravate self-contempt, machismo, and even homophobia. As a modern and modernist *wenren*, Xu calls up ways of being manly without resorting to physical, economic, or political power. I focus primarily on three features that aggregate as his masculine appeal: his immersion in multinational literature (of China, France, Germany, India,

Italy, the United Kingdom, and the United States); his individualist bravura and pursuit of romantic love; and his appreciation and support of men *and* women of letters, instilling in them his esprit de corps. Like the *caizi* in the traditional scholar-beauty genre, he seeks not just good-looking women but friends and lovers who are also soul mates. These dimensions of Xu are evident in both biographical and fictional accounts. Hence, I shall highlight some salient details of his life before analyzing the literary texts. (Throughout this chapter, I use Xu to refer to the historical figure; Hsu or Hsü according to how his name is spelled by other authors in their texts.)

A Modernist *Wenren*

Leo Ou-fan Lee, in *The Romantic Generation of Modern Chinese Writers*, has pointed out that the concept of *wenren* underwent significant changes in the 1920s, that the emergence of *wenren* as a social group with literature as vocation is "a modern phenomenon" related to sociopolitical vicissitudes, especially to the termination in 1905 of the examination system that was the institutional scholar-official channel for Chinese men, thereby turning their focus from the state to society (248, 250, 251). The modern *wenren*, Lee notes, differed from the traditional *caizi* in that he was "modernized" with "foreign fads and new-style thinking," impressed by "the love affairs of Byron, the sad ending of Keats or Shelley, or even the daring amours of George Sand"; he was also good with networking: retaining old friends and making new national and international friends, contributing to journals or newspapers, publishing his own magazines and books, and sponsoring other writers (38). Lee, who devotes two chapters to our poet in this book (spelled Hsü Chih-mo therein), obviously has him at the back of his mind in characterizing the new-style *wenren*. As the most popular literary figure during his lifetime and perhaps even more so in the decade after his death, Xu is remembered for his avant-garde poetry, his mastery of both Chinese and European (especially British Romanticist) literature, his individualist pursuits of romantic love, and his wide yet intimate circles of national and international friends.

Born in Haining, Zhejiang, to a banker's family, Xu had started his Chinese education with a tutor at the age of four. At 11 he enrolled in a modern school that taught Western subjects, where he was called "Boy Wonder," and became class president by virtue of his academic record (Chang 74). He married Zhang Youyi/Chang Yu-i 张幼亿 (1900–1989) at the age of 18 but soon left her to study law at Beiyang University and

Peking University. In 1918, he traveled to the United States to study banking and sociology at Clark University, from which he graduated with high honors in June 1919. He then went on to study economics and political science at Columbia University, where he earned a Master of Arts degree in 1920. That fall he gave up his doctoral studies at Columbia and left for King's College, Cambridge University, where, with the help of China enthusiast G.L. Dickinson (1862–1932), he specialized in English and Romantic poetry and French symbolist poetry. In 1922, Xu returned to China and became a leader of the modern poetry movement, founding the Crescent Moon Society 新月社 (named after *The Crescent Moon* by Tagore), a literary community that consisted mostly of returnees from Europe and America (with Lin Huiyin and Ling Shuhua being the only two female members) and which operated until his death in 1931; the group also launched the periodical *Xinyue* 《新月》, the *Crescent Monthly*.

When Tagore visited China in April 1924, Xu, an admirer who had orchestrated the visit, served along with Lin Huiyin as interpreters. According to Leonard K. Elmhirst, an Englishman who raised funds for the visit, "Tagore immediately recognized in [Xu] first of all a fellow poet, secondly a man with a sense of humor, thirdly a man through whom he felt he could get into touch with the spirit of the Chinese, especially the spirit of the younger Chinese" (Elmhirst 11; cited in Leo Lee 146). Xu worked as an editor and professor at several schools before dying at the age of 34 in a plane crash while en route from Nanjing to Beijing. In 2008, a white marble stone was installed at the back of King's College, Cambridge on which is inscribed four lines from Xu's best-known poem, "Farewell Again, Cambridge" 《再別康橋》, also translated as "A Second Farewell to Cambridge": "輕輕的我走了／正如我輕輕的來／我揮一揮衣袖／不帶走一片雲彩" (see Fig. 4.1). In English: "Quietly I take my leave / As quietly as I came / Lightly I flick my sleeve / Without walking off with a single petal from the iridescent sky" (my translation). A photographic exhibition celebrating the relationship between Xu and King's College was held in the antechapel of King's College Chapel in 2014 (Fig. 4.2).

In his time and today, in life and literature, Xu is known for his charisma. Having sieved through both biographical and literary accounts, I ascribe his reputedly mesmeric personality to his cultural hybridity, inner spirit, unabashed sentimentality, and intellectual generosity—which he extends freely to women. It is not my intent to idolize Xu, however, especially given his caddish treatment of his first wife, his ubiquitous wild oats, and his elitist class background (though he died a poor man on account

Fig. 4.1 Marble inscribed with excerpt of Xu Zhimo's "A Second Farewell to Cambridge" 《再别康桥》

Fig. 4.2 Plaque describing the inscription on the marble

of his second wife's opium addiction). Nevertheless, he provides a shining contrast to Hollywood's stock images of insipid Asian men, who are almost invariably presented as deficient in sexual, romantic, and lyrical ardor. In Xu, whose physical, emotional, and literary passion knew no bounds, we witness a historical precedent who had won the hearts of women and men of diverse nationalities. Xu was patently no nerd.

Xu anticipated many transnational intellectuals today in his vagrant identity and cultural hybridity, in his proclivity to be at home in multiple places. He was possibly the first Chinese writer to claim a strong affinity with a place other than the native land. "If Shaoxing of China is identified with Lu Xun, West Hunan with Shen Congwen and Beijing with Lao She, then the mention of Xu Zhimo … will invoke the image of Cambridge among readers of modern Chinese literature," Lai-Sze Ng and Chee-Lay Tan observe (575). In an essay published in 1926 entitled "The Cambridge I Know," Xu uses the term *Sixiang* 思乡 (nostalgia) in recalling his Cambridge days (Hu Shi; Ng and Tan 576). "Farewell Again, Cambridge" has been included in Chinese literature textbooks throughout Asia.

Furthermore, Xu made a marked impression upon a wide range of English intellectuals at a time when racism was rampant in the West. After Xu enrolled, with the help of G.L. Dickinson, as a special student at King's College, he befriended several members of the Bloomsbury Group: "He came here once and won our hearts completely. Stayed with Roger" (letter from David Garnett to Julian Bell, 1935; quoted in Laurence 132). Xu's own letter to Roger Fry notes: "I have always thought it the greatest occasion in my life to meet Mr. Dickinson. It is due to him … that my interest in literature and art began to shape and perpetuate itself" (Mody 10). According to Gaylord Leung, Xu remained friends with Dickinson, Dadie Rylands, H.G. Wells, Roger Fry, and Bertrand Russell. He was also introduced to Arthur Waley, who along with Dickinson facilitated the connections between Bloomsbury and China (Leung; Laurence 129; Wood 191). Elmhirst, the supporter of Indian and Chinese causes who accompanied Tagore to China, also struck up a friendship with Xu that was to last until his death. Elmhirst was the one who sent Xu passage money when he sailed for England for the third time in July 1928 (Stirling 88); in a letter to Ling Shuhua in 1971, Elmhirst writes that he likes Xu for his "abundant charm, his sensitivity, his poetic imagination and his warmth of affection" (Laurence 145).

As a masculine figure, Xu combines the *wen* of the East and the Romanticist spirit of the West. He resembles the traditional *caizi* in Chinese classics and drama, enticing because of his gentle demeanor and artistic sensibility. As well, Xu is an admirer of British Romantic poets, and also of Thomas Hardy, James Joyce, and especially Katherine Mansfield; he advocates, upon his return to China, the expressions of "true personality" of the individual, including the passions of the body (Laurence 126). He writes in "Art and Life" (published originally in *Chuangzao jikan*《创造季刊》in 1922): "If the materialistic West is a civilization without a heart ... [ours] is one without a soul, or at any rate with no consciousness." "If the Westerners are being dragged along by their own machinery of efficiency," he continues, "my almost brutal imagery of the society we know would be a deadly stagnant pool of water ... *we have no art precisely because we have no life*" (Xu 169, 172). Xu's reverence for the inner life makes his a refreshing voice in the materialistic West and in a China roiled by nationalist, socialist, and communist ideologies. Nicknamed "the Chinese Byron" and "the Chinese Shelley" (Spurling 174), he infuses his Chinese lyrics with Western forms of rhyme and meter and douses them with his romanticist spirit. He breaks away from the rhyming pattern of traditional Chinese poetry "to substitute an essentially Western form of versification with rhyme" (L.O.-f. Lee 147). His enduring literary impact in China speaks to the potential of intercultural poetics, to the way Western literature can be seeded in and made to produce new strains on Chinese soil, much as Chinese literature has taken root in the West.

Both in his lifetime and beyond, Xu's spontaneous individual expression and keenness for literature have galvanized an entire literary community. Wilma Fairbank ascribes the success of the Crescent Moon Society to Xu's "uncanny ability to find and gather" like-minded folks and to ignite in them "new concepts, new aspirations, and, not least, new friendships" (Fairbank 12). Nora Stirling, one of Pearl Buck's biographers, notes that Xu's "international background and winning personality" made him much in demand as teacher and editor; as faculty at Peking University and as editor of the *Peking Evening News*, "his generous help to both students and writers made him almost a legend among his colleagues" (Stirling 88). As the editor of the *Morning Post Literary Supplement* and of the *Crescent Monthly*, he helped launch the literary careers of talented writers such as Ding Ling 丁玲 (1904–1986), Shen Congwen 沈从文 (1902–1988), and Ling Shuhua 凌叔华 (1900–1990), an intimate friend (who surfaces again in my discussion of Min's *Pearl of China*). Jonathan Spence writes that

Xu helped Ding Ling and her friends in "some of their earliest literary ventures" (Spence 151). Jeffrey C. Kinkley (Shen's biographer) considers Xu, who was "instrumental in publishing Shen's first works," to be Shen's most helpful professional friend and an abiding source of inspiration: "It was through [Xu] and his encouragement that Shen first earned a bare subsistence by his pen." Upon Xu's death Shen tried to "assimilate the 'afterglow'" of Xu's life into his own works (Kinkley 82, 224). (Shen's *Autobiography* is discussed in Chapter 6.)

The free rein Xu gave to his emotions and passions earned him a large following. Patricia Laurence considers "feeling" in Xu to be "a transgressive act" at a time when self-expression and the sentimental were associated with "the weakness of 'feminine' or individual indulgence in emotion" in China, England, and America (Laurence 155). Xu's determination to pursue partners of his own choosing (rather than settling for his arranged marriage) was reminiscent both of the defiance embedded in the traditional scholar-beauty genre and of Western romantic love. His love interests were legion (and legendary). He sought a divorce with Zhang Youyi, apparently on the advice of Bertrand Russell (Leung 29; Wood 194), after falling in love with Lin Huiyin 林徽因 (1904–1955).[3] Lin Huiyin remained his friend and correspondent till his death, but she chose to marry Liang Sicheng 梁思成 (1901–1972), Liang Qichao's eldest son and a fellow architect. Xu was en route to attend a lecture by Lin Huiyin on Chinese architecture at Peking University when his plane crashed (Chang 199). (In Anchee Min's fictional account, he is on his way to a rendezvous with Pearl Buck when he dies in the accident.) After Lin Huiyin's marriage, Xu fell in love with Lu Xiaoman 陆小曼 (1903–1965), a glamorous socialite married to a military officer, whom she divorced to marry Xu.[4] Their widely publicized affair, as Leo Lee observes, "seems to have been taken directly from traditional Chinese novels" (141), to wit, the scholar-beauty genre featuring a gifted scholar and an accomplished beauty. Lee observes that Xu's courtship of Lu "left posterity a piece of confessional literature of unprecedented candor," that "these outbursts from a poet's heart exerted tremendous impact upon millions of Chinese youth," that as Tagore's interpreter and Lu Xiaoman's suitor, Xu had become a national celebrity (L.O.-f. Lee 141, 142).[5]

Xu's romantic entanglements do not end with Lu. According to some Chinese and English sources, Xu was the lover of Ling Shuhua, a painter and writer dubbed by Xu as "the Chinese Katherine Mansfield" (Welland 149). As I shall advance later, this often overlooked relationship is possibly behind Min's characterization of Willow, Pearl's lifelong friend in *Pearl of China*. After Xu's death, Ling was approached by Xu's father to provide a poetic epitaph for his tombstone, to supplement Hu Shih's insufficiently lyrical inscription. Modifying a line from *Dream of the Red Chamber*, she obliged with the following line: "冷月照诗魂 [A cold moon shines on the poet's soul]" (Welland 224). Xu's liaisons with Chinese women are the subject of a popular China-Taiwan-Hong Kong TV drama serial *April Rhapsody*《人间四月天》(2000). Less publicized were his encounters with American journalist Agnes Smedley (1892–1950) and Nobel Laureate Pearl Buck (1892–1973). According to Janice MacKinnon and Stephen MacKinnon, Smedley's biographers, "Smedley's first Chinese contacts were with Western-educated intellectuals," including Hu Shi and Yang Quan, but she was most attracted to Xu, "the perfect union of East and West": "By midsummer of 1929, he and Smedley were having an affair" (MacKinnon and MacKinnon 143). In their endnote to this information, the MacKinnons tell: "About two years earlier, Xu had an affair with Pearl Buck" (366n17).[6] The liaison between Xu and Buck, real or imagined, is dramatized in Min's *Pearl of China*.[7]

Whether or not there were frequent assignations between Xu and Buck, the two were indeed kindred spirits, by virtue of not only their common cultural hybridity (for there were many other bicultural Chinese intellectuals during the 1930s) but also their ability to level incisive critique about their own culture on account of their insights into the "other" way of being. Like the exiles evoked by Edward Said, Xu and Buck's plurality of vision gave rise to a contrapuntal awareness—"juxtapositions that diminish orthodox judgment and elevate appreciative sympathy" (Said 148). Both writers had lived what Said calls a "nomadic, decentred, contrapuntal" life, one "led outside habitual order" (Said 149). Buck, despite being a missionary child and wife, spoke vehemently against missionary condescension (see Chapter 7). In this regard, she is the American counterpart to G.L. Dickinson, Xu's best friend in Cambridge, though her knowledge of China was far deeper than Dickinson's. Xu, on his part, pointed out Dickinson's romanticized mystification of China before losing his own unflinching critique of the same culture. Acknowledging the compliments of "sincere friends" like Dickinson and Bertrand Russell regarding "our dispassionate attitude toward life, love of moderation," he asked: "What is a dispassionate attitude toward life but a patent negation of life by smothering the divine flame of passions almost to extinction? What is love for moderation but an amiable excuse for cowardice in thought and action?"

And answered: "We have come to be, indeed, too rational and reasonable for passionate love, as for passionate religious thoughts" (Xu 173). Xu clinches his jeremiad about the suppression of the spirit and the senses in traditional Confucian culture with a mordant allegory:

> Subtract the element of sexual passion and all that radiates from it and you will be shocked to see the irretrievable bankruptcy of European literature and arts.... Had the tree of knowledge been planted in the middle of the Chinese Empire... Adam and Eve would have remained superb creatures, blind of heart as of eye and insensible to the life promptings within, and God Himself would have been spared all the indignations and troubles consequent of the snake's heroism and Eve's curiosity. (Xu 172, 174)

The qualities that several Bloomsbury members admire in the Chinese are not unlike the Confucian ethics lauded by American conservatives vis-à-vis the stateside model minority. Xu, a *wen* exemplar who blasphemed Confucius—the *wen* God—was one of the first Chinese to question a life of conventionality and social conformity.

Xu was unquestionably no Confucian in his unbridled expressions in life and in poetry. Leo Lee aptly compares him to Icarus, insofar as the poet shared the "ascensionist" personality described by Dr. Henry A. Murray as Icarus syndrome: "'passionate enthusiasm, rapid elevations of confidence, flights of imagination, exaltation, inflation of spirits, ecstatic mystical up-reachings'" (Murray; L.O.-f. Lee 173). Xu writes in his essay "Wanting to Fly"《想飞》: "Who does not dream of soaring up in the sky to watch the earth roll like a ball in infinite space? ... If this fleshy carcass of ours is too heavy to be dragged along, throw it away." Xu then intimated his impending mortality: "Suddenly the wings are slanting, and a ball of light swoops all the way down, clashing in a boom—and breaking up my imaginings while in flight" (quoted in L.O.-f. Lee 172, 173; Kai-yu Hsu's translation). When the plane that was supposed to take Xu along with two pilots from Shanghai to Beijing went down in flames after hitting a peak near Shandong on November 19, 1931, Xu "died a truly Icarian death" (L.O.-f. Lee 173).

The poet—whose lines about softly taking his leave and not taking with him a single iridescent petal are literally inscribed in stone—did not leave the world quietly but with a big bang and, as far as his incalculable dear friends were concerned, took with him all the variegated splendor of the sky. The irrepressible emotional flow of the lyrical Icarus was matched by the torrential literary outpouring of grief that flooded the press at his death. Xu died at the age of 34—at the same age Katherine Mansfield had died. Ling Shuhua (the Chinese writer he had likened to Mansfield) lamented: "Didn't you say to me ... before we leave this life, we must use all our power to add some beauty to an ugly world ... This world now grows uglier and cheaper by the day, how could you have the heart to steal away?" (Welland 223). Lin Huiyin wrote: "The news is like a needle puncturing the hearts of many friends, turning the morning as dark as ink... What we have lost is not just a friend, just a poet; we have lost the rarest, the most endearing character" (Lin Huiyin 2, 6, 7; my translation). Hu Shi, alluding to lines from Xu's poetry, bemoaned: "after the gust, our sky turns bleak and lonesome, only then do we realize that the loveliest petal of cloud has been carried off, never to return ... [but] we will never forget the sparks exchanged during the fleeting contact" (Hu Shi; my translation). The fact that Xu was so deeply and publicly mourned by Chinese intellectuals reflected not only his magnetic personality but also his impact as a *wenren* of his time.

Younghill Kang's *East Goes West*

Among those who have mourned Xu in tears and in ink is the narrator of *East Goes West* (1937), a semi-autobiographical Korean American classic. The narrator, Chungpa Han, an emigrant from Korea, describes his struggle with assimilation in the United States and Canada. Having left Korea because of its colonization by Japan, Han hopes to transplant his Korean roots in the soil of the New World. In New York, he strikes up a friendship with To Won Kim, another Korean expatriate. Both Han and Kim are steeped in Asian (Chinese, Japanese, and Korean) and Western (French, German, British, and American) literature. Through Kim, Han meets Hsu Tsimou (Kang's variant spelling of Xu's name). The Chinese poet—perhaps on account of his literary renown—is one of the very few historical figures not given a fictitious name in this novel, which encapsules his peerless attraction in a cameo appearance. Kang uses Hsu and Kim as character foils to symbolize the frustrating endeavors of grafting Asian culture onto Western civilization and vice versa.

Han pits Hsu's optimistic spirit against the pessimism of Kim, who feels that Korea is doomed culturally and politically. Hsu tries to persuade Kim to go with him to Shanghai, to join him in revivifying the East: "And this East is not dead as you say. The desert is soon going to bloom. When all the bad old ways are cut off and thrown away—underneath the roots are still green—grafting of new life will take place. The best of the West upon the undying roots of the East" (208). Kim remains unpersuaded. Kim is deeply in love with Helen, a white woman, but her family soon puts a stop to the courtship. Despite his bicultural sophistication, Kim finds the West, as symbolized by Helen, out of reach. After being rejected by her family, Kim becomes despondent and eventually commits suicide. Han, shocked and devastated upon reading Kim's obituary in an Asian newspaper, writes immediately to Hsu: "And though I did not know it, I was writing to another dead man. The joyous Chinese lyricist had been killed in an airplane crash, but on his native soil, expressing his firm belief in the future of Western science transported to China" (364). The contiguous deaths of Kim and Hsu suggest that neither China nor the United States was ready to embrace the blending of cultures heralded by these two modernist *wenren*.[8] Kim's suicide reveals his despair at not being accepted in the West on account of his Asian face. Xu was relatively successful in grafting romanticist ideals onto Chinese poetry during his lifetime, but we know with historical hindsight that a severe backlash against the West took place shortly after his death. Had he not died young, he would have been relentlessly persecuted after 1949 and certainly during the Cultural Revolution. Just as the West regarded Asia with Orientalist condescension, China eyed the West with distrust and soon shut it out completely by lowering the bamboo curtain. In light of Xu's revival in China today, however, the poet may be said to have had the last word.

To the Korean American narrator and presumably to the author, Hsu certainly embodies optimal cultural intermixing: Western and Asian gallantry, heady receptivity to the West and strong attachment to the motherland. Unlike Kim, who is "in all things an observer, especially toward the West," Hsu not only espouses Western ideas but also immerses himself in them: "[Kim] might be as familiar as Tsimou with Browning, Shelley, and Keats, but he did not swim, breathe, and have his being in exuberant romantic waters. Hsu Tsimou did. He was a romanticist pure and simple" (205–206). Han goes on to describe Hsu's enviable physique: "a very handsome oval face, and black eyes full of fire, and an unconquerable zest for life. Hsu Tsimou was so handsome, indeed, that he looked like a character out of an old Chinese novel—such as *Dream of the Red Chamber*. His whole personality reflected radiance and enthusiasm" (206). Hsu's inalienably Asian masculinity stands out from the American brawny variety.

Yet Hsu is neither model minority nor model Chinese. Conducting his life with infectious gusto, he flagrantly defies Chinese social conventions in his celebration of love, sacred and profane: "Love is my inspiration, as Death to François Villon, as the wine to Li Tai Po... The world is full of rain, wind, and bitter air, but that does not matter... With love I can sleep in the moonlight without food or bed" (206). We do not know whether these words were actually spoken by Xu, but they are in keeping with what the Chinese poet says about love in "Art and Life," as "transcendental and transfiguring, and being transfigured through that mysterious force one's mortal eyes are, for once, to behold visions that belong to the spiritual realm" (Xu 174). His love goes beyond his prodigious amorous pursuit to literature and culture. This nomadic poet cuts a most quixotic figure in Kang's novel: "He had only arrived from Europe that day, and had come straight to Kim's place, suitcase in hand. In that one suitcase he could travel all over the world and had done so many times. And even it was full of books" (208). Hsu is determined to make a difference in Chinese literature, being "an ardent supporter of the new literary movement under Hu Shih" (205). And a believer in Lu Hsün (Lu Xun): "What is it that Lu Hsün says? First there is no road always: the feet of many people put one there" (208). The poet envisions himself to be a literary path-breaker who enriches Chinese soil with Western learning.[9] Kang's portrait of the artist illustrates that feasting on Western culture does not signify a lack of appetite for one's own. Hsu's pioneering spirit and zeal for his motherland distinguish him from Kim, who "showed no enthusiasm for going back" (208). By contrast, the native soil is so dear to Hsu that he wishes to nourish it with imported nutrients.

Though a peripheral character in Kang's novel, Hsu's friendship with Kim and the narrator conveys the poet's easy camaraderie with Asian men of another nationality as well as the amazing intellectual openness and world literacy of all three expatriates, and perhaps also a special affinity between the Korean immigrant writer and the migrant poet-scholar. These two writers seem to have more in common with each other than either of them had with their fellow Chinese or Asian American writers. It is outside the scope of this book to draw the many parallels between the two, but Kang can almost be imagined as Xu's double (or vice versa) in his exceptional multilingual expertise, poetic and romantic temper, and ability to integrate into broad Asian and Western literary circles. "I am a poet," said Kang in a 1946 lecture cited by Sunyoung Lee, who remarks that this self-identification is less a description of occupation than "a deceptively concise distillation of [Kang's] passions and convictions" (S. Lee 375). Kang writes in *Grass Roof* (1931), his first novel: "the poet alone has no home nor national boundary... His nearest kin is the muse up in the clouds, and his patriotism goes to the ethereal kingdom" (3:376). The line could easily have been written by our Chinese lyricist. Both writers frowned on the chauvinism of their countrymen; both were effervescent and romantic, pulling out all the stops in their amorous pursuits; and both were catholic in their empathy and sympathy, mingling easily with people of different ethnicities and races. Even the Chinese poet's interracial liaisons had parallels in Kang's fiction and life. "At a time when, on the opposite coast in California, anti-miscegenation laws banning Asian/white marriages were still in place," S. Lee relates, Kang "married Frances Keely, the pampered daughter of a Virginia industrialist turned professor" (S. Lee 375).[10] Presumably Kang also prevailed upon Keely with his *wen* allure.

Yet there was one striking difference between the two modernist *wen-ren*. While Kang too was able to befriend white (and black) folks and to rub elbows with Western literary giants, including Rebecca West, H.G. Wells, and Thomas Wolfe, he "suffered the inevitable humiliations of America's entrenched racism," as both his biographical accounts and his autobiographical novel *East Goes West* attest (S. Lee 396). How did Xu escape similar mortification in the West? Or, as the grandniece of his first wife puts it: "How did he do it, become friends with Westerners and not have them call him 'chink,' not have them call him names?" (Chang 110).

Pang-Mei Natasha Chang's *Bound Feet and Western Dress*

Bound Feet and Western Dress is a dual memoir by Chang Yu-i 张幼仪 (Zhang Youyi), the first wife of Xu Zhimo (spelled Hsü Chi-mo therein) and her American-born grandniece Pang-Mei Natasha Chang, whose grandfather is Yu-i's younger brother. Yu-i married Hsü at 15 and gave birth to a son at 18 and another at 22, the same year that Hsü divorced her—"the first modern divorce in China" (5). Throughout their arranged marriage, Hsü was apparently never in love with Yu-i, and her memory of their brief matrimony is understandably unflattering. In 1920, Yu-i left China to join Hsü in London; she recalls his chilly welcome when she disembarked from the steamer: "His carriage was unmistakable...the only one in the crowd of receivers who looked as though he did not want to be there" (103). When she got pregnant for the second time, Hsü asked her to seek an abortion, a very risky procedure at the time. Yu-i refused, whereupon Hsü left her alone in London to fend for herself. She only refrained from suicide because of the cardinal rule of filial piety: "your body with your hair and your skin is a gift from your parents. You must treasure this gift to be filial" (125). To his wife's befuddlement, the missing husband wrote some of his best-known lyrics during this spell, "experiencing his epiphany" while inflicting "pain on everyone who loved him" (147). Yu-i later gave birth in Germany, and Hsü turned up with the divorce papers. Their second son Peter died at the age of five because Yu-i did not have enough money to send him to a good hospital.

Given Hsü's callous behavior, one would expect a damning portrayal of the poet by both Yu-i and Natasha, her devoted grandniece, but after the initial complaint, just about the opposite is the case. Instead of excoriating her heartless ex-husband, Yu-i expresses heartfelt gratitude: "I want to thank Hsü Chih-mo for the divorce. Without it, I might never have been able to find myself, to grow. He freed me to become someone" (201). Her words echo a letter by Xu written in March 1922 demanding a divorce, declaring that a marriage not based on love was intolerable, that "freedom should be repaid by freedom." "Both of us have minds set on reforming society . . . on achieving well-being for mankind. This all hinges on our setting ourselves as examples. With courage and resolution, with respect to our personalities, we must get a free divorce" (quoted in L.O.-f. Lee 134). It is true that after a harrowing period of scrambling alone and losing her second child, Yu-i studied in Germany and subsequently carved out a distinguished career, becoming the vice-president of the Shanghai Women's Savings Bank. But instead of crediting her success to her own strength of character, she feels beholden to Hsü, whose abandonment supposedly had allowed her to live up to her full potential: "I always think of my life as 'before Germany' and 'after Germany.' Before Germany, I was afraid of everything. After Germany... I was a much stronger person who feared nothing" (149). Furthermore, "I actually got along with [Hsü] better after our divorce... He and I actually became close to each other" (187–188).

Notwithstanding the excessive credit given to Hsü, Yu-i's account reveals two important points. First, it supports Friedan's finding that the "feminine mystique" concocted by men (that most women are happy with their traditional roles as wives and mothers) is far from true, that many women in fact derive enormous satisfaction from their careers and from living up to their intellectual potential. Second, Hsü, the male idol of his time, was also one of the first Chinese men who show a distinctive preference for strong, accomplished women to demure companions. His increasing regard for Yu-i was no doubt brought about by her transformation from a submissive housewife into a self-possessed career woman. If Hsü had despised his former spouse for being a country bumpkin, he came to admire the divorcée who had become as transnational and multilingual as he, not unlike the other women he adored throughout his life.

Hsü's susceptibility to independent women is part of his own appeal. Hsü differs from many traditional Chinese men wary of women who are their equals or superiors. All of his sweethearts, whether lovers or soul mates, were formidable intellectuals or artists. Lin Huiyin was a poet and the first female professor of architecture in China. Lu Xiaoman, his second wife, was described by Hu Shi as "a painter, singer, writer, and a speaker of French and English" (Laurence 148). Ling Shuhua was a painter and writer, whose autobiography, *Ancient Melodies*, was published by the Hogarth Press in 1953 (Laurence 84).[11] Agnes Smedley was a gritty journalist, whose activism on behalf of the dispossessed led to "accusations of espionage, forcing her to flee America and die abroad" (Wood, 209). Pearl Buck was the 1938 Nobel Laureate of literature. Xu also worshipped Katherine Mansfield, whom he met for only 20 minutes (through the arrangement of her husband John Middleton Murray) and whose stories he translated (Laurence 203). Surely an impressive roster of talented women. The men who held Xu in high esteem—Shen Congwen, Hu Shi, Younghill Kang (in the guise of Chungpa Han), G.L. Dickinson, E.M. Forster, I.A. Richards, and Rabindranath Tagore—were likewise pioneering figures and renowned authors. Most of these men and women were also progressive thinkers ahead of their time.

Just as Hsü learned to appreciate the transformed Yu-i, so her impression of her ex-husband also changed with time. In the beginning, Yu-i told Natasha that he divorced her because of Lin Huiyin, "but by the end she said he divorced her because he respected women and did not want to see them compromised." "Which was the truth?" asked Natasha. "Had Yu-i taken her anger toward Hsü Chi-mo and twisted it into love and gratitude?" (192). Natasha's question remains unanswered. All we know is that "Yu-i made Hsü Chih-mo sound so heroic" (192). The response of Natasha to Hsü is no less unexpected. She sees her aunt as a feminist predecessor, much as the narrator of *The Woman Warrior* claims her no-name aunt and her mother as her forerunners. In the course of chronicling Yu-i's life, however, Natasha finds herself again and again coming back to Hsü, who has transfigured into another role model for her:

> Hsü Chih-mo's journey to the West infused him with a desire to change his ways... [He] devoted himself to becoming a living embodiment of those virtues and traits that he most admired in the West: love, passion, honesty... I hated the way [he] treated Yu-i, but... I could not help but feel tremendous admiration for him and his work... I hoped to be like him, one infused with both Western and Eastern learning. (94)

Even though Natasha resents Hsü's treatment of Yu-i, she envies his biliteracy, his courage in defying received mores, and his friendship with illustrious English writers and critics. During her visit to Cambridge University in the summer of 1989, she imagined the "sensation" Hsü created there in 1921 and 1922: I.A. Richards invited him to "join in the activities of the Heretics' Club"; E.M. Forster described meeting Hsü as "one of the most exciting things that ever happened to him"; G.L. Dickinson "wore continually the Chinese cap" Hsü had given him in admiration (110).

An aside about Dickinson (1862–1932): as an admirer of a foreign culture and a critic of his own, he is a chiasmic counterpart of the Chinese poet. Dickinson was a British historian, political activist, poet, a close associate of the Bloomsbury Group, and a lecturer of history at Cambridge from 1886 to 1920. In 1901, in the wake of the Boxer Uprising and the harsh reprisals from a multinational expeditionary force against China, Dickinson published a series of articles in the *Saturday Review*, collected and published anonymously as *Letters from John Chinaman* in Britain in 1901 and as *Letters from a Chinese Official* in the United States in 1903, wherein he chastises England, condemning "the damage done by both imperialist armies and Christian missionaries" (Wood 191–193; see also Harding 29, Laurence 167, 169). This "Chinese official" reminds the British that the first English traders in China were the opium dealers, selling a drug that destroyed many Chinese lives, and closely followed by Christian missionaries who compelled the Chinese to receive their religion in the 1840s. He then exclaims in the final letter: "Irony of ironies—it is the nation of Christendom who have come to teach us by the sword and fire that Right in this world is powerless unless it be supported by Might!" (Auden and Isherwood 197).[12] Dickinson did not simply write under the guise of a Chinese. He told Roger Fry during his travel to China in 1913–1914: "I feel so at home. I think I must have been a Chinaman once... What a civilized people they have been" (Laurence 135). Despite his quixotic view of China, his anti-imperialist satire, as Patricia Laurence argues, anticipates postcolonial theory today in exposing England's ethical weakness

(Laurence 167). In Xu and Dickinson, one can discern a kind of reverse symmetry. Dickinson was as atypical an Englishman as Xu was iconoclastic as a Chinese; in both, relish of the "other" civilization was in tandem with a chastening introspection: "each looks at the other's culture and art and then critiques his own" (Laurence 176).

There might even have been a certain homoerotic attraction. Through Dickinson's arrangement, Xu enrolled in Cambridge as a "special student" at King's College. Frances Wood corroborates Natasha's observation about the Chinese cap: "One of the most famous images of Dickinson is a photograph in which he wears the black satin Chinese hat given him by Xu Zhimo" (Wood 194). Dickinson was gay; during his stay in China, he expressed embarrassment in being taken to a banquet of "sing-song girls," adding, "I wish they were boys!" (quoted in Laurence 188). E.M. Forster, Dickinson's friend and biographer, and author of six novels including *A Room with a View* and *Howards End*, also was gay. One wonders whether their effusiveness over Hsü might have been more than purely intellectual. Unlike American notions of masculinity, the *wen* ideal tends to elide the putative differences between gay and straight physiognomy and deportment, and endorses a mien that behooves men of any sexual orientation.

In any case, the Chinese poet got along famously with diverse Cambridge dons. Natasha muses: "How exotic, quixotic Hsü Chih-mo must have seemed to his Western friends: an intelligent, extravagantly romantic Chinese discovering kindred spirits and traditions in the West." She thinks Hsü was better able to mix in the Western world than she could, who was brought up in the West: "How did he do it, become friends with Westerners and not have them call him 'chink'"? (110–111). How indeed did he accrue the admiration of compatriots and Westerners alike? Not only have Yu-i and her grandniece forgiven Hsü for the immense suffering he wreaked on his first wife, the two women—like so many trans-Pacific and trans-Atlantic intellectuals in his day—*idolized* Hsü. His charisma in *Bound Feet & Western Dress*, as in Kang's novel, seems inseparable from his fusion of the East and West and the ease with which he moves between worlds, befriending everyone in the vicinity. As Natasha admits, even an American-born person of Chinese descent like herself still feels, to this day, like an ethnic outsider. Hsü's popularity in the West at a time when Asians were stereotyped as heathens and coolies speaks to his allure as a modernist *wenren*. The proliferation of books by and about Xu published in China and in America in the last decade, the commemorative marble in Cambridge University, the publication of his selected poems by Oleander

Press in 2012, and the photo exhibition in the Chapel at King's College in 2014 signal his continuing glow across oceans.

The dual memoir proper concludes with Yu-i's answer to Natasha's recurrent question about whether she loved Hsü: "If caring for Hsü Chih-mo and his family was love, then maybe I loved him. Maybe, out of all the women in his life, I loved him the most" (Chang 208). Pearl Buck, however, might beg to differ.

ANCHEE MIN'S *PEARL OF CHINA*

Pearl of China is a biographical novel about the Nobel Laureate Pearl S. Buck, whom Anchee Min was forced to denounce as American cultural imperialist during the Cultural Revolution. Even though she had not read anything by Buck at the time, as a protégé of Mao's wife Jiang Qing (1914–1991), Min was pressed to write an essay criticizing Buck in a campaign to orchestrate popular opposition against her 1972 visit to China with Richard Nixon (Min, "Q&A" 279, 280). Buck died the following year of lung cancer. Years later, when Min read *The Good Earth* in the United States, she savored Buck's narrative about Chinese peasants and regretted being one of a generation that had been "indoctrinated" to think poorly of the American author (Min, "Q&A" 279; see also Yue Cheng). *Pearl of China* is, in a sense, a "novel atonement" (Basu). Like *East Goes West*, it combines historical and imaginary figures.[13] (Throughout this section, I use Buck to refer to the writer, and Pearl to the fictional counterpart.) The "Author's Note" indicates that Min wants to see Buck as her fellow Chinese saw her, and therefore, she writes from the point of view of Willow, Pearl's lifelong Chinese friend in the novel—a composite character created by merging Min's own life with the lives of a number of Buck's actual friends from different phases (Min, "Note" 277). Min reveals that as a child she spent time in a small village town called Tangza in Jiangsu province, just an hour and a half's drive from Zhenjiang, where Pearl grew up: "I lived what Pearl Buck described in her novels" (Basu 19).[14] The author describes how the liaison between Pearl and Hsu (spelled Hsu Chih-mo in this novel), easily the most engaging segment of this biographical saga, was hatched in her mind: "The possibility of a romantic relationship between the two has been rumored for years... These were two great individuals who possessed both the Eastern and Western cultures and worlds—they were bound to admire and love each other" (Min, "Q&A" 282). Like Kang and Chang, Min adverts to Hsu's bicultural sensibility. Here the poet also finds in Pearl an echoing soul.

Both Nora Stirling and Peter Conn, Buck's biographers, seem to believe in the rumored love affair between the two writers. Conn initially relates the affair as a matter of fact: "Perhaps in retaliation [to her husband's infidelity] Pearl took a lover, an extraordinary Chinese poet named Hsu Chih-mo ... intermittently until Hsu's death in a plane crash" (Conn 103). Conn then casts some doubt in an endnote: "Nora Stirling reconstructed the details of Pearl's affair" based on interviews, but there is "some dispute about whether the affair actually took place" (Conn 397, n63). Stirling, Conn's source, speculates frequent meetings between the two writers, for "both traveled often between Peking, Nanking and Shanghai on literary matters," and describes how Hsu's shadow hung heavily over Buck's life during the mid-1920s (Stirling 96).[15] A romance between the two writers is also suggested by an evocative passage in Buck's memoir, quoted in Conn's book and echoed in Min's novel: "One handsome and rather distinguished and certainly much beloved young poet was proud to be called 'the Chinese Shelley.' He used to sit in my living room and talk by the hour and wave his beautiful hands" (Buck, *My Several Worlds* 178–179; Conn 103; Min, *Pearl* 131). The sobriquet "the Chinese Shelley" gives away the young man's identity. The poet also looms over Buck's *A Chinese Woman Speaks* (1925), which evolves into *East Wind: West Wind* (1930), a novel that, according to Stirling, "had been inspired by Pearl's fantasy of being Hsu's wife" (Stirling 97). But Conn observes that there was never any question of marriage between the two: "Both were married, and, despite the fantasies of *Letter from Peking* (1957), neither of them would actually have married across racial lines" (103).

The romance is writ large in *Pearl of China*, though Hsu does not appear until a third of the way through the novel, when Pearl is still suffering from an unhappy marriage and struggling to be a writer. From 1917 to 1935, Buck was married to John Lossing Buck [Lossing in Min's novel], a missionary agriculturalist who worked in China from 1915 to 1944, and Min adheres quite closely to this chronology. The reason for their divorce was not publicized, but Min supplies three answers in her fiction. Their daughter Carol, born 1920, was afflicted with phenylketonuria, an inherited disorder that causes permanent intellectual disability. In Min's tale Carol's condition, Lossing's affair with Lotus, a Chinese translator, and Lossing's discouragement of Pearl's creative pursuit contribute to the marital discord. When Hsu appears, both Pearl and Willow are living in Nanjing (where historically the Bucks made their home from 1920 to 1933). Pearl is an English instructor at University of Nanking (金陵大学); Willow, a journalist for *Nanking Daily*. Even before the two women meet Hsu for the first time, Willow has been a fan of the Chinese poet, with whom she later becomes deeply infatuated: "I learned that I was among thousands of women who dreamed of Hsu Chih-mo. We threw ourselves at him like night bugs at a light" (119).

In *Pearl of China*, Hsu figures as a character foil to both Absalom Sydenstricker, Pearl's father, and Lossing Buck. Absalom is so fixated on saving Chinese heathens that he is totally oblivious to his wife Carie and their daughters, so much so that Carie forbids him from visiting her when she is dying. "You go and save your heathens" were her last words to him (97). Lossing, an agricultural expert who marries Pearl in part so she can serve as his field translator, disparages her writing endeavors: "if Pearl has ambition, she has little skill or training… She is bound to lose if she tries to make it as a writer." When Pearl protests that he has no right to stop her from writing, Lossing counters: "You well know that without your help I can't do my job. You treat your writing as if it is a job, but… I am the one who earns the money." He then addresses Willow: "Who wants to read her stories? The Chinese don't need a blond woman to tell their stories, and the Westerners are not interested in China" (107, 108). Unlike Absalom, Hsu is always solicitous of the women in his life (in Min's novel there is no mention of the aggrieved first wife); in stark contrast to Lossing, who disparages Pearl's potential as a writer, Hsu encourages Pearl all the way.

Like "The Story of a White Woman Who Married a Chinese" by Sui Sin Far/Edith Eaton, *Pearl of China* sets off a nurturing Chinese companion against an insensitive white husband. But unlike the Chinese husband in Far's tale, Hsu is not only caring but also irresistibly handsome, artistic, and attuned to Pearl's corresponding forte. Willow recalls: "After he left, I couldn't escape the sound of his voice praising Pearl. 'Pearl and I are soul mates!' '*The Good Earth* is like no other novel I have ever read. It's a masterpiece!' 'It takes a humanitarian to be a good novelist'" (140). The compliments Hsu lavishes on Pearl further suggest that the love between them is the centripetal pull of like minds, reciprocal admiration, and mutual understanding. "Pearl makes me happy," Hsu tells Willow. "She's brilliant, cunning, and funny. The mix of Chinese and American cultures in her fascinates me always" (142). Thus, both *Bound Feet and Western Dress* and *Pearl of China* depict women who seek fulfillment beyond conventional conjugal and maternal roles and who hold the man who encourages their professional pursuits in the highest esteem.

In the case of Pearl and Hsu, intellectual affinity soon flares into incandescent love. The two writers, in fiction as well as in life, hold quite a few things in common. Both are in an unhappy marriage, their respective spouses having taken on a lover. Both are sympathetic to the plight of peasants. Pearl is determined to make peasants the subject of her fiction; Hsu, to "promoting the working class's right to literacy" (116). Both are thoroughly versed in Chinese and Western literature. Buck translated *Water Margin* (discussed in Chapter 2), which she titled *All Men are Brothers*. Xu translated, among others, Byron, Shelley, and Mansfield. Both are compulsive persons of letters for whom writing is living. Hsu tells Willow: "The inner force is far more important than talent ... writing is my rice and air. One shouldn't bother picking up a pen if that is not the case" (123). "That is exactly the case with my friend Pearl Buck," Willow replies (124). Both are stout individuals who do not yield to the tide of politics, public opinion, or dogma. They share what Said calls an exile's "contrapuntal" awareness, which can become highly gratifying "if the exile is conscious of other contrapuntal juxtapositions that diminish orthodox judgment and elevate appreciative sympathy" (148). People capable of such sympathy are often drawn to one another, as in the case of G.L. Dickinson and his Chinese protégé, but even more so in Pearl and Hsu. Like Dickinson and Xu/Hsu, both of whom were highly critical of their own cultures, Buck/Pearl remonstrated against American missionaries: "I have seen the missionary narrow, uncharitable ... so scornful of any civilization but their own ... so coarse and insensitive among a sensitive and cultivated people, that my heart has fairly bled with shame" (Buck, "Case" 144). Min quotes Buck, almost verbatim, when she has Pearl, despite her own status as a missionary child and wife, speaking vehemently against missionary condescension: "So scornful of any civilization except their own ... so coarse and insensitive among a sensitive and cultivated people that my heart has fairly bled with shame" (187).

Pearl and Hsu also admire what is atypical in each other. "Hsu Chih-mo is the only Chinese man I know who was true to himself ... daring and almost impulsive," Pearl tells Willow. "I couldn't help but love him" (155). Hsu, on his part, was "convinced that Pearl was more Chinese than he was." "He was especially thrilled when she cursed in Chinese. He loved 'the Chinese soul under the white skin'" (141). The love between the two, as Min renders it, seems a kind of love of negation: Pearl loves what is *not* traditionally Chinese about Hsu, and Hsu loves what is *not* Western in Pearl, as though each sees the inverted self in the other.[16] More than mutual appreciation of hybridity, they marvel that each can hold their own, be their own person.

What sets this fictional Hsu apart from both the Chinese and the Western intelligentsia are his respect for Pearl long before she is recognized, his encouragement of her writing, and his sincere admiration of her work. Their literary conversations (like the correspondence between the poet and Lin Huiyin, and between him and Lu Xiaoman) smack of the Chinese scholar-beauty drama. At one point they discuss the famed Chinese erhu player Ah Bing (阿炳) (also known as Hua Yanjun 华彦钧 1893–1950), a beggar turned artist, and their ideas bounce deftly off each other: "It was in music that Ah Bing escaped the life he was living," Hsu intones. "Yes," Pearl replies. "Through music Ah Bing became the hero he desired to be." After a pregnant pause, Hsu is overheard by Willow as saying: "That is how I felt when I read your manuscript" (133), drawing a flattering analogy between Ah Bing's music and Pearl's manuscript for *The Good Earth*. The love between them, as Willow painfully witnesses, is sparked by this verbal pas de deux: "They spoke as if I were not in the room… I could feel the force pulling them closer … my real-life Romeo and Juliet, the Butterfly Lovers" (132). Words are the magnets doing all the pulling here.

The two plays that enter Willow's mind are revealing. The first conversation between Romeo and Juliet takes the form of a sonnet. Even more telling is the allusion to *The Butterfly Lovers*, a classic scholar-beauty drama in which Zhu Yingtai 祝英台, the "beauty," has to cross-dress to attend an academy, where she becomes the doting roommate of Liang Shanbo 梁山伯. Upon the completion of their study, Yingtai suggests that Shanbo marry "his" sister, who resembles "him" in every way, and Shanbo readily consents. The attachment between these two is akin to that of soul mates, at least on Shanbo's part at the beginning; their regard for each other is first and foremost fostered by literary exchange, much like the classical scholar-beauty analyzed by McMahon, in which a man and a woman "get to know each other, often through the exchange of literary messages, especially poetry. It becomes spontaneously apparent that they are meant for each other" (McMahon 230). Min follows this typical plot in recreating the deepening affection between Pearl and Hsu. Willow's allusion to *The Butterfly Lovers* accentuates the main attraction between the writers to be their common intellectual and artistic sensibility, which is further corroborated by Willow's eyewitness accounts: "Hsu Chih-mo believed that Pearl was a true artist, the Ah Bing of literature." Pearl tells Willow: "He is the only other Chinese person besides you who understands my writing... He inspires my confidence and creativity" (135). Because this love is much more than physical, it persists in Pearl even after Hsu dies and after she leaves China. Min borrows a passage verbatim from Buck's memoir: "He claimed me with his love, and then he let me go home. When I arrived in America, I realized that the love was with me, and would stay with me forever" (Min, *Pearl* 131).

Their admiration of each other's bicultural receptivity further cements their bond. Hsu confesses to Willow: "The mix of Chinese and American cultures in her fascinates me always" (141). Pearl likens her enthrallment to "an addict running toward opium" (148), perhaps seeing in Hsu her own reflection. Willow, who has known Pearl's loneliness since they were children, recounts: "She had always searched for her 'own kind.' That didn't mean another Westerner. It meant another soul that experienced and understood both the Eastern and Western worlds. It was in Hsu Chih-mo that Pearl had found what she was looking for" (150). This intercultural balance becomes a fatal attraction. "Their separations had never lasted. It was like cutting water with a sword," Willow observed, echoing Li Bai's famous line "water keeps running no matter how sharply you split it with a sword [抽刀断水水更流]." In the novel, Hsu takes a free plane ride with his pilot friend three times a week to be with Pearl and the pilot allows him to borrow his farmhouse near the airport for their trysts (147–148). On one of these rides, the plane crashes.

The Chinese Shelley, rumored to be the "friend" instrumental in preventing Buck's publisher from cutting the manuscript of *The Good Earth* (Stirling 102–103), died in 1931, the same year the novel was published, earning Buck the 1932 Pulitzer Prize and catapulting her into literary limelight. But during his funeral, Pearl (and also Buck) was conspicuously absent, in person and in written memorial. Buck, who should have been elated by her success, continued to be depressed during this period. Stirling attributes her despondence to Xu's death even though Buck "remained silent" (Stirling 116). Min fills this silence by having Pearl keep a private vigil for Hsu at the pilot's hut, where Willow finds her: "She had been performing the traditional Chinese soul-guarding ceremony for Hsu" (149). Pearl, after reading the package of Hsu's lyrics for her delivered by Willow, composes a valedictory poem (151). Willow muses: "In the future I would understand the connection between Pearl's accomplishments as a novelist and her love of Hsu Chih-mo." Willow surmises that Pearl carries on a posthumous affair in the scores of books she writes over her lifetime. "Writing a novel is like chasing and catching spirits,"

Willow quotes Pearl. "The novelist gets invited into splendid dreams. The lucky one gets to live the dream once, and the luckiest over and over." Willow concludes that Pearl is the "luckiest one," who "must have met with [Hsu's] spirit throughout the rest of her life," adding, "I consider myself lucky too" (151). Pearl is able to continue to commune with Hsu after his death because it is the mind rather than the body that has so tantalized the lovers.[17]

But why does Willow consider herself "lucky"? Before venturing an answer, I would like to return to my aforementioned hunch that Ling Shuhua (who, along with Zhang Youyi, Lin Huiyin, and Lu Xiaoman, was part of Xu's Chinese love pentagon) might be behind Min's characterization of Willow and the novel's love triangle. Min reveals that she "combined a number of Pearl's actual friends at different times throughout her forty years in China to create the character Willow. Looking back, I think it was the best choice I made." It was indeed a felicitous choice. To the medley of personages that have engendered Willow, I would add Ling Shuhua. She is better known in the West as the lover of Julian Bell, Virginia Woolf's nephew, who mentioned her "having been passionately in love with Xu Zhimo" (Laurence 70; Welland 250). When Xu left for Europe for the second time in 1925, in part to escape from the wrath of Lu Xiaoman's husband, Xu asked Ling for two favors on the eve of his departure: to encourage Lu Xiaoman to "cultivate more literary habits such as painting and keeping a diary" and to safeguard his "Eight Treasures Box," a small chest containing his diaries, letters, and notes (Welland 175). This exchange between Xu and Ling provides several clues into the poet's character. First is how much he appreciated literary predilection in women, as much as the fictional Hsu did in Pearl's. Next is the extent to which his romances were kindled and kept aglow by epistolary exchanges. Third is his special relationship with Ling. He told her he did not want to leave the box with Lu Xiaoman, for his early diary entries about Lin Huiyin would arouse Lu's jealousy; Xu also told Lu that "of my female friends, Shuhua is my comrade" (Welland 175). Ling's feelings for Xu were apparently much stronger in comparison, according to Ying Chinnery, Ling's daughter, who believes that her mother was deeply in love with the poet, but she ended up marrying Chen Yuan/Chen Xiying (1896–1970), founder and editor of the *Contemporary Review*, and Xu's steadfast friend.[18]

The parallels between Ling and Willow—as the poet's unrequited lover, confidante, safe-keeper, and wife of his bosom friend—cannot be merely coincidental. Ling's strong feelings for the poet were unilateral, and unspoken. So were Willow's. During Hsu and Pearl's discussion on Ah Bing, Willow as onlooker has found herself "both witness to and victim of a great love," "touched by their birth of feeling but sad beyond description" on account of her own crush on Hsu (132). Ling told Bell "she'd once been in love with Xu Zhimo, but couldn't admit it at the time, and married Xiying out of duty" (Welland 250); Willow, too, never discloses her love and later marries Dick Lin: "Looking back, I realized that it was Dick's love for Hsu Chih-mo that bound us together" (155). Both Ling and Willow meet their future husband through the poet, who introduced Ling to Chen, and whose fictional counterpart introduces Willow to his best friend Dick Lin, editor of the *Shanghai Avant-Garde Magazine*. Ling was asked to safekeep Xu's love letters; Willow was asked by Hsu to be his courier, delivering his poetic missives to Pearl. Xu entrusted Ling with his intimate correspondence so as to avoid arousing Lu Xiaoman's jealousy; Hsu asks Willow to keep all his precious manuscripts, including his poems for Pearl, for the same reason. With these many parallels in mind, it is impossible to read Willow's attempt at self-consolation after Hsu's death without conjuring up Ling: "I considered myself lucky too. Although Hsu Chih-mo didn't love me, he trusted me. It made our ordinary friendship extraordinary." "Hsu Chih-mo had asked me to keep the original manuscripts of his poetry. His wife had threatened to burn them because in the pages she 'smelled the scent of another woman.' ... I'd like to think that Hsu Chih-mo loved me in a special way" (151).

Besides this "special" affection, Willow is also indebted to the poet (and to Pearl) for stimulating her intellectual growth. She tells that Pearl, who was attracted to challenges, never "looked up to anyone until Hsu" (155). For Willow, both Pearl and Hsu are her challenges. Perhaps she can afford to be generous toward both because they have admitted her into the charmed triangle: "Without Pearl and Hsu Chi-mo in my life, I never would have been the person I am today," someone who "published and impressed others as a writer" (155–156). Dick Lin, now Willow's husband, feels equally beholden: "If I am a giant today, it is because Hsu Chih-mo taught me the difference between physical and intellectual height" (155).

I dwell on the correspondences between Ling and Willow at length because both fact and fiction reveal a singular dimension of Xu: his "challenging," "stimulating," and succoring presence, which his beneficiaries kept evoking even after his death. The helping hand he extended to female artists in a patriarchal society must have been cherished to no end.

Ling Shuhua and Buck, Willow and Pearl are historical and fictional examples of women indebted to his intellectual gallantry, even in the absence of amorous interest on his part. Xu, as noted previously, was also the one who had launched Ling's literary career by publishing her early works. Buck's biographers—Stirling, Conn, Spurling—all acknowledge Xu's role in encouraging Buck to become a professional writer. After Buck's success with *The Good Earth*, *Colophon*, a literary magazine, invited her to relate the publication history of her first novel. Buck wrote, in tacit reference to the Chinese poet, that "a friend who was always urging me to write asked if I had not something to show him" and upon reading "told her to submit it for publication" (Stirling 97). Xu's inclination to treat women as intellectual equals and to urge them to reach their full potentials must have contributed to his immense popularity.

Though not a central character in any of the three Asian American works, Xu registers high on the scale of symbolic significance. His popularity with Chinese women and men requires no elaboration, but the three texts additionally manifest his cross-cultural panache. *East Goes West* reveals the hold he has on Asian intellectuals in the United States, where he represents the possibility of fully imbibing different cultures without choosing one over another, without rejecting one's own. Unlike his two Korean friends, who have given up on Korea under Japanese occupation, the Chinese lyricist is eager to rejuvenate China and enrich his native soil with Western ideas, though his effort is nipped in the bud. *Bound Feet & Western Dress* depicts the spell this migrant poet-scholar casts on Cambridge dons, among others, in stark contrast to the stereotypical Chinaman in the popular Western imagination. *Pearl of China* delineates the mutual attraction of two writers of different national origins who are conversant with the Other's worldview. The beloved poet figures as Pearl's artistic "challenge" and someone who takes women seriously and feelingly as intellectual equals.

Like the Cambridge immortalized in his best-known poem, Xu himself is a timeless personification of the confluence of cultures. His enduring legacy in multiple circles testifies to the value of crossing oceans and swimming in exuberant waters, redounding to the benefit of *wenren*. This signature masculinity of Xu takes three distinctive forms. First, his *wen* is as variegated as the opalescent clouds that recur in his poetry: Chinese, British, French, Indian, and American; his transnational and multicultural literacy is perhaps matched only by Lu Xun and Younghill Kang in his time. Second, it flies against the Western masculine codes; it demonstrates that what is labeled "feminine"—gentle deportment, emotional expressiveness, lyrical effervescence—can very much become a man, behaviorally and stylistically. Not to gainsay the importance of "writing is fighting" put forward in the previous chapters, in Xu writing is *loving*. Xu makes palpable the sensuous power of the pen, whereby he captures hearts and minds of his contemporaries. Third, Xu's *wen* is reflexive—mutually enabling and entrancing. In particular, Xu should be credited for appreciating *wen* in women and in people from a different shore. Where Kam Louie considers *wen* to be an exclusive masculine yardstick, Xu freely applies it to the opposite sex, so that for him a *cainü* 才女 (female literary or artistic talent) was no less captivating than a *caizi*, a male poet-scholar. Xu was drawn to both Chinese and American women of letters, and to male mentors and friends who rivaled his own ability to appreciate an(other) world and to critique their own.

As a forerunner for those who believe in claiming and promoting a multicultural world heritage, in mingling with people of all stripes, Xu combines the individualism touted in the West with the communal or interdependent ethos inculcated in the East. His ability to open himself to foreign influence and to experiment with eclectic poetics is complemented by his propensity to appreciate, encourage, excite, and inspire people of like multicultural mind, a quality that endears him to an array of intellectuals. Hu Shi, in his elegy to Xu, is speaking on behalf of Xu's many friends: "Zhimo did not enter this world in vain; because we had befriended him, we could comfort ourselves that our lives too have not been in vain" (Hu Shi; my translation). Xu remains an indelible presence in the lives of writers and scholars as diverse as Pearl Buck, Chen Yuan, G.L. Dickinson, E.M. Forster, Roger Fry, Younghill Kang, Liang Qichao, Lin Huiyin, Ling Shuhua, Shen Congwen, and even his first wife. His romantic (soul)mateship did not discriminate between women and men, gay and straight, lovers and ex-lovers. Therein lies, perhaps, Xu Zhimo's *wen* aura and masculine mystique.

Notes

1. For an excellent study of Cantonese opera, see Bell Yung, *Cantonese Opera: Performance as a Creative Process*.
2. Most remarkably, Xu remained lifelong friends with two husbands whose wives were rumored to be his lovers: Chen Yuan/Chen Xiying (1896–1970), husband of Ling Shuhua and founder of the *Contemporary Review*; and Liang Sicheng, husband of Lin Huiyin. Xu's "presence alone …

was enough to draw Chen Yuan to Beijing" (Laurence 104). Liang Sicheng was visiting Shandong Province when Xu's plane crashed there: "He and his friends were in the first of the search parties" (Chang 199).
3. Lin Huiyin, who later became the first professor of architecture in China, was also the aunt of Maya Lin, designer of the Vietnam Veterans Memorial in Washington, DC. Xu met the 17-year-old Lin Huiyin and her father in London in the summer of 1920 through his mentor, Liang Qichao 梁启超, an intellectual vanguard in the twentieth century (L.O.-f. Lee 127). According to Wilma Fairbank, Lin's close friend, "Lin Huiyin loved Hsu Chih-mo [Xu Zhimo]" but "could not imagine being in a relationship in which a woman had been cast aside for her" (Chang 162).
4. "Legend has it that Hsü and Lu met on stage when he played an old scholar and she a cute maid in a charity performance; no sooner was the play over than the hero and heroine fell madly in love with each other" (L.O.-f. Lee 140). Xu had also acted with Lin Huiyin. When Tagore turned 64 on May 8, the Chinese scholars gave a party in his honor, which featured a performance of his short play, "Chita," with Lin "in the role of a princess and [Xu] as the god of love" (L.O.-f. Lee 146).
5. After Xu's death Lu "made the most of the public attention, giving permission for publication of their ardent correspondence written during their courtship" (Stirling 116).
6. Smedley and Buck actually crossed paths around 1942, when the journalist was in dire financial straits and Buck and her second husband Richard Walsh offered to help: "The two women had more in common than they realized: they did not know that at different times each had had an affair with Xu Zhimo" (MacKinnon and MacKinnon 253). Mari Yoshihara echoes: "[Buck and Smedley] had more in common than they had expected. At different times, each had had an affair with a romantic Shanghai poet Xu Zhimo" (Yoshihara 149–150).
7. Stirling and Peter Conn, another biographer of Buck, also believe that she was Xu's lover (Conn 103; Stirling 86). Stirling traces the affair to 1928, after the Bucks moved from the politically unstable Nanjing to Shanghai. While the "romantic news that Pearl had had a lover was known for some time by three of her intimates," the lover's identity was unknown until Stirling's 1978 interview with "Sara Burton" (assumed name of Lillieth Bates, Buck's housemate in Shanghai): "Hsu Chih-mo [Xu Zhimo] ... was four years younger than Pearl... Pearl and Hsu no doubt met in Nanking. As an English teacher, she would certainly have attended Tagore's lecture. And it is not difficult to imagine Hsu's impact upon her, joyous in his own success and yet warmly responsive to others, while she was at her nadir, locked into a dead marriage with a hopelessly ill child (Stirling 86, 87). Buck was apparently intermittently involved with Xu until 1931 (Conn 103),

though Hilary Spurling, another of Buck's biographers, thinks that an affair between them seemed "unlikely, if only because he was one of the stars of his literary generation, while she was at best an onlooker." But even Spurling allows that Buck fantasized about Xu: "Pearl admitted long afterward that, when she wrote 'A Chinese Woman Speaks,' she imagined herself ... marrying a young man such as Xu Zhimo" and that "she put something of Xu into the half-Chinese hero of *Letter from Peking*" (Spurling 175).
8. Han, also the narrator of Kang's first novel *The Grass Roof*, shares Kim's view of a moribund Korea under Japanese occupation and dream of planting Korean culture in the rest of the world: "Korea ... was called to get off the earth. Death summoned. I could have renounced the scholar's dream forever ... and written my vengeance against Japan in martyr's blood... Or I could take away my slip cut from the roots, and try to engraft my scholar inherited kingdom upon the world's thought" (2:8–9).
9. Given that Xu was later branded by post-1949 critics as anti-communist and anti-leftist, it is noteworthy that Kang remembers him as an admirer of Lu Xun, the writer venerated by the Communist regime.
10. Their daughter Lucy Lynn Kang would write about her parents in 1972, before her father's death in the same year: "He regarded her as the princess with the many mattresses on top of the pea, and he was the foreign prince. In Don Quixote fashion, nothing was impossible" (L. Kang 3; S. Lee 376).
11. See Shu-mei Shih, *The Lure of the Modern* (204–228) for an analysis of the fiction of Lin Huiyin and Ling Shuhua.
12. Dickinson continues: "You are arming a nation of four hundred millions! A nation which, until you came, had no better wish than to live at peace... In the name of Christ you have sounded the call to arms!" (Auden and Isherwood 197).
13. There is an incidental connection between Younghill Kang and Pearl Buck. When *The Good Earth* was published in 1931 to rave reviews, Kang was one of the few lukewarm critics. Conn relates that Kang "complained that Pearl had falsified the reality of Chinese gender relations, first by involving her main characters in a 'western-style' romantic plot, and then by depicting a landlord's sexual use of his slaves, which Kang claimed—erroneously—could not happen" (Conn 126) (Y. Kang, "China"). Interestingly, Kang has no compunction speaking as an authority on Chinese culture, while his narrator in *East Goes West* is distressed that Kim, found dead in his apartment, is mistaken for a "Chinaman," a common mistake at the time. Kang's review and Kim's mistaken identity demonstrate how East Asians were all too interchangeable in the USA during the first half of the twentieth century.
14. But she altered the actual dates of two historical events "for the sake of the story": the year Absalom Sydenstricker (Pearl's father) died and the year of

the Nanking Incident, both of which she marks as occurring years after Hsu's death in 1931, but which should be 1931 and 1927, respectively (Min, "Note" 277).
15. All of Buck's biographers agree that a quarter-century after the poet's death, Buck memorialized her former flame in *Letter from Peking* in the figure of Amerasian Gerald: "I saw Gerald run with his striking grace ... the glint of the sun on his black hair, the lively glance of his black eyes, and the clear smoothness of his cream skin." The portrayal is highly reminiscent of Kang's sketch of the lyricist in *East Goes West*. In Buck's novel, a sexual union definitely occurs: "It was in this house that we first consummated our eternal love... I have never told our heavenly secret to anyone, nor has he" (Buck, *Letter* 90; Stirling 88).
16. I thank Robert Kyriakos Smith for this insight.
17. Before Pearl and Willow had met Hsu in person, Pearl had sent Willow a section of Hsu's essay "Morality of Suicide," with her own note enclosed: "Let me know if you don't fall in love with the writer's mind" (117). It is therefore plausible that Pearl, and perhaps Buck as well, continues to consort with his spirit by reading his work and by writing about him under various guises, as Buck's biographers educe.
18. Chinnery discloses in an interview with Laurence that her mother "was chasing after Xu" though "Xu only regarded her as a confidante" (Laurence 70–71). According to Chinnery: "[Xu] left a lot of letters and diaries with [Ling Shuhua when he went abroad (1923–1924)]. It was still with her when he died. I think there were a lot of upsets when Xu's widow tried to retrieve the letters. Xu was also in love with Lin Huiyin who also wrote letters to Xu. I don't understand why there isn't one scrap of letter or poem by Xu in my mother's place. My guess is that she was jealous of Xu's friends and might have become a secret enemy of Xu. My father was his best friend ... introduced by Xu to my mother" (Laurence 70–71). Chinnery's rather confusing statement seems to suggest that Ling deliberately destroyed Xu's papers out of jealousy.

Works Cited

Auden, W. H., and Christopher Isherwood. *Journey to a War*. London: Faber and Faber, 1973.
Basu, Chitralekhha. "Novel Atonement." *China Daily*, 4 June 2010: 19.
Buck, Pearl S. "Is There a Case for Foreign Missions?" *Harper's Magazine*, 1 December 1932: 143–155.
——. *Letter from Beijing*. New York: Pocket Books, 1957.
——. *My Several Worlds: A Personal Record*. New York: John Day, 1954.

Chang, Pang-Mei Natasha. *Bound Feet & Western Dress: A Memoir*. New York: Anchor-Random House, 1996.
Chen, Chih-shen, ed. *Tang Po-hu tien Chiu-hsiang/yuan chu kao Pa-chih*. Taipei: Kai Hui, 1981.
Conn, Peter. *Pearl S. Buck: A Cultural Biography*. New York: Cambridge University Press, 1996.
Elmhirst, Leonard K. "Recollections of Tagore in China." 3 March 1959.
Fairbank, Wilma. *Liang and Lin: Partners in Exploring China's Architectural Past*. Philadelphia: University of Pennsylvania Press, 1994.
Friedan, Betty. *The Feminine Mystique*. New York: W. W. Norton, 1963; 1981.
Gao, Heng-wen 高恒文, and Nong Sang 桑农. *Xu Zhimo and the Women In His Life*《徐志摩与他生命中的女性》. Tianjin: Tianjin People's Publishing Co. [天津人民出版社], 2000.
Harding, Jason. "Goldsworthy Lowes Dickinson and the King's College Mandarins." *Cambridge Quarterly* (2011): 26–42.
Hu Shi 胡適. "追悼志摩 [Mourning Zhimo]." <http://w3.loxa.com.tw/fxp6033/01-data2.htm> (accessed 22 July 2015).
Hwang, David Henry. *M. Butterfly*. New York: Penguin, 1986.
Kang, Lynn. "Thoughts of the Times." *Korea Times*, 16 July 1972: 3.
Kang, Younghill. "China Is Different." *New Republic*, 1 July 1931: 185–186.
——. *East Goes West: The Making of an Oriental Yankee*. New York: Kaya, 1997.
——. *The Grass Roof*. New York: Charles Scribner's Sons, 1931.
Kimmel, Michael S., and Michael A. Messner. *Men's Lives*. Boston: Allyn and Bacon, 1995.
Kinkley, Jeffrey C. *The Odyssey of Shen Congwen*. Stanford: Stanford University Press, 1987.
Lau, D. C. "Introduction." *Confucius: The Analects*. Trans. D.C. Lau. Harmondsworth: Penguin Books, 1979. 9–55.
Laurence, Patricia. *Lily Briscoe's Chinese Eyes: Bloomsbury, Modernism, and China*. Columbia: University of South Carolina Press, 2003.
Lee, Leo Ou-fan. *The Romantic Generation of Modern Chinese Writers*. Cambridge: Harvard University Press, 1973.
Lee, Sunyoung. "The Unmaking of an Oriental Yankee." In *East Goes West: The Making of An Oriental Yankee*. Ed. Younghill Kang. New York: Kaya, 1997. 375–399.
Leung, Gaylord Kai Loh (Liang Hsi-hua). *A New Biography of Xu Zhimo*. 2nd Edition. Taipei: Lien Qing, 1994.
Lin Huiyin 林徽因. "悼志摩 [Mourning Zhimo]."《你是人间四月天 [You are the April of the World]》. Beijing: Tongxin Chubanche 同心出版社, 1931; 2015. 2–9.
Louie, Kam. *Theorizing Chinese Masculinity: Society and Gender in China*. Cambridge: Cambridge University Press, 2002.

MacKinnon, Janice R., and Stephen R. MacKinnon. *Agnes Smedley: The Life and Times of an American Radical.* Berkeley: University of California Press, 1988.
McMahon, Keith. "The Classic 'Beauty-Scholar' Romance and the Superiority of the Talented Woman." *Body, Subject & Power in China.* Ed. Angela Zito and Tani E. Barlow. Chicago: University of Chicago Press, 1994. 227–252.
Min, Anchee. "Author's Note." *Pearl of China.* New York: Bloomsbury, 2010a. 277.
Min, Anchee. *Pearl of China: A Novel.* New York: Random, 2010.
———. "Q&A with Anchee Min." In *Pearl of China.* Ed. Anchee Min. New York: Bloombury, 2010b. 279–284.
Mody, Perveez. "Xu Zhimo, Cambridge and China." *King's Parade: Magazine for Members and Friends of King's College, Cambridge* (Summer 2014): 10.
Murray, Henry A. "American Icarus." *Clinical Studies of Personality.* Ed. Arthur Burton and Robert E. Harris. Vol. 2. New York: Harper, 1955. 615–641.
Ng, Lai-Sze, and Chee-Lay Tan. "Two Tiers of Nostalgia and a Chronotopic Aura: Xu Zhimo and His Literary Cambridge Identity." *IPEDR.* Singapore: IACSIT Press, 2011. 575–580.
Pan, Chun Ming 潘君明, ed. *Tang Po Hu Wai Chuan*《唐伯虎外传》Chiang-Su: Ku wu hsuan chu pan she [古吴轩出版社], 1993.
Said, Edward W. *Reflections on Exile and Other Essays.* Cambridge: Harvard University Press, 2002.
Song, Geng. *The Fragile Scholar: Power and Masculinity in Chinese Culture.* Hong Kong: Hong Kong University Press, 2004.
Spence, Jonathan D. *The Gate of Heavenly Peace: The Chinese and Their Revolution 1895–1980.* New York: Viking, 1981.
Spurling, Hilary. *Pearl Buck in China: Journey to The Good Earth.* New York: Simon & Schuster, 2010.
Stirling, Nora. *Pearl Buck: A Woman in Conflict.* Piscataway: New Century Publishers, Inc., 1983.
Wang, Zilan, and Alan Macfarlane. *Xu Zhimo: Cambridge and China*《徐志摩：剑桥与中国》San Bernadino: CreateSpace Independent Publishing Platform, 2014.
Welland, Sasha Su-ling. *A Thousand Miles of Dreams: The Journeys of Two Chinese Sisters.* New York: Rowman & Littlefield, 2007.
Wood, Frances. *The Lure of China: Writers from Marco Polo to J.G. Ballard.* San Francisco: Long River Press, 2009.
Xu, Zhimo. "Art and Life (1922)." *Modern Chinese Literary Thought: Writings on Literature, 1893–1945.* Ed. Kirk A. Denton. Stanford: Stanford University Press, 1996. 169–181.
Yang, Bojun 杨伯俊, trans. *The Analects Translated and Annotated.*《论语译注》. Beijing: Zhonghua shuju, 1958.
Yoshihara, Mari. *Embracing the East: White Women and American Orientalism.* New York: Oxford University Press, 2003.

Yue Cheng 岳诚. "美国万花筒:闵安琪与赛珍珠 [American Kaleidoscope: Anchee Min and Pearl Buck]." *Voice of America*. 8 May 2010. <http://www.voachinese.com/content/article-20100716-anchee-min-pearl-buck-100054624/516808.html> (accessed 23 May 2016).

Yung, Bell. *Cantonese Opera: Performance as Creative Process*. New York: Cambridge University Press, 1989.

Zhong, Xueping. *Masculinity Besieged? Issues of Modernity and Male Subjectivity in Chinese Literature of the Late Twentieth Century*. Durham: Duke University Press, 2000.

CHAPTER 5

Art, Spirituality, and *Ren* or the Ethics of Care: Shawn Wong, Li-Young Lee, and Russell C. Leong

The editors of *Aiiieeeee!* believed that the invisibility of Asian American men in North America is due in part to the dearth of Asian American writers in the 1970s and to the "lack of a recognized style of Asian-American manhood" (xxxviii). They saw this absence as analogous to castration: "Language is the medium of culture and the people's sensibility... Stunt the tongue and you have lopped off the culture and sensibility ... a man in any culture speaks for himself. Without a language of his own, he no longer is a man" (xlvii–xlviii). In *The Big Aiiieeeee!* the editors attempted to refashion Asian American masculinity by espousing an "Asian heroic tradition" that glorifies the martial heroes featured in classical Chinese and Japanese epics as some kind of ancestral models for contemporary Asians. Notwithstanding their masculinist leanings, their arguments concerning the denigration of Asian men in American popular culture remain valid today. What has changed is the growing number of Asian American male writers who have been reconfiguring the contours of Asian American masculinity. Yet much of the refashioning, including recent works like Ed Lin's *Waylaid* (2002) and Eddie Huang's *Fresh off the Boat*, is mired in patriarchal notions of manliness, whether of Asian or American origin. Chapter 3 demonstrates, through analyzing the work of Gus Lee and David Wong Louie, that the two Chinese American writers have either inverted racist stereotypes by creating pugnacious heroes or internalized these stereotypes by reproducing diffident Chinese lovers. I contend that from both cultural nationalist and feminist standpoints, a quest for Chinese American manhood should allow for an alternative cast rather than mere imitations of Western heroes. Chapter 4 uses both Chinese opera and the figure of Xu Zhimo to revive an alternative model, that of the *wenren* or poet-scholar, known variously as *caizi* or *shushen*, who is seductive because of his gentle demeanor, wit, and artistic sensibility. The poet-scholar often prides himself on being indifferent to wealth and political power, and seeks women and men who are his equals in intelligence and integrity. Such a model not only counters the cultural invisibility of Asian Americans but also offers a mode of conduct that breaks down the putative dichotomy of gay and straight behavior.

But the model of poet-scholar, especially in the figure of Xu Zhimo, may seem too detached from worldly politics to inspire those whose very consciousness as "Asian Americans" came in the wake of the civil rights movement. Advocating such a model may further smack of elitism in view of the neglected education of migrant children in China and high dropout rates of underprivileged youngsters in high schools and colleges in the United States. As explained in the Introduction, however, *wen* is supposed to be a vehicle of moral education and it is incumbent on *wenren* to change social mores and better the world. This chapter uncovers Chinese American counterparts of this traditional model: men who influence social events through both rhetoric and social action, who cultivate an inner life, or who exhibit a humanist ethic that harks back both to the Confucian notion of *ren / jen* 仁 (person-to-person care or mutual kindness) and to what Nel Noddings, taking her cue from Carol Gilligan, calls the "ethics of care," which she describes as a "feminine approach to ethics." *Ren*—the component of *wen* boldfaced in this chapter—is, pace Confucius, who allegedly associated it with the ruling class (Louie 48)—attainable by people from any segment of society.

Both the conjuncture and disjuncture between Confucian *ren* and feminist caring are remarkable. Confucius (551–479 BC) associates *ren*—glossed by James D. Sellmann and Sharon Rowe as "person to person care" and by Joseph R. Levenson and Franz Schurmann as both "human-kindness" and "humankind-ness"—as the key ingredient of the *junzi* 君子 or the superior man (Sellman and Rowe 2; Levenson and Schurmann 42). Sellmann and Rowe argue for the "family resemblance" between this Confucian notion of *ren* and the feminine ethics: both are about "giving and receiving care that is fitted to the needs of particular people in specific situations"; both emphasize "interdependence (over individualism)"; both are "context dependent (not independent);

... circular (not linear); ... [placing] virtue over justice" (3). To preempt objections from critics who balk at their linkage of the feminist ethics with the Sage, Sellmann and Rowe distinguish Confucius teachings from their sexist transmission by the Literati School (*Rujia* 儒家): "The strong presence of humanistic values and loving care and concern expressed in Confucius' philosophy would not serve the power politics of imperial China," and therefore its presence was eclipsed by doctrines that support patriarchal hierarchy (Sellman and Rowe 1–2). Sellman and Rowe believe one of Confucius's many innovations was transforming the traditional concept of *ren* "understood to be the 'loving affection between close relatives' ... to mean the 'loving care between two people'"; "he wanted to extend the loving care of close family relationships to others beyond the family or clan bond. The care one learns at home is extended outward ... to others" (4). Yet no amount of Confucian apology, I am afraid, can sugarcoat the fact that Confucius, like his Chinese coevals, was inveterately sexist, so that when he talked about *ren*, he was thinking primarily of man-to-man (rather than person-to-person) care. In fact, there is a well-known derogatory proverb called *furen zhiren* 妇人之仁 (womanly *ren*) ("woman" is here used in the sense of "Frailty, thy name is woman!"), referring to a kind of mawkish, syrupy, and effusive (to the extent of clouding judgment) soft-heartedness that is often confined to kin, as opposed to the big-hearted magnanimity that supposedly only superior men can exude and that allows them to cherish and lavish favors on great men of the same ilk.[1] Notwithstanding this phallocentric purview of *ren*, its emphasis on interpersonal attentiveness, on giving and receiving care, does have the merit of offsetting a putative bane of "manhood" dubbed "male ego" in popular parlance.

Noddings, by contrast, associates the ethics of care—emphasizing relationships, mutual care, and the importance of context dependent ethics—with women, though she is quick to add that "men might also share this experience" (xxiv). My intention in coupling the Confucian *ren* and the feminist care ethics is not to recuperate Confucius (as Sellman and Rowe have tried to do) but to decouple caring from femininity lest caring men be deemed "effeminate" in the West. Biased in the opposite direction, Confucius actually considers *ren* to be the paramount manifestation of superior *men*. This chapter focuses on this longstanding virtue—masculine solicitude—as a viable alternative to macho aggression.

Like the fiction covered in the previous chapters, Shawn Wong's *American Knees* (1995), Li-Young Lee's *The Winged Seed* (1995), and

Russell Leong's "Phoenix Eyes" (2000) attest to the inextricability of gender, race, ethnicity, and sexuality and the importance of foregrounding what Kimberlé Crenshaw calls "intersectionality." Unlike Frank Chin, Gus Lee, and David Wong Louie, however, the three writers in this chapter counter the "emasculation" of Asian men without falling into the trap of reinstating hegemonic masculinities. Among their characters are artists, poet-scholars, caring fathers, Christians, and Buddhists—all of whom provide counterexamples to the pervasive association of masculine power with physical prowess or economic success.

Through my analysis of these figures, I further demonstrate how geographical locations—Asia, Europe, and North America—affect the overlapping axes of race, class, and gender, particularly the contours of masculinity. Susan Stanford Friedman argues that the "new geographics of identity" involves moving from the concept of a unifying self to a "discourse of spatialized identities constantly on the move." The three works analyzed point to such geographics, which "figures identity as a historically embedded site, a positionality, a location, a standpoint, a terrain, an intersection, a network, a crossroads of multiply situated knowledges" (Friedman 17, 19). Wong's protagonist, a cocksure Chinese American affirmative action officer, cannot wrap his head around his lover who is a refugee from Vietnam; Ba, Li-Young Lee's father, goes from being venerated as a charismatic minister in Hong Kong to being a slighted foreign pastor in the American Midwest; Leong's narrator in "Phoenix Eyes" gains a new apprehension of, and appreciation for, Asian virility in Taipei.

American Knees[2]

Shawn Wong's *American Knees* at once undermines traditional Chinese patriarchy, explodes American mythology about Asian men, and reveals the difficulties faced by a Chinese American in defining his masculinity independently of Chinese filial obligations and American stereotypes. Raymond Ding, the protagonist, recalls how children used to tease him in the schoolyard:

> "What are you—Chinese, Japanese, or American Knees?" they'd chant, slanting the corners of their eyes up and down, displaying a bucktoothed smile, and pointing at their knees. When Raymond, not liking any of the choices, didn't answer, they'd say, "Then you must be dirty knees." (12)

Though the title conveys how Asian Americans have long been subjected to racial slurs in the United States, "American Knees" also encapsulates Raymond's liminal status: he is too American to abide by Chinese patriarchal injunctions, but he also cannot be accepted fully as "American" by the dominant culture.

Raymond, who works in the affirmative action office of a San Francisco college, finds it difficult to fulfill Chinese expectations of filial piety. When the novel opens he is going through a divorce from Darleen, his Chinese wife, an event which triggers an internal dialogue with traditional Chinese beliefs, such as the stigma associated with divorce, the taboo against marrying outside one's race, and the responsibility incumbent on male offspring to have children so as to perpetuate the family name. Upon seeing his father, Woodrow/Wood, Raymond is conscious of an "ominous unspoken thought" that goes through both their minds: "Raymond would never again marry a Chinese woman and would thus be the first in his thin branch of the family tree not to be married to a Chinese. He was already the first to divorce" (23). While Chinese patriarchy is often equated with male privilege, it also imposes a special burden on male heirs, especially number-one sons: "The first son in a Chinese family has certain duties to family as well as to himself, and over time the performance of these filial obligations is a test of patience and tolerance against personal ambition" (32). Darleen, on the other hand, is free from such obligations: "She understood that the power in the family rested on the shoulders of the men. This wasn't the legendary and oppressive Chinese patriarchy at work; it was freedom and the luxury of choice for Darleen" (17). While Wong makes light of sexism here, he exposes the contradictions inherent in Chinese patriarchy—especially the way it afflicts those it supposedly favors.

Through Raymond's appreciation of Wood, Wong undercuts conventional Chinese and American codes of manhood. Wood breaches the code of the stoic and invincible Chinese father when he asks his son to sleep next to him two nights after Raymond's mother's funeral: "There's too much space there" Wood laments (28). Raymond considers the voicing of this request—this reaching out to the son for solace and intimacy—to be "the bravest thing his father had ever done" (28), thereby inverting the conventional notion of manly courage. Raymond also redefines the paternal ideal to include the ability to relinquish authority. Unlike Darleen's father—the typical Chinese patriarch who dictates the lives of all his sons and sons-in-law—Wood gives Raymond "his place in the family by not telling him, by not asking, by not saying what was in his heart. It was the manly way of doing things. This was how Raymond became a man" (31). The silence is Wood's way of making room for Raymond's independence.[3]

Through his protagonist, Wong also overturns American stereotypes about Asian men. Raymond often measures himself against both the ideal Chinese son and the American "model minority"—only to deconstruct both. His racy seduction of a red-haired wine rep is juxtaposed, for instance, against his putative "image": "Raymond was a good Chinese boy who never cut class … never tore up a parking ticket, didn't burn his draft card" (18). We later learn that this semblance of the stereotype is a result of fear and subjugation during his military service in the Vietnam War. All Raymond can remember of the war is "the fear he'd felt when the sergeant had called him a 'gook.' That, and the desire he'd brought back from his few months in the army to be anonymous in the world. There was safety in being Asian American at home in America. *We work hard. We keep quiet. I am the model minority*" (59). The model minority is merely the flipside of being deemed a gook: the solution to being treated as enemy alien is to be a member of a docile and silent minority. Both the derogatory and laudatory epithets "unman" the Asian male.

Wong then proceeds to delineate an alternative masculinity. Raymond's two-year courtship and affair with Aurora Crane, who is half Irish and half Japanese, shows he is far from quiet and self-effacing and challenges the widespread perception, propagated by the media, about Asian "preference for lovers not of their own race" (40). Being handsome, witty, articulate, and sexy, Raymond bears no resemblance to America's "stereotypical wimpy Asian nerd" (103). Instead he brings to mind the classical Chinese *fengliu caizi* 風流才子 (flirting scholar). The most famous classical exemplar, known as Tang Yin 唐寅 or Tang Bohu 唐伯虎, is a renowned poet drawn to women who are not only attractive but also intelligent—capable of outwitting the male suitor (Chen; Pan Chun Ming 23–26), in accordance with the scholar-beauty genre discussed in Chapter 4. Raymond has a few lessons coming to him from women, to be sure. But he also disabuses Aurora of her stock images. On first seeing him at a party, Aurora, who has absorbed many stereotypes about Asian men, "searched for the most typically Chinese feature about him, but couldn't find the usual landmarks: cheap haircut with greasy bangs falling across the eyebrows, squarish gold-rimmed glasses, askew because there's no bridge to hold them up, baggy-butt polyester pants" (36). During their initial "long distance phone sex" (47), Raymond further chips away at her presuppositions. Like Tang Yin and his beloved maid, Qiuxiang 秋香, or Shakespeare's Benedick and Beatrice, their initial courtship is a saucy battle of wits:

"I didn't know forty-year-old Asian men masturbate."...
"We can even use the other hand to calculate logarithms on our Hewlett-Packard calculators."...
"How big is this golden aura of manhood?"
"How big do you want it to be?"
"Big as a cucumber."
"How about a pickle?" (46, 48)

Wong insistently stresses Raymond's verbal felicity. After they become lovers, Raymond spins an erotic tale for Aurora whenever they make love: "In Aurora's bedtime stories Raymond learned to flirt, be romantic, be seductive, and undress her all at once, making love to her in complete sentences and full paragraphs" (47–48).

Part of his appeal to Aurora is his knowledge and sensitivity about Asian American history: "Their conversation was complementary. She offered information, and he filled in the blanks without asking embarrassing questions" (42). Aurora finds Raymond seductive not because he conforms to dominant masculine ideals, but precisely because he differs from matinee idols and pushy adolescents: "She thought about how some men kissed like they had learned to kiss by watching James Bond movies and fishing shows on television, coming at her with their mouths open... Raymond preferred to take turns kissing... His hands applied no pressure on her bare skin" (82–83). His masculine attraction stems from his tenderness, his lack of bluster. What Aurora finds "sexiest" about him is his "patience with women": "I've noticed it's how you flirt with women. You sit and listen. You actually want to be friends" (65). Raymond's eloquence, refinement, and attentiveness align him with Chinese poet-scholars, rather than with mainstream idols. Insofar as masculinity in North America is associated with domination, Raymond exemplifies a refreshing alternative.

But he has a propensity for intellectual condescension. Aurora, though drawn to Raymond the romantic poet, soon finds Raymond the didactic ethnic scholar patronizing: "She hated his instructive tone" (58). Instead of accepting her biracial status, he tries to raise her Asian quotient: "He thought his ancestry was a gift. Their union was never just love and desire and friendship to him" (54). When Aurora resists his efforts, he reprimands her, "I guess you haven't learned a thing. Don't you know in America skin color is your identity? This is a racist country. You can't be invisible" (55). Aurora retorts, "Not everyone can be a professional affirmative action officer like you. I'm your lover, not a case history" (57). To be fair to Raymond, age difference, gender, and race do account for important differences between these two. The political consciousness of Raymond, who is 41, has been forged in the crucible of the civil rights movement, which has dismantled the most blatant forms of inequality; Aurora, still in her twenties, is a beneficiary of the struggle. They also have different experiences in a "culture that says Asian women are beautiful and acceptable and Asian men aren't"; being beautiful and biracial, Aurora is much less susceptible to racism's sting. It strikes her that "Raymond had become, on a more complicated level, like the people who asked Aurora what she was and where she came from. The ignorant were rude; Raymond was educational" (81). She decides to end their relationship.

Raymond as forsaken lover is perhaps at his most attentive and caring: "In the end, Raymond moved and Aurora stayed in the apartment because he could not bear to see her leave... He couldn't live in the apartment that held the memory of the two of them... His leaving was love ... his silence was love" (74). No sooner have they separated than they commit a mutual relapse. Aurora calls her (own) apartment to leave a message for him; Raymond, who should not be there, picks up the phone. She invites him for dinner, and he brings her favorite dessert: "It wasn't fair to expect him not to know things about her, not to remember a passion for peach pie or her taste in clothes, not to be able to read her mind, not to know that there was a reason they often said the same things at the same time" (80). His attentiveness and understanding continue to disarm Aurora, though Raymond has meanwhile become involved with Betty Nguyen, his co-worker.

Where Raymond has tried to shape Aurora's life, to study her as a case history, Betty refuses to reveal her painful past to Raymond; she does not want him to bear "the responsibility of knowing" (85). When pressed by Raymond, the details she supplies remain nebulous, so that Raymond or the reader is never sure whether she is revealing the truth.[4] We are told that she is a refugee from Vietnam who was cruelly abused by her former husband, to whom she lost custody of their daughter, who has been told that her mother is dead. No amount of intellectual analysis and political correctness can assuage this kind of grief. Nevertheless, Raymond learns to love her "completely," with all his heart, without trying to nail down or pontificate about her identity, as he has done with Aurora (189). Unlike Aurora, who has complained to Raymond, "I don't see me anywhere in you" (70), Betty tells him she doesn't want to be "the object and purpose" of his life (189). When she later realizes that Raymond still loves Aurora, Betty decides to remove herself for good.

Raymond and Aurora are given the opportunity to meet again over the hospitalization of Wood, who has suffered a brain aneurysm. Aurora notices changes in her former lover:

> He *was* different ... as if some sudden pain preoccupied him. She sensed the faintest edge of insecurity around him. Perhaps thinking about his father's mortality had made him fragile and uncertain. His eyes were more open, but also less confident, less guarded. They no longer flirted in their familiar way. He looked the way people look when they grieve a lost love. (228)

Aurora is drawn back to a chastened Raymond. From having entered another's sorrow, Raymond learns his limits and loses his cocksureness and self-possession, his insouciance and insolence. Aurora sees his diffidence and insecurity as indications of his increased sensitivity, not as weaknesses. His care, grief, and loss have made him a better person—a better man.

In *American Knees*, Wong succeeds in evoking a form of masculinity that goes against the dominant grain. There are, however, also limits to his attempt at redefining Asian American manhood. Even as the author attempts to overturn stereotypes through his protagonist, he also reinforces them by portraying Raymond as an exception to the rule. After Aurora's initial search "for the most typically Chinese feature about him," she begins "looking for and analyzing the most un-Asian features about him" (36). What Aurora finds attractive in Raymond at first sight seems to be his "most un-Asian features." Raymond, who himself complains that Aurora is "not culturally sensitive enough," describes his Uncle Ted's son as "an undergraduate nerd with a slide rule, on his way to becoming a nerd of a nuclear engineer" (120). His comment echoes one made earlier by Darleen's roommate, who "convinced Darleen that the Asian guys in the public administration program were less nerdy than the ones in the business school" (13). Finally, when Raymond and his friend Jimmy examine the stereotypes of Chinese men in the book *Chinese Girls in Bondage* (an invented title), they conclude facetiously that it is "better to be evil and Chinky than sexless and obsequious" (150). The slanted perspectives of the characters demonstrate that stereotypes are not just imposed on Asians by the dominant culture but also perpetuated by Asian Americans themselves. Even as the exception, Raymond lends credence to the oppressive rule. He is so conscious of the stereotype of Asian men as asexual that he comes across at times as merely its deliberate inversion. He has to be exceptionally good in bed to be good enough;

has to be hyperactive sexually to be considered masculine. In magnifying Raymond's sexual prowess and in devoting many pages of the novel to graphic scenes of lovemaking (49–52, 81–85), Wong underwrites the dominant culture's overemphasis on sexual potency as an index of masculinity.[5] *American Knees* at once offers new ways to think about masculinity and attests to the ubiquity of the stereotype about Asian men and the difficulty of disentangling entirely from the dominant ideology. James Moy has observed concerning Asian American drama that often the playwrights are complicit in disfiguring Asian men (Moy 115–129). The same holds true in Chinese American fiction; even Wong cannot refrain from off-color jokes at Asian men's expense.

Nevertheless, Wong's novel does deconstruct its own racial and gender preoccupations and caution against ideological stringencies, suggesting that Asian Americans who allow race and gender to become primary considerations in their interpersonal encounters, no matter how correct politically, are simply doing the obverse of what the dominant culture has been doing to racial and sexual minorities. It is tempting to think about the book as in some way reflecting the intellectual trajectory of the author, one of the editors of *Aiiieeeee!* (1974) and *The Big Aiiieeeee!* (1991). Both the Preface and "An Introduction to Chinese- and Japanese-American Literature" in *Aiiieeeee!*, which judge Asian American writing according to what the editors deem to be politically correct but which many critics (including myself) consider to be sexist and homophobic criteria, are underwritten by the four editors, Shawn Wong included. In *The Big Aiiieeeee!*, Frank Chin is the sole author of the 92-page essay explicating the Asian Heroic Tradition and arbitrating what he considers to be authentic works, possibly suggesting that the other three editors may not fully share his criteria for the "fake" and the "real" Asian American literature.

In *American Knees* (1995), Raymond goes from being a high-handed and condescending affirmative action officer who pegs everyone (father, wife, and girlfriends included) according to race and culture to being a much more sensitive individual who no longer defines people by their pedigree. Wong seems to imply that Asian Americans too must guard against essentializing race and identity, and treating fellow Asians as racial specimens or turning race, gender, and culture into the central axes of a person's identity. Raymond has learned from Aurora and Betty that he must not try to read or shape them according to his Asian American cultural nationalist ideology. He comes to see that even his father is defined less by culture than by his profession as an engineer: "The more he read [his father's engineering manuals], the more he came to understand that his father was not so much traditionally Chinese as he was a typical engineer who measured the world as a structure and applied the principles of building to families, lovers, dreams" (237).

Just as Wood applies the principles from his training as engineer to his personal life, Raymond's profession as affirmative action officer has also crept into his earlier interactions with Darleen and Aurora, when he is obsessed with his position as a Chinese American male defending or staking out his territory in white America. His setbacks with Aurora and Betty, and Wood's near-death encounter, have made him more introspective, becoming more alive to the feelings of others and to his own. The ending of the novel, which is suffused with tenderness between father and son, mother and son, Aurora and Raymond, and Raymond and Betty, reflects this inward turn. This coda begins with Wood transplanting a 40-year-old bonsai pine from his house to Raymond's house and giving Aurora the garden gloves of Raymond's mother, Helen:

> [Raymond] thinks about the woman he loves—the one who is embedded in the heart and life lines of his palms, the one who makes love to him on a tiny bed ... the one who sends him a picture of herself cuddling an infant... He wishes he could mark his life at each of these points so that he could come back later with the memory and knowledge of how to occupy the heart in order to find solutions, discover a sense of place, reach home, explain his love. (239–240)

At the beginning of the novel, Raymond felt like a failed Chinese son on account of his divorce, and his failure to perpetuate patrilineage. This ending shows that things are passed on from one generation to the next nonetheless, albeit not in the traditional way. The bonsai pine is transplanted by Wood to the son's house; Aurora inherits Helen's gloves. Betty, meanwhile, has given birth to a girl, albeit yet unbeknownst to the father. So the family line goes on through this daughter. Instead of thinking about racial pedigree and gender warfare, Raymond now just wishes he could reach out to each of the women he still loves—Helen, Aurora, and Betty— to find a place in the heart of another, and vice versa, to allow another to occupy a space in his. This wistful invocation has in a way allowed the inner spaces of thought and memory to open up, to summon all his beloved home: "He crosses the bridge between them" (240).

THE WINGED SEED

It has been nearly four decades since the editors of *Aiiieeeee!* deplored "the failure of Asian-American manhood to express itself in its simplest form: fathers and sons" in early Asian American literature (xlvi–xlvii). Since then, the field has witnessed some memorable father-son relationships in Peter Bacho's *Dark Blue Suit* (1997) and *Leaving Yesler* (2010), Frank Chin's *Donald Duk* (1991), Chang-rae Lee's *Native Speaker* (1995) and, as discussed above, in Wong's *American Knees*. Li-Young Lee's *The Winged Seed*, a memoir, revolves entirely around the narrator's formidable father—Ba (Chinese vocative for Father)—a political prisoner under President Sukarno of Indonesia. After 19 months in prison, Ba escapes with his family to the United States, settling first in Pennsylvania and then in Chicago. The narrator is haunted by him, an ambivalent figure who teeters between saint and taskmaster, magnanimous minister and exacting father, invincible man of God and vulnerable man of flesh, and who falls somewhere between alternative and hegemonic masculinities. Through the narrator's fluctuating emotions toward his father as they move from various Asian countries to the United States, we witness how perceptions about masculinity are inseparable from race and nationality, and how they shift with the environs.

The narrator registers his admiration for Ba's artistic and spiritual resolve during the family's odyssey, when Ba occupies himself by constructing a model of Solomon's Temple. This painstaking achievement illustrates both his Christian and paternal devotion: "What it took a great king seven months to accomplish with stone and three hundred thousand slaves, it took my father nearly four years to complete out of cardboard and paper, a feat of love, or someone serving a sentence" (37). The replica has been intended as a gift for his daughter's 11th birthday: "And the real genius of the thing was ... its portability. For each piece could be gently dismantled, unfolded, spread flat, and put into a box to be carried across borders" (38). This labor of love, together with consummate craftsmanship, "indicating the obsessive and aching hand of a maker whose playfulness was surpassed only by his determination" (40), comes across as artistic and spiritual testimony to Ba's masculinity. The word "maker" has the effect of elevating Ba to the level of the biblical creator, an association that will be developed further.

Ba's manual dexterity is matched by his virtuosity as a preacher: "On the island of Hong Kong he drew crowds in such numbers that rows of folding chairs had to be set up in the very lobbies of the theaters where his revival meetings took place ... where throngs of sweating believers stood for hours in the sun, listening to him speak and pray" (73). His pastoral efficacy is the more remarkable when set against the frailty of a body ravaged by his long imprisonment, as though the two were inversely proportional, as though his spiritual ascent were propelled by the downward momentum of dying. In an interview, Li-Young Lee discusses this opposite yet connected momentum: "The momentum of dying and the act of making art are opposing forces. Making art opposes dying, but at the same time it gets all its energy from this downward momentum, this art into the abyss that all of us are a part of, that's the tension we feel in art which we enjoy" (J.K.-J. Lee 274). Ba's close encounter with death in prison seems to bleed into his creative and spiritual endeavors.

Besides expressing his faith by deploying his hands and tongue, Ba puts his Christian faith and universal love to practice by attending to the "'shut-ins,' those who never left their houses, mainly old, infirm, crazy, or dying" (67). One of them is a "frighteningly little bag of bones ... and you couldn't tell she wasn't a corpse until you heard her wheeze" (71). Ba sincerely cares about everyone in his congregation which, as the author wryly notes, is made up largely of people who look askance at him: "he loved each and every one of them and more than I ever felt they deserved, they who referred to him as their heathen minister, these alcoholic mothers ... delinquent children, shell-shocked bus-drivers, pedophilic schoolteachers, adulterous barmaids... Perhaps it was my father's calling to love every mangled or lost or refused soul" (82). Ba's behavior seems to accord well with both Confucian *ren* and the care ethics designated by Noddings as "feminine."

Yet there *is* a palpable difference between Ba's altruistic caring and Noddings's model, especially with regard to Ba's own children. Noddings states that "when the attitude of the one-caring bespeaks caring, the cared-for glows, grows stronger, and feels ... that something has been added to him" (20). When it comes to his children, Ba seems to take something away from them, as symbolized by the narrator's response as he sketches their portraits: "As his hand moved to make a face or an arm appear on a white tablet... I could feel large parts of myself being vanquished by his gaze and his drawing hand, as though, being translated that way to rough page and graphite by my father, there would soon remain nothing of me" (56). Despite a certain paradox suggested by the narrator ("For he was making me go away so completely, I was beginning to arrive" (56), there is something unsettling about Ba's obliterating strokes. Unlike the relationship between Wood and Raymond in *American Knees*, in which father and son give each other room to grow, Ba overshadows his offspring. Instead of inspiring confidence, he elicits fear and longing for recognition from his children, who vie with one another to please their sire. Ba's mode of caring differs from Nodding's ethics and resembles what Sellman and Rowe call Confucian "phallo-centric care" (2). Whereas Confucius extends kindred regard to social relationships, however, Ba places his pastoral duty above paternal concern. One recalls similar split devotion in *Fighting Angel* (1936), Pearl Buck's biography about her missionary father Absalom Sydenstricker, who was so obsessed with converting Chinese into Christians that he gave callous short shrift to his wife and children (Buck; see also Chapter 4). One is also reminded of the Buddhist father in Hisaye Yamamoto's "The Legend of Miss Sasagawara" (1950): "This man was certainly noble... The world was doubtless enriched by his presence. But say that someone else, someone sensitive, someone admiring, someone who had not achieved this sublime condition and who did not wish to, were somehow called to companion such a man. Was it not likely that the saint, blissfully bent on cleansing from his already radiant soul the last imperceptible blemishes ... would be deaf and blind to the human passions rising, subsiding, and again rising, perhaps in anguished silence, within the selfsame room?" (33). In both Christianity and Buddhism, men who seem selfless and saintly in the public eye can paradoxically be the most negligent and even abusive fathers. These men could use a corrective dose of *furen zhiren*, feminine caring.

The narrator reveals the peculiar relationship between father and son through a tacit linkage of the earthly father and the heavenly Father:

> We would fashion our souls to fit the grip of God... [We] who would fashion ourselves thus were earlier than sparrows, though never earlier than our father, who would never have the light find him supine... Our sincerest wish was ... to be seen, truly seen, seen once and forever, by our father... It was, then, for love, that we got on with it: for love of him who was remote and feared, that we fashioned ourselves. (43–44)

In this conflation of God and Ba, we can divine the narrator's filial ambivalence. Ba elicits intense devotion from his children, who ironically worship him rather than God. Yet his rigorous discipline and supreme standards also render him implacable and forever inaccessible to his children. His godlike demeanor inspires in them awe, respect, and love, but not intimacy. On rare occasions, he is capable of tenderness, as when he massages the narrator's feet after their endless voyage across the Pacific: "My father put down our suitcase, untied my shoes, and rubbed my feet, one at a time and with such deep turns of his wrist. I heard the water in him through my soles. Since then I have listened for him in my steps" (42). The lyrical and almost numinous manner in which this moment is reminisced suggests its rarity, its preciousness, and its lasting impression on the narrator—who is "never allowed to look ... straight into his [father's] eyes" (60).

More often, the son is made to follow in his father's footsteps, literally, as when he accompanies Ba on his endless rounds to tend the poor and lost souls on communion Sundays, weekly rituals that for the son constitute a "trial" (68). The father is more attentive to his religious duties than to his son's fatigue as a long day draws to a close around ten o'clock at night: "I was hungry, impatient, my feet freezing, and my trouser legs damp. My father smiled at me and said, 'One more visit ... then we'll have done a little good.' A glum fourteen, I was not cheered" (70). Besides his physical discomfort, the son is also tormented by uncertainty about whether Ba is indeed doing good: "If those communions were difficult, were they empty?... Was my father wasting his time?" (73).

The disjuncture between Ba's single-minded devotion to his congregation and his inability to monitor his son's physical and mental distress recalls the classical division of private and public spheres, the latter traditionally associated with men. While Ba can "love every mangled or lost or refused soul" (82), he is oblivious to his own children's suffering. His behavior, like that of Absalom and Reverend Sasagawara, remains governed by the traditional code of masculinity—stoicism that in these cases translates into callousness toward one's closest kin—as well as by orthodox religions, which put much greater stock in public than in private life. One cannot help but wish that Ba, who has such a magnetic hold over both his congregation and his family, could also step down from the altar to play with his children and harken to their growing pains.

There is, however, another way to interpret the narrator's increasing grudge against his father. As long as Ba is in Asia, his authority as a minister and as a patriarch is never questioned, notwithstanding his long imprisonment. All that changes when the family arrives in the United States. Just as Raymond's "masculinity" is enviable among Asian men but is invisible to white men, Ba, a renowned preacher in Asia, is dubbed a "heathen minister" by the lowest of the low, the pariahs of society in Pennsylvania. The narrator, meanwhile, also has to adjust to the status of being a poor and dumb alien. He confesses feeling "a mixture of sadness and disgust, even shame" when years later he encounters a man who had been a great fan of his father's powerful sermons in Hong Kong. Rather than feeling pride, the narrator recoils:

> Why did I feel disgust?... I was almost ready to disavow everything. Why? What makes a person want to disavow his own life? When I was six and learning to speak English, I talked with an accent anyone could hear, and I noticed early on that all accents were not heard alike by the dominant population of American English speakers... More than once I was told I sounded ugly. My mouth was a shame to me. (75–77)

What good were the father's moving sermons in another language to the tongue-tied son? Ba's eloquence and fame in Asia cannot remove the narrator's speech impediment in the United States, cannot blot out the stigma of his "ugly" accent. The narrator's diminishing esteem for his father—a movement from awe to something akin to pity and contempt—seems closely tied to Ba's "emasculation" in North America and to the narrator's own sense of abjection and rejection.

"Identity depends upon a point of reference," Friedman observes. "As that point moves nomadically, so do the contours of identity, particularly as they relate to the structures of power" (Friedman 22). Friedman's feminist insight applies just as aptly to permutations in masculinity. Even in Lee's intensely personal memoir, paternal authority and filial devotion are inflected by nationality, race, and place. Unlike Ba's dexterity, epitomized by his Solomon's Temple, which is eminently portable, his gift of tongue is dislodged and his patriarchal sway attenuated in crossing the Pacific. The question remains as to whether the forms of masculinity that can be so easily stripped away are truly desirable. What do Asian American men mean and want when they try to reclaim their masculinity? Do they seek to (re-)occupy positions of dominance or do they envision a world free of domination? What is inalienably manly, and what are merely masculine trappings?

"Phoenix Eyes"

Russell Leong's "Phoenix Eyes," which features a gay protagonist, provides perhaps the most radical alternative to hegemonic masculinity. Although debates about gender have been simmering in Asian American studies since the 1970s, discussions around themes of sexual orientation remained relatively hushed until the 1990s. The cultural nationalist movement designed to give voice to Asian Americans also repressed (homo)sexual difference. The editors of *The Big Aiiieeeee!*, in their preoccupation with manhood as traditionally defined, come close to making homophobic pronouncements: "It is an article of white liberal American faith today that

Chinese men, at their best, are effeminate closet queens like Charlie Chan and, at their worst, are homosexual menaces like Fu Manchu... The good Chinese man, at his best, is the fulfillment of white male homosexual fantasy" (xiii). Leong, whose highly elliptical "Rough Notes for Mantos" is included in *Aiiieeeee!* under the pseudonym Wallace Lin, reveals how "in the late 60s and 70s there was simply no room for sexuality that diverged from the conventional, even within Asian American movement or literary circles" (R.C. Leong, "Writing Sexualities"). The Asian American gay subject, as David Eng and Alice Hom have pointed out, is also marginalized in queer studies, which generally casts "the white, European, middle-class gay man as the unacknowledged universal subject" and ignores "how other axes of difference form, inform, and deform the queer subject" (12). Not surprisingly, it has taken a long time for gay Asian American writers to break out of the closet. But their writing plays an important role: "Through literature, queer Asian Americans have constructed a space where they maintain control over representations of queerness and at the same time illuminate the complexities of queer identity as it relates to ethnicity, gender, and the body" (Sohn 101).

Tackling crisscrossing lines of difference, Leong's articulation of a gay Asian American male subjectivity in "Phoenix Eyes" disrupts not only Asian patriarchy and American racial hierarchy, but also the unacknowledged universal subjects of Asian American studies and queer studies. The story follows the career of Terence, the narrator, a college graduate with a degree in theater arts and business communications. After being rejected by his parents because of his homosexuality, he lights out for Asia—Taipei, Hong Kong, and Osaka—where he works for a living as an escort.[6] The title calls attention to the possibilities of seeing outside the "normal" vision of the white and the Asian (American) heterosexual male subject. Terence elaborates on the meaning of "Phoenix Eyes" when he describes his work for the *hung kung hsien*, the international call line:

> We were all accessories. Whether we were from the country or the city, whether pure-blooded Chinese or mixed with Japanese genes... Or Malay. It didn't matter. We were beads on a string. A rosary of flesh... There was some room for variation, for beauty was in the eye of the beholder. I myself was called *feng yen* or "phoenix eyes" because of the way the outer folds of my eyes appeared to curve like the tail of the proverbial phoenix. Such eyes were considered seductive in a woman, but a deviation in a man. Thus, the male phoenix sings by itself, as it dances alone. (135)

Terence's "phoenix eyes" invite various interpretations. As a symbol of rebirth in Western mythology, the phoenix anticipates the theme of reincarnation that emerges at the end of the story. In the immediate context, however, the "phoenix eyes" call attention to the arbitrariness of societal standards and regulations. That the same shape of eye is seen as desirable in women but deviant in men underlines the vagaries of gender distinctions, of what constitutes feminine and masculine beauty. The synecdoche also hints at Terence's sexual orientation, which deviates from heterosexual norms. Such norms isolate gay people who, like the male phoenix that dances alone, must keep to themselves. In the light of Terence's profession, in which generic Oriental bodies are bought and sold, the phoenix eyes are likewise symbols of objectification: one is desired or shunned on account of some accident of phenotype. However, in the context of the narrative as a whole—which is seen from the point of view of those eponymous eyes—the object becomes the subject: the allegedly aberrant eyes of Terence look critically at Chinese patriarchy and the Orientalism of his white and Asian patrons. Through these eyes, Leong also provides us with glimpses of alternative masculinities.

Terence's optic provides, for instance, a sobering look at the neo-Confucianism and its attendant Chinese family values touted during the economic bloom in Asia in the 1980s. Leong, building on Dana Takagi's argument, has observed elsewhere that "the domain of the Asian American 'home' is usually kept separate from the desire of the sexual and emotional 'body'" (R.C. Leong, "Introduction" 5). Like Raymond in *American Knees*, Terence chafes under Chinese patriarchal mores. He is banished by his parents after he reveals his intention to remain single: "Ba and Ma had high hopes of me, of a wife and children soon... When I told them I would never marry, they threatened to disown me. It was as if I, the offending branch, had been pruned from the family tree" (130). Since traditional Chinese filial piety is defined partly by the obligation to beget offspring, to ensure the continuing growth of the family tree, Terence's refusal to marry and procreate is tantamount to a betrayal of the patrilineal family.[7]

In addition to confronting Chinese patriarchy, Terence also faces racism in the United States, where Asians are cast as hyper-feminine, awaiting the white male's consumption. He notes that when he was a student on the West Coast, "Asian men going together was considered 'incestuous'" (131), as though it were a perversion for Asians to be attracted to one another.[8] However, in Taipei, where Asians are the majority, Terence resents the objectification and exploitation of Asian bodies. Instead of worshiping white men, he is drawn to Asian males who are sexually, intellectually, and spiritually appealing. Where Ba in *The Winged Seed* is disempowered by his immigration to the United States, Terence is empowered by his sojourn in Asia. Instead of seeing fellow Asians as nerdy or wimpy, he soon encounters Chinese men whose virility is variously expressed.

Terence's phoenix eyes are thus not merely objects of the Orientalist gaze; they also stare back at the Orientalists and register their folly. One of the most insidious aspects of Orientalism—the equation of human bodies with art objects, or as props to bolster aesthetic appreciation—is relayed by Otto, a Swiss manufacturer of cookware who has a predilection for "slender Asians in their twenties, and important antiques" (135). No less vexing are those who view Oriental beauty as frozen in the past and who use the natives to enhance their admiration of classical art or poetry: "A certain Ivy League professor known for his translations of Sung poetry, loved whenever he was in Taipei, to … have Wan [Terence's co-worker] undress and dress for him" (133). Terence is told that these "horny American Sinologists … were suitable for conversation and culture … but not for their allure or their dollars. They were the Orientalist tightwads of the Orient" (133).

Orientalism is not confined to whites, however. Asians, especially wealthy males and females, also participate in the somatic objectification. A Chinese art connoisseur in Hong Kong has an eye for old Chinese paintings and young male bodies: "At the same time that he could appreciate esoteric old masters … his sensual tastes ran to young, unschooled hairdressers and bartenders with thick hair and bright eyes" (137). Businessmen's wives with unfaithful husbands pay for the spectacle and service of younger men: "We would set up parties for these *tai-tais*, who paid well for good-looking men. Struggling (but handsome) students, and out-of-season soccer players were my specialty. Women, we found, went for the strong thighs and tanned calves of the players, which performed more diligently than the listless limbs of their pale husbands" (137). Physical attributes such as "strong thighs" and "tanned calves" are ostensible accouterments of manhood. Yet the ways these brawny bodies are being used in the service of rich elderly women and men ("We gave up our youth to those who desired youth") (135) are viscerally emasculating.

Ironically, it is when Terence encounters an armless artist who paints with his toes and mouth that he has an epiphany about virility: "I looked at the crayfish emerging as his toes deftly controlled the bamboo brush… [Then] he bent over, inserting the brush into his mouth… The green carapace of a grasshopper emerged… How did he bathe or cook or make love? Despite his lack of arms, he seemed to have a part that I lacked" (139–140).⁹ The "part" that Terence—a dilettante in love and art—lacks may be a sense of purpose, commitment, or transcendence. But the phrase, coming right after the query about lovemaking, also links the lack to a sense of castration. The association of the armless artist with sexual potency is later made explicit when Terence induces the ejaculation of a Japanese businessman without using his arms or hands: "Flexing my calves and thighs, I pressed my feet together until finally he could not contain himself. At that moment, in my mind, I could see the painter" (141). Up against an artist whose inner determination transcends his physical handicap, Terence feels inadequate. Setting off this artist who uses his defective body to create beauty against young men who sell their beautiful bodies, Leong redefines masculinity as emanating from artistic and spiritual resources rather than from physical endowments.

Two other episodes stand out from the ubiquitous commerce of flesh to highlight Asian masculinity. The first is a sexual encounter between Terence and a Chinese waiter. The scene is, as far as I know, one of the first portrayals of passionate sex between two Asian men in American fiction. Like the lovemaking between Raymond and Aurora and between Raymond and Betty, it is an unabashed refutation of the pervasive belief in North America that Asians are not sexually drawn to one another. It is, therefore, not a coincidence that Terence has his uninhibited flings with Asian men in Taiwan, and not in the United States. The effete images of Asian men on American movie screens are a far cry from the passionate lovemaking between Terence and the waiter atop two red vinyl banquettes: "We lay on the slick vinyl, sweating and breathing hard... In the darkness, I fumbled for the ... sesame oil ... steadily working the oil and sweat between his legs" (136). The next day the waiter, who has to pay for his brother's tuition, asks Terence whether he can connect him with some American "friends." Terence immediately pulls out $50 for him, but the waiter vehemently refuses: "No... Brother, you are Chinese. We look the same... *I ch'uang t'ung meng*—though we sleep in different beds, we have the same dreams!" (137). The needy waiter has more compunction about commodifying Chinese than Terence's rich clients, and even Terence, who do not hesitate to exploit fellow Asians. Nevertheless, it is important to note that although Terence is of Chinese descent, he is an American citizen. His ready acceptance by the waiter as being "the same" by virtue of his race invites comparison with the primacy of race in determining whether one is granted or denied acceptance in North America, where

European immigrants are readily accepted because they "look the same," but Americans of Asian descent are regarded as perpetually foreign. In this light, "Phoenix Eyes" also risks reverse-stereotyping at times. The scathing portrayals of white characters such as Otto and the American literary scholar come across as caricatures. The Chinese waiter's willingness to fleece non-Chinese exclusively is likewise a form of racism.

The second episode also involves a bonding between a Chinese American (Terence) and a Chinese—P., the man who introduces Terence to the call line.[10] Just as the potent figure of the armless artist casts doubts on the often skin-deep attributes associated with masculinity, the tender friendship between Terence and P. challenges the common representation of gay relationships as driven primarily by sex. Terence first meets P. at the National Palace Museum in Taipei—another repository of art and artifacts. Yet the repartee between the two knowingly parodies class cleavages and the objectification of human bodies: "'You'd have been a good model for a stable boy.'... I retorted: 'And you are a Tang prince waiting to mount the horse?'" (132). Although P. and Terence come from disparate economic strata, both of them work as call boys, Terence for a living and P. for pocket change: "Sometimes after double-dating with clients... P. and I would fall asleep on the same bed, feeling safer in each other's arms" (134). During a visit to a lotus pond, P. tells Terence about his grandmother, who had the lowest status in the large household because she had not produced a male heir, but who had adopted and raised P. as her own son:

> Upon seeing [the white lotuses], he began to tremble. I put my arm around his shoulder. His grandmother ... had always looked forward to ... the blooming of lotuses... Each year, during the two or three weeks that lotuses were in full bloom, she would, just before dusk, pour clean water onto the bulb of each pale flower. At dawn, she would, with a tiny spoon, collect what remained on the flowers into a jar. This precious liquid, mixed with morning dew, would make the purest water for tea, enough to brew a single cup, which she would sip with him. (134)

P.'s explanation of the grandmother's lowly status is another indirect indictment of Chinese patriarchy, which disfranchises son-less mothers, daughters, and gay men. In contrast, the passage above adumbrates alternative forms of kinship. It registers a tender moment not only between the grandmother and P. but also between P. and Terence. The kindred feeling between the grandmother and P. is affiliative rather than biological. Similarly, the friendship between P. and Terence is akin to a fraternal bond. Analogous to the white lotuses that "pushed themselves up to reach the sun" from "the depths of mud and dark water" (134), the friendship between the two rises above the sordid commerce of their quotidian occupation. Like the grandmother sharing a special cup of tea in a manner reminiscent of communion, P. shares his precious past with Terence. The grandmother's nurturing presence also anticipates the mutual caring of the two sensitive men.

As indicated earlier, one of the strongest objections to homosexuality in traditional Chinese culture has to do with procreation or the perpetuation of the bloodline. Consequently, a heteronormative Chinese family home can become the most homophobic space. In "Phoenix Eyes," Leong offers several instances of virtual kinship independent of biological connection and based instead on *ren* or the ethics of care, including the relationship between P. and his grandmother, and between P. and Terence. The call line makes possible yet another affiliative family. Leong juxtaposes two parallel scenes to contrast Terence's filiative and affiliative families. At his biological father's 70th birthday banquet, which takes place after Terence's return to the United States, Terence feels uneasy accompanying his parents from table to table, imagining questions from the smiling guests, including: "Where are his wife and children? Why isn't he married yet?" (142). He is relieved upon reaching the last table to toast: "We lifted our last shots of brandy, like I had at my own farewell meal [in Taipei]… There, the members of my adopted family—P., Marie, Wan, Tan Thien, Otto, Li-ming, and the others whom my blood family would never meet— used me as an excuse to toast each other… I suddenly felt orphaned with my memories" (142). Terence feels much more attached to this alternative family than to his biological family. These forms of affiliation not only circumvent the heterosexist mandate of consanguinity but also, as Cynthia Liu rightly notes, aligns with Leong's activist pursuit: "Leong's self-awareness about the importance of community distinguishes his fiction from other attempts to merge an uninterrogated American individualism with Buddhism" (Liu 1; see also Chapter 9).

Leong resumes his critique of Chinese patriarchy when he discloses its treatment of family members with AIDS. After Terence returns to the United States, settling in Los Angeles, he receives a foreboding postcard from P., who has moved to San Francisco. Three days later he learns about P.'s death:

No funeral services were held in the states. His family ... were not alone in their desire not to see or hear about AIDS. In Asian families, you would just disappear... They simply could not call AIDS by its proper name: any other name would do—cancer, tuberculosis, leukemia. Better handle it yourself, keep it within the family. Out of earshot. (143)

Worse than being objectified is being treated as a cipher. For a man to contract AIDS in a homophobic culture is perhaps the ultimate "emasculation." The person needing utmost care and psychological and emotional support may instead become a source of shame and disgrace. If many Asian gay sons and lesbian daughters already feel ostracized in their filiative homes, those who are afflicted with AIDS are further quarantined and "shut up" (see also my analysis of Leong's "Your *Tongzhi* Body" in Chapter 9). Leong contravenes this erasure from the family by having Terence name his comrade at the end: "Only now I can say his name, because now it doesn't matter. Peter Hsieh, the beloved grandson of the general" (143).

Leong further gives P. another life by placing this sensual and sensuous tale within a Buddhist narrative frame. One of the unique features of this story is its blending or reconciliation of (homo)sexuality and spirituality, two areas that have been presented in agonistic terms in both orthodox Christianity (Sodom and Gomorrah; *Corinthians* 7) and in Buddhism, which considers desire and attachment the roots of human suffering. "Phoenix Eyes" opens in a Buddhist temple where P. and Terence used to go. Terence is listening to the five Buddhist precepts, saying "yes" to all but the last: "Do not have improper sexual relations" (130). The rest of the story is told, while Terence stalls for time, as a flashback of his life in Asia and the United States.

Throughout this flashback, Leong uses religious symbols to link the carnal and sacred realms, as in his description of the escorts as "beads on a string. A rosary of flesh"; in his reference to the phoenix, at once a glance at Terence's sexual orientation and a symbol of rebirth; and in his reference to the lotus blossom, a Buddhist emblem of purity and reincarnation and a reminder of the Platonic albeit also homoerotic friendship between P. and Terence. After P.'s passing, Terence reflects: "I thought that I was prepared to accept the news of his death. But I wasn't. Rereading his card, I began to tremble from the fear and beauty of his words, 'A new birthday in a new month.' Being nominally Buddhist, he believed in rebirth, and in good or bad karma begetting similar karma" (144). Terence's tremor recalls P.'s at the sight of the lotus flowers. Just as the flowers prompt P. to recall his grandmother's loving gestures, so P.'s beautiful words evoke memories of the now deceased speaker, the moment of tenderness between P. and Terence by the lotus pond, and the possibility of rebirth or transfiguration. The two remembrances not only illustrate that those who have passed away continue to live in the memories of those who love them but also imply, through the Buddhist allusions, that the beloved will live again in another life. By the end of the story, the narrator, who has balked at the fifth precept about abstaining from "improper sexual relations," finally says "yes." He senses P.'s visitation at that instant: "I could sense his presence nearby. He was not the one whom my eyes had sought and loved, or the one who had already lived and died. He was another—the one still waiting to be born" (144). It is possible that Terence, in answering affirmatively, has decided to forswear same-sex love, judged improper according to conventional Buddhist practice.

Yet the palpable presence of P. suggests another interpretation: Terence no longer considers homosexuality to be "improper." His relationship with P. surely rises above the liaisons, whether straight or gay, of the clientele at the call line or of the wealthy Hong Kong housewives and their boy toys. In this richly ambiguous ending, Terence could be saying "yes" simultaneously to the Buddhist precept against "improper" sex and to same-sex desire and love, thereby validating the homoerotic attraction between P. and himself as "proper."[11] Departing from the traditional Buddhist belief that desire leads only to attachment and suffering, Leong in a conference paper expresses the need "to overcome the split, fractured ways in which we analyze our nature," that desire "is inclusive of suffering, sexuality, and joy" (R.C. Leong, "Writing Sexualities"; unpublished conference paper). As Cynthia Liu puts it nicely, for Leong "the dialectic of mud and lotus is founded in their intimate coexistence" (Liu 1).

"Phoenix Eyes" thus exposes Orientalist exploitation of Asian bodies, reclaims same-sex love among Asians, and gives voice to marginalized men, including perhaps the most silenced—Asian AIDS victims. Leong defamiliarizes the racism against Asians and the stereotyping imposed on them in North America by setting the first part of his story in Taipei, in which whites are the foreigners, thereby reversing the Orientalist gaze and the racial hierarchy. Unlike the "typical" Oriental courtesan in French and English literature who, in Edward Said's words, "never spoke of herself … never represented her emotions, presence, or history" (6), the Chinese hustler in Leong's story is the one who gets to represent the "Occidental" clients.

More importantly, in speaking out against the heterosexual mandate of Chinese patriarchy, which makes AIDS unspeakable and its victims invisible and inaudible, and in memorializing an AIDS victim, Leong makes room in "Phoenix Eyes" (as in his poem "The Country of Dreams and Dust") for an alternative masculinity in sickness and restores dignity to the afflicted and the dying.

It is perhaps an odd choice for a feminist scholar to play fast and loose with a Chinese American flirting scholar, an evangelical preacher, and gay hustlers. Through my analysis of these male figures, I hope to unyoke masculinity from dominance or invincibility—traditional accoutrements of manhood. What Leong says of P.'s family in "Phoenix Eyes" is also true of men who still abide by the conventional code of masculinity: They are not willing "to admit at all that the myth of … invulnerability is simply a myth" (143). It would be both presumptuous and counterproductive for me to present "perfect" models, which do not exist, and arguably imperfection or vulnerability is what makes the figures analyzed endearing. The figure *that* most approximates a godhead is Ba in *Winged Seed*, who is also the most forbidding. Despite his altruism, he strikes his children (and the reader) as remote and elusive. By contrast, Wood, Raymond's father in *American Knees*, is deemed heroic by his son precisely because he has the courage to reveal his vulnerability. P., a source of disgrace for his Chinese family, is beautiful in Terence's (phoenix) eyes.

The three works covered all unsettle patriarchal, religious, and sociopolitical mores, questioning both much-vaunted Chinese family values and the die-hard racism in North America and revealing the crosscutting vectors that bear on manhood. The narrator in *The Winged Seed*, much as he venerates his father, critiques the conventional patriarch and the zealous evangelist in him who can be blind to the psychological needs of his own offspring. Both Raymond in *American Knees* and Terence in "Phoenix Eyes" resist their filial duty to marry and procreate. Leong exposes the compulsory heterosexuality that excommunicates gay progeny. He also subverts the Christian and Catholic bifurcation of body and spirit, as well as the Buddhist teaching of detachment, by reconciling sexuality and spirituality. Wong suggests that all kinds of ideologies and orthodoxies, including those pertaining to race, gender, and culture, can be reductive, vitiating interpersonal empathy.

Above all, these three works illuminate how manhood is inflected by various interlocking determinants, including position on the map. In *American Knees*, the difference in age, gender, and racial makeup between

Raymond and Aurora accounts for their varying degrees of "political correctness" and self-esteem. Though male privilege pervades both the US and Chinese cultures, men of Asian descent in North America may be subject to more negative stereotypes and greater social rejection than their female counterparts. Terence, who finds it awkward to date Asians on the West Coast, has no trouble consorting with Asian men in Taipei, where he prefers Asian to Caucasian lovers. Ba, a famous preacher in Hong Kong, becomes a "heathen minister" in the United States, scorned even by those he takes pains to succor. Perceptions about masculinity, and performances of gender, also fluctuate within the same country depending on the surroundings. Raymond, whose physical appearance arouses envy among Asian men, is invisible to white men; Ba, an impeccable and constantly available minister in public, can be a tyrannical and inaccessible father to his own children. Sexual orientation can nullify masculine prerogatives altogether under patriarchy. Leong illustrates that the discrimination faced by gay Chinese men is not just a sum total of their oppressions as gay men and as men of color. As gay Asians they are outside the definitions of manhood altogether in both American and Chinese cultures. Customary Chinese male privilege does not extend to gay sons; Chinese AIDS victims are often marooned and silenced by their own families.

While the characters in these works are far from paragons, they all subvert hegemonic masculine ideals and sociopolitical orthodoxies. Ba, Raymond, Wood, P., the armless artist, and Terence also furnish examples of alternative masculinity. Eloquent and sensitive, they belie the stereotype of Asian men as asexual nerds, contradicting the distorted representation of Hollywood movies, in which Asian men are almost never presented as desirable partners, whether for Caucasian women and men or for women and men of color. Instead of being males who dominate others by physical, economic, or political power, they manifest their masculinity through art, spirituality, and *ren* or care ethics. Art takes the form of Raymond's bedtime stories, Ba's handicraft and sketches, and the armless artist's paintings. Spirituality takes the form Raymond's increasing empathy for his father and partners, Ba's Christian devotion, the armless artist's inner resolve, and Terence's Buddhist quest. *Ren* or caring is embodied in Raymond's small acts of love toward Aurora and Betty, Ba's indefatigable ministration to the needy, and the reciprocal solicitude of Terence and P. In questioning received patriarchal values and political and religious orthodoxies, and in invoking alternative strengths, the authors prompt us to entertain other (hu)manly possibilities.

Postscript: I mentioned in the introduction the alarmingly sexist attempt in Chinese schools to address the "problem" of too many female teachers by recruiting more male teachers so as to instill "valor" in boys. But there is, thankfully, a counterpoint. During my recent sojourn in Shanghai (September 2015–August 2017), I learned a term for a new masculine ideal: *nuan'nan* 暖男, literally "warm male." The online *Chinese Urban Dictionary* defines the neologism as "a man who is friendly, caring, and positive"; "He might not be wealthy, but he's rich in empathy and positivity" (Li). This new model is attentive and understanding; at the same time "he is no wimp but a person of principle 暖男不能成为软男 … 要坚持原则" ("暖男"). This new ideal bodes well for some of the alternative attributes presented in this chapter. Whether this new model will travel across the Pacific remains to be seen.

Notes

1. This proverb can be traced to *Records of the Worthies* 《史记·淮阴侯列传》 by Sima Qian 司马迁: When Liu Bang 刘邦, who founded the Han Dynasties in 202 BC, asked his generals why he was able to defeat his rival Xiang Yu 项羽, he was told that *furen zhiren* was his rival's weakness, that Xiang Yu practiced nepotism and neglected talents outside his charmed circle. See http://chengyu.t086.com/cy3/3469.html. Confucius was no less reactionary toward class as toward gender. Citing Zhao Jibin, Kam Louie observes: "The 'people' in '*ren*' did not extend beyond the ruling class" (Zhao; Louie 48).
2. The novel has been adapted into *Americanese* (2006), a memorable film by Eric Bryer, starring Chris Tashima, Allison Sie, and Joan Chen. I thank Shawn Wong for bringing the DVD to Shanghai and for an evening of memorable conversation over dragon well and chrysanthemum tea.
3. I discuss similar silence as nonverbal expression of affection in *Articulate Silences* (Cheung, *Silences*).
4. Shawn Wong points out that Betty is a woman "comfortable with living without a defined past" (email correspondence October 20, 2015).
5. Cornel West argues that "Americans are obsessed with sex and fearful of black sexuality" (83). And one may add, oblivious of Asian male sexuality.
6. Sau-ling C. Wong describes this demimonde in Taipei as "the underside of the much vaunted Asian economic boom of the 1970s and 1980s" (94).
7. According to a Chinese saying, "There are three ways of being unfilial, the worst being childlessness 不孝有三, 无后为大" (my translation).

8. David Henry Hwang makes a similar observation in the Afterword of *M. Butterfly*: "Gay friends have told me of a derogatory term used in their community: 'Rice Queen'—a gay Caucasian man primarily attracted to Asians. In these relationships, the Asian virtually always plays the role of the 'woman'; the Rice Queen, culturally and sexually, is the 'man.' This pattern of relationships had become so codified that, until recently, it was considered unnatural for gay Asians to date one another. Such men would be taunted with a phrase which implied they were lesbians" (98).
9. This portrait is based on an actual artist Leong encountered in Chongqing, China. See Leong, "Memories of Stone Places" (9).
10. Leong reveals that P. is based in part on the famous Chinese writer Kenneth Pai (Bai Xianyong 白先勇) and his brother, offspring of a famous KMC general (personal communication, February 14, 2015).
11. Departing from the traditional Buddhist belief that desire leads only to attachment and suffering, Leong holds that desire "is inclusive of suffering, sexuality, and joy" and urges us "to overcome the split, fractured ways in which we analyze our nature" ("Writing Sexuality" 11).

Works Cited

Buck, Pearl S. *Fighting Angel*. New York: Pocket Books, 1936, 1964.

Chan, Jeffery Paul, et al. *The Big Aiiieeeee!: An Anthology of Chinese American and Japanese American Literature*. New York: New American Library-Meridian, 1991.

Chen, Chih-shen, ed. *Tang Po-hu tien Chiu-hsiang/yuan chu kao Pa-chih*. Taipei: Kai Hui, 1981.

Cheung, King-Kok. *Articulate Silences: Hisaye Yamamoto, Maxine Hong Kingston, Joy Kogawa*. New York: Cornell University Press, 1993.

———. "Of Mice and Men: Reconstructing Chinese American Masculinity." *Other Sisterhoods: Literary Theory and U.S. Women of Color*. Ed. Sandra Kumamoto Stanley. Urbana: University of Illinois Press, 1998. 173–199.

———. "The Woman Warrior Versus The Chinaman Pacific: Must a Chinese American Critic Choose between Feminism and Heroism?" In *Conflicts in Feminism*. Ed. Marianne Hirsch and Evelyn Fox Keller. New York: Routledge, 1990. 234–251.

Chin, Frank, et al. *Aiiieeeee! An Anthology of Asian-American Writers*. Washington, DC: Howard University Press, 1974/1983.

Crenshaw, Kimberlé. "Demarginalizing the Intersection of Race and Sex: A Black Feminist Critique of Antidiscrimination Doctrine, Feminist Theory and Antiracist Politics." *University of Chicago Legal Forum* (1989): 139–167.

Davis, Angela Y. *Women, Race, and Class*. New York: Vintage, 1983.
Eng, David L. *Racial Castration: Managing Masculinity in Asian America*. Durham: Duke University Press, 2001.
Eng, David L., and Alice Y. Hom, eds. *Q & A: Queer in Asian America*. Philadelphia: Temple University Press, 1998.
Friedman, Susan Stanford. *Mappings: Feminism and the Cultural Geographies of Encounter*. Princeton: Princeton University Press, 1998.
Fung, Richard. "Looking for My Penis: The Eroticized Asian in Gay Video Porn." In *How Do I Look? Queer Film and Video*. Ed. Bad Object-Choices. Seattle: Bay Press, 1991. 145–168.
Harris, Cheryl I. "Finding Sojourner's Truth: Race, Gender, and the Institution of Property." *Cardozo Law Review* 18.2 (1996): 309–409.
hooks, bell. *Feminist Theory from Margin to Center*. Boston: South End, 1984.
Hwang, David Henry. *M. Butterfly*. New York: Plume/Penguin, 1989.
Lee, James Kyung-Jin. "Li-Young Lee: Interview by James Kyung-Jin Lee." In *Words Matter: Conversations with Asian American Writers*. Ed. King-Kok Cheung. Honolulu: University of Hawai'i Press, 2000. 270–280.
Lee, Li-Young. *The Winged Seed: A Remembrance*. New York: Simon & Schuster, 1995.
Leong, Russell Charles. *The Country of Dreams and Dust*. Albuquerque: West End, 1993.
———. "Introduction: Home Bodies and Boy Politic." In *Asian American Sexualities: Dimensions of the Gay and Lesbian Experience*. Ed. Russell Leong. New York: Routledge, 1996. 1–18.
———. "Memories of Stone Places." *Emergence* 9.1 (1999): 149–162.
———. *Phoenix Eyes and Other Stories*. Seattle: University of Washington Press, 2000.
———. "Writing Sexualities: Death, and Rebirth in the Gay Diaspora." *Remapping Chinese America: An International Conference on Chinese American Literature: Program & Papers*. Taipei: Institute of European and American Studies, Academia Sinica, 1999.
Levenson, Joseph R., and Franz Schurmann. *China: An Interpretive History*. Berkeley: University of California Press, 1969.
Li, Mia. "That's Beijing." 15 December 2014. http://www.thatsmags.com/beijing/post/7989/chinese-urban-dictionary-nuannan (accessed 16 January 2016)
Ling, Jinqi. "Identity Crisis and Gender Politics: Reappropriating Asian American Masculinity." *An Interethnic Companion to Asian American Literature*. Ed. King-Kok Cheung. New York: Cambridge University Press, 1996. 312–337.

Liu, Cynthia. "'Phoenix Eyes and Other Stories' by Russell Charles Leong." *Tricycle* Spring 2001: 1–2.
Louie, Kam. *Theorizing Chinese Masculinity: Society and Gender in China.* Cambridge: Cambridge University Press, 2002.
Lowe, Lisa. *Immigrant Acts: On Asian American Cultural Politics.* Durham: Duke University Press, 1996.
Moy, James S. *Marginal Sights: Staging the Chinese in America.* Iowa City: University of Iowa Press, 1993.
Noddings, Nel. *Caring: A Feminine Approach to Ethics & Moral Education.* Berkeley: University of California Press, 1984.
Palumbo-Liu, David. *Asian American: Historical Crossings of a Racial Frontier.* Stanford: Stanford University Press, 1999.
Pan, Chun Ming, ed. *Tang Po Hu Wai Chuan.* Chiang-Su: Ku wu hsuan chu pan she, 1993.
Said, Edward. *Orientalism.* New York: Vintage, 1979.
Sellman, James D., and Sharon Rowe. "The Feminine in Confucius." *Asian Culture* 26.3 (1998): 1–8.
Sohn, Stephen Hong. "'Valuing' Transnational Queerness: Politicized Bodies and Commodified Desires in Asian American Literature." In *Transnational Asian American Literature: Sites and Transits.* Ed. Shirley Geok lin Lim, et al. Philadelphia: Temple University Press, 2006. 100–122.
Spelman, Elizabeth V. *Inessential Women: Problems of Exclusion in Feminist Thought.* Boston: Beacon, 1988.
Tajima, Renee E. "Lotus Blossoms Don't Bleed: Images of Asian Women." *Making Waves: An Anthology of Writings by and about Asian American Women.* Ed. Asian Women United of California. Boston: Beacon, 1989. 308–317.
Takagi, Dana Y. "Maiden Voyage: Excursion in Sexuality and Identity Politics in Asian America." *Asian American Sexualities: Dimensions of the Gay and Lesbian Experience.* Ed. Russell Leong. New York: Routledge, 1996. 21–35.
West, Cornel. *Race Matters.* Boston: Beacon, 1993.
Wong, Norman. *Cultural Revolution.* New York: Persea Books, 1994.
Wong, Sau-ling Cynthia. "Circuits/Cycles of Desire: Buddhism, Diaspora Theory, and Identity Politics in Russell Leong's *Phoenix Eyes*." *Amerasia Journal* 37.1 (2011): 87–111.
Wong, Shawn. *American Knees.* New York: Simon & Schuster, 1995.
Yamamoto, Hisaye. *Seventeen Syllables and Other Stories.* New Brunswick: Rutgers University Press, 1998.
Zhao, Jibin 趙紀彬. 《論語新探 [A New Exploration of the Analects]》. Beijing: Renmin chubanshe, 1962.

PART II

Genre and Form

CHAPTER 6

In(ter)dependence in Chinese/American Life-Writing: Liang Qichao 梁启超, Hu Shi 胡适, Shen Congwen 沈从文, Maxine Hong Kingston, William Poy Lee, and Ruthanne Lum McCunn

Is there an autobiographical tradition in China? Does the answer matter? Is there anything distinctive about Chinese American life-writing? In an essay entitled "This Is Not an Autobiography," Frank Chin denounced autobiography as a "peculiarly Christian literary weapon" that has "destroyed knowledge of Chinaman history and culture" (109).[1] Chin's animus toward the genre, as I posit in my second chapter, was a reaction to the ways in which early Asian American writers have had to employ autobiography as a means to be published and read by a mainstream audience. That these prototypes of ethnic life-writing might have accommodated to the tastes of American mainstream audiences should not warrant a blanket dismissal of the genre, however. What Chin sees as self-subordination in Chinese American writing has little to do with Christian influence but much to do with an interdependent mode of subject-formation that informs both the Chinese and Chinese American texts I analyze in this chapter.

Gish Jen, in *Tiger Writing: Art, Culture, and the Interdependent Self*, elaborates on "two very different models of self-construal" developed by cultural psychologists:

> The first—the "independent," individualistic self—stresses uniqueness, defines itself via inherent attributes such as its traits, abilities, values, and preferences, and tends to see things in isolation. The second—the

"interdependent," collectivist self—stresses commonality, defines itself via its place, roles, loyalties, and duties, and tends to see things in context. (7)

Jen connects the individualistic self with the West, especially America, and the interdependent, collectivist self with the East, including China, but she is quick to add that between these two lies "a continuum along which most people are located" and that individuals do not always abide by these "cultural templates" (7).[2] Still, these opposite modes engender "profoundly different ways of perceiving, remembering, and narrating both self and world" (8). Such differences in "narrating both self and world," I contend, account for some notable convergences (and also some divergences) in Chinese and Chinese American life-writing.

I disagree with F. Chin that there is no Chinese autobiographical tradition. While there might not have been any book-length autobiography in China before the nineteenth century (when Shen Fu沈复's posthumous *Six Records of a Floating Life*《浮生六记》became an instant best seller in 1877), there were always autobiographical sketches, in prose and poetry, such as the postscript to the *Shiji/Shih-chi*《史记》(*Records of the Grand Historian*) (c. 91 BC) by historian Sima Qian/Ssu-ma Ch'ien 司马迁 and "The Life of the Sire of Five Willows"《五柳先生传》(AD 392) by poet Tao Yuanming 陶渊明, both of which predated St. Augustine's *Confessions* (AD 398), which F. Chin considered to be the Ur-autobiography.[3] But my intent in this chapter is not so much to refute F. Chin's claim as to usher in a transpacific exchange that illuminates the interdependent self and directs attention to three Chinese American writers' polyphonic approaches to lifewriting; to cast a different light on some pertinacious controversies sparked by F. Chin in Asian American literary studies; and to reiterate a call made by him in the same essay for bicultural literacy, a plea eclipsed by his diatribe against autobiography. I use the term "life-writing" here to cover autobiography, memoir, biography, and even one biographical novel. I juxtapose three pre-World War II Chinese works—Liang Qichao 梁启超's "My Autobiographical Account at Thirty"《三十自述》(1902), Hu Shih 胡适's "An Autobiographical Account at Forty"《四十自述》(1933), and Shen Congwen 沈从文's *Autobiography*《从文自传》(1934)—with three postwar Chinese American works—*The Woman Warrior* (1976), William Poy Lee's *The Eighth Promise* (2007), and Ruthanne Lum McCunn's *Wooden Fish Songs* (1995). My comparison underscores what is distinctive about Chinese American life-writing, residing as it were somewhere along the "continuum" of interdependence and independence.

The first part of this chapter connects interdependent subject-formation with polyphonic life-writing by highlighting the constant fusion of autobiography and biography (especially that of the author's mother) in the two national clusters. It also shows how the two American ethnic memoirs differ from the Chinese self-portraits in cutting the individualist self greater slack. The second part situates interdependence in the extensive sociohistorical contextualization of Chinese (American) life-writing and traces the emergence of a distinctive ethnic subjectivity from uneven social relations. The third part intervenes in the critical controversies in Asian American literary studies concerning the use of exotic material, and recommends multicultural literacy as a means to obviate cultural misreading.

Before monitoring transpacific convergences and divergences, I need to note the differences within each group. Liang (1873–1929), Hu (1891–1962), and Shen (1902–1988), already introduced briefly in Chapter 4 as Xu Zhimo's close friends, were all eminent Chinese intellectuals. Liang, a political reformer and philosopher who advocated for Western reform during the reign of the last Qing emperor, had to flee China when the Empress Dowager launched a coup and put a price on his head. Hu was a vanguard in the movement promoting the use of vernacular Chinese in literature, and later the Republic of China's ambassador to the United States (1938–1942); he studied under John Dewey at Columbia and became a lifelong advocate of pragmatism. Shen was a prolific writer whose career came to an abrupt halt in 1949, when his works were banned on both sides of the Taiwan Strait. Under the Communist regime, he suffered a political purge, a mental breakdown, and a failed suicide attempt. Of all the modern Chinese writers, Shen, who was of partial Miao/Hmong descent, was most attuned to ethnic sensibility and "native soil" or local color.[4] Mo Yan, the 2012 Nobel laureate, compares himself with Shen: "I left school as a child and had no books to read. But [like] Shen Congwen, I had an early start on reading the great book of life" (2012).[5] Shen himself was twice nominated for the Nobel Prize in literature, in 1980 and 1988, and was slated to win in 1988, but he died (at age 85) before it could be awarded. He would have been the first Chinese writer to receive the award.

The three Chinese accounts vary in content and style. Liang's somewhat stilted treatise tells us less about the author than about his illustrious teachers and peers. The author acknowledges his debts to his various mentors, especially Kang Youwei/K'ang Yu-wei 康有为 (1858–1927), political thinker and reformer of the late Qing Dynasty, and painstakingly catalogs all their students. Hu's account, written in vernacular Chinese, is much more personal than Liang's in tone. He stresses how specific events and people shaped his intellectual development and how an individual may serve as an index of the time. Shen's autobiography, which describes his youthful encounters in Feng Huang 凤凰, his hometown in western Hunan, is much more literary than Liang's and Hu's, replete with colorful and astonishing reminiscences. In China, Liang's account is classified as autobiography and Shen's as literary autobiography, with Hu's open to debate as to which category it should fall under. I select these three texts because they exemplify interdependence and because they were published before 1949, before the maelstrom that roiled the Chinese literary tradition in the wake of the Communist Revolution.

Kingston (1940–), Lee (1951–), and McCunn (1946–) are known primarily as writers, not public figures, though Kingston has also achieved international fame since the publication of *The Woman Warrior* (1976).[6] Lee is a lawyer/banker turned writer. *The Eighth Promise* is a dual memoir (of the author and his mother), in which turbulent national and international events bleed into family history. McCunn has authored numerous biographical vignettes and five biographical novels. *Wooden Fish Songs* is about Lue Gim Gong (1858–1925), a horticulturist from Southern China. These three works were all published during or after the civil rights and Asian American movements; consequently, we find therein a certain ethnic gumption missing from earlier Chinese American writing.

The appeal of the accounts by Liang and Hu, owing to their statures as public intellectuals, is quite different from the hold of the other four works, whose fascination is in part ethnographical. This difference matters when it comes to the politics of representation. Those who read Shen are drawn by his literary ingenuity and regional flavor. Readers (especially non-Asians) who read Kingston, Lee, and even McCunn for ethnographic reasons may assume that their work is representative of the Chinese American experience, much in the way *The Narrative of Frederick Douglass* tells about the black ordeal of slavery. Behind this assumption also lies a certain condescension that American writers of Asian descent are only capable of unmediated representations and are not creative enough to venture beyond their own life experiences.

I select the Chinese American texts largely on formal grounds, to show how the three authors remodel life-writing with a dialogical structure. *The Woman Warrior*, in devoting a chapter each to a different woman, real or mythical, spearheaded a multivocal approach to autobiographical writing.

The Eighth Promise, in alternating the voice of the mother (recorded in her native Toisanese before being translated by the author into English) and that of the American native son, embarked on an interlingual memoir that is perhaps also the first mother-son duet in Asian American literature, a notable counterpart to James McBride's dual memoir *The Color of Water: A Black Man's Tribute to His White Mother*. *Wooden Fish Songs*, which triangulates the perspectives of a Chinese, a white, and a black woman, models a transnational and interracial approach to life-writing. As with the ethnic memoirs, interdependence informs both the "life" in question (in this case the subject of the biographical novel) and the narrative strategy of the author—to the extent McCunn can compose the biographical subject through the perspectives of three women who are close to Lue (whose own voice is palpably absent). McCunn constructs this central figure via an intercultural context through the vantage points of three intimate participant observers.

Interdependent Self, Genre Fusion, and Maternal Legacy

The notion of the interdependent self, which "finds meaning in affiliation, and duty, and self-sacrifice" (Jen 3), seems to have direct bearing on the fusion of biography and autobiography, the emphasis on maternal legacy, and extensive contextualization in Chinese and Chinese American life-writing. The interdependence implicit in the Chinese accounts takes the form of multiple points of view in the Chinese American texts. Unlike Liang's and Hu's self-representations, however, Kingston's and Lee's memoirs, perhaps owing to American individualist emphasis and diminishing regard for authority, exhibit greater nerves in setting the self in relief within an interdependent web and in allowing family secrets to come out of the closet.

The plural voices informing the two clusters suggest cultural persistence rather than Christian influence. Yu-ning Li, the editor of *Two Self-Portraits: Liang Ch'i-Ch'ao and Hu Shih*, gives a different reason for the self-effacement F. Chin imputes to Christianity. After tracing the beginning of Chinese autobiography to Sima Qian's *Shiji*, Li notes how "cultural expectations, such as modesty, reticence about one's abilities and achievements, and even self-deprecation, as well as keeping family affairs private, placed severe restrictions on the development of this genre" (Li 8). Li credits the West for bringing about "daring innovations in autobiographical and biographical writing" in the twentieth century (Li 8).

F. Chin is therefore right about the impact of the West in advancing Chinese (American) autobiography, but the de-emphasis of the self that he attributes to Christian self-loathing has more to do with Chinese cultural expectations, which have kept the self from being the centerpiece in the Chinese (American) texts, as evinced by the merging of autobiography and biography and the placement of personal narrative within a broad sociohistorical context. "Neither Liang nor Hu made a theoretical distinction between the principles of biography and the principles of autobiography," observes Li (9). He ascribes Liang's catalogues of his mentors and their students to an investment in group membership: "people are important not for their individual characteristics or actions, but for ... their participation in collective actions" (12). The "I" in Liang's and Hu's accounts, in Shen's autobiography, and to a lesser extent in Kingston's and Lee's memoirs, is either overshadowed by, or jostles against, other members of the family, historical and legendary figures.

The collectivist self noted by Li corresponds to the "interdependent self" expounded by Jen. The narrator of *The Woman Warrior* captures piquantly the difference between the Chinese collectivist identity and the American uncompromising individuality when she describes her difficulty in wrapping her head around the morphology of self-references in the two languages:

> I could not understand "I." The Chinese "I" has seven strokes, intricacies. How could the American "I," assuredly wearing a hat like the Chinese, have only three strokes, the middle so straight? Was it out of politeness that this writer left off strokes the way a Chinese has to write her own name small and crooked? No, it was not politeness; "I" is a capital and "you" is lower-case. (166–167)

While the narrator's perplexity might have nothing whatsoever to do with the etymology of *wo* 我—the Chinese "I"—and of the American "I," the two words furnish provocative visual metaphors for the position of the self—especially that of a child—in a traditional, extended Chinese family, in contrast to that of an European American self, which is often encouraged from a tender age to assert its "capital" individualist identity, especially in a nuclear family. The Chinese child in a traditional family is taught to honor all her elders in a hierarchical order according to age and gender, but because women are the ones who take care of children at home conventionally, the person with the strongest impact on the child is most likely to be the mother.

Thus, the profiling of maternal figures and the frequent fusion of autobiography and biography in the two clusters speak to the cultural persistence of interdependence. The works by Hu, Shen, and the three Chinese American writers all spotlight filiation. The first, and arguably best, chapter of Hu's autobiographical account is devoted entirely to his mother's betrothal and subsequent widowhood; it is therefore, strictly speaking, a biography. *Autobiography* by Shen focuses on his extended family, especially its Miao branch. In the chapter "My Family" 《我的家庭》, he traces his Miao ancestry through his grandmother, who, because of her low Miao status, was sent away by the grandfather's family to a remote region once she had given birth to two sons. In reclaiming his ethnic provenance, Shen has chosen to identify with his forsaken grandmother rather than with his powerful grandfather, an official under the Manchu government.

Kingston's memoir features five kindred and legendary women. The narrator boldly recreates a matrilineal tradition by casting her no-name aunt, her mother (Brave Orchid), her mother's sister (Moon Orchid), the legendary Mulan of her fantasy, and poet T'sai Yen as her "forerunners." In particular, she sees her mother as her Muse: "I too am in the presence of a great power, my mother talking story" (19–20). In fact, the text often conflates mother and daughter by encrypting crossidentifications. As Anne Anlin Cheng shrewdly observes: "Is not Brave Orchid, by name as well as by deed, the true Woman Warrior in the book?... Even the novel's subtitle ('Memoirs of a Girlhood among Ghosts') produces a confusion between narrator and mother" (Cheng 87).

The subtitle of Lee's memoir is expressly "Tribute to His Toisanese Mother." The "Eighth Promise" refers to the vow extracted by the author's grandmother from his mother to be compassionate to everyone. Told in the alternating voices of mother and son, this (auto)biography maintains that the mother's Toisanese tradition has enabled the family to survive a tragedy involving a homicide conviction of Lee's younger brother: "This is the story of my mother as my greatest wisdom teacher, who ensured that I received the best of my Toisanese heritage, the story of how my mother's Eighth Promise kept the ways of Toisan strong within us through life's ten thousand joys and ten thousand sorrows" (5).

Although maternal legacies inform both clusters, the two American memoirs differ from the Chinese counterparts in being much more self-assertive and much less reticent in venting family secrets. The narrator of *The Woman Warrior* acknowledges her mother as her inspiration, but depicts this maternal Muse as a domineering one whom the daughter must constantly butt against. The agonistic pas de deux distinguishes this American narrative from Hu's account, which pays unqualified homage to the mother. Another difference is Kingston's emphasis on the narrator's sedulous "self-invention"—an art that Paul John Eakin associates specifically with Western autobiography.[7] Even though the book features five women, the narrator is more interested in empowering herself through matrilineal help than in simply honoring her female ancestors. This memoir charts, paradoxically, an interdependent construction of an independent self, a collectivist making of a self-made woman.

Similarly, unlike the Chinese accounts in which the self is invariably upstaged, *The Eighth Promise* concentrates on Lee's tortuous journey to find himself during the fraught political climate of the 1970s, including nightmarish brushes with the American judicial system. Though the mother figures as a sustaining presence throughout this journey, most of the time she remains in the wings. Nevertheless, this portrait of a second-generation Chinese American offspring contrasts sharply with autobiographical antecedents such as Pardee Lowe's *Father and Glorious Descendant*, which flaunts how assimilated or Americanized the eponymous duo are, or Jade Snow Wong's *Fifth Chinese Daughter*, which relates how the daughter must overcome daunting patriarchal obstacles in her Chinese family to become a distinguished American woman. Lee's (auto)biography honors an empowering inheritance: the Toisanese maternal legacy that enables Lee and his family to triumph against formidable odds in the New World.

Wooden Fish Songs, told from the viewpoints of three women—Sum Jui, the mother in China, Fanny, the white adoptive "mother" in the United States, and Sheba, an African American maid (who eventually becomes a voluntary caregiver)—uses female voices to undermine patriarchal, Eurocentric, and Sinocentric views. Early Chinese American history has tended to focus on the predominant male population living in California Chinatowns. This biographical novel demonstrates that the first Chinese settlers are not all members of "bachelor societies," that women are fully influential in the immigrants' lives, and that their viewpoints are essential and irreplaceable in filling in those details missing from official annals. McCunn thus practices what Jenny Sharpe, speaking of the process by which an author reconstructs "a range of subjectivities from the fragmentary appearance of slave women in the historical records," describes as "literary archeology" (Sharpe xiv). In doing so, McCunn imaginatively pieces together the lives of her three female narrators from sketchy historical and legal documents.

The salience of maternal legacy is both a striking transpacific correspondence mirroring interdependence and a robust deviation from Chinese patrilineage. History, including Chinese family history, chronicles primarily if not exclusively the exploits of men. Jen mentions the common practice among Chinese families to keep a clan register; such a genealogical record, another index of interdependence, apparently enables her father to trace his pedigree back through 28 generations (Jen 12). In *Wooden Fish Songs*, the removal of the protagonist's name from such a clan register as punishment for Lue Gim Gong's escape, on the eve of his arranged marriage, to North America is the most draconian measure meted out by his clan in publicly disowning and disinheriting him, analogous to the prohibition against mentioning the No Name Aunt's name in Kingston's memoir, which McCunn consciously echoes: "if Gim Gong was struck from the *ga bo* [家谱, clan register], he would … forever be an outsider … a no-name man, a hungry ghost" (316). In the hope of forestalling such a hapless fate, Sum Jui begs Oi Ling (the daughter-in-law who has gone through the wedding ceremony with a rooster and who has already served as a "widowed" daughter-in-law for over 15 years) not to leave the family lest her husband be struck from the *ga bo*. "Am I in the *ga bo*?" Oi Ling retorts. "Are you?" She is then told by her father-in-law: "The names of daughters and wives are never entered" (364). McCunn thus pointedly indicates that women's names do not even ever "register" in a clan register.

Against such a long and extensive patriarchal history of female anonymity and invisibility, the life-writing of Hu, Shen, Kingston, Lee, and McCunn stands out conspicuously as counternarratives, as a calculated attempt on the part of these authors to write against the dominant patriarchal grain. The personal tenor of autobiography and the biographical novel gives the authors leave to recollect with honesty the persons whose influences have been the strongest on their lives; that these individuals happen to be their mothers is then no more surprising than the tributes paid by Malcolm X., Alice Walker, James McBride, and Mo Yan to their mothers in *The Autobiography of Malcolm X* (1965), *In Search of Our Mothers' Gardens* (1983), *The Color of Water* (1996), and "Nobel Lecture: Storytellers" (2012), respectively. *The Woman Warrior* is one of the first works that breaks away from an earlier Asian American autobiographical tradition by embracing Brave Orchid as a font of talkstory. No less generative, as cultural transmitter and enduring resource, is the mother in *The Eighth Promise*.

But the treatment of family history in the two national clusters diverges sharply. Liang and Hu magnify the creditable aspects. Li observes, "everything [Liang] says about his family is complimentary" (Li 11). Although Hu frowns on the "requisite encomium" (Li 11), he too puts his mother on a pedestal: "I lived under my mother's guidance for nine years, and was profoundly influenced by her. ... If I have learned one thread, one strand of good disposition ... if I am able to forgive and sympathize with others, I must thank my loving mother" (Hu 78). By contrast, the American ethnic writers do not scruple to pull the plug on family secrets, including maternal errancy. Kingston publicizes the rape of her father's sister as well as the mental breakdown of her mother's sister. Lee discloses not only his brother's conviction but also his mother's protracted love affair with a family friend. Such conventionally unseemly particulars concerning kinsfolk, let alone about one's mother, are seldom broadcast in the broad daylight of a Chinese autobiography, which routinely abides by the traditional precept to "keep family scandals from leaking out [家丑不出外传]."

The decisions by Kingston and Lee to share secrets unspeakable in China reflect both different moral codes in the ancestral and adoptive countries and the authors' awareness of the Chinese (and also American) double standard toward women and men. In Kingston's memoir, when the No Name Aunt was discovered to be pregnant during her husband's long absence, the villagers hounded her to death even though her pregnancy most likely resulted from a rape. The husband of another aunt—Moon Orchid—married again in San Francisco and repudiated Moon Orchid, but he got away scot-free. Lee's mother, who had had an affair with a family friend in San Francisco for many years till the lover died, would have never been able to do so, even with her husband's and sons' connivance, had she remained in her Toisan village. Perhaps it was because her lover, in being a most congenial paternal figure, was the antithesis of Lee's volatile father that both the biological father and the children accepted this alternative familial structure, which is yet another reconfiguration of interdependence. Publicizing these extramarital liaisons allows Kingston's narrator to reclaim her No Name Aunt and Lee to express his understanding of his mother's need for a gentle companion and to uncover patriarchal abuse and female strategies of resistance and accommodation.

Sociohistorical Contextualization and Ethnic Subjectivity

Gish Jen uses her father's autobiography, written when he was 85, to give her audience a feel of "how an interdependent self might narrate a life" (8). Jen Sr. begins his piece not with his birth but with a section entitled

"Ancient History," drawing from his aforementioned family's genealogy book and tracing his ancestry back 4500 years to the Yellow Emperor. "To trace your family back to the Mayflower is one thing," Jen muses. "This is more like tracing your family to Adam and Eve" (14). No less paramount is the sense of place, in its both physical and metaphorical sense: "Traditionally your hometown meant everything—interweave that it was of your physical context, your historical context, and your relational context; and a certain density of weave being common in China" (15).

The extensive background in the personal narrative cited by Jen brings us to another convergence between the Chinese and Chinese American texts, in which interdependence is extended to a macrocosmic context and, in the cases of Shen, Kingston, and Lee, to the formation of ethnic subjectivity. Liang contextualizes his birth with political events in Europe as well as in China: the Taiping Rebellion, the Franco-Prussian War, and the unification of Italy. The few lines about his birth, Li observes, "dramatically shift the context of Liang's life from a family which for generations had cultivated the land in an isolated rural setting" to the world of "modern international strife and change" (Li 11). Indeed, Liang's participation in the movement for a constitutional monarchy almost cost him his life when the Empress Dowager's coup put an abrupt end to the "Hundred Days' Reform" (1898). Hu similarly describes how he has been embroiled in the major controversies of his day. As a staunch champion for vernacular writing and democratic governance, he was subject to a lengthy suspension at his university.

International events equally impinged on the Chinese American lives that must come to terms with their ties to two nations. The collective consciousness evinced by Kingston and Lee in the wake of the civil rights movement resonates with an interdependent subject-formation that embraces a plural perspective of the world. Kingston's narrator shows how the Communist Revolution in China affected the life of her family in California and how World War II and the Korean War rendered Asian American children in public schools as alien others. The constant negotiation between divergent geopolitical perspectives and between conflicting Chinese and American norms nevertheless expanded the narrator's worldview: "I learned to make my mind large, as the universe is large, so that there is room for paradoxes" (Kingston, *WW* 29).

Lee, who participated personally in the San Francisco State University demonstrations for the establishment of Ethnic Studies, directly links his brother's troubles with the civil rights movement, and openly acknowledges its impact on his own ethnic awakening. His memoir implicitly aligns the mother's interdependent village life with her (and later her son's) active engagement with the diverse communities of San Francisco, all of which work to instill multiple ways of seeing. Lee learns from his mother's example when he tries to anchor himself during the tumultuous seventies: "In my odyssey, other tongues, intelligible voices, had been speaking to me and I was listening" (137). He tuned in to the voices of the Committee Theater Improvisation Troupe, City Lights Bookstore, the anti-Vietnam War movement, the counterculture, and the Southern civil rights movement. These motley constituencies were even more important than his biological family during his late adolescence in offering a sense of belonging, inculcating a sense of accountability, and fostering coalitions for social change. Just as the mother's upbringing in a Toisanese clan sisterhood allows her to embrace the different ethnic communities in San Francisco as an extended family, William's ethnic and racial consciousness is eclectically begotten, molded by people of all stripes and hues. The mother's interdependent ethos dovetails perfectly with the variegated formation of William's ethnic subjectivity, whose manifold origins also prevent identity politics from devolving into another exclusive entity.

Not that interdependence will automatically guarantee tolerance. Quite the contrary, it can sometimes degenerate into oppressive clannishness, in the form of malicious gossip, herd mentality, and ubiquitous surveillance, resulting in ruthless persecution of individuals who refuse to abide by communal mores. While Lee accentuates the nurturing dimensions of clan sisterhood in his memoir, Fae Myenne Ng, describing the community of sweatshop seamstresses who are the protagonist's mother's fellow workers in *Bone*, offers a more balanced view: "how often the sewing ladies were a gossiping pain and equally how often they were a comfort" (Ng 105). Communal gossip can turn easily into what erin Ninh calls "disciplinary technology," as surveillance (Ninh 129, 132–135). Jen too points out this "less salutary side" of interdependence: "the horror and *angst* of leaving an interdependent household or group can be inconsiderable" and "group policing can be intense and ruthless" (Jen 125, 126). In *River Town*, Peter Hessler notes that while a collectivist sense of self was conducive to social harmony, "once that harmony was broken the lack of self-identity made it hard to put things back together again"; personal accounts of the victimization during the Cultural Revolution "were surprisingly full of shame," with many victims believing "they were somehow flawed." It was like "a target of McCarthyism immediately breaking down and admitting that he was wrong" (cited in Jen 125–126).

A harrowing instance of group policing against the errant, nonconforming individual—the No Name Woman—opens *The Woman Warrior*. In *Wooden Fish Songs,* the victim is male. McCunn shows Lue's experience as a double exile during the second half of the nineteenth century when many Chinese laborers in California and Massachusetts were either driven out by white workers or lynched. Even Americans sympathetic to the Chinese considered them heathens who must be "civilized" by being converted to Christianity. Upon his return to China, Lue was harassed and persecuted by Chinese villagers on account of his conversion to Christianity. The immense pressure exerted on Lue by his white patrons in the United States to become Christian was matched only by the fanaticism with which his Chinese family attempted to exorcise the "Holy Ghost" from him. Thus, an interdependent orientation is neither good nor bad in itself. Depending on how it is inculcated, it can encourage tolerance or heighten bigotry, foster an inclusive community that values divergent perspectives or harden into a policing squadron that abets mass hysteria.

When the nonconformist is ethnicized or racialized, she will try to either "pass" (if there is a choice) and dissolve into the dominant culture or develop an ethnic consciousness, which can gather strength in the face of dominant suppression. In terms of a deliberate evocation of ethnic sensibility, cultural identification, and social awareness, Shen Congwen's *Autobiography* is a remarkable precursor to the American ethnic texts. Shen attributes his lifelong ambivalence toward mainstream society to his early exposure to the fringe environment, to his rural upbringing in the backwater of Chinese society before he moves to Beijing, the imperial capital. As an author of mixed Han and Miao descent who grew up in a terrain fraught with tension both between the Han immigrants and the Miao aborigines, and between the imperial soldiers and the local inhabitants, Shen details the peculiar practices of his ethnic community and the dominant culture's regulatory technologies.[8] In the chapter "A Lesson from the Xinhai Revolution"《辛亥革命的一课》, he divulges Manchu incursions in which soldiers randomly beheaded Miao villagers in the name of executing revolutionaries. After a few days of indiscriminate killings, the officials allowed the remaining captives to draw lots to determine who were to be executed. This chapter, which begins airily with excited teenagers (the author included) doing a literal head count, ends on a somber note: "I can never forget the desolate and plaintive expressions of those destined to die but unable to take their minds off their little ones at home.

What I saw gave rise to my lifelong revulsion against the abuse of authority and power" (24; my translation).

The two Chinese American memoirs are no less concerned with ethnic equality and social justice. The narrator of *The Woman Warrior* recalls her boss's glee in coining the phrase "nigger yellow" to describe a paint color at an art supply store; her objection to the offensive term was ignored. Another boss fired her for refusing to type invitations for a land developers' association that chose to hold a company banquet in a restaurant being picketed by CORE and the NAACP. In *The Eighth Promise*, Lee was suspended by his high school for protesting against the unfair treatment of the Chinese there. His parents decided to talk to the white principal. "But the principal got up from his desk, charged at Father, and started to scold him like a child, his fingers pointing in his face." In response, Lee's father "jumped up from his chair, and with his own fingers jabbing back like in a swordfight, scolded him back." The principal then "retreated behind his desk" (171–172). As a result of this dramatic showdown, which provides a cathartic moment in the memoir, young William was permitted to resume his study.

The three autobiographical texts as well as McCunn's novel also include culturally specific practices that can come across as "strange" to outsiders. Yet these practices may be integral to affirmation of a marginalized culture, or to the exposure of social inequality. In the chapter "What I Saw during *Qingxiang* [Purging of the Village]" 《清乡所见》, Shen remembers an incident involving a young tofu vendor who had disinterred a young girl from her grave and spent three nights with the body prior to returning it to the coffin. The vendor was arrested and sentenced to death. Just before his execution, young Shen asked him why he slept with the corpse; the vendor just smiled as though the inquirer were too callow to understand love, before muttering to himself, "Exquisite, exquisite [美得很,美得很]" (105; my translation). This incident left an indelible impression on the author.

Outlandish descriptions are also found in the three American texts. Ghosts of all kinds haunt *The Woman Warrior*. The narrator confides at the end of her second chapter (about the No Name Aunt): "My aunt haunts me—her ghost drawn to me because ... I alone devote pages of paper to her" (16). *The Eighth Promise* describes in detail the Toisanese nuptials between the author's parents and also many Chinese New Year rituals, selected recipes for "qi soup" requiring rare ingredients, and practices associated with the indigenous clan sisterhood. *Wooden Fish Songs*, like *The Woman Warrior*, recounts sundry supernatural visitations; and as does *The Eighth Promise*, it introduces an ethnic sisterhood—in this case a community without men altogether: "These women don't have to suffer childbirth or the responsibility of bringing up children ... and they govern themselves" (McCunn 363). All these texts incorporate beliefs and customs unfamiliar to mainstream and even Asian American readers.

The tendency to read Asian American life-writing as (auto)ethnography, however, makes some Asian and Asian American readers uneasy with these "exotic" descriptions and, as I mention in Chapter 2, partially explains the divided reception of *The Woman Warrior*. Well worth heeding is James Clifford's caveat that the traditional belief in the transparency of ethnography has crumbled, that "culture is composed of seriously contested codes and representations," and that "the poetic and the political are inseparable" (Clifford 2). In Shen's autobiography, Kingston's and Lee's memoirs, and McCunn's biographical novel, poetics and politics are thoroughly enmeshed to illuminate a marginalized cultural tradition. These texts all deplore the invidious treatment of people on account of ethnic, racial, or religious differences.[9] None of the (auto)biographers covered in this essay uses the genre, pace F. Chin, to express personal feelings alone. They use the form to wage some kind of war—be it political, linguistic, ethnic, or racial. In light of the works analyzed, autobiography is anything but a "Christian contraption" laden with "perpetual self-contempt and redemption, self-hatred and forgiveness, confession" (Chin, "Autobiography" 112). Here it is a vehicle of ethnic and feminist self-fashioning.

Bicultural Literacy as a Solution to Critical Conundrums

Because of the prevalence of ethnographic fallacy, the inclusion of sensational tidbits in Chinese American writing sometimes ruffles fellow Asian Americans who deem such material to be "Orientalist" or detrimental to the communal image. The anxiety is less about its circulation within the ethnic enclave than about its mainstream reception, its exposure to the non-Asian public. It arises, in my opinion, from a prescriptive interdependence between writers and audiences. To expect ethnic writers to be constantly on guard against the impressions non-Asians may get from their work is, however, a form of censorship. Furthermore, to suppress cultural difference so as to escape the stereotype of being a perpetual foreigner is to underwrite the most hegemonic form of assimilation.

Transpacific dialogues about autobiography can generate certain fresh insights into some standing controversies concerning genre, content, and audiences. Foremost in the divisive uproar over *The Woman Warrior*, both in China and in North America, is whether autobiography should admit fictional techniques and imaginative detail. Liang's account chronicles various historical events and consists entirely of facts. The reason, as Zhao Baisheng 赵白生 observes, is that Liang treats (auto)biography merely as a "branch of history 历史的一个分支" (7; my translation). Liang, in Zhao's opinion, does a disservice to biography which, unlike history, should focus on everyday anecdotes that reveal character or what Plutarch, in "The Life of Alexander the Great," calls "marks and indications of the souls 心灵的证据" (12; my translation). Even Hu's more literary account primarily tracks his intellectual growth. Although he borrows narrative techniques from fiction in the "Prelude: My Mother's Betrothal," describing his parents in third person and keeping the reader in suspense till the end that the elderly gentleman and the young girl portrayed in the preceding pages are his father and mother, the rest of his autobiographical account is told chronologically in the first person.

Shen, Lee, Kingston, and McCunn, on the other hand, disturb the distinction between (auto)biography and novel. Shen compiles a series of actual events during his childhood and youth, but skillfully filters them through the eye of a naïve narrator; the reader must read between the lines of his cavalier descriptions to see the skeletons beneath many a breezy yarn. Lee similarly uses literary techniques to organize his memoir and to build up to the harrowing events surrounding his brother's conviction. In *The Woman Warrior* and *Wooden Fish Songs*, fiction and nonfiction are thoroughly interwoven. Kingston collapses fact and fantasy as well as disparate Chinese legends, such as those of Hua Mulan and Yue Fei. In a chiasmic genre reversal, McCunn embeds into her novel countless factual details, accrued through her meticulous historical research about the protagonist's life.

How one evaluates genre fusion depends on how strictly one wishes to maintain taxonomical boundaries, and on whether one wishes to align biography with history or with literature. Disciplinary and genre distinctions remain sharp in China. Zhao Baisheng, echoing Mark Schorer's remark that "as a writer of fiction he was a free man; as a biographer, he is writing in chains" (Schorer 249), affirms that "biographers must wear a chain of facts" (B. Zhao 6). At an international biographical conference in Beijing (December 2010), one eminent Chinese scholar insisted on the sanctity of straightforward factual (auto)biography and considered a *literary* (auto)biography (传记文学) an adulteration. Yet back in 1902, Liang, notwithstanding his adherence to facts in his own autobiographical account, enunciated: "all the literature is history" (Liang, *Yinbingshi heji* 《饮冰室合集》 111; cited in X. Xu 17).[10]

I too would like to defend the value of "literary autobiography." Since autobiography is inseparable from "self-invention," imagination is always involved unless the chronicle consists only of externally attested facts. Shen apparently only records firsthand events in his *Autobiography*, but his delectable prose makes it read like a picaresque novel. The episodes are spiked with liberal dashes of authorial imagination, drawing the reader to its moral compass. The literary quality does not detract from its ethnographic or historical value; on the contrary, it enables Shen to impugn the Manchu regime's repressive measures: random killing of Miao civilians in the name of suppressing a rebellion and exterminating mavericks and potential dissidents in the name of purging a village. Though Shen was insinuating against a regime that already had been overthrown, similar abuses by the ruling power persist. Had these analogous repressions, along with the author's condemnation, been presented openly, Shen probably would not have been granted a hearing, even before 1949. His way around the restrictions was to couch political critiques in quaint vignettes.

In the West, "literary autobiography" is often designated as memoir, but the distinction between autobiography (supposedly factual) and memoir (which allows for poetic license) remains fuzzy. Western intellectuals such as Jean-Paul Sartre, Hayden White, and Jean-François Lyotard have cogently challenged the line between subjectivity and objectivity, fiction and nonfiction, literature and history (Sartre; White; Lyotard). Whatever the classification, a certain fictive element is assumed in life-writing. As Peter France and William St. Clair put it, "Biography is fiction, but without the freedom that the novel bestows on the writer" (France and St. Clair 1). The "distinction between reality and psychical reality," as Cheng notes, is especially thin (Cheng 119). As long as scholars are vigilant in differentiating original myths from inventive adaptations and in probing into the reasons why some authors wish to combine fact with fiction and objective observations with subjective impressions, we may unearth deeper truths in literary memoirs than in putatively factual autobiography. An author's reasoning may be literary, political, or both. Superimposing the story of Yue Fei on that of Mulan allows Kingston to redefine heroism by transferring power from "sword" to "word"—using the pen as weapon. As a writer and a feminist pacifist, Kingston has both literary and political stakes in imagining a woman warrior who defeats her enemy with words. Her "art of self-invention," as I argue in Chapter 2, involves rewriting patriarchal myths and turning jingoistic war cries into pacifist songs.

Another bone of contention among Asian Americanists concerns the use of alien or outlandish material (Chin, "Come"; Ma; Zhao Wenshu). Some critics balk at Chinese American writers' descriptions of rare or antiquated Chinese customs, such as the cutting of human flesh to express filial piety seen in Amy Tan's *Joy Luck Club* or the monkey feast related in *The Woman Warrior*. Yet analogous sketches in Shen's *Autobiography* have not aroused similar discomfort in China. The reason may lie in his avowal of "eccentric" behavior in his hometown: the author has informed the reader in the second chapter, "The Milieu of My Upbringing"《我所生长的地方》, that his village is regarded by urban folks as a "weird place [古怪地方]." Implicitly, he is asking mainstream Han readers to refrain from hasty judgment and to take in the locale's unique ambience.

Apropos of the episode about the necrophiliac tofu vendor, Shen's intention is not to use the macabre detail to titillate but to goad readers to see the incident through the perpetrator's eyes and to question the decapitation meted out by the Manchu officials. After all, the vendor has not committed any rape or murder, but he is executed for loving a young girl beyond the grave. His behavior is akin to Shakespeare's Romeo who, as soon as he learns about Juliet's death, resolves to "lie with" her that very night (5.1.34) and who has come down through literary history as the preeminent romantic hero. Shen's chapter exposes the ruthless practice of the Manchu soldiers, who see it fit to dispatch any minority member (in this case a cave dweller) who deviates from the established social norm. The nuanced ending of the chapter dispels any doubt as to where the author's sympathy lies:

> Vexed by the vendor's unremorseful demeanor, a soldier yells at him: "Rabid dog, aren't you afraid to die? I'm going to chop off your nutty head this very next minute!" The man only smiles softly and keeps quiet. His smile seems to register: "Who knows who's nuts here." This smile has not faded from my memory all these years. (55; my translation)

Shen's interpretation of the vendor's expression subtly reverses the official conception of sanity and insanity and casts a dubious shadow over the bloody purge of civilians who fail to conform to the national self-image.[11]

Had Shen published his *Autobiography* in English in North America, would he have been censured for using lurid details to regale Western audiences? In the early years of the People's Republic, Shen was purged for being "peach-pink" (i.e. pornographic) and "uncommitted" to the New

China (Kinkley 266), not for crowd-pleasing; whereas criticism regarding contemporary Chinese American writers' use of sensational material stems from anxiety over white audiences' (mis)perceptions. As Katheryn M. Fong complains in an open letter to Kingston regarding *The Woman Warrior*: "I read your references to mythical and feudal China as fiction.... The problem is that non-Chinese are reading your fiction as true accounts" (Fong 67). The mainland Chinese readers, familiar with the mainstream Chinese culture, are not troubled by Shen's inclusion of shocking incidents, just as American readers are not vexed by regional writers' display of local color, however eerie, as in Faulkner's "A Rose for Emily" (verily a Western "bedfellow" to Shen's "What I Saw during *Qingxiang* [Purging of the Village]," in plot and allegorical import). Put otherwise, critical discomfort with Orientalist content has less to do with whether it is "authentic" than how it may come across to a mainstream American audience that assumes the work to be representative of the author's ancestral culture or the immigrant community.

McCunn seems to have hit upon a methodological solution to this quandary. Although *Wooden Fish Songs* contains as many exotic details as does *The Woman Warrior*, she deflects the Orientalist gaze by juxtaposing Chinese beliefs in assorted ghosts with Quaker beliefs in a "Holy Ghost." Unlike works that set "odd" Chinese traditions against European American "norms," McCunn tells by turns the strengths and the blind spots of Chinese, European American, and African American cultures. The novel's three narrative viewpoints, which exemplify dialogic ways of seeing structurally and thematically, accentuate the importance of tuning in to voices from various quarters. The biographical novel shows how Lue's life is ravaged by the anti-Christian hysteria in China and by the racist laws in the United States—turning him into a pariah in both countries. Yet it is also on account of his ability to combine his hands-on knowledge of planting gleaned from Sum Jui, the botanical instruction given by Fanny, and the folk wisdom passed on by Sheba and her spouse that he achieves national renown as a horticulturist with an orange named after him in Florida. In synthesizing the contesting visions that Said attributes to exiles, Lue and the reader gain a triple "awareness of simultaneous dimensions" (Said 148).

Intercultural literacy, as exemplified by McCunn, offers perhaps the most effective solution to the problems arising from American audiences' unfamiliarity with Chinese literature. But for too long, Eurocentric education in the United States has worked against a heterogeneous approach to literature and culture. Unpersuaded as I have been by most of the assertions made by F. Chin in "This Is Not an Autobiography," I could not more fully agree with his plea for greater world literacy. Here I quote in full his imagined dialogue (alluded to in the second chapter) with his Berkeley dons:

> I am so fluent in your culture... Your language is mine down to the maggoty red raunch, for I know where it comes from. I went to school with your kids and know the lullabies you sang to them, the stories you told, the Aristotle, the Plato, the Homer, the Bible, the Shakespeare.
> But you don't know our lullabies and heroic tales, the myth and drama that twangs and plucks our sense of individuality, our personal relations with the authorities and the state. You should know. (Chin, "Autobiography" 118)

Both writers and readers who tackle Chinese archives need to do the requisite preparation, and certainly not all deviations from the original can be chalked up to artistry. There are differences, for instance, between Milton's and Christa Wolf's subversive revisions of Homer, the open admission by Kingston's narrator of cultural confusion as a *pre*text to engage in gender bending and artistic amalgamation, and the glaring mistelling of Chinese lore out of ignorance. Amy Tan, for instance, frequently "retells" traditional stories incorrectly. In *The Valley of Amazement* (2013), her latest novel, a celebrated fable by Tao Yuanming entitled "Peach Blossom Spring" 《桃花源记》 (summarized in Chapter 8), a utopian tale about an egalitarian society without government, is retold by a Chinese courtesan as a story promising "eternal youth" through sex: "If told in the right way, any man who hears it will wish to have your youth rub off on him. The actual rubbing, of course, will not happen until your defloration" (143). Since Tan's raconteur (unlike Kingston's narrator) was born and raised in China, one can only attribute the inaccurate rendition of "the story everyone knows" (144) to the author's negligence or unabashed foisting of spurious erotica. (*The Valley of Amazement* is much more "peach-pink" than anything Shen has ever penned.) Lapses along the same vein abound as well in Tan's *Joy Luck Club* and *Kitchen God's Wife*, as Sau-ling Cynthia Wong has shown. In order to judge whether Kingston's fusion of Mulan and Yue Fei, or Tan's transformation of a social utopia to an erotic paradise, is an innovative adaptation or a flagrant misrepresentation of Chinese legends, one must have a firm grasp of the sources used. Increasing intercultural literacy, as F. Chin urged almost three decades ago, ought to be taken up as one of the goals of transnational American studies. It would help writers better deploy, and critics better assess, intertexts in Asian American literature.

F. Chin was also half right about the considerable Western impact on the evolution of Chinese American autobiography. Although the self-subordination that he attributes to Christianity is actually very much a Chinese cultural legacy, the increasing lack of inhibition about disclosing psychological struggle and family secrets in contemporary Chinese (American) life-writing can well be attributed to Western influence. In his preface to "An Autobiographical Account at Forty," Hu was the first to acknowledge "the lack of biographical literature in China" and to admit he had urged friends to write their autobiographies to fill this gap (Hu 32). It was not until the twentieth century, thanks to Western influence, that the genre blossomed.

Many Western thinkers even extoll biography as the quintessential genre, perhaps because it swings the farthest to an independent self-construal. Dr. Johnson wrote in *Rambler*, N. 60 (13 October 1750): "No species of writing seems more worthy of cultivation than biography, since none can be more delightful or more useful, none can more certainly enchain the heart by irresistible interest, or more widely diffuse instruction to every diversity of condition" (Johnson 110). In "History" (1841), Emerson proclaims: "We are always coming up with the emphatic facts of history in our private experience, and verifying them here.... There is properly no history; only biography" (Emerson 4). Yeats surmises in his introduction to "The Resurrection" (1927): "We may think that nothing exists but a stream of souls, that all knowledge is biography" (Snukal 28).[12] The individualist emphases of these men of letters certainly have had a strong impact on Chinese and especially on Chinese American life-writing. I do not see this impact as a problem or as an adulteration. Each work discussed in this chapter puts a premium on competing modes of viewing life and society. Both Liang and Hu argue for the need to learn from the West.[13] Shen is mindful of preserving a record of the life of the Miao minority against the homogenizing influence of the Han mainstream. Kingston and Lee draw on maternal legacies to combat dominant American culture, thereby also decentering the patrimony vaunted in the works by and about the founding fathers. Where Liang and Hu use autobiography to promulgate Western knowledge, Shen, Kingston, Lee, and indeed F. Chin press (auto)biographical writing (or its parody in Chin's case) into the service of ethnic reclamation. McCunn's novel cautions against the bigotry fermented by an insistence on nativism, whether of Chinese or American vintage. Lue tells Sum Jui that just as he is able to produce a more hardy fruit by crossing different strains, "people can be improved the same way," that the "the strength of [the] Gold Mountain comes not from guns but from mixing together different peoples and new ideas" (McCunn 224). It is, therefore, especially ironic and counterproductive for Chinese and stateside critics to denounce a genre that has, on account of its mixed origins, been singularly amenable to cross-cultural imaginings. The point, surely, is not to eschew Western influence on Chinese (American) literature but to reclaim and promulgate—as Chin has attempted to do—a Chinese cultural legacy in America. Life-writing has facilitated ethnic and feminist awakening and cross-fertilization between worlds.

The texts analyzed in this chapter exemplify inventive crossings. There are obvious correspondences between the two national clusters. The melding of autobiography and biography, the emphasis on maternal legacies, and the contextualization of the self within familial, social, and political milieus all reflect interdependence and cultural persistence. The emphasis on female lineage can also be imputed to the genre itself. Unlike androcentric history, autobiography allows the author to pay tribute to the person—in many cases the mother—who most shapes his or her life. In addition to claiming a maternal legacy, Shen, Kingston, and Lee, who share a common authorial status as members of an ethnic minority, reclaim a marginalized cultural identity and uphold ethnic or racial equality. There are also notable divergences between the two clusters, owing to the dilution of ancestral culture across the Pacific. As Jen reminds us, "culture is not fate; it only offers templates, which individuals can finally accept, reject, or modify, and do" (7). Writing from the opposite shore, the American authors no longer feel constrained by disciplinary and genre boundaries between history and fiction, autobiography and literary memoir, and fact and fantasy; nor by qualms about airing dirty linen in public.

In addition to staging intercultural comparisons, I intervene in the literary controversies concerning the deployment of autobiography and the Chinese material therein. I posit that Kingston and Lee use their memoirs to wrestle with, rather than conform to, the dominant culture. By juxtaposing their works with Shen's autobiography, I show that what is seen as potboiler excess in one context may be appreciated as ethnic color in another, depending on the audience's cultural literacy. Taking cues from F. Chin and McCunn, I suggest two strategies to forestall tendentious "misreading": the decentering of cultural norms, as McCunn has done in *Wooden Fish Songs*; and the promulgation of Chinese cultural literacy, as espoused by F. Chin. This literacy nevertheless must go beyond the heroic tradition championed by the (s)wordsman to include, among others, the Chinese autobiographical tradition he claims to be nonexistent.

This interdependent autobiographical tradition redounds to the dialogism in the Chinese American texts. In the hubbub over Western influence on life-writing, no one, it seems, bothers to look the other way: to examine how Chinese and especially Chinese American writers have transformed (auto)biography, how they have infused multi-subjectivity into this most subjective "Western" genre. While writing from the perspective of more than one character has been a common fictional technique, Kingston might have been the first to orchestrate divergent viewpoints and to herald a matrilineal legacy in her self-portrait of an artist as a young woman. Instead of stewing about the excessive Western influence on ethnic autobiography, let us marvel at how the writers have refashioned life-writing in the process of self-fashioning. Kingston, Lee, and McCunn have turned what Yu-ning Li considers to be restraining Chinese protocols into narrative strengths by staging their memoirs and biographical novel with various speaking parts. If one of the greatest challenges in deploying more than one narrator in fiction is keeping the story focused, the individualist "life" featured in the three American texts provides a unifying "subject" for the ensemble. Negotiating between independence and interdependence, Kingston, Lee, and McCunn have transformed the most navel-gazing genre into a convivial literary rendezvous—bringing into conversation voices across generations, nations, epochs, race, gender, class, languages, accents, even across fact and fiction.

Notes

1. Chin states that, whereas "Chinese civilization is founded on history" (115), Western civilization is based on religion, and that the church and state are two sides of the same coin demanding the submission of the individual. Referring to *My Life in China and America* by Yung Wing 容閎 (1828–1912), he declares: "The first Chinese-American autobiography in English appears in 1910 [actually 1909], by a missionary boy… The first Chinese language autobiography of any kind appears in 1920. The Christian Chinese American autobiography is the only Chinese American literary tradition" (109). In *The Big Aiiieeeee!*, he further disparaged Yung as a "tourist guide" providing "titillation by his exotic and quaint revelations" (Chin, "Come" 11; see Floyd Cheung for a revaluation of Yung's autobiography).

2. Jen carefully avoids viewing the two modes of self-construals hierarchically, but presents them as equally viable ways of being that only come into conflict when jostling against each other.
3. Even if we fast-forward to the twentieth century, "My Autobiographical Account at Thirty" 《三十自述》 (1902) by Liang Qichao 梁启超 was written seven years before the publication of Yung Wing's book.
4. See Xinjian Xu (2009) for an overview of multiethnic literature in China.
5. *Soul Mountain* by Gao Xingjian, the 2000 Nobel Laureate, in which autobiographical anecdotes are animated by artistic finesse, is also highly reminiscent of Shen's *Autobiography*.
6. Former Presidential Press Secretary Bill Moyers said in his interview with Kingston on 25 February 1990 that her books were "the most widely taught on college campuses today, of any American author" (Tucher 11). In 1997, Kingston was awarded the National Humanities Medal by President Bill Clinton.
7. Among Eakin's examples are the autobiographical works of Mary McCarthy, Henry James, Jean-Paul Sartre, Saul Friedlander—and Kingston.
8. See Qi An for a historical analysis of this triangular tension in the Miao frontier.
9. Hence I take exception to Chin's insistence on autobiography being a Christian genre—as an extensive confession designed to gain acceptance by God or by the state. The works analyzed show little evidence of Christian motivation. Both Liang and Hu are known for their pragmatism. In the chapter "From Spirit Worship to Atheism," Hu emphatically states that he had stopped "believing in ghosts and souls" from a young age (88). Shen is intent on disclosing the spiritual practices of the Miao minority, especially the practices of the shamans. Kingston and Lee are Buddhists. Lee mentions that he attended a Christian church during high school, but he soon left it on account of its racist sermons.
10. In Chinese: "何止六經皆史…也可以説諸子皆史,詩文集皆史, 小説皆史, 因爲裏頭一字一句都藏有極可寶貴的史料, 和史部書同一價值" (《饮冰室》 111; cited in X. Xu 17).
11. Shen's chapter reminds me of Hisaye Yamamoto's "The Legend of Miss Sasagawara," an allegorical tale in which the narrator also reverses our notion of who is sane and who is mad at the end.
12. See Zhao Baisheng's *A Theory of Auto/Biography* 《传记文学理论》 for a thoughtful analysis of various theoretical currents about life-writing in China.
13. Liang recounts his momentous first encounter with Kang Youwei, when this reformer made him see the urgent task of acquiring knowledge of Western history.

Works Cited

An, Qi. "Protecting the 'Children': Early Qing's Ethnic Policy Towards Miao Frontier." *Journal of Cambridge Studies* 4.2 (2009): 24–36.

Cheng, Anne Anlin. "The Melancholy of Race." *Kenyon Review* 19.1 (1997): 49–61.

Cheung, Floyd. "Early Chinese American Autobiography: Reconsidering the Works of Yan Phou Lee and Yung Wing." In *Recovered Legacies: Authority and Identity in Early Asian American Literature*. Ed. Keith Lawrence and Floyd Cheung. Philadelphia: Temple University Press, 2005. 24–40.

Chin, Frank. "Come All Ye Asian American Writers of the Real and the Fake." In *The Big Aiiieeeee! An Anthology of Asian American Writers*. Ed. Jeffery Paul Chan, et al. New York: New American Library-Meridian, 1991. 1–92.

———. "This Is Not An Autobiography." *Genre* 18.2 (1985): 109–130.

Clifford, James. "Introduction: Partial Truths." In *Writing Culture: The Poetics and Politics of Ethnography*. Ed. James Clifford and George Marcus. Berkeley: University of California Press, 1986. 1–26.

Eakin, Paul John. *Fictions in Autobiography: Studies in the Art of Self-Invention*. Princeton: Princeton University Press, 1985.

Emerson, Ralph Waldo. "History." In *Self-Reliance, the Over-Soul, and Other Essays*. Claremont: Coyote Canyon Press, 1841, 2010. 1–18.

Fong, Katheryn M. "An Open Letter/Review." *Bulletin for Concerned Asian Scholars* 9.4 (1977): 67–69.

France, Peter, and William St. Clair. "Introduction." In *Mapping Lives: The Uses of Biography*. Ed. Peter France and William St. Clair. New York: Oxford University Press, 2002. 1–5.

Hessler, Peter. *River Town: Two Years on the Yangtze*. New York: Harper Perennial, 2006.

Hu, Shih 胡適. "An Autobiographical Account at Forty" 《四十自述》." In *Two Self-Portraits: Liang Ch'i-Ch'ao and Hu Shih*. Ed. Yu-ning Li. Trans. Yu-ning Li and William A. Wycoff. Bronxville: Outer Sky Press, 1933, 1992. 32–188.

Jen, Gish. *Tiger Writing: Art, Culture, and the Interdependent Self*. Cambridge: Harvard University Press, 2012.

Johnson, Samuel. *Selected Essays from the "Rambler", "Adventurer" and "Idler"* (Yale Edition of the Works of Samuel Johnson). Ed. W. J. Bate. New Haven: Yale University Press, 1968.

Kingston, Maxine Hong. *The Woman Warrior: Memoirs of a Girlhood among Ghosts*. New York: Vintage International, 1976, 1989.

Kinkley, Jeffrey C. *The Odyssey of Shen Congwen*. Stanford: Stanford University Press, 1987.

Lee, William Poy. *The Eighth Promise: An American Son's Tribute to His Toisanese Mother*. New York: Rodale, 2007.

Li, Yu-ning. "Introduction." In *Two Self-Portraits: Liang Ch'i-Ch'ao and Hu Shih*. Ed. Yu-ning Li. Bronxville: Outer Sky Press, 1992. 1–19.
Liang Ch'i-Ch'ao, 梁启超. 《飲冰室合集:文集》 [*Yinbingchi heji: Wenji*]. 14 vols. Beijing: 中華書局 [Zhonghua Shuju], 1941.
Liang Ch'i-Ch'ao, 梁启超. "My Autobiographical Account at Thirty 《三十自述》." In *Two Self-Portraits: Liang Ch'i-Ch'ao and Hu Shih*. Ed. Yu-ning Li. Trans. Yu-ning Li and William A. Wycoff. Bronxville: Outer Sky Press, 1902, 1992. 1–30.
Lyotard, Jean-François. *The Postmodern Condition: A Report on Knowledge*. Minneapolis: University of Minnesota Press, 1979, 1984.
Ma, Sheng-Mei. *Deathly Embrace: Orientalism and Asian American Identity*. Minneapolis: University of Minnesota Press, 2000.
McBride, James. *The Color of Water: A Black Man's Tribute to His White Mother*. New York: Riverhead Books, 1996.
McCunn, Ruthanne Lum. *Wooden Fish Songs*. Seattle: University of Washington Press, 1995, 2007.
Mo Yan, 莫言. "Nobel Lecture: Storytellers." 4 November 2014. http://www.nobelprize.org/nobel_prizes/literature/laureates/2012/yan-lecture_en.html
Moyers, Bill. "[Talk with] Maxine Hong Kingston [25 February 1990]." *World of Ideas*. http://www.pbs.org/moyers/journal/archives/kingstonwoi.html (accessed 15 September 2015).
Ng, Fae Myenne. *Bone*. New York: Hyperion, 2008.
Ninh, erin Khuê. *Ingratitude: The Debt-bound Daughter in Asian American Literature*. New York: New York University Press, 2011.
Roosevelt, Theodore. *The Works of Theodore Roosevelt*. 20 vols. New York: Scribner, 1926.
Said, Edward W. *Reflections on Exile and Other Essays*. Cambridge: Harvard University Press, 2002.
Sartre, Jean-Paul. *Nausea*. Trans. Lloyd Alexander. New York: New Directions, 1938, 2013.
Schorer, Mark. "The Burdens of Biography." *Michigan Quarterly Review* (1962): 249–258.
Sharpe, Jenny. *Ghosts of Slavery: A Literary Archeology of Black Women's Lives*. Minneapolis: University of Minnesota Press, 2003.
Shen Congwen 沈從文. *Autobiography* 《从文自传》. Beijing: Renmin Wenxue Chubanshe 人民文学出版社, 1934, 1988.
Snukal, Robert. *High Talk: The Philosophical Poetry of W. B. Yeats*. New York: Cambridge University Press, 1973.
Tan, Amy. *The Valley of Amazement*. New York: HarperCollins, 2013.
Tao Yuanming, 陶渊明. "The Life of the Sire of Five Willows 《五柳先生传》." In 《古诗文英译集: *An Anthology of Ancient Chinese Poetry*.》 Ed. Sun Dayu, 孙大雨. Trans. Sun Dayu, 孙大雨. Shanghai: Shanghai Foreign Language Education Press, 1995. 72–75.

T'ao, Ch'ien. "Peach Blossom Spring [《桃花源记》]. In *Anthology of Chinese Literature: From Early Times to the Fourteenth Century*. Ed. Cyril Birch. Trans. Cyril Birch. Vol. 1. New York: Grove Press, 1965. 167–168.
Tucher, Andie, ed. *Bill Moyers: A World of Ideas*. Vol. 2. New York: Doubleday, 1990.
White, Hayden. *Metahistory: Topics of Discourse*. Baltmore: John Hopkins University Press, 1978.
Wong, Sau-ling Cynthia. "'Sugar Sisterhood': Situating the Amy Tan Phenomenon." In *The Ethnic Canon: Histories, Institutions, and Interventions*. Ed. David Palumbo-Liu. Minneapolis: University of Minnesota Press, 1995. 174–210.
Xu, Xinjian. "On Historical View of Multiethnic Literature." *Journal of Cambridge Studies* 4.2 (2009): 15–23.
Yung Wing 容闳. *My Life in China and America*. New York: Henry Holt, 1909.
Zhao Baisheng, 赵白生. *A Theory of Auto/Biography*《传记文学理论》. Beijing: Peking University Press, 2003.
Zhao Wenshu, 赵文书. "Why Is There Orientalism in Chinese American Literature?" In *Global Perspectives on Asian American Literature*. Ed. Guiyou Huang and Wu Bing. Beijing: Foreign Language Teaching and Research Press, 2008. 239–258.

CHAPTER 7

Theorizing in Narrative Form: Bing Xin 冰心

"The Photograph"《相片》—a short story appearing originally in Chinese in 1934—puts across a sophisticated representation of transcultural and interracial dynamics and heralds many of the theoretical insights later articulated by postcolonial scholars and Asian American critics. Its author—Bing Xin (pen name for Xie Wanying 谢婉莹, 1900–1999)—began her literary career around the time of the May Fourth Movement (1919) and earned her master's degree from Wellesley College (under the name of Wan Ying Hsieh) in 1926. Though one of the most esteemed Chinese authors of the twentieth century, Bing Xin is known principally as an author of literature for children and young adults. This very different story, published during a period in China (1917–1937) that Shu-mei Shih has termed "semi-colonial" (x–xi), advances—along with the writings of Pearl Buck—a trenchant assessment of racial hierarchy and cultural imperialism. Its configuration of transnational contact crosses the boundaries of Chinese, Chinese American, gender, ethnographic, and postcolonialist studies; critiques both American colonialist assumptions and Chinese traditional values; and casts innuendoes about cultural approaches to transracial adoption. It also sheds new light on an author who, I believe, has been subjected to a gendered reception in China. The May Fourth Movement, for all its rhetoric of emancipation, tended to discount political and cultural critiques by women writers, much as the cultural nationalist movements during the US civil rights era tended to eclipse or compartmentalize the intellectual contributions of women.[1]

While "The Photograph" has received scant critical attention in China, it is anthologized in *The Short Story and Photography 1880's–1980's*, edited by Jane M. Rabb, in which Bing Xin is the sole Chinese author and one of only three women writers included alongside luminaries such as Raymond Carver, William Faulkner, Thomas Hardy, Eugène Ionesco, Thomas Mann, and Cynthia Ozick. This story charts an unusual East-West encounter through a detailed psychological portrait of Madam Simpson, an American who has spent 28 years in China. Retiring from her post as a music teacher in a missionary school, she adopts eight-year-old Shuzhen after the death of Mister Wang—the girl's father and Madam's Chinese tutor. When Shuzhen is 18, Madam takes her to New England, where they meet Reverend Li and his son Tianxi; a friendship and a nascent romance develop between the two young persons. On seeing a photograph of Shuzhen taken by Tianxi, Madam abruptly announces her intention to return to China. This tale is told in third person, two-thirds of it from the limited point of view of the white expatriate; but there is a section—during the time when Madam and Shuzhen are in New England—in which the author shifts to an omniscient point of view, thereby affording a glimpse beyond Madam's tunnel vision. At first Madam comes across as a cosmopolitan and compassionate woman; unlike her missionary compatriots in New England, who view China as a backward heathen country, she prefers China to the United States. Reading between the lines, especially through the perplexing ending, however, the reader can discern troublesome undercurrents of Orientalist condescension and colonial possessiveness on the part of Madam, and of self-repression and internalized stereotyping on the part of Shuzhen.

The story exemplifies and predates, almost by half a century, Edward Said's well-known pronouncements in *Orientalism*: "When one uses categories like Oriental and Western as both the starting and the end points of analysis ... the result is usually to polarize the distinction ... and limit the human encounter between different cultures, traditions, and societies" (45–46). Since Said's seminal study about the tendentiousness of bifurcating peoples as Orientals and Occidentals, there have been numerous interventions, including his own *Culture and Imperialism* (1993), about colonialist legacies. Especially relevant to my literary analysis are the works of Ali Behdad, Vincent John Cheng, Frank Chin et al., Rey Chow, Arif Dirlik, David L. Eng, Dominika Ferens, Christina Klein, Susan Sontag, and Mari Yoshihara. While taking cues from these scholars in teasing out the multiple strands in "The Photograph," I marvel at how the narrative anticipates many of their insights, at how the Chinese author—like the black female writers lauded by Barbara Christian—has engaged in "theorizing ... in narrative forms" (52).

Bing Xin was undoubtedly influenced by her contemporary and friend Pearl Buck in deploring American missionaries' condescending attitudes toward the Chinese. Like Buck and Xu Zhimo (the semi-fictional lovers in Anchee Min's *Pearl of China*, discussed in Chapter 4), Bing Xin had lived in both China and the United States and was thoroughly conversant with both cultures. Where familiarity with another world allowed Buck and Xu to look critically at their own, Bing Xin alone unmasked, via fiction, the complicity of America and China in concocting what has come to be known as Orientalism.

Buck, though acute in criticizing American arrogance vis-à-vis China, still presented in *The Good Earth* a timeless and typological view of the Chinese as hard-working, land-loving, long-suffering and, in the case of O-lan, the "heroine," silent and self-sacrificing. These "favorable" images of the Chinese might be a far cry from Fu Manchu and Charlie Chan, but they smack of what the *Aiiieeeee!* editors have described as "racist love." Bing Xin, by contrast, adumbrates not only the sinister aspect of racist love but also its shaping power on the beloved who takes pains to conform to the image of a compliant subject.

COMMODIFICATION AS CHINOISERIE AND AS AFFECTIVE LABOR

Madam Simpson's juxtaposition of China and the United States seems of a piece with the American white, middle-class mentality during her time. As Mari Yoshihara notes in *Embracing the East*, in the wake of industrialization, commercialization, and urbanization, "Americans were anxious to assert and maintain the ideas and values considered to be lost in modern society, such as purity and sincerity" (Yoshihara 26). Thus, the most prevalent Orientalist conception between the 1870s and 1940s was an association of "the powerful West ... with virile masculinity, and [of] the subordinate East with passive femininity" (4), along with "premodern simplicity, naturalness, tradition" (26). Anxious to retain values considered to be lost in the age of industrialization and associating anti-modernist qualities with Asian arts and artifacts, Americans turned to "the production, use, and display of Asian-style goods [to] represent and promote their moral and cultural refinement" (26). Such consumption and display, Yoshihara observes, reinforced the white, middle-class women's place in Victorian domesticity while veiling the underlying "gender and racial ideologies" (26).

Madam Simpson, notwithstanding her extensive sojourn in China, exhibits the same nostalgia for a pre-modern tradition when she is back in the United States—which she deems less refined than China. When she returns to her New England home every seven years, it no longer feels like home to her, and she is annoyed by the uncouth American youth who "would quickly show their lack of interest or respect, and on occasions would even laugh and sneer at her." At such times she would retreat into herself with "thoughts, fond thoughts, of another place far to the east, where she truly felt at home ... [where] she had raised the quiet and virtuous Shuzhen" (Bing Xin, *Photograph* 234–235; all English citations are to this edition). Throughout the story, Madam and other Americans consistently equate Chinese virtue with reticence: "The girl had a certain quality and character that simply could not be found in Western girls. She possessed a quiet depth" (241).

This polarization of the United States and China—especially the association of verbal restraint with Eastern decorum—places Madam squarely in the company of American Orientalists. Frank Chin et al., the editors of *Aiiieeeee!*, specifically impute the Western association of Asian virtue with silence to "racist love" (Chin et al. xxv; Chin and Chan, "Racist"). Although the editors have in mind the stereotypes imposed on Asian Americans, their deliberation is equally applicable to American perceptions of the Chinese:

> One measure of the success of white racism is the silence of that [minority] race and the amount of white energy necessary to maintain or increase that silence... The stereotype operates as a model of behavior... [resulting] in the neutralization of the subject race as a social, creative, and cultural force... Given fear of white hostility and the white threat to the survival of the subject minority ... embracing the acceptable stereotype is an expedient tactic of survival. (Chin et al. xxv–xxvii)

The editors assert that European Americans divide racial minorities by commending Asians who are quiet and submissive to white authority while reproving other racial minorities—notably African Americans—who challenge white supremacy. Furthermore, this maintenance of racial hierarchy requires ethnic cooperation, a point also made by Arif Dirlik when he observes that Orientalism calls upon "the complicity of [Asians] in endowing it with plausibility" (Dirlik 108). Madam Simpson may not be consciously imposing a confected perception on Shuzhen any more than Shuzhen is consciously living the stereotype, but the reiteration of the adoptee's laudable reserve strikes an all too stereotypical note. Since the white mother is literally the benefactor, the orphan may have embraced the cherished image as an "expedient tactic of survival."

The dynamics in the adoptive relationship in "The Photograph" appear invidious not only in the older woman's equation of Shuzhen's taciturnity with Eastern mystique but also in her objectification of the girl, who is recurrently compared to exotic flora:

> One summer day, like a dainty willow blossom borne on a summer breeze, Shuzhen fell gently into the courtyard of her heart... The girl was as frail as a willow blossom, thin, sickly, and pale. But there was something about this young thing that so contrasted with the dark and lifeless atmosphere around her that Madam Simpson could not forget the little girl. (237, 239)

Yoshihara writes that American catalogs of East Asian merchandise around the turn of the twentieth century contain "photographs and illustrations not only of items being sold—such as ivory carvings, embroideries, porcelains ... but also of landscapes, people, and various images of the Orient" (Yoshihara 31; see also Behdad). In Madam's mind, Shuzhen seems to blend imperceptibly with Chinese sceneries and curios. Such a "package deal" may explain why the white woman, whose "life was stagnating like a pond in summer with no source water and no outlet" (237), adopts the Chinese girl on a Christmas Eve:

> In the light of the blazing fire the older woman looked into the gaunt and timid face and those deep-set black eyes: there was something so mysterious, so desolate in this tiny thing. Madam Simpson slowly reached out and touched the hand of the girl... She slowly began to sense that it was not just the hand of a little girl that she was holding; she was now grasping Mister Wang's poetry, Mrs Wang's exquisite embroidery; she was holding the very essence of Eastern womanhood, all the silent mystery of ancient China. (240)

One cannot find a more telling inventory of Orientalism. Instead of embracing Shuzhen in flesh and blood, Madam regards her as an exotic Christmas present—a cryptic parcel of Chinoiserie, the very embodiment of ancient China. Bing Xin reinforces her characterization of Madam as someone enamored of old China by using, whenever she enters the expatriate's mind, stylized poetic similes such as "a dainty willow blossom borne on a summer breeze" and "a stream in a meadow" in contrast to her unadorned presentation of the thoughts of Shuzhen or of the conversation between Shuzhen and Tianxi. One is reminded of Buck's prose in *The Good Earth*, which also uses rather stylized language to describe Chinese rural life.

To Madam Simpson, Shuzhen stands as an automated China doll. She therefore does not seem particularly concerned with the adoptee's emotional well-being, though she is fully aware of the girl's physical, verbal, and emotional inhibition:

> And so for the next ten years Shuzhen grew up at the side of Madam Simpson. The girl was like a stream in a meadow, its slow water too deep to gurgle, too placid to be heard. Although well cared for, Shuzhen remained a short and skinny girl, and her face was always a sad, pale shade. She never showed sorrow, never showed joy. She answered when spoken to, but no more, and she went around the house as silently as if she were on tiptoes. (241)

This depiction reminds one of a timeless Chinese tableau rather than of a budding teenager. Considering that the girl is constantly *beside* Madam, her reserve may have emanated from a sensing of an unremitting maternal surveillance. Madam certainly finds the hushed yet solicitous presence to be a solace. The attention she bestows on Shuzhen is requited manifold by the girl—the daughter who plays the role of a scrupulous handmaiden, ever mindful of her adoptive mother's needs and silently active in the wings.

> Whenever Madam Simpson was sick, the lass would quietly and meticulously take care of the older woman with gentleness and genuine feeling. Whenever Madam Simpson would look up from her bed, Shuzhen was always sitting at her side... "You're like an angel sent from Heaven!" Madam Simpson would always want to say, but as she looked into that ashen face and sorrowful eyes, she would hold back her words. (241)

Shuzhen is, in effect, performing what David Eng terms "affective labor." Calling attention to "the racialization of intimacy in our global age," particularly to the widespread adoption of Chinese girls by US citizens, Eng cautions: "we need to consider how the stereotype of the hard-working, agreeable, and passive Asian girl, ever eager to please, works to smooth over political problems, economic disparities, and cultural differences" (Eng 109, 110). Madam subscribes to such racial categorization and takes for granted Shuzhen's constant vigil. She seems content as long as the rueful teenager "serves" as her guardian angel. Not once does she attempt to find out the cause of the girl's timidity or plumb the depth of her sadness. Shuzhen later confides to young Tianxi: "Since my father died, I have always felt no one understands me in my silence" (253).

Not that an emotional bond is absent between the adoptive mother and the child. But what connects the two is not mutual understanding but forlorn co-dependence:

> Both of them felt like outcasts in the world, lonely fragments that fit only into each other. The sense of loss and loneliness brought them closer together that day [after sweeping Mister Wang's tomb during Qing Ming Festival]. As they walked home, Shuzhen could feel herself being bathed in the motherly love and compassion that Madam Simpson had for her. They never went out much; Madam Simpson slowly lost contact with most of her friends, and she even lost interest in collecting antiques. Her life was now centered on this fair and delicate willow blossom, Shuzhen. (242)

Madam Simpson's fondness for the girl is clearly due in part to their similar personalities: gentle, reticent, withdrawn, despondent, and self-conscious. The fact that the twain share these attributes suggests that they are, *pace* Madam, neither exclusively Chinese traits, nor the epitome of Eastern womanhood. Her maternal devotion, however palpable in the passage, is undercut by her acquisitiveness and possessiveness, and her unwitting exploitation of Shuzhen. In a Chinese article on "The Photograph," Qiu Yanping 邱艳萍 and Li Baiqing 李柏青 notice that Madam stops keeping a dog and collecting antiques soon after the adoption, as though "Shuzhen were merely 'a little dog' and an 'antique' to allay her loneliness" (27). Although Qiu and Li have not linked such fungibility with what has come to be associated with Orientalism, they rightly characterize Madam's maternal love as abnormally domineering.

Especially unsettling is the American mother's fear of losing her daughter to marriage: "There was something in that thought that froze her heart… Loneliness, a chilling sadness overwhelmed her… She trembled … and pushed that terrifying thought out of her mind"; "if anyone should broach the subject of Shuzhen's marriage, Madam Simpson would simply smile smugly, and with practiced tact change the subject" (242, 243). The translation "terrifying" fails to capture the sense of the original Chinese expression "*buxiang* [不祥]" (Bing Xin 397), meaning *inauspicious* or *ominous*. Few mothers would consider with trepidation the prospect of a daughter's marriage. Presumably Madam is perturbed by its consequence of her being left alone. Her selfishness in wishing Shuzhen to remain with her forever is a far cry from maternal love but is perfectly in line with her commodification of the girl: as antique, pet, and handmaiden all in one.

RACIST LOVE

The asymmetrical relationship between the two is even more pronounced after Shuzhen accompanies Madam Simpson to New England, where the American mother is occasionally "asked to speak at the church on the present situation in China" while the Chinese daughter "would quietly sit and listen. . . . Everyone thought she was adorable. Her quiet and respectful disposition was especially admired by the older women who showered the girl with little gifts" (245). Madam is regarded as the authority on China; Shuzhen, as the demure Oriental. The white woman fits the profile of what Dirlik calls "Sinified Westerner" whose "'Orientalization' was what qualified [her] to speak for the Orient"; Shuzhen, on the other hand, is emblematic of "self-Orientalization" (Dirlik 110, 111). The church ladies' eleemosynary attitude, along with Madam's "matronizing" behavior, also brings to mind what Stacilee Ford terms "maternal exceptionalism"—in reference to American women "who drew on their national and gender identities, particularly their 'feminine' roles as mothers and/or nurturers, to claim a certain authority" in Asia (Ford 114).

Bing Xin's oblique remonstration of orthodox Christian attitudes toward the Chinese was no doubt inspired by Pearl Buck's unflinching criticism of missionary condescension in an essay entitled "Is There a Place for the Foreign Missionary?" published in *The Chinese Recorder* in 1927 and its sequel "Is There a Case for Foreign Missions?" published in *Harper's Magazine* in December 1932, just over one year before "The Photograph" appeared in print. In the first piece, Buck asked her readers "the question of whether or not any one has the right to impress upon another the forms of his own civilization, whether those forms be religious or not" (Buck, "Place" 102). In November 1932, Buck delivered a speech for a Presbyterian gathering at the Astor Hotel, in which she related her "findings in four decades as a mission child, wife, and teacher" (Spurling 204) and deplored the conceited attitudes of Christian missionaries who considered themselves dispensers of civilization charged with enlightening backward Chinese heathens:

I have seen the missionary narrow, uncharitable, unappreciative, ignorant
... so filled with arrogance in his own beliefs ... so lacking in sympathy for
the people they were supposed to be saving, so scornful of any civilization
but their own ... so coarse and insensitive among a sensitive and cultivated
people, that my heart has fairly bled with shame. (Buck, "Case" 144)

Buck went on to point out the futility of sending out missionaries who were not only arrogant but oblivious of the people they were trying to convert and their civilization: "I grew up among these and I know them," she said bitterly, describing an entrenched white community that refused to look beyond its own received opinion and rigid codes of conduct. "Very nearly was I moved to turn against all Christianity and all missionary work" (Buck, "The Whole Christ" 450). Buck laid bare the underlying missionary assumption that has preempted treating the other as equals:

We have approached these foreign countries not in the spirit in which Christ approached men. We have come too often in lordliness and consciousness of race superiority... We have had the abominable attitude of one who confers a favor. We have felt we were making a sacrifice... We have ... so entangled the simple, clear teachings and life of Christ with the trappings of our western civilization that we are now fairly open to the accusation that we have come seeking to impress our civilization upon the civilization of another race. (Buck, "Place" 104, 105)[2]

Buck is both an astute postcolonialist precursor and a brazen Orientalist. Chinese scholar Guo Yingjian 郭英剑 extols Buck as "a pioneering figure of postcolonialist literature" ("后殖民主义文学的先驱者") (24). What Buck and contemporary postcolonialist scholars have in common, Guo observes, is their multicultural awareness, their determination to promote the "other" culture in the West and their boldness in chastising Eurocentrism. He adds that not only did Buck anticipate Said's seminal critique but, as someone who focuses on China, she also filled a massive gap in Said's *Orientalism* (25). Despite her disapproval of missionary superciliousness toward the Chinese, however, Buck still succumbs in her fiction to the "discourse of Orientalism," which Yoshihara believes to have contributed immensely to the popularity of *The Good Earth*: "Through her mastery and display of ethnographic details and her construction of an authorial narrative voice, she simultaneously established her position of expertise vis-à-vis her Western readers and gained authority over her Chinese subjects ... placing Buck in a position of superiority over her Chinese subjects" (Yoshihara 152–153).

Bing Xin shares Buck's distaste for haughty American missionaries, but she also indirectly exposes, in the guise of another white female narrator in "The Photograph," Buck's own "position of superiority" as discursive authority over China. The two female writers were no strangers. Chen Shu 陈恕, Bing Xin's son-in-law and biographer, relates that the two women became friends when Buck returned to China in 1933 (after winning the 1932 Pulitzer Prize for *The Good Earth*) and that Bing Xin organized a press conference for Buck at the University of Nanking 金陵大学. In 1936, when Bing Xin and her husband, both teaching at Yenching University 燕京大学 at the time, were about to go abroad for their sabbatical, she received a telegram from Lossing Buck, Buck's first husband, inviting the couple to stay with him in Nanjing (Chen 157). Bing Xin most probably would have read Buck's "Is There a Case for Foreign Missions?" and related essays.

The subject of American missionary condescension toward the Chinese is explicitly broached in "The Photograph" by Tianxi, who feels pinioned by white patronage:

> I also am the product of a missionary school... Last year the church sent Father here to study more theology, and they also have supplied me with a very generous stipend so I can come and attend classes. The sad part is that I would prefer to study art, but because of the conditions set up by the church, I must attend classes on theology. They want to make me into a pastor ... but I have no desire to wear a black robe and stand behind a pulpit all my life! (251)

The missionary treatment of Tianxi dovetails with the manner in which Shuzhen is molded by Madam. Both young persons have been recipients of white beneficence with invisible strings attached. Tianxi receives a missionary stipend to study theology at the expense of pursuing his own interests; he is expected to serve the church in return for the evangelical assistance. Similarly, Shuzhen is expected to repay Madam's kindness by attending to her adoptive mother at the expense of her independence, personal growth, and pursuit of happiness.

Through Tianxi—who chafes under the ethnographic gaze of the American missionaries and questions their premise of cultural superiority and their supposition that Cathay can be easily encapsulated and known (specifically through him as a participant-observer)—Bing Xin anticipates Said's critique of a reductive colonialist epistemology and its attendant hierarchy:

To speak at the church and have people come up to me afterwards and ask questions about China scares me to death. From my scant twenty years of life, what do I know about four thousand years of Chinese history and what it means to us today? The very idea of doing that annoys me... What rattles me even more is when people say that China had no culture before the coming of Christianity. At the seminary they ... call me a "model Chinese youth." Some of the educators who have been in China ... like to take me with them on their fundraising campaigns... [They] introduce me to the audience with something like, "Just look at the kind of Chinese youth our education there has produced!" Isn't that just the way a circus man shows his trained monkey to the crowds? (251)

Tianxi's scathing comments about Christian educators prefigure not only Said's arguments but also those of the editors of *Aiiieeeee!* concerning "racist love," of Ferens regarding the white gaze, and of other Asian Americanists (such as Victor Bascara, David Eng, David Palumbo-Liu, and Lisa Lowe) who have demystified the dubious construction of the "Asian American model minority."

In accordance with "racist love" and "racist hate"—white approbation of tractable racial minorities and condemnation of those who challenge white supremacy—the American missionaries at the turn of the twentieth century took pride in the Chinese who accepted Christianity and denounced as heathens the adherents of ancestral worship. Tianxi complains that even Chinese Christians are subject to the white gaze, paraded as the trophies of evangelical triumph. His description of the farewell ceremony for a missionary about to leave for China further reveals the dismal American view of indigenous Chinese culture: "The missionary candidate ... says a final sad but stirring farewell, and everyone shows the person the utmost respect and pity as if the fellow was heading for some disease-infested jungle full of savages!" (252).

This negative association of China with malaise and barbarism seems antithetical to the assessment of Madam, who holds a highly positive, if also romanticized, view of the culture—so much so that she has virtually made the country her home. She so prefers respectful Chinese youth to their boisterous American counterparts that she scrupulously brings up Shuzhen as pure "Chinese":

> Everyone praised Madam Simpson for how she raised Shuzhen: for the ten years that she took care of her in China, Shuzhen remained entirely Chinese in looks, action, and spirit. She never wore Western clothes. Except when

with folks who could not understand Chinese, Madam Simpson never spoke to the girl in English. If any of the boys from the school came to their house for an occasional party, Shuzhen would timidly stay at the Madam's side and would never enter into the games or bantering. Even when she passed the candied fruit or other refreshments, she would always keep her eyes modestly downcast and speak in a whisper. (243)

Madam's sinophile attitude may seem a welcome exception to American missionary vilification of China. But in ensuring that Shuzhen conforms to her notion of a Chinese paragon, the adoptive mother is no less self-serving and guilty of typecasting than her compatriots. The racist love she showers on Shuzhen is merely the flipside of the racist hate of her peers who openly revile Chinese culture. Shuzhen's Chineseness is being inculcated not through interaction with other Chinese but by being confined to "Madam's side," under the maternal assumption that the "get-togethers ... most young people enjoy so much were uncomfortable times for Shuzhen, and she never liked them" (243). Once removed from Madam's watchful eye, however, Shuzhen relishes the companionship of young people (especially Tianxi's) in New England. Thus, one must interpret the alleged preference for solitude as a concession to maternal wishes, to the alien mother's "Chinese" upbringing of her.

Contesting Epistemologies

In *Cold War Orientalism*, Christina Klein distinguishes between European texts about Asia published before World War II, which generally paint Asians as racially inferior, and postwar American texts that tend to espouse "racial tolerance and inclusion" and serve as "the official ideology undergirding postwar expansion." She argues that by forging "emotionally satisfying bonds across the divides of difference ... the sentimental could serve as an instrument for exercising power" (Klein x–xi, xiv–xv). Although "The Photograph" was published before World War II, it brings out the two forms of Orientalism expounded by Klein—one dismissing Asians as inferior and the other demonstrating white sympathy. Of specific relevance is Klein's point about the "double-edged" power of sympathy in interracial adoption. Adducing the example of the Welcome House, an adoption agency that Pearl Buck launched in 1949 "to find families for Asian and part-Asian children born in the United States whom other agencies refused to handle," Klein connects adoption across racial boundaries with Cold War Orientalism: "The white mother that figured so prominently in postwar middlebrow culture ... possessed a complex genealogy... The infantilization of racialized Others and marginalized social groups has been a standard rhetorical means of legitimating unequal power relations" (175).

Madam Simpson seems a precursor to the postwar middlebrow white mother figure in her unwitting assumption of control over Shuzhen. Her possessiveness, already perceptible in China where she would brush aside any thoughts of Shuzhen's marriage, becomes manifest in New England when she comes across Tianxi's photo of Shuzhen:

> Madam Simpson suddenly froze in shock!
> In the background was the thick, gnarled bough of an old oak, its branches adorned with new leaves, at the bottom was a lush green lawn, and in the middle was Shuzhen. Her hands were on a picnic basket that she was opening ... her face reflected all the young woman's spirit, personality, and joy. Her perfect smile revealed her beautiful white teeth, and in her eyes there was a vitality that Madam Simpson had never seen in the girl for the ten years she had known her!
> Madam Simpson trembled slightly. A deep and dark feeling suddenly seized her. It was not fear, nor was it anger, it was not even remorse... She clutched the photograph tightly as she stared at it. (257)

In the Chinese original, Shuzhen's expression registers more than "vitality": "her face is awash with coyness; her smile is suffused with rapture and tenderness [满脸的娇羞,满脸的笑,惊喜的笑,含情的笑]" (《相片》 405). The original leaves little doubt that Shuzhen is in love with Tianxi, a development that startles Madam. The photographic image is her first glance at Shuzhen's passion, spirit, and womanhood. Because of her vested interest in keeping the adoptee primly Chinese, she is alarmed by the lusty metamorphosis.

The reader, on the other hand, has already witnessed the girl coming to life before Tianxi after she meets him at a dinner. Upon listening to his critique of the American missionaries, she feels galvanized by his presence, which she likens to "an illuminating light so warm and powerful that it penetrated and enveloped her very soul. As she looked into Tianxi's face, his cheeks burning and eyes blazing with passion for the truth he spoke, tears began to well up in her eyes" (252). Tianxi's impassioned speech obviously strikes a deep chord in Shuzhen, who realizes, perhaps for the first time, the extent to which she has been constructed and conditioned by her adoptive mother. Unlike the mother, who has persisted in seeing Shuzhen as the embodiment of ancient Chinese art, Tianxi "could immediately sense the 'new China' ... a dynamic and progressive China" in Shuzhen (253). Tianxi and Madam Simpson clearly do not see eye to eye. Whether or not his perception is any more accurate than hers, the discrepancy suggests that the image of an impassive daughter is largely a maternal fantasy, perhaps reinforced by the role Shuzhen has felt compelled to inhabit beside Madam.

Instead of being pleased by the photo, which foregrounds a sensuous and vibrant young lady, Madam is distraught. Her ineffable bewilderment may be diagnosed as a form of "Orientalist melancholia"—a term coined by Rey Chow to describe those white sinologists who feel contemporary Chinese writers cannot live up to age-old Chinese literary criteria: "But this moralistic indictment of the other's infidelity masks a more fundamental anxiety ... that the Chinese past which [the sinologist] has undertaken to penetrate is evaporating and that the sinologist himself is the abandoned subject ... [that] the historical relation between the 'first world' and the 'third world' is reversed" (Chow 4). Madam experiences a similar "dis-Orientation" brought on by the stark new impression of the Chinese girl she has presumed to "know" so well hitherto. She feels destabilized by another subjectivity, displaced by an alternate epistemology.

SUBVERSION OF THE MASTER'S TOOL

"The most grandiose result of the photographic enterprise is to give us the sense that we can hold the whole world in our heads—as an anthology of images... It means putting oneself into a certain relation to the world that feels like knowledge—and, therefore, like power ... it turns people into objects that can be symbolically possessed," Susan Sontag observed (3, 4, 14). The Orient serves as a prime example. "At the origin of photography is 'the Orient,'" Ali Behdad reminds us, noting that Paul Nibelle, one of the early advocates of this technology in the Middle East, remarked that "'perhaps for the first time we will have truth in place of fiction'" (Behdad 1; Nibelle 64). But Nibelle's statement cannot be farther from the "truth." Photography in Sontag's formulation and Behdad's rendition constitutes a perfect trope for the relationship between the colonizer and the colonized.

Bing Xin's title conjures up this fraught relationship, albeit with a subaltern twist, calling attention to both hegemonic and *Other* ways of seeing. Most of the narrative sketches of different characters are mediated by Madam's limited perspective, filtered through her Orientalist lens. In making Tianxi the photographer in the story, the author wrests the authority from Madam and enables the reader to detect the distortions and oblique angles in her framing of the Chinese characters, particularly Shuzhen. If camera work is often made to serve possessive colonialist ends, Bing Xin—by using Tianxi's eyepiece to contest the essentialized image of the deadpan Chinese girl—shows it is possible to use the master's tool to deconstruct the master's predatory vision.

Madam Simpson is shaken by Tianxi's snapshot because the image is so different from her own "still life" picture of the girl. She may even feel betrayed or deceived by Shuzhen's Oriental veneer that she herself has taken such pains to construct and preserve. Moreover, her response to the youthful image inverts another one of Sontag's premises: "All photographs are *memento mori*. To take a photograph is to participate in another person's (or thing's) mortality, vulnerability, mutability ... to contact or lay claim to another reality" (Sontag 15). Far from allowing Madam to participate in *another person's* mutability or to lay claim to another reality, the image of her daughter exuding "the fragrance of youth" trains her eyes on her own fading beauty and mortality: "She looked across the room at the mirror on her vanity. Her hair was disheveled ... and her face was ashen white. She peered at her own bloodshot eyes, and at the wrinkled face" (259). Madam had affixed the adjective "ashen" to Shuzhen previously; now the relation between the "first world" and the "third world" (to echo Chow) and between the subject and object is reversed.

Above all, the photograph intensifies her greatest fear all along: the adoptee's marriage. Though she does not explicitly trace her consternation to that dreaded prospect, her reaction upon viewing the picture replicates her earlier jitters at the thought of Shuzhen's marriage: "there was something in that thought that froze her heart... She trembled ... and pushed that terrifying thought out of her mind" (242). In both instances, she "froze" and "trembled." The close-up undoubtedly telescopes in her mind's eye the looming possibility of losing Shuzhen to Tianxi, and this time she cannot simply banish the thought. The tightness with which she clutches the photo reflects her nervousness about losing both cognizant and physical grasp of the girl and her determination to hold on to the adoptee.

The snapshot had been taken in Madam's absence during an excursion. Being ill, she could not join the young people for the outing: "She was going to ask Shuzhen to stay home and take care of her, but ... because she assumed that Shuzhen would not go alone anyway, she said half-heartedly that the girl should go on ahead with them" (258). Her inner thought betrays her manipulative control and her limited understanding of the adoptee for, to her surprise, Shuzhen "smiled and told the group she would join them, and they all ran down the porch steps and disappeared in the car" (258). The teenager's readiness to leave Madam behind puts one in mind of Zora Neale Hurston's folktale "'Member Youse a Nigger'" in which the white master expects his slave John to stay with his "loving" family after emancipation. Yet John is more than happy to leave: "Ole Massa kept callin' 'im and his voice was pitiful. But John kept right on steppin' to Canada" (Hurston 90). Shuzhen may feel grateful enough to Madam, but she too wishes to unloose herself from the white matron.

In New England, Shuzhen has become an evolved fledgling eager to take wing. Her repression and inhibition hitherto have been to a large degree conditioned by Madam rather than intrinsic to her Chinese character. By the same token, her transformation into an outgoing woman can be credited to the influence of Tianxi as well as to the American ways to which they both have been exposed. Tianxi encourages Shuzhen to mingle with American youth and to entertain the idea of attending college in the United States. The idea of an American college education for Shuzhen had, in fact, occurred to Madam, but shortly after seeing the photograph she changes her mind and announces, "through her tears," what becomes the tale's clincher: "I'm thinking, daughter, about returning to China" (259). Not "daughter" but "haizi [孩子]" or "child" is the vocative used in the Chinese original. Since one does not leave a child to fend for herself in a foreign country, Madam clearly intends to return to China with Shuzhen.

Taking Shuzhen back just when she is blooming, falling in love and exploring life on her own, makes little sense and seems outright cruel. But Madam is intent on nipping Shuzhen's maturation in the bud. She seems to think that once back in China and away from Tianxi, the adoptee will resume her wonted role as the quiet ward who will remain by her side out of filial piety. Despite good intentions in adopting Shuzhen, Madam bears the colonialist mark in viewing the adoptee as an Other and as a dependent who should repay maternal care with lifelong servitude. Because the story ends with Madam's teary announcement, Shuzhen's response is withheld from the reader. She may decide to stay against her adoptive mother's wishes, or Tianxi may decide to go back to China with her, and both of them may put romantic love above filial piety. Since the story was published at a historical juncture in China when Western influence was spreading rapidly and when the received code of conduct was being challenged, the open ending leaves ample room for each reader's imagination.

Published decades before Said's *Orientalism* and the *Aiiieeeee!* anthology, the story already contains the kernels of these later theorizations. Scholars routinely apply existing theories to literature; it is equally apposite and productive to generate theory from fiction, as Said has done with Victorian texts. Bing Xin is far ahead of her time in divulging the colonialist mindset of Madam Simpson beneath her admiration of Chinese culture and her affection for Shuzhen, and in roundly censuring, via Tianxi, the condescending white missionary gaze prior to World War II. "Defining Asia" over the course of the nineteenth century, Dominika Ferens points out, "was largely the province of missionaries and lay travelers" (Ferens 19). "The Photograph" provides an early literary glimpse of how New England missionaries sought to garner ethnographic knowledge and of how Madam raised Shuzhen in accordance with such stereotypical understanding of the Orient. Tianxi's advice to Shuzhen to learn about another culture by hanging out with Americans offers a much more viable way to know the "other." While he also generalizes about the West—"I have always respected Westerners' courage and zest for life. I very rarely find an American young person perpetually somber and pensive like we are" (253–254)—his observations are derived from everyday encounters and not from ethnography. The white mother, despite spending decades in China, has chosen to admire the culture in the form of ancient art and, soon after the adoption, to occlude herself and her child from mingling with living Chinese.

The story thus offers a pungent critique of reductive ways of knowing and illuminates Said's dictum that "the line separating Occident from Orient ... is less a fact of nature than it is a fact of human production" (Said, "Orientalism Reconsidered" 211). Bing Xin disputes the line by indicating that Madam and Shuzhen share many attributes as introverts; that the adoptive mother sees the adoptee as embodying pre-modern Cathay, while Tianxi regards her as epitomizing new China; that Madam and her missionary compatriots hold divergent views of China—as the cradle of civilization and as a hotbed of barbarians, respectively; that Tianxi's impressions of outgoing Americans hardly apply to Madam. These contradictory clues all go to show the need to transcend binary oppositions. Biological origins should not dictate essentialist upbringing, as racial difference does not preclude cultural commonality.

"THE PHOTOGRAPH" AS SINOPHONE ASIAN AMERICAN LITERATURE

This narrative also blurs the distinction between Chinese and Asian American writing. In interweaving three strands of Orientalism—Madam Simpson's racist love, the American missionaries' racist disdain, and Shuzhen's unwitting enactment of the "model minority" stereotype—it foreshadows many of the key themes elaborated by Chin et al. in their introduction to *Aiiieeeee!* In portraying the loneliness of a white woman in China and the alienation of Chinese youth in North America, the story bespeaks the thorny process of transpacific migration and acculturation, in both directions. The sense of double exile felt by Madam in China and the United States resonates with the experiences of many early Asian immigrant characters, including the protagonist in Younghill Kang's *East Goes West* (1937), the farmer in Bienvenido Santos's "Scent of Apples" (1955), and the parents in Jhumpa Lahiri's *The Namesake* (2003). The sense of displacement felt by Shuzhen and Tianxi in New England recalls the autobiographical "Leaves from the Mental Portfolio of an Eurasian" (1909) by Sui Sin Far/Edith Eaton, credited by Li Guicang 李贵苍 as the *bizu* 鼻祖 (progenitor) of Asian American literature (Li; more on Far later). The objectification of Shuzhen and Tianxi further brings to mind the eponymous Sakura Jiro in Onoto Watanna/Winnifred Eaton's "The Loves of Sakura Jiro and the Three Headed Maid" (1903), in which a Japanese immigrant must earn his keep in the New World by making a voyeuristic spectacle of himself.

"The Photograph" bears especially close resemblance to Ruthanne Lum McCunn's biographical novel *Wooden Fish Songs* (discussed in Chapter 6), which depicts the adulterated love of Fanny (a white woman) for her adopted Chinese son Lue Gim Gong (1858–1925). The two adoptive mothers hold much in common. Fanny considers Lue her "creation" and treats him both as a "field Negro" who tends her orchard and a "house Negro" who attends her sickbed. Madam fashions Shuzhen per her own Orientalist image and expects unconditional gratitude. Where Fanny takes credit for Lue's Christian demeanor, however, Madam ascribes Shuzhen's sedateness to Eastern femininity. Given the many parallels between "The Photograph" and the foregoing Asian American texts, it deservedly belongs to Sinophone Chinese American literature that stands alongside Anglophone works by Chinese nationals such as Chiang Yee, Lin Yutang, Yung Wing, and Wu Ting Fang—which already fall within the rubric of early Chinese American writing. Bing Xin—an author who spent substantial time in the United States and who (at least in this story) depicts experiences of Asians in North America—fits the comprehensive definition of Asian American author put forward in *Asian American Literature: An Annotated Bibliography* (Cheung and Yogi v–vi). In calling attention to the experience of an American woman in China, she nicely complements most of the other pre-World War II authors who focus on the experience of Chinese in North America.

The story's affinity with Asian American literature is particularly evident in its dual critique of American Orientalism and Chinese patriarchal familism. Wu Bing, pioneering scholar of Asian American literature in China, founder of the Center of Asian American Literary Studies in Beijing, as well as a daughter of Bing Xin, has published an essay entitled "Reading Chinese American Literature to Learn about America, China, and Chinese America." "The Photograph" sheds light on all three terrains through its depiction of the Christian churches in New England, life in pre-World War II China, and the experiences of Chinese in America. Wu's appraisal of Chinese American literature as "introspection literature 反思文学" ("Reading" 105; "Concerning" 20) for Chinese readers and specifically her critique of the obligation to reciprocate favors and express disproportionate gratitude (滴水之恩,泉涌相报) ("Concerning" 20) also apply to the narrative, given its ambivalence toward traditional values. erin Khuê Ninh has demonstrated forcefully that the model minority designation is more than "a discursive instrument used by whiteness to discipline other nonwhite minorities," that there is an undeniable connection between Chinese "model minority and model filiality" (epitomized by a withering hortative: "Get your filial child, your doctor/lawyer, your model minority here"), and that the "psychic costs of this subject formation," including the feeling of "being trapped inside that house," still stay with many immigrant daughters (Ninh 8, 162, 2). Ninh boldly asserts: "The assimilationist, individualist, upwardly mobile professional class of the model minority is, for familial intents and purposes, Asian America's model children" (Ninh 11). And, let me add, China's model children traditionally.

Unlike Qiu and Li, who hold up Shuzhen as the exemplar of two commendable constitutions of Chinese culture—the traditional virtues of Old China and the progressive virtues of New China (Qiu & Li 22)—I suspect Bing Xin invites us to look critically at the conventional inculcation of reticence, filial obligation, and inordinate expression of gratitude. In having a white woman be the one to exact such normative behavior and to expect gratitude in the form of servitude, the author bares the underbelly of these vaunted assets. These values, defamiliarized through Madam Simpson's Western eyes, take on a troubling light, allowing the author to critique American Orientalism and conventional Chinese feminine ideals simultaneously. In reinforcing "Eastern" politesse and in believing that Shuzhen will remain forever filial and obliging after returning to China, Madam is not simply showing her stereotypical vision. Other than her anxiety about losing Shuzhen through marriage, her familistic notions—perhaps just as inimical to a youngster's self-development—are not so different from those of many traditional Chinese parents. Shuzhen herself, before encountering Tianxi, has been conforming not only to maternal expectations but also to patriarchal protocols for Chinese women. In sitting quietly in the New England congregation while Madam lectures on China, she abets Orientalist representation and bolsters cultural hegemony by giving the American woman the power to speak for the Other. Although Tianxi also balks at speaking about China in front of an American audience, his reluctance stems from his sound reasoning that any generalizations about this vast country inevitably come up short. Furthermore, his vision of "new China"—lively, passionate, and expressive, as captured in his photograph of Shuzhen—offers an appealing alternative to the timid willowy figure inscribed in traditional Chinese paintings and cherished by Madam.

INTERNATIONAL ADOPTION

The assignation, preservation, and reinscription of traditional values have far-reaching repercussions today on account of widespread inter-country adoption. Klein contends that transracial adoption of Asian orphans during the Cold War era was not just an individual private practice but a cultural issue fraught with political ramifications. The interracial adoption in "The Photograph," which may be read as a precedent to Klein's Cold War examples, can serve as a sobering contribution to the ongoing debate over the viability of various cultural approaches to raising adoptees whose racial and national origins differ from the adoptive parents'—especially in cases of Chinese girls with European American parents. Cynthia Callahan notes that attempts to compensate for the losses experienced by international adoptees include "cultural preservation practices such as language classes and culture camps, as well as other ways to help adoptees feel connected to their birth culture" (131). Whether these adoptees should be brought up according to conventional Chinese values or to the customs and beliefs of the adoptive parents remains a conundrum.

Vincent J. Cheng argues that issues surrounding transracial and intercountry adoption are "important reflections of Western cultural attitudes toward cultural identity and authenticity" (64). He communicates his misgivings about the popular "heritage industry" putatively designed to help Chinese adoptees in North America to learn about their culture:

> Such choices are not likely or frequently to be made ... on the basis of actual lived experience, but rather on the basis of cultural stereotypes ... resulting most frequently (and unconsciously) in Orientalisms and fetishizations of an exoticized otherness, evocations of an exoticized but dead past, or exercises in what ... Renato Rosaldo has so aptly coined "imperialist nostalgia"... We would not apply the same dynamics of authenticity when there is no racial difference involved, that is, with white babies. (79–80)

Unless the white babies are adopted by parents of color, as in the case of Sui Sin Far's short story "Pat and Pan" (1912), a story that provides an instructive contrast with "The Photograph." In Far's tale, Pat, the white boy adopted by Chinese American parents, is later taken away by white authorities on account of the intervention of Miss Harrison, an American missionary who thinks that "for a white boy to grow up as a Chinese was unthinkable" (161). Pat is then adopted by a white couple, who would "raise him as an American boy should be raised" (164). Callahan notes how Far uses the transracial adoption to "critique the assimilationist agenda of religious missionaries" (Callahan 158). Though the ethnicities of parent and child are reversed in "Pat and Pan" and "The Photograph," both stories challenge the use of biological or racial determinants to demarcate difference.

Racial distinction, compounded by personal preference, accounts for Madam Simpson's calculated attempt to shield Shuzhen from her maternal Western heritage. The white mother has herself gone through considerable Sinification in her long sojourn. She might have started out like her American contemporaries seeking for aesthetic Orientalism, but her long stay in China has also turned her against the insubordination of American youth, even as she remains a perpetual foreigner in her beloved China. Hence, there is an equal measure of identification with and alienation from China. Despite or because of her own bicultural marginality, she seems determined to "preserve" Shuzhen's culture as a static constant. By refraining from speaking English to the adoptee and by not teaching her about American culture, Madam deprives her daughter of a valuable bilingual and bicultural upbringing. It is Tianxi, vehement critic of Western missionaries, who nevertheless stresses the importance of cross-cultural interchange: "I believe we ought to use our time abroad ... to travel," he tells Shuzhen. "I have always respected Westerners' courage and zest for life ... you ought to join them sometime; it would really broaden your horizon" (254). Madam's nostalgic, culturalist construction of the adoptee is unhinged by his aforementioned impression of a vivacious Shuzhen embodying "New China"—an image surely no less authentically Chinese during and after the iconoclastic May Fourth era, a period from about 1919 to 1926 that witnessed the erosion of Confucian culture and the ascendency of Western ideals.[3] Though published well before adoption across racial lines began to gain currency, this early transnational tale is the first to insinuate the hazards of essentializing and fetishizing adoptees and regarding them as cultural acquisitions.

Gendered Reception

Finally, this story raises the question of the author's gendered reception. Bing Xin is venerated as one of the vanguards of the May Fourth vernacular movement, but her works are taught primarily as juvenile texts in Hong Kong and China. The reason is in some way self-imposed: she explicitly devoted the bulk of her writing *To Young Readers*—the title of her famous collection of "letters." Nevertheless, her gender has further inflected the ways she has been compartmentalized as a foremost representative of the Boudoir Lady School (*guixiu pai* 闺秀派), an author engaged with "domestic" rather than national and international issues. Shu-mei Shih has also called attention to the tendency in modern Chinese literary history to "trivialize the importance of women writers," observing that the writings of Lin Huiyin and Ling Shuhua (both of whom are introduced in Chapter 4) were also sidelined during the May Fourth Movement: "It was the male voice propounding an agenda of national cultural rejuvenation that ironically displaced the feminist agenda of women's liberation" (Shih 204). Shih posits that Ling Shuhua has been perceived as a "minor" writer in Chinese literary history because "her stories deal with seemingly trivial events surrounding women and children rather than grand social issues"; Ling was identified by male critics of her time and after as a representative of the New Boudoir Lady School" (*xin guixiu pai* 新闺秀派), thereby "conflating Ling's gender with her work" (221).

Style and gender were likewise conflated in the case of Bing Xin, Ling's classmate at Yenching University. Although Bing Xin fared better as a writer and had a much stronger literary reputation, she too suffered from similar constraints, of which she was all too aware. In an essay about her beloved author Ba Jin 巴金, Bing Xin discloses that at one point she adopted the pseudonym "Male [男士]" for her book *On Women* 《关于女人》 out of financial necessity to get "more fees for her writing" (Bing Xin, "About Men" 400). Her situation was analogous to that of Pearl Buck, who published many of her later novels under the pen name John Sedges because despite "her high acclaim as 'the popular expert' on China ... her work was continually regarded as 'women's literature' which supposedly used the language of moral suasion and sentimentality, unlike the works of male Great Authors" (Yoshihara 168). The corresponding Chinese "male Great Authors" belonging to Bing Xin's generation, such as Ba Jin, Lu Xun 鲁迅, and Lao She 老舍, are noted for their political insight and criticism of feudal China, while the female authors' reputations rest mainly on their luminous prose, psychological subtlety, and philosophy of love.

Bing Xin is perhaps the first Chinese writer to reverse the one-sided gaze by creating a story about an American woman. According to historian David Roediger, "White writers have long been positioned as the leading and most dispassionate investigators of the lives, values, and abilities of people of color... Writers of color ... are cast as providing insight, often presumed to be highly subjective, of what it is like to be a 'minority'" (Roediger 4). From this vantage point—and extending it to a Pacific Rim context—Bing Xin's experimental appropriation of white authority is nothing short of insurgent. Aside from Tianxi's conversation with Shuzhen, the narrative is told from the perspective of a white woman who is oblivious to her Orientalist bent. Just as the eponymous photograph inverts the colonialist relationship noted by Sontag, the short story confounds the established Orientalist hierarchy. Madam regards her Chinese ward as an ethnographic subject, but she herself is simultaneously subjected to the critical gaze of the Chinese author.

Far more nuanced than the one-dimensional maternal view is Bing Xin's portrayal of Madam Simpson, whose psychological complexity rivals that of Megan Davis, the white female protagonist in *The Bitter Tea of General Yen* (1933), a film directed by Frank Capra. Megan, an expatriate romantically drawn to but culturally repulsed by the eponymous Chinese general, vacillates "between wanting to escape from Yen and wishing to convert him to Christianity" (Palumbo-Liu 59). Madam's attitude toward China is no less vexed. Her decision to stay in the country attests to her feminist independence and her willingness to become assimilated into an alien culture. Yet her attempt to domesticize and preserve the adoptee as a China doll betrays her "Orientalist melancholia" and "imperialist nostalgia."

Unlike ethnocentric Chinese or American writers, Bing Xin delicately balances chiasmic registers in the story. On the political level, the author's sympathies are with the young Chinese against the American Orientalist ideology embodied by Madam Simpson and the New England missionaries. On the cultural and psychological level, the dynamic is reversed: the narrative champions American individualism and self-development over identification with family and nation. On this level, Madam's attraction to China is no more peculiar than Shuzhen's growing fascination with the United States and the author's sympathy would seem to lie with the white expatriate. Although I have focused on interracial politics in order to emphasize the author's foresight regarding Orientalism, the nuanced sketch of Madam—a superb character study of an aging woman who has chosen to remain single and to spend most of her life in an Other world—merits no less scholarly attention. To borrow Dirlik's words, Madam exemplifies "the Orientalist [who] is 'Orientalized' ... herself in the very process of entering the 'Orient' intellectually and sentimentally" (Dirlik 119).

Viewing "The Photograph" with the hindsight of postcolonial, Asian American, and gender studies allows us to see the prescient and subversive author in a new light. The literary audacity whereby Bing Xin arrogates to herself the "authority" of a white woman, the artistic finesse with which she represents the tenor of interracial adoption, and the sensitivity with which she attends to the political and psychological dimensions of the narrative continue to radiate across borders and decades. Because of gender biases, however, the author has been celebrated exclusively as someone who writes eloquently about matters of the heart, especially of maternal love. Completely overlooked is her critique of Chinese Confucian hierarchy, especially its emphasis on filial obligation, and of American missionary condescension. At a time when most Chinese writers level their critiques at Chinese feudalism and look to the West as a source of salvation, Bing Xin homes in on the unequal relationship between the United States and China and offers caveats against imperialist perils. She conveys the difference, in 1934, between Orientalism and an evolving Chinese culture, and between Eurocentrism and universality.

NOTES

1. For a meticulous and exhaustive biography and complete works of Bing Xin, see Chen Shu 陈恕.
2. Spurling notes that when Buck had been asked to give a talk to missionary trainees in Nanjing in 1923, she urged her students to never operate "on anything less than an absolute equality": "We simply cannot express the Gospel with any force if we have hidden within us a sense of racial superiority... We are no better than anyone else, any of us" (Spurling 204–205).
3. It was around this time, during the early 1930s, that Brave Orchid, the feisty mother in *The Woman Warrior*, left her village for medical school: "Brave Orchid represents the quintessential modern Chinese woman, independent-minded and self-determining, leaving her home village to sail, alone, to an urban center to train in that most modern of scientific vocations, medicine" (Kong 149). Bing Xin and her contemporaries such as Lin Huiyin and Ling Shuhua (introduced in Chapter 3), not to mention writers Ding Ling and Aileen Chang, are all examples of modern Chinese women that belie Madam Simpson's Orientalist image of silent and supine femininity.

WORKS CITED

Behdad, Ali. *Camera Orientalis: Reflections on Photography of the Middle East*. Chicago: University of Chicago Press, 2016.

Bing Xin 冰心. "相片 [The Photograph]. 《冰心作品精编》 *Bing Xin Zuopin Jingbian*]. Ed. Ru 卓如 Zhuo. Guilin: 漓江出版社 [Lijiang Chubanshe], 2006/1934. 393–406.

——. "关于男人(之八):一位最可爱可佩的作家 [About Men (8): The Most Endearing and Admirable Author]." 《冰心集》 [*Collected Works by Bing Xin*]. Ed. Huanting 贾焕亭 Jia. Guangzhou: "华城出版合 [Huacheng Chubanshe], 2005/1989. 399–401.

——. "The Photograph." *The Short Story and Photography 1880's–1980's: A Critical Anthology*. Ed. Jane M. Rabb. Trans. Jeff Book. Albuquerque: University of New Mexico Press, 1998. 121–137.

——. "The Photograph." *The Photograph*. Trans. Jeff Book. Beijing: Panda Books, 1992. 234–259.

Buck, Pearl S. "Give China the Whole Christ: To the Editor of The Chinese Recorder." *Chinese Recorder*, July 1932: 450–452.

——. "Is There a Case for Foreign Missions?" *Harper's Magazine*, 1 December 1932: 143–155.

——. "Is There a Place for the Foreign Missionary?" *Chinese Recorder*, February 1927: 100–107.

Callahan, Cynthia. *Kin of Another Kind: Transracial Adoption in American Literature*. Ann Arbor: University of Michigan Press, 2011.
Chen Shu, 陈恕. 《冰心全传 [*Complete Biography and Works of Bing Xin*]》. Beijing: 中国青年出版社 Zhongguo Qingnian Chuban She, 2011.
Cheng, Vincent John. *Inauthentic: The Anxiety over Culture and Identity*. New Brunswick: Rutgers University Press, 2004.
Cheung, King-Kok, and Stan Yogi. *Asian American Literature: An Annotated Bibliography*. New York: Modern Language Association, 1988.
Chin, Frank, and Jeffery Paul Chan. "Racist Love." *Seeing Through Shuck*. Ed. Richard Kostelanetz. New York: Ballantine, 1972. 65–79.
Chin, Frank, Jeffery Paul Chan, Lawson Fusao Inada, and Shawn Hsu Wong, eds. "An Introduction To Chinese- and Japanese-American Literature." *Aiiieeeee! An Anthology of Asian-American Writers*. Washington, DC: Howard University Press, 1974/1983. xxi–xlviii.
Chow, Rey. *Writing Diaspora: Tactics of Intervention in Contemporary Cultural Studies*. Bloomington: Indiana University Press, 1993.
Christian, Barbara. "The Race for Theory." *Cultural Critique* 6 (1987): 51–64.
Dirlik, Arif. *The Postcolonial Aura: Third World Criticism in the Age of Global Capitalism*. Boulder: Westview Press, 1997.
Eng, David L. *The Feeling of Kinship: Queer Liberalism and the Racialization of Intimacy*. Duke University Press, 2010.
Ferens, Dominika. *Edith and Winifred Eaton: Chinatown Missions and Japanese Romances*. Urbana: University of Illinois Press, 2002.
Ford, Stacilee. *Gendered Exceptionalisms: American Women in Hong Kong and Macau*. Hong Kong: University of Hong Kong, 2002.
Guo Yingjian, 郭英剑. 《全球化语境下的文学研究》[*Literary Studies in the Context of Globalization*]. Beijing: Foreign Language Teaching and Research Press, 2010.
Hurston, Zora Neale. "Member Youse a Nigger." *Mules and Men*. New York: Harper & Row, 1934/1990. 70–90.
Klein, Christina. *Cold War Orientalism: Asia in the Middlebrow Imagination, 1945–1961*. Berkeley: University of California Press, 2003.
Kong, Belinda. "Theorizing the Hyphen's Afterlife in Post-Tiananmen Asian America." *MFS Modern Fiction Studies* (2010): 136–159.
Li, Guicang 李贵苍《书写他处:亚裔北美文学鼻祖水仙花研究》. [*Championing Chinese Ethnicity: Sui Sin Far and Her Writing*]. Beijing: Chinese Social Sciences Press 中国社会科出版社, 2014.
Nibelle, Paul. "La photographie et l'histoire." *La Lumière*, 22 April 1854: 64.
Ninh, erin Khuê. *Ingratitude: The Debt-bound Daughter in Asian American Literature*. New York: New York University Press, 2011.
Palumbo-Liu, David. *Asian/American: Historical Crossings of a Racial Frontier*. Stanford: Stanford University Press, 1999.

Qiu Yanping, 邱艳萍, and 李柏青 Li Baiqing. "镜像中的文化与人性——冰心小说《相片》读解" ["Culture and Character in the Mirror: An Analysis of Bing Xin's 'The Photograph'."] 《琼州大学学报》 *Xiongzhou University Newsletter* 1 (2000): 21–32.

Roediger, David R., ed. *Black on White: Black Writers on What It Means to Be White.* New York: Schocken Books, 1998.

Said, Edward W. *Orientalism.* New York: Vintage, 1979.

———. "Orientalism Reconsidered." *Literature, Politics, and Theory: Papers from the Essex Conference, 1976–1984.* Ed. Francis Baker et al. London: Methuen, 1986. 210–229.

Santos, Bienvenido. "Scent of Apples." *Scent of Apples: A Collection of Short Stories.* Seattle: University of Washington Press, 1979/1955. 21–29.

Shih, Shu-mei. *The Lure of the Modern.* Berkeley: University of California Press, 2001.

Sontag, Susan. *On Photography.* New York: Farrar, Straus and Giroux, 1973.

Spurling, Hilary. *Pearl Buck in China: Journey to The Good Earth.* New York: Simon & Schuster, 2010.

Sui Sin Far, [Edith Eaton]. "Pat and Pan." *Mrs. Spring Fragrance and Other Writings.* Ed. Amy Ling and Annette White-Parks. Urbana: University of Illinois Press, 1995/1912. 160–166.

Watanna, Onoto [Winnifred Eaton]. "The Loves of Sakura Jiro and the Three Headed Maid." *"A Half Caste" and Other Writings.* Ed. Linda Trinh Moser and Elizabeth Rooney. Chicago: University of Chicago Press, 2003/1903. 60–66.

Wong, Sau-ling Cynthia. "The Yellow and the Black: Portrayal of Chinese- and African-Americans in the Work of Sinophone Chinese American Writers." *Chung-wai Literary Monthly* 34.4 (2005): 15–53.

Wu Bing, 吴冰. "关于华裔美国文学研究的思考 [Concerning Asian American Literary Studies]." 《理论研究》 *Foreign Literary Criticism* 2 (2008): 15–23.

———. "Reading Chinese American Literature to Learn about America, China, and Chinese America." *Amerasia Journal* 34.2 (2008): 99–108.

Yoshihara, Mari. *Embracing the East: White Women and American Orientalism.* New York: Oxford University Press, 2003.

CHAPTER 8

(Im)migrant Writing, Moving Homelands: Ha Jin 哈金

A 2012 issue of *Amerasia Journal* (38.2), "Towards a Third Literature," features prominently Ha Jin, a multi-award-winning writer from China who has published prolifically in English. In the 1980s, given the *Aiiieeeee!* editors' insistence on American nativity and on distinguishing Chinese American from Americanized Chinese writers, an author like Jin was unlikely to appear, let alone serve as a centerpiece, in this flagship journal of Asian American studies. As Belinda Kong points out in "Theorizing the Hyphen's Afterlife in Post-Tiananmen Asian America," Jin presents "a compelling challenge to older conceptions of Asian-American identity." "Against Kingston's early formulation of 'claiming America,' he may be said to be 'claiming China' and advancing a model of Asian-Americanness that reads the hyphen backward" (138; see also my Introduction). In her article, Kong deliberately reinserts the hyphen to redistribute the weight between "Chinese" and "American," but she herself tends to tilt to its left. Jin, I contend, straddles the hyphen. I use the visual parenthesis advisedly to mark "(Im)migrant" in the title of this chapter because Jin's consciousness—as evinced in both *The Writer as Migrant* (*Migrant* hereafter), his first book of nonfiction, and *A Free Life* (*AFL* hereafter), his only novel set primarily in the United States hitherto—is neither entirely immigrant nor entirely diasporic, but something in between. Instead of looking askance at such fluid identity as betraying a "dual personality," Asian American literary studies can encompass such a sensibility as conducive to intercultural poetics and to tolerance of differences. American transnationalism must

© The Author(s) 2016
K.-K. Cheung, *Chinese American Literature without Borders*,
DOI 10.1057/978-1-137-44177-5_8

likewise harken to these new accents in the English language, and weave into itself new strands of being and becoming American.

This chapter links the notion of a borderless homeland with migrant poetics, which I use to illuminate Jin's work instead of assessing it against Chinese and American canons. Jin's experience as an intellectual migrant, embedded in *Migrant* and *AFL*, generates probing questions about the writer's role, the hazards and possibilities of wielding an adoptive language, and definitions of home(land). Both books engage in a kind of double-voiced discourse. On the surface, *Migrant* (based on his Campbell lectures delivered at Rice University in 2006) is a commentary on fellow transplanted writers, including C. P. Cavafy, Joseph Conrad, Milan Kundera, Lin Yutang, Vladimir Nabokov, and V. S. Naipaul. Yet one can discern many parallels between Jin and the men of letters discussed. Even more pronounced are the convergences of Jin and Nan Wu, the protagonist in *AFL*. Both Jin and Nan were doctoral students at Brandeis in 1989 who decided to stay in the United States after the Tiananmen crackdown; both have become personae non grata in China. Before becoming an English writer, Jin traveled a route similar to Nan's. One cannot help sighting autobiographical traces in the novel, especially regarding authorial struggle and aesthetic philosophy. Indeed, the novel is dedicated to Jin's wife and son, who expressly "lived this book." Unlike those who assume artistic works that are to some extent "autobiographical" to be less "creative," I show how life experience can catalyze original art forms—in this instance a distinctive migrant aesthetics, a bilingual grafting that collapses national borders.

In addition to decoding veiled self-references in both the nonfiction and fiction, I use *Migrant* to shed light on *AFL*. Because *AFL* tracks the life of a Chinese writer as migrant, many of the ideas articulated in *Migrant* pertain at once to Jin and his protagonist Nan, an aspiring poet. For Jin and Nan, the (im)migrant journey coincides with a rhetorical expedition, in which the attempt to build a home in America is also a metanarrative about finding a foothold in the vast expanse of English letters. In undergoing a double—physical and linguistic—exile, Jin and Nan also acquire a new subjectivity, grasping the world and their place in it anew. For both, the serene landscape etched deeply in their psyche by traditional Chinese poetry and painting can now be found only outside their native country. They publish in English not only to avert Chinese censors but also to reinvent themselves, to blaze an individual trail. Nevertheless, this reinvention still takes in the native land, both geopolitically and linguistically. It is my contention that in *Migrant* and *AFL,* Jin bestrides both sides of the hyphen in equal measure.

The Chinese Writer as Migrant

While *Migrant* focuses on a slate of international luminaries, its insights seem to derive from Jin's own migrancy. The volume comprises three essays entitled "The Spokesman and the Tribe," "The Language of Betrayal," and "An Individual's Homeland" respectively. The themes therein are not unlike those explored in Salman Rushdie's "Imaginary Homelands" (1991) and Edward Said's "Reflections on Exile" (2000) (Rushdie 9–21; Said, "Exile" 137–149). "The Spokesman and the Tribe" uses the cases of Alexander Solzhenitsyn and Lin Yutang to affirm literature as self-validating and to dispute the viability of serving as a spokesperson for one's compatriots. "The Language of Betrayal" wrestles with the questions of whether writing in a second language amounts to sedition against one's native country (a charge to which Conrad was subjected) and whether using a foreign literary medium inevitably constitutes a drawback (an insinuation Edmund Wilson made about Nabokov). "An Individual's Homeland" draws on Cavafy, Kundera, Naipaul, and Sebald to explore four conceptions of homeland: country of birth, adopted country, mother tongue, and an imagined habitat spun by the artist. Unlike Rushdie and Said, Jin often skirts volatile political issues affecting his own literary career; nevertheless, an autobiographical counterpoint is audible throughout his scholarly discourse.

The telling correspondences between Jin and the authors he invokes manifest themselves in his critique of Lin Yutang as spokesperson for China; in his detailed account of a Polish critic's attack on Conrad as having betrayed his country and in his comment on Edmund Wilson's condescending advice to Nabokov; and in his discussion of Cavafy's "Ithaka" and his nuanced discussion of Odysseus's homecoming. In "The Spokesman and the Tribe," Jin explicitly compares himself with Lin, who attempted to be his native country's spokesperson—a role from which Jin has refrained. In Jin's view, Lin's novel *Moment in Peking* (1939) suffers as literature on account of Lin's impulse to present a favorable image of Chinese to Americans—which results in a one-dimensional, Pollyannaish portrayal of Modern China (Jin, *Migrant* 17). Jin has shifted from considering himself a spokesman for the oppressed to defining himself as artist. Whereas he envisioned himself, in the wake of the 1989 Tiananmen repression, as writing "on behalf of the downtrodden Chinese" in *Between Silences* (1990), his first book of poems, he soon recognized the "unfeasibility of the position" for someone who is observing China from abroad (Jin, *Migrant* 3–4) and concluded instead that writers must subordinate political causes to their craft.

Despite his stance that writers should only write for themselves, however, Jin is scrupulously heedful of his social responsibility and acutely sensitive to both American and Chinese critics. Notwithstanding his resolve to put down roots in the adoptive land, he engages in a *sotto voce* parley with his country of birth and strives to reach the offshore audience. Far from espousing a purely formalist position, Jin still shares Lin's belief in a writer's ethnographic and historiographical mission. Combatting "historical amnesia" is for him the key function of literature. He laments the silence surrounding the Anti-Rightist Movement in China in the late 1950s: "Millions of people suffered persecution, tens of thousands of intellectuals perished, yet not a single piece of literature with lasting value emerged from this historical calamity." "What was needed was one artist who could stay above immediate social needs and create a genuine piece of literature that preserved the oppressed in memory," Jin submits (29–30). All of Jin's novels, particularly *War Trash* (2004), *Nanjing Requiem* (2011), and *A Map of Betrayal* (2014) attempt to preserve history. What is left unsaid in his high valuation of literature, however, is that its historiographical function can hardly be realized in a country that polices and regulates publications, lest the underbelly of official history be exposed.

"The Language of Betrayal" can be read as Jin's oblique reproof of repressive official policies in China and their repercussions. The authors discussed in this essay—whether accused of being renegades for using a second language, reprimanded for being sellouts by critics from their native countries, or nitpicked by native English speakers for verbal infelicities—also mirror Jin's predicament. Charges of betrayal have been leveled at Jin in China. Though he does not delve into his experience, the following passage carries distinct autobiographical undertones: "Historically, it has always been the individual who is accused of betraying his country. Why shouldn't we turn the tables by accusing a country of betraying the individual?… The worst crime the country commits against the writer is to make him unable to write with honesty and artistic integrity" (31–32). Jin had previously made these points, almost verbatim—with specific reference to himself—in an op-ed in the *New York Times*: "To some Chinese, my choice of English is a kind of betrayal. But loyalty is a two-way street. I feel I have been betrayed by China." "I have tried to write honestly about China and preserve its real history," he continues. "As a result, most of my work cannot be published in China" (Jin, "Exiled" 2009). As Taiwanese scholar Te-hsing Shan 单德兴 wryly observes, "Among overseas Chinese writers, Jin has had the most awards and the greatest number of books translated into Chinese and banned" (Shan 20, my translation).

Jin is therefore rehearsing his own case in "The Language of Betrayal" when he both defends other authors' adoption of a second language and deplores the control exerted by a given country over its native sons. A couple of uncanny (albeit tacit) similarities surface between Jin and the two writers he recurrently champions—Conrad and Nabokov. The first is between a Polish scholar's attack on Conrad and a Chinese professor's denunciation of Jin. Just as Eliza Orzeszkowa (1841–1910), "the grande dame of the Polish literary circle" (36), had accused Conrad of betraying his country by writing in English and of reducing his writing to the level of a peddler (37), Jin was lambasted in almost identical terms by Liu Yiqing 刘意清, a prominent Professor of English (now Emeritus) at Peking University, who attended a reading by Jin of his award-winning novel *Waiting* (1999) during her stay in Chicago. In a Chinese essay pointedly entitled "拿诚实作交易 [Trading upon Integrity]," Liu fumes: "Jin has paid too high a price for his National Book Award, for which he has … bad-mouthed his compatriots and become an instrument of the US media in vilifying China" (刘; my translation). Jin later revealed in an interview entitled "曾有人说我是卖国贼 [Someone Has Accused Me of Being a Traitor]" how much he had been stung by Liu's remarks. His staunch defense of Conrad against Orzeszkowa in *Migrant* thus comes across simultaneously as vicarious self-defense. He argues that the Polish critic only "read about" but had "not actually read" Conrad's books and ignored Conrad's "dire financial straits" at the time: "In essence, hers is a collective voice, which demands the writer's unconditional dedication and sacrifice but does not care whether he could survive in a foreign land" (Jin, *Migrant* 38). Like Orzeszkowa, Liu had apparently neglected to read *Waiting*, at least in its entirety, before she published her scathing critique, for she based her attack primarily on what she deemed to be the Orientalist appeal of the novel's *appearance*: the allegedly anachronistic bound feet of a character, the picture of a man's queue on the book's cover, and the way the book was publicized in the *Chicago Tribune*, displaying images of both the bound feet and the queue. Like the Polish matron, Liu views Jin's writing in commercial rather than existential terms (as livelihood and artistic calling). As though in answer to Liu, Jin explains in *Migrant* that when he tells people he writes in English "for survival," he is not just referring to basic needs: "To exist also means to make the best use of one's life, to pursue one's vision" (32).

Jin's discussion of Wilson's cavil about Nabokov's English also casts a reflexive glance. Wilson told Nabokov: "Do please refrain from puns, to which I see you have a slight propensity. They are pretty much excluded from serious journalism here" (Wilson 34; quoted in *Migrant* 50). No less irksome to Nabokov was Wilson's backhanded compliment—"Mr. Nabokov's English almost rivals Conrad's" (Karlinsky 283n3)—to which the Russian author retorted: "Conrad knew how to handle *readymade* English better than I... He never sinks to the depth of my solecisms, but neither does he scale my verbal peaks" (Nabokov 282; quoted in *Migrant* 92n27). Jin obviously recalled this exchange between Wilson and Nabokov upon reading John Updike's lukewarm review of *AFL*: "Ha Jin's English in *A Free Life* shows more small solecisms than in his Chinese novels" (Updike 101). In an essay entitled "In Defence of Foreignness," Jin couches his objection to Updike's review in terms strongly reminiscent of his defense of Nabokov: "Once we enter a foreign terrain in our fiction, standard English may have to be stretched to cover the new territory. Ultimately this is a way to expand the capacity of the language, a kind of enrichment" (Jin, "Defence" 466). What Updike considers "solecisms," Jin contests, are deliberate coinage designed to render Chinese expressions that have no ready Anglophone equivalents. No mention of Updike's review is made in *Migrant*, but its vindication of Nabokov can be read as Jin's indirect rebuttal.

Finally, the images of "homeland," always in flux, that appear in "An Individual's Homeland" apply both to Nan's search for home and Jin's own, which involves rooting in another language and residing in a house of fiction. Jin is not alone in troping language terrestrially. Costica Bradatan, for instance, observes: "To practice writing is to grow roots into [a] language... Literary virtuosity almost always betrays a sense of deep, comfortable immersion into a familiar soil" (Bradatan). For a writer to switch to a different linguistic medium is, therefore, painfully unsettling—an uprooting as radical as emigration. Yet the experience can also be regenerative, for language is not merely a means of articulation but also "a mode of subjective existence" and "a constitutive part" of oneself; therefore, "to abandon your native tongue and to adopt another is to dismantle yourself ... and then to put yourself together again, in a different form" (Bradatan). Bradatan's ideas apply to both Jin and his protagonist in *AFL*, Nan Wu.

A Free Life as Chinese American Pastoral

AFL recounts the dismantling and remaking of the writerly self. In Nan (and Jin) the process involves not so much a radical uprooting as grafting—drawing inspiration from both Chinese and American pastoral and cross-stitching Chinese and American expressions to stake out a geographical and literary homeland across national borders. The novel traces a Chinese family's adjustment to life in the United States, particularly the patriarch Nan Wu's meandering trek to be a poet while supporting his wife (Pingping) and son (Taotao). Lest his poetic talents rust unused, Nan must unfetter himself from various chains that constrain his literary ambition—Chinese state power that impels him to write in English, American materialism that stalls his artistic development, the Chinese tenet of parental sacrifice that tells him to place his son's welfare before his own, and the commonplace conception of the American dream that places accumulation of wealth above higher pursuits.

Echoing the themes explored in *Migrant*, *AFL* revolves around finding a habitation that permits Nan to write without political or financial anxieties and to root himself in a new soil that allows him to shed received values and to apprehend a different way of being, seeing, and becoming. The solitude Nan espouses at the novel's end combines the reclusiveness of traditional Chinese writers who live close to nature to escape from politics and commerce and the nature-loving and nonconformist spirit championed by American literary giants such as Emerson, Frost, Whitman, and Faulkner. Nan's dual odyssey brings out the overlapping contours of geographical and rhetorical crossings, of ecological and moral landscapes, and of pastoral and existential solitude.

In traditional Chinese literature environmental and ethical well-being are viewed as interdependent; therefore, an earthly paradise must be situated as far as possible from centers of power and commerce.[1] This pastoral tradition is associated with the reclusive poets, especially Tao Qian/T'ao Ch'ien/Tao Yuanming 陶潛/陶淵明 (365–427 CE) of the Six Dynasties. In "Peach Blossom Spring"《桃花源記》, his well-known fable, a fisherman roams through a grove of peach trees aflame with blossoms to a natural spring. He then discovers a village founded long ago by refugees escaping taxation, economic rivalry, and political persecution. No potentates or bureaucrats control the population in this egalitarian community, where villagers make their living by farming and raising cattle. The fisherman then returns to his own prefecture and tells his magistrate about the unique village (against the wishes of its inhabitants), but it cannot be found again. Tao's implication is that Peach Blossom Spring exists only in the imagination.[2] Chen Guangchen points out that rural life in Tao's village is set against political tyranny with attendant literary implications: "nature writing is an escape from literature serving propaganda purposes," implicitly pitting "the Confucian ideal of the literati's social responsibility" against "the Taoist pursuit of individual freedom" (Chen 178, 179). In Tao's fable (as in much of traditional Chinese literature) most of the ills in society come from the ruling class; officials often reek of oppression, toadyism, and rapaciousness. Both officialdom and wealth (which tend to go in tandem) are deemed corrupting and adverse to artistic integrity.

American pastoralism, according to Leo Marx, is similarly grounded in "the presumed opposition between the realm of the collective, the organized, and the worldly on the one hand, and the personal, the spontaneous, and the inward on the other" (Marx 44). Emerson's ruminations about solitude and nature, as I have argued elsewhere ("Affinity"), provide the closest American counterpart to the Chinese reclusive ideal: "If a man would be alone, let him look at the stars. The rays that come from those heavenly worlds will separate him and what he touches... The stars awaken a certain reverence, because though always present, they are inaccessible" (Emerson, "Nature" 9). Emerson suggests that solitude is a sublime experience privy to the responsive mind in nature's presence. Like the Chinese reclusive poets, he marvels at the power of the natural world to heal the workaday soul: "To the body and mind which have been cramped by noxious work or company, nature is medicinal and restores their tone. The tradesman, the attorney comes out of the din and craft of the street, and sees the sky and the woods, and is a man again" ("Nature" 14). But unlike the self-effacing Chinese pastoral poets, Emerson sees nature as ancillary to the "realized will" of a human being—"the creator in the finite" ("Nature" 28, 43). Each person must learn to "detect and watch that gleam of light which flashes across his mind from within" and answer his inner calling without being beholden to public approbation ("Self-Reliance" 139). For "society is a joint-stock company in which the members agree, for the better security of his bread to each shareholder, to surrender the liberty and culture of the eater." Against such feckless conformity Emerson recommends self-reliance. Hence the oft-quoted corollary: "Whoso would be a man must be a non-conformist... Nothing is at last sacred but the integrity of your own mind" ("Self-Reliance" 141). Self-reliance and solitude are allied for Emerson, but the latter does not entail isolation: "the great man is he who in the midst of the crowd keeps with perfect sweetness the independence of solitude" ("Self-Reliance" 143). Reprising both Chinese and American pastoral, *AFL* cautions against the pitfalls of power, wealth, and society, and embraces self-reliance and solitude.

The Nation-State and the Individual

Emerson's resistance against society's demand for conformity—what Stanley Cavell calls "aversive thinking" (135)—has made an impact on contemporary Chinese intellectuals, such as Nobel laureates Gao Xingjian 高行健 and Liu Xiaobo 刘晓波. Both have coupled solitude with self-reliance; both have been displaced (Gao exiled and Liu incarcerated) by the Chinese government for their dissident views. Liu asserts: "Solitude implies independence, self-reliance; it means not following the crowd… For Chinese intellectuals, solitude must start with a complete negation of the self, because … [they] were never independent thinkers … but 'court literati.'" He echoes Emerson when he continues: "Whoever wants to possess the universe must first possess an independent self" (Liu 207–209). Gao Xingjian defends artistic autonomy from the encroachment of politics and maintains that literature must not "tolerate having restrictions imposed upon itself … for the sake of the nation or the party, the race or the people" (Gao 67). He sees loneliness as an affirmation of one's personal worth—"a prerequisite for freedom" (Gao 164–165)—and decries the dehumanization under both communism and capitalism. Whether figured as a cultural bureaucracy abetting careerism, a panopticon policing its citizenry, or a "joint-stock company" with dividends for the shareholders, society for Liu, Gao, and Emerson represents collective pressure that threatens to smother the individual. Jin, who mentions Emerson repeatedly in *AFL*, also puts a premium on intellectual autonomy. Like Gao and Liu, he too is rejected by his country of origin.

In line with Chinese and American pastoral, *AFL* shows the inverse relationship between individual well-being and state power, between wholesome living and affluence, and between self-fulfillment and the accouterments of the American dream. In the course of the novel, Nan bucks against the nation-state, rises above conventional values of property and fame, embraces the mind as his poetic touchstone, and dares the world to whip him with its displeasure. His agonistic stance toward the Chinese communist government recalls conventional distrust of the ruling class. His generation lived through the ruthless persecution of intellectuals during the Cultural Revolution and again during the 1989 Tiananmen crackdown. Nan tells how, after watching *Doctor Zhivago*, both he and his wife Pingping feel sick for days because it reminds them of their life in China where "human lives had been worthless, where hatred and blind rage had run amok, and where the gun ruled the law" (516). Nan himself has suffered the wrath of the Chinese authorities. The political fallout of Tiananmen ricochets thousands of miles away into his life in the United States when his Chinese passport is revoked, transforming him overnight from foreign student to immigrant laborer.[3] "What a misfortune it was to be born Chinese, for whom a trifle like a passport renewal would be tantamount to an insuperable obstacle!... Any petty official could torment you and ... demand your obedience" (71). After settling down in the United States, Nan and Pingping are constantly reminded of their patriotic obligation as Chinese expatriates. Nan, who thought he could live a "reclusive" life by severing his family from the Chinese community, soon realizes that "China would never leave them alone" (235). The comment conveys his sense of unremitting political harassment.

Nan is adamantly opposed to subordinating poetics to politics, perhaps in part as a reaction to Mao's 1942 guidelines, established in Yan'an, about the social and political function of literature, which stipulate that literature and art must serve the State and the people. Just as Jin maintains in *Migrant* that poetry should transcend history and outlast politics, Nan takes exception to the conflation of political and literary merits by a fellow emigrant poet who declares that the entire body of his poetry is worth less than "'*one drop of the blood shed by the martyrs in Tiananmen Square*'" (95; italics in the original indicates that the conversations are conducted in Putonghua). Nan's views accord with those of Jin, who states in *Migrant* that a writer must subordinate politics to literary and historical purposes.

Both Nan and Jin refuse to be bound by nationalism. When Nan's friend Danning Meng insists that decent human beings must always love their native country, Nan testily retorts: "*I wear my nationality like a coat* [because China] *treats its citizens like gullible children and always prevents them from growing up into real individuals*" (96). In an almost verbatim reiteration of the author's op-ed piece in the *New York Times* (Jin, "Exiled"), Nan tells Danning: "*To me loyalty is a two-way street. China has betrayed me, so I refuse to remain its subject anymore*" (96). He attributes his "truncated and enervated" life as a migrant writer to the turmoil in his motherland (471). When he visits China twelve years after emigration, he feels alienated even in his hometown. The smog sickens him, as does the similarly hazy political climate, in which one has to "bribe and feast others to get anything done"

(568). By refusing to pledge allegiance to a country that does not allow writers to express themselves freely and that does not treat its citizens as independent thinkers, Nan indicates that it is not any abstract interpellation by Chinese authorities but the environment that governs his choice of abode. This belief, as will be shown later, will eventually lead to a radical redefinition of "homeland." Meanwhile, the connection between topos and ethos is further stressed when Nan is asked to bring the ashes of a dissident scholar to the New World because the former patriot "*wanted to be buried in a clean place*" (570).

SURVIVAL AND TRANSPACIFIC MATERIALISM

Jin notes in *Migrant*, regarding Orzeszkowa's attack on Conrad, that the Polish critic ignores the question of how Conrad could otherwise "survive in a foreign land" (*Migrant* 38). *AFL* shows that while one must have the financial means for basic survival before pursuing a higher calling, obsession with material accumulation, which goes against both forms of pastoral living discussed earlier, can snuff out the artistic soul. Nan must learn to balance two forms of survival, "to survive as an artist while making one's art thrive" (*Migrant* 80), and to go beyond making a living to making a life. He eventually becomes what Te-hsing Shan calls a "multiple other: a person who leaves his home country behind out of disillusionment with the Communist regime, a foreigner in the US ... and an idealist who decides to abandon his hard-won business and materialistic American Dream and to devote himself to poetry writing" (74).

Material pursuit has taken over in both China and America, at the expense of ecology, artistry, and spirituality. After living in the United States for over a decade, Nan realizes that his native country has fully caught up with the New World in its venal fixation. Danning tells Nan that the people there are "*obsessed with getting rich, and money has become God*" (593). During a stay with his family in Harbin, Nan and his brother Ning visit a nearby riverbank. There had once been a park there, "but now most of the plants were gone and there were booths and kiosks everywhere ... like a marketplace"; the concrete ground was "strewn with melon rinds, ice cream cups, crushed eggshells. Popsicle sticks and wrappers, cigarette butts" (552–553). Ning, who is considering emigration to Australia, views this urban squalor as mirroring a general moral turpitude. He relates how the smog has become so thick that one has to wear a surgeon's mask, that countless Chinese have lung problems "*because China has no lungs any more—all the forests are gone. Worst of all, there are lots of criminals roaming around*" (555). Ning reveals that human avarice and bureaucratic corruption have become endemic in China, jeopardizing the natural environment, the body politic, and the physical and moral health of its citizenry. With the toxic territory comes rampant disease and deceit.

America, where one's worth is "measured by the property you owned and by the amount you had in the bank," is no less susceptible. Recalling a lonely hearts section of the *Boston Herald* in which a man labels his profession as "millionaire," Nan infers: "money was God in this place" (66). Nan regards making money as marketing himself. When he withdraws from his graduate program to work, he frets: "I don't know how to sell myself here" (55). But knowing his freedom is dependent upon financial stability, he, like many immigrants, takes up odd jobs—security guard, night watchman, and sous-chef. He becomes so tired of working for hire and the accompanying indignities that at one point he begs a traffic cop to shoot him. He is even more uneasy about those who commodify their art. He frowns on the way distinguished American poet Edward Neary behaves like a "business magnate" who harps on power and money (304), the way his poet friend Nick Harrison frets about the sale of his books and his speaking fees, and the way painter Bao Yuan tries to get rich by churning out a painting a day "like a manufacturer" (451). If state power keeps writers under the thumbs of bureaucrats, the lure of profit drives some artists to produce corporatized art that is no less compromised.

But Nan's American struggle also teaches him that poverty is anything but uplifting. Even though he shares traditional Chinese poets' reservations about earthly riches, he explodes the myth held by the reclusive poets (and some American nature writers) that art could improve under adverse conditions. He observes that it is impossible "for an unfettered genius to rise from a tribe of coolies ... possessed by the instinct for survival" (109), that "too much hardship could dull a poet's sensibility," just as prolonged hard work has "stunted his growth as a poet" (426). When the Wus buy a restaurant business and put a down payment on a ranch-style house in Georgia, necessitating an extensive interruption in his writing, his own poetic endeavors have to take a back seat. The family work so hard that in a few years they attain the classic American dream. Impressed by how much the Wus have gained in a year, their former landlady exclaims: "This can happen only in America" (390).

Instead of brimming with pride, Nan becomes despondent, feeling "as though the whole notion of the American dream was shoddy, a hoax"

(418). He comes to realize that his failure to follow his own dream has robbed him of a sense of fulfillment, that he has devoted all his energy to the restaurant business out of fear for "the overwhelming odds against writing in English artistically, against claiming his existence in this new land, and against becoming a truly independent man who followed nothing but his own heart" (472). He is disgusted with himself for being fainthearted, for temporizing. He detests himself even more after coming across a quotation from Faulkner (in a book entitled *Good Advice on Writing* but originally from his acceptance speech of the Nobel Prize): "The writer must teach himself that the basest of all things is to be afraid" (604). It dawns on Nan that his reasons for putting off writing are all excuses—"his sacrifice for his son, his effort to pay off the mortgage, his pursuit of the American dream … his family's need for financial security" (605). He runs out of excuses once he has paid off his mortgage.

Through this wrenching epiphany, Nan questions the philistine aspect of the American dream and the Asian commendation of parental sacrifice. Many immigrant parents, including the Wus, work around the clock for the benefit of the next generation. Nan puts it acerbically: "The first generation was meant to be wasted, or sacrificed, for its children, like manure used to enrich the soil so that new seeds could sprout and grow" (419). His friend Shubo, on hearing Nan chide himself for his lack of literary productivity, tells him that writing poetry professionally should be reserved for immigrants' grandchildren and reiterates the Chinese bromide: "That's how we Chinese survive and multiply—each generation lives for the next." Nan counters: "'Sacrifice' is just an excuse for our cowardice and laziness. My son has his life and I must have mine." When Shubo adds that even Ben Franklin's father forbade his son to be a poet and dismissed most verse makers as beggars, Nan snaps back, "*Then Franklin's dad was a major American philistine*" (420, 421). Jin suggests that no one—Chinese or American—should compromise his or her vocation out of parental obligation or pusillanimous pragmatism.

Furthermore, while many East Asian cultures have exalted parental devotion as noble and altruistic, the novel pries into its underside. erin Khuê Ninh has pointed out how some Asian parents, whether consciously or not, use sacrifice as a form of capitalist investment and, as shareholders, try to control the lives of their children, who are supposed to show thanks by obeying (Ninh). This theme plays out in the lives of several of the novel's characters. Nan, a former college instructor in China, was scorned by his father for being unable to find decent housing for his family. Danning's daughter, who loves painting and wants to major in fine arts, is asked by her parents to specialize instead in ad design, which is more likely to lead to a lucrative profession. Pingping similarly disregards Taotao's desire to major in French and urges her son to become a doctor. Taotao protests: "I don't like medical science. How about art history or English?" "Zen you will be a poor scholar for zer rest of your life," Nan answers. When Taotao responds that he doesn't care, Pingping retorts: "You don't care because we work night and day to make money for you... You act like rich kid who don't need profession" (504). Parental sacrifice, then, sometimes can be a form of economical manipulation, as crippling as financial hardship or political control. Such generational transactions, Jin implies, can thwart the aspirations of parents and offspring alike.

Nan sees his pecuniary preoccupation as largely responsible for derailing his literary progress. He has set out to do "*something moneyed people can't do*" (42), but at some point he became dazzled by dollar signs. While he had no choice but to put his nose to the grindstone initially, even after the family restaurant business has taken off, he continues to work long hours. He now excoriates himself for being "just a channel of food, a walking corpse" (419). Like the Canadian geese in his yard, which have exchanged their inborn abilities as migratory birds for daily feedings, Nan has ensconced himself in the restaurant (ironically called the Gold Wok) instead of taking wing as a poet. In a poem entitled "My Pity"—in which the speaker feels sorry for those "who love security," who are "content to live in cellars where / Food and drinks are provided," whose "lungs are unused to fresh air," and whose "salvation depends on a powerful man" (636)—Nan pitches homespun living against craven security, material comfort, and obsequious existence. At this juncture, however, Nan is not too different from the object of pity, as the equivocal pronoun of the poem's title suggests.

Jin implies that a person enchained by a philistine dream risks forfeiting freedom even in the fabled "land of the free." After reading Faulkner's aforementioned remonstrance against fear, Nan suffers a "paroxysm of aversion" verging on a nervous breakdown. He removes all the banknotes from the restaurant's cash register and then ravages the altar of the God of Wealth, to whom the Wus have been making regular offerings. He then thrusts a five-dollar bill on the flame of a candle, crying, "I want to burn it all, all zis dirty acre," when he had meant to say "filthy lucre" (605–606). In this dramatic scene, Nan revolts against the transpacific idolization of the money god. By both burning an American bill and desecrating the

Chinese God of Wealth, Nan recants his blind devotion to household livelihood, spurred by the Protestant work ethic, the Asian imperative of parental sacrifice, and the common understanding of the American dream. The slippage of "dirty acre" and "filthy lucre" nicely blends the two forms of acquisition—real property and cash—that undergird that dream. It also suggests the convergence of earthly and spiritual wasteland. For the scholar who wishes to be buried in a "clean place," urban pollution mirrors social degradation in China; for Nan, the American acre acquired with US lucre looms as the expatriate writer's graveyard.

Nan's incendiary act may be regarded as both an exorcism and a rebirth through fire—renunciation of his mercenary self and resuscitation of his inner poet. The Gold Wok figures as both an albatross and a crucible for the born-again Nan, who now rouses himself from the addictive dream of economic prosperity. When Pingping suffers a back injury, forcing the Wus to sell their restaurant business, it is almost a blessing in disguise. Because of his wife's expensive medical treatment, Nan finds a job as a front desk clerk at the Sunflower Inn, which offers adequate medical insurance for the family. Despite the reduced family income, he is glad to be free at last of the restaurant; he is able to find the quiet setting and repose of mind needed to read and write during his night shift, instead of toiling like an automaton to climb the economic ladder. Sitting by himself at the front desk from 11 p.m. to 7 a.m., Nan comes to a new understanding of the American dream as "something to be pursued only": "To be a free individual, he had to go his own way ... to be brave enough to devote himself not to making money but to writing poetry" (619). Unlike other immigrant tales that glorify the American dream or bemoan its elusiveness, *AFL* impugns the economic impetus that drives the conventional dream and redefines it as a process of self-actualization.

Linguistic Deterritorialization and Tripartite Solitude

Nan's rebirth is bound up with his literary initiation in a foreign tongue. Bradatan believes that the process of literary switching to another language is not unlike a "death-and-rebirth experience," wherein "the world is born anew" and the authorial self is reincarnated: "as you do it something happens to you, the language acts upon you" (Bradatan). Nan's determination to pursue his own American dream by writing poetry at the risk of utter failure and his unlearning of received Chinese values such as parental sacrifice and uncritical patriotism stem in part from this performative dimension of language, from his plunge into English letters—a move that is fraught with perils even as it allows Nan to rise as a revenant that accesses the world afresh.

Jin, who espouses enriching standard English with polyglot intonation while covering a foreign territory (Jin, "Defence"), answers his own call in *AFL*. Nan, in comforting himself for being unable to publish in Chinese and for having to confront the "wall" of writing in a second language, calls forth two lines from "Bidding Farewell on an Ancient Grassland"《賦得古原草送別》by Tang poet Bai Juyi 白居易 (AD 772–846): "No prairie fire can burn the grass up / When the spring breeze blows, it will again sprout [野火烧不尽,春风吹又生]" (*AFL* 408–409). He extrapolates from these lines that "however thick and impenetrable the wall before him," he must go on "like the invincible grass with blades," emulating Whitman's "American spirit" (409). In this notable act of literary code-mixing, Nan not only appropriates Bai's conceit about the resilience of nature to refer to his own poetic genius—dormant seeds awaiting auspicious elements to burgeon—but also weaves Whitman's leaves of grass in the New World with the wild grass of the Chinese prairie. Though no explicit mention is made of "Song of Myself," the reference to Whitman jostles the reader's memory of the other vegetation pullulating and "growing among black folks as among white" (Whitman 29). In doing so, Nan / Jin has surreptitiously added yellow folks to the racial spectrum. Through such interplay of languages, Nan begins to fashion his own multihued esthetics.

In addition to reconvening in print two forms of pastoral, *AFL* threads together three strains of solitude—pastoral reclusiveness, political independence, and linguistic marginality—as the resolution of Nan's psychic crisis. The transition from the *Gold* Wok to the *Sunflower* Inn recalls traditional Chinese poets' retreat from high society to a life close to nature. For Nan, however, sitting at the front desk alone, "thinking and writing devotedly," is sufficient for composure. He notes, "Even Pingping's back injury had done him a service, forcing him to change his life," adding: "How fortunate he was to have Pingping as his wife and fellow sufferer" (616). The repeated references to his spouse suggest that Nan's idea of a secluded existence—in contrast to the cocooning of Emily Dickinson—comports with the Chinese tradition in which poets who sequester themselves from public life still enjoy being around their families. Nan for a long time has been unable to love Pingping deeply because of his infatuation with another woman, but her presence (as someone who shares and understands his pain) has sustained him through the years. It is beyond the scope of this chapter to delve into gender asymmetry, but I wish to observe in passing that for both the reclusive poets and for Nan, the boon of having a wife who takes care of domestic chores and child rearing must have facilitated their solo creative endeavors. Whether intentional on Jin's part or not, Pingping's back injury conjures up the twin image of what Harryette Mullen pungently terms "Muse & Drudge"—which can also be construed as muse and mule—the female back upon which Nan (Chinese homonym for male) partially stands to write his poetry.

What Nan appreciates most about his current occupation is the freedom to apply himself without distractions, a preferred modus operandi akin to the author's. "When I was a young boy, I often dreamed of becoming a stonemason who worked alone at a quarry in a distant mountain," Jin discloses in a personal vignette. "Somehow the image of that solitary worker has possessed me... I aspire to write books as solid as rocks, both useful and artistic" (Jin, "A Stonemason" 1). Nan comes close to being Jin's alter ego when he reckons poetry to be a "craft, not very much different from carpentry or masonry" (628), and when he resolves to produce works that "possess more strength than beauty" (473). Associating writing with masonry and carpentry, crafts that employ natural resources, concords with the pastoral convention that poetry issues most spontaneously from nature. Perhaps Nan's work as a clerk at the appositely named Sunflower Inn writing poetry during predawn hours is the closest the protagonist can get to the work of a stonemason. Nan, who curbs his hearty appetite to live an austere life after selling the restaurant, is able to recreate in an urban setting the tranquil and ascetic lifestyle relished by Chinese literati and by Jin.

Despite his alienation and deracination from his native land, Nan takes after his reclusive forebears. Although his sanctum is not an actual mountain retreat, the bucolic surrounding of the Wus's residence in Georgia and the quiet night shift at the Sunflower Inn approximate their salubrious milieu. An appendix entitled "Poems by Nan Wu," attached to the novel proper, further implies that the ambience of the Sunflower Inn and Nan's renewed appreciation of his household indeed befit him and his art.[4] On Christmas Eve, Nan is able to pen a verse for Pingping "naturally and effortlessly," much to his surprise: "Never had he been able to write with such fluency and feeling" (619, 620). The poem, entitled "Belated Love," ends with the line "My love, I've come home" (620)—a tacit acknowledgment of Pingping's abiding companionship, which may have kept Nan's solitude from congealing into loneliness. *AFL* indicates that a poet requires a peaceful niche in which to compose (and, one might add, a wife in the offing), and that an obsession with bills and property can sabotage creativity. When Nan turns down a promotion to motel manager that would bring a big pay raise, he does so not just out of paternal duty (to pick up his son from school in the afternoon) but also in favor of his nightly vigil, which is conducive to both creativity and spiritual independence.

The mentality that Nan admires is encapsulated in a poem entitled "A Eulogy," in which he expresses his appreciation for someone who "loving a country, never lets this love / outweigh his love for a woman and children," who "accepts disaster and triumph equally," who "treats ... a palace as no more than a dwelling," and who, "while having coffee with a dignitary, / doesn't hesitate to step out the door for a breath of fresh air" (657). Valuing pure air over social stature and equating a palace with a mere dwelling are consonant with traditional Chinese pastoral. Nan's poem also alludes to *Yueyang Lou Ji* 《岳阳楼记》, a well-known verse by Fan Zhongyan 范仲淹 (989–1052)—a prominent literary figure, educator, and statesman during the Song dynasty. The lines about being unflappable in the face of disaster or triumph echo Fan's couplet: "Not gratified by external gains, not distressed by personal losses 不以物喜，不以己悲." But Nan also undercuts Fan with his insistence on putting one's kin above one's country, thereby upending Fan's hortative clincher: "Place the country's concerns before your own; put your own welfare behind the country's 先天下之忧而忧，后天下之乐而乐" (Fan; my translation).[5]

Whereas Nan's cherished quietude has roots in traditional Chinese poetry, the restive independence that he embraces sets him apart from an insouciant Taoist or a dutiful Confucianist. His determination to set the terms of his own life by braving a new linguistic frontier and his refusal to kowtow to a higher authority have a definite American ring that reverberates with Emerson's cadences. He learns from Emerson, as well as Whitman, Thoreau, Faulkner, and Frost, that he must heed his own calling without dreading public censure or hankering after popular acclaim. Both author and protagonist have taken an individualist literary path. Bettina Hofmann observes that Jin abides neither by the social commitment of many American writers of color who try to express a communal vision nor by the artistic goal of *Künstlerroman* to create beauty (Hofmann 185). Instead, Nan blends his bicultural legacies to herald a migrant poetics. Just as he takes liberties with Chinese texts and modulates the trope of rustic solitude according to his urban situation, his assimilation of American aphorisms, as Arnold Pan astutely points out, is "never a one-way street, since his cultural familiarity with idiom and language are re-routed and interpreted through an immigrant experience" (Pan 24). For example, the authorial "fear" against which Faulkner admonishes becomes for Nan the angst of blazing his trail through foreign words. Unlike the great American authors, his challenge as poet is compounded by his adopted linguistic medium.

His redefinition of the American dream—as "something to be pursued only"—likewise turns on his *sui generis* explications of Emerson and Frost:

> This must be the true meaning of Emerson's dictum "hitch your wagon to a star." To be a free individual, he had to … endure loneliness and isolation, and had to give up the illusion of success in order to accept his diminished state as a new immigrant and as a learner of this alphabet. (619)

Nan's inference seems at odds with the purport of Emerson's motto and with its standard glosses. Emerson uses the sidereal metaphor twice (albeit with variant possessives) in *Society and Solitude*: "Now that is the wisdom of a man, in every instance of his labor, to hitch his wagon to a star, and see his chore done by the gods themselves." And: "Hitch your wagon to a star. Let us not fag in paltry works… Work rather for those interests which the divinities honor and promote" (Emerson 25, 27). Deployed in the first instance to describe human ingenuity in harnessing elemental forces and in the second to goad humankind to harbor high principles, the phrase has become, in common parlance, a hortatory adage for lofty ventures. But Nan conflates this maxim with another by Emerson—"If a man would be alone, let him look at the stars"—while developing an idiosyncratic line of thought. Gone is the grand entelechy epitomized by Emerson's metaphor, which shines instead as a lone beacon for Nan, beckoning him to either look to himself for contingent fulfillment or brace himself for probable fiasco: "He had to take the risk of wasting his life without getting anywhere and of becoming a joke in others' eyes" (619).

Nan's words echo Jin's soul-searching before the author decided to use English as his creative medium: "I had to ask myself whether I could accept failure as the final outcome … which meant having wasted my life without getting anywhere" (Jin, "Exiled" 119). In place of Emerson's confident proclamation, "Speak your latent conviction, and it shall be the universal sense" ("Self-Reliance"138), Nan expresses the tangible loneliness of groping in the margins. He sees his solitude as an existential condition for those relegated to the linguistic fringes. His invocation of Emerson to reflect his own tenuous plight is doubly ironic. Nicknamed by his classmates at Brandeis as "Mr. Wagon Man" for often quoting Emerson, Nan was told by a Chinese historian "not to '*parrot that so-called New England sage*' who was a racist and always despised the Chinese" (55).[6] The way Nan / Jin bends the poet-prophet's pronouncement to the measure of his own Chinaman's chance can thus be considered as either a tribute or retribution.

Robert Frost's pregnant question concerning "what to make of a diminished thing" is similarly retooled as a poignant self-reference by Nan—an unknown poet wielding a second tongue who must accept his "diminished state" as a novice in English letters (619). Although Nan echoes Emerson's conviction that the mind alone suffices as self-validation and that the individual surpasses any collective, his credo stems from his precarious situation as a linguistic amphibian exposed to the sharp tongues of Chinese and English critics. Mei Hong, a fellow emigrant, accuses Nan of betraying China and its language: "*That's why you've been writing in English and dreaming of becoming another Conrad or Nabokov... You are just making another buffoon of yourself!*" (496). No less caustic is the taunt of an English editor: "I admire your courage, but ... you are wasting your time. English is too hard for you." This editor later quotes Yeats: "No poet who doesn't write in his mother tongue can write with music and strength," adding: "Can you imagine your work becoming part of *our* language?" (626, 628; my emphasis). This prickly question is clearly meant to be rhetorical: Nan, a non-native English writer, cannot possibly enrich American literature, let alone the timbre and texture of its poetry. The editor's reference to English as "our" language casts Nan as a brazen interloper.[7]

Just as Jin argues for the need to "stretch" standard English to cover a foreign terrain, Nan, in his response to the editor in his personal journal, advances an elastic view of the language: "that xenophobic question ... ignores the fact that the vitality of English has partly resulted from its ability to assimilate all kinds of alien energies" (628). On a metanarrative level, by infiltrating American English with his peculiar conceits, Jin has already answered the editor's sardonic question. He has engendered a form of linguistic deterritorialization by adapting Chinese lines into English lyrics and by imbuing oft-quoted lines by Faulkner, Frost, and Emerson with shades peculiar to his own struggle as an émigré writer, thereby inflecting "standard" lexicons with singular tonalities. Weaving Chinese poetry into English texts and infusing an immigrant sensibility into the common understanding of the American literary canon dissolve cultural borders, keeping the ethnic legacy alive while expanding the American heritage.

Brought on in part by a shift into another tongue, Nan's solitary stance is likewise a hybrid variation on American rugged individualism and the Chinese reclusive ideal. Having entered the interstices between languages, even accepted the possibility of falling into the abyss, Nan senses a certain ontological and linguistic liberation in passing through the void, as the concluding tercet of his poem "An Exchange" signifies: "To write in this language is to be alone, / to live on the margin where / loneliness ripens into solitude" (659). Jin has said in an interview that English gives him "freedom ... of a different kind, closer to solitude," enabling him to be "independent and work alone" (Kellman 83). *AFL* suggests that the optimal habitat for a poet is not so much restorative as invigorating; the "self-made man" is not someone who has "made it" in monetary terms but rather a pilgrim who dares to spurn worldly profit and glory, chase after a personal ideal, and make something of himself against formidable odds. Jin does not downplay the importance of economic independence, legal citizenship, and domestic stability, all of which contribute to Nan's peace of mind. But he cautions against the craving for public veneration, obsessive accumulation of wealth, and the abandonment of personal objectives in the name of domestic responsibility or political expediency, or at the risk of intellectual or moral bankruptcy. Having overcome the menaces to self-trust that had prevented him from pushing his limits, Nan seems to have succeeded in attaining the kind of indomitable selfhood lauded by Emerson: "Think alone, and all places are friendly and sacred. The poets who have lived in cities have been hermits still. Inspiration makes solitude anywhere" (Emerson, "Literary Ethics" 58). Nan, who used to chafe at work and at home, now cherishes both localities, thanks to his ability to "think alone."

Concurrent Homelands

The ideas about home(land) presented in *AFL* find parallel exposition in *Migrant*. Although both fiction and nonfiction counsel against nostalgia, these two works evince what Ketu H. Katrak, in tracing the "parameters of literary imagination" in South Asian American writers, calls "the *simultaneity of geography*—namely, the possibility of living here in body and elsewhere in mind and imagination" (Katrak 201). With Jin and Nan, the concurrence lies not so much in being in one place physically and another mentally as in being unable to leave the former homeland behind, in still carrying it around melancholically on American shores.

Freud's notion of "melancholy" seems especially resonant here. Freud sees melancholia as a pathological manifestation of mourning, because the melancholic, instead of overcoming loss (the object of which can range from a "loved person" to "fatherland") through mourning, incorporates loss as part of the ego, because the remembrance of loss is so persistent that it becomes part of the self (Freud, "*Mourning*" 164). What Anne Anlin Cheng said about home and homelessness in *The Woman Warrior* is even more true, literally and psychologically, of Jin: "For Kingston's narrator, most at home when she is not at home, has surely fashioned for herself a subjective map that guarantees perpetual unease. If one cannot go home again ... there is often the other half of that prescription: and yet one always has to" (Cheng 67).[8]

Both "simultaneity of geography" and "melancholy" are captured in Jin's explication of Cavafy's "Ithaka" in *Migrant*. Jin notes in "An Individual's Homeland" that although Cavafy's title alludes to Odysseus's homestead, "Ithaka is a symbol of arrival, not of return. It represents what can be gained, not regained" (62). Jin may be speaking from his personal experience as both exile and immigrant. Jin posits that nostalgia "often deprives [migrants] of a sense of direction and prevents them from putting down roots anywhere" (63). After a prolonged departure, Jin adds, the ancestral land may become foreign to the native, as in the case of Odysseus, who fails to recognize Ithaca upon landing for two reasons: "first, in his twenty years of exile, he has changed and so has his memory of his homeland; second, his homeland has also changed, no longer matching his memory of it"; hence "one cannot return to the same place as the same person" (66). In dwelling on Odysseus's harrowing homecoming, including the cold welcome by most of the Ithacan citizenry (Penelope's suitors who have turned against the hero), Jin is registering his own estrangement, not unlike Nan's, from his native land. Nan expresses deep reservations upon visiting China after more than ten years abroad. He finds Beijing "hardly recognizable" and his home in Harbin alienating: "How lonely he felt in his parents' home, as though he hadn't grown up in this very apartment. Perhaps he shouldn't have come back in the first place" (*AFL* 530, 560).[9] Jin, who has been repeatedly denied a visa to China, does not even have the choice of return. His repudiation of nostalgia thus smacks of a defense mechanism, perhaps even sour grapes.

Yet Jin cannot extirpate himself psychologically from his native country, though he is haunted more by melancholy than by nostalgia. Unlike a typical immigrant tale, *AFL* indexes far more than Nan's acculturation in the New World. Much of *Migrant* and *AFL* reflects Jin's incessant wrangle, whether within earshot or not, with his native country, especially over official censorship—a primary reason why both Jin and Nan choose to write in English. Jin observes that for emigrants who find a physical return to their native country disappointing, the mother tongue could still make them feel virtually "at home" (*Migrant* 72–74). He discloses in his preface to the Chinese edition of *A Good Fall* (2009) that by translating this collection of short stories into Chinese, he has alleviated his own homesickness: "I have infused this self-translated text of mine with a measure of [nostalgia], using my native language to erect a small 'villa'—a way station, as it were, in my extensive odyssey" ("序 [Preface]" 7; my translation). But that collection is published in Taiwan, not the mainland, where most of Jin's works are still banned. In the United States, Jin is writing primarily for an English-speaking audience. He may be mulling over his own dilemma when he notes in "An Individual's Homeland" that for some writers, "the mother tongue is an unavailable 'home' … and their survival may lie in another language" (79–80).

For a writer, Jin implies, home is wherever one finds freedom. Both *AFL* and *Migrant* suggest that the art of writing must override other considerations. Nan, as mentioned earlier, is annoyed by an emigrant poet who gauges literature by its impact on the motherland. In *Migrant,* Jin asserts that the "first responsibility" of writers is "to write well" (28), that nothing is more important than "making one's art thrive." Hence, migrant writers must distance themselves from a native country that throttles creativity and invest in a new "homeland" and "do everything" to find their place in the adopted language (59).

All the same, Jin admits that a writer is always laden with a personal history: "no matter where we go, we cannot shed our past completely" (*Migrant* 86). What he says of "Ithaka" also applies to his own voyage. He points out that although Cavafy changes the symbolic meaning of Odysseus's homeland, the title still carries with it the entire "cultural baggage": "The beauty and the subtlety of the word 'Ithaka' resides in its mythological resonance, which evokes something in the past in the traveler's origin—something that has shaped his imagined destination." Therefore, the speaker's "arrival cannot be completely separated from his point of departure, because his journey was effected by the vision of a legendary city whose historical and cultural significance constitutes part of his heritage" (*Migrant* 62). Analogously, the indelible imprint of the Chinese past creeps into Jin's *Migrant* and *AFL*. It is evident in the author's social commitment, notion of translation, preoccupation with the nation-state, and indirect critique of its literary establishment. Nan complains that no matter how hard he tries to dissociate his family from the old country, he can never extricate them completely: "Wherever they went, the old land seemed to follow them" (*AFL* 235). Insistently the old land seems to be lurking around the corner for Jin as well. Its presence suggests that even someone who vows to "stand alone" as a writer (*Migrant* 28) cannot insulate himself from his cultural legacies and geopolitical realities.

In Jin the inalienable heritage often takes the form of a nagging, if contradictory, desire to decry the ideological constraint of contemporary China and to be read and cherished by readers in his native land, to whose ethos, judgment, and approbation he remains susceptible. Inculcated since his youth with the social function of literature, Jin has not entirely jettisoned such a precept in favor of art for art's sake, but is ever mindful of his public responsibility as writer. Taught to venerate New China as a sacrosanct entity, Jin continues to be haunted by its looming shadow. The narrator in Kundera's *Ignorance* observes: "the Communist countries hurled anathema at emigration, deemed to be the most odious treason" (Kundera 17). In reversing the charge of an individual betraying a country to that of a country betraying the individual, Jin still adheres to the notion of a monolithic nation, whose grip on him is all too palpable. His reluctance to refer to himself and his work directly in *Migrant* is also in keeping with Chinese cultural expectations, such as self-effacement and reticence about personal struggle and accomplishment (see Chapter 6). Despite his attempt to turn his back on China, it remains the primary setting and inspiration of his fiction. Beneath Jin's restive energy and the determination to "move forward" in *Migrant* is a keen sense of rejection by the country of origin.

Although Jin considers to be irrational the belief that "success means much more if it is appreciated by the people of one's native land" (65), he too, it seems, yearns to be validated by his Chinese compatriots. Although he acknowledges that finding one's place in an adopted language may involve sacrificing the mother tongue, he maintains it is still important to retain the native language's "strength and resources" (60). It matters to him that a work, when "rendered into different languages, especially into the language spoken by the people the author writes about ... still remains meaningful" (59). Apropos of Chinua Achebe's criticism of Conrad's *Heart of Darkness* (for failing to resonate with Africans, who are not treated "as normal human beings"), Jin asks his readers to envisage "what kind of work it would become if the people it portrays could accept the story as literature that speaks also to them." He then supplies the answer himself: "The novella would grow into a masterpiece of universal significance and appeal" (59).

This subjunctive remark seems to convey his own unspoken longing to be read and appreciated in mainland China. One also catches a certain self-reflection when Jin relates that Conrad declined honorary degrees offered by Oxford and Cambridge, and a knighthood. "What he really wanted was the Nobel Prize," Jin deduces, "to mend the division within his identity. The Nobel Prize would also have brought honor to the Poles and therefore would have redeemed him from the guilt for his 'desertion' of Poland" (34). Global recognition would also mend the inner division of Jin, who has implicitly set his life and work alongside Conrad, Nabokov, Kundera, and Naipaul, thereby establishing a transnational migrant pedigree.

For Jin the breach is created not only by his emigration and his Anglophone writing but, above all, by official censorship in China. In a country where the media and the arts are still enlisted to serve politics, writers tread dangerous waters when they tackle delicate topics such as the Anti-Rightist Campaign, the Great Leap Forward, the Cultural Revolution, or the Tiananmen Incident. When Jin complains about the absence of any literature depicting the Anti-Rightist Movement in the late 1950s, he is all too aware of the ongoing political pressure perpetuating this silence. His criticism of Lin Yutang's sanitized portrayal of China is, I believe, also an indirect indictment of the current Chinese government's effort to promote an unblemished national image at the expense of honest documentation. In "The Censor in the Mirror," Jin comments on the pernicious effects of censorship: "it's not only what Chinese Propaganda Department does to artists, but what it makes artists do to their own work"—turning themselves into self-censors ("Censor" 26). His own Chinese editor told him in 2004 that his novels *The Crazed* (with the Tiananmen Incident as backdrop) and *War Trash* (about the Korean War) could not be published, owing to their sensitive subject matter; after the Shanghai censorship office rejected his collection of short stories *Ocean of Words* in 2005, the editor abandoned the project of publishing Jin's work in China altogether ("Censor" 26).

The sizable portions of *AFL* devoted to Nan's gambit to write in English and the vicissitudes of Danning and other writers and artists in China testify to Jin's unceasing preoccupation with artistic freedom in his Asian homeland. He no doubt draws on his own experience when he has Nan address the difficulties of continuing to write in Chinese and publish in China. Nan stops submitting work to China for publication after an editor there has asked him to delete several lines judged "too sensitive politically" (*AFL* 409); he learns about a group of novelists in Toronto whose manuscripts have been rejected in China due to the subject matter. Friends of his who have repatriated end up writing hackneyed or tepid work because of official censorship or the dictates of the publishing marketplace. Danning tells Nan that he is "living in a net, having to navigate through many invisible holes" (257). Even though Danning later becomes a popular writer in China, he remains stymied: "*The higher ups want us to write about dead people and ancient events ... to make us less subversive and more inconsequential*" (532). By hamstringing creative effort, Jin insinuates, the government has turned the country into a cultural desert that produces only arid works peripheral to lived experience. When Danning visits the Wus in Georgia, he not only admires the countryside scenery but also connects it with honest living and enduring art: "*Your life here is so clean and decent.*" He grumbles that "*significant work is impossible in China at present*" (593), that as a "*petty cadre at the writers' association*" he is prohibited from seeking spiritual enlightenment in a church or temple, that he is like a small fish yearning for "*clean water*" (602). The simile links cultural bureaucracy with muddy waters from which no one can emerge unpolluted.

In "An Individual's Homeland," Jin meditates on the title's two meanings—as one's provenance and as "the land where one's home is at present" (65). He concludes the essay in the first person plural: "no matter where we go, we cannot shed our past completely—so we must strive to use parts of our past to facilitate our journeys. As we travel along, we should also imagine how to rearrange the landscapes of our envisioned homelands" (86). Jin answers the challenge of rearranging the linguistic topography of the new homeland in *AFL*, in which the past winds its way to the present in the form of geopolitical reflection and cultural heritage. The novel ends on Christmas Day, with imagery that aligns pristine, if austere, nature with Nan's newfound strength as poet: "The sky was overcast and the wind chilly... Nan felt sleepy ... yet he was strong in spirit ... he mustn't nod off on his way home" (621). "Belated Love," "Homeland" (another poem by Nan), and the novel proper all end with the word "home." Nan, like the author, has chosen to savor the solitude of displacement and settle down in an outpost that will allow him to breathe freely, if not free of melancholy. After being virtually exiled from his native land, then adrift and tongue-tied in the New World, he has finally arrived at a place where he can feel more or less at home, both physically and linguistically.

But only more or less. One does not sense a full crossing over to the New World in *AFL*, or in Jin's life. Nan remains deeply entangled within his Chinese homeland's affairs. Even though he has settled down permanently in Georgia, he is still teetering on the hyphen psychologically. The same is true of Jin. Notwithstanding his inability to set foot in China again, he still attempts to salve his nostalgia by writing not only about China but also, increasingly, in his mother tongue. In addition to translating *A Good Fall* into Chinese, he has recently published a volume of Chinese poetry, entitled 《另一个空间》 (*Another Space*) (2015). He explains in its "Afterword 后记" that he had intended to draft the poems in Chinese first and then translate them into English, thereby "using Chinese to enrich English" (as I argue Jin has done in *AFL*). But he soon discovers that the Chinese language unfurls for him a "boundless vista, unlimited opportunity," and he therefore decides to compose in his "first language" in earnest (Jin, "Afterword" 138; my translation in this and subsequent citations therein).[10] What he says about this "return" to Chinese is achingly revealing:

> Using Chinese to write these poems has brought me tranquility and joy I have not relished for years. These poems can only resonate lyrically in Chinese… For me the process of penning this collection is … a glorious excursion that affords me serene bliss… But this happiness is only an interlude, for eventually I must return to the strenuous labor of writing in English, continuing all the way the path I myself have paved. I can't say I have no regret… But we must accept our personal exigencies and losses, and find meaningful work in the space allotted us, and build our home. (Jin, "Afterword" 138–140)[11]

This passage intimates the difference between writing in the first and the second language. Just before this intimation, Jin has quoted Gao Xingjian as saying: "If I write in French, the energy it takes to write one novel is equivalent to the energy expended on ten Chinese novels" (137). Jin uses Gao's words to flesh out the extra effort it takes for a writer to write in a second language. After decades of publishing in English, Jin still feels untold pleasure in revisiting his mother tongue. Using an image reminiscent of Bradatan's terrestrial trope, he likens his ease with Chinese to "plowing in familiar soil, turning it over effortlessly" (138), an analogy that is almost the very antithesis of the simile that looms before Nan when he is thinking of giving up his mother tongue and trying to become an English lyricist: "It was as if in front of him stood a stone wall inviting him to bump his head against it" (*AFL* 409). Although Jin has obviously scaled or circumnavigated the stone wall, it does not mean, in light of his Chinese "Afterword," that he feels perfectly at home in the new alphabet.

Jin has nevertheless discovered the hard-earned freedom and opportunity associated with liminality. Both *Migrant* and *AFL* remind me of the ending of Edward Said's memoir *Out of Place*, in which Said relates that his "search for freedom, for the self beneath" could only have begun because of his "rupture" from his natal family and native land: "So I have come to think of it as fortunate, despite the loneliness and unhappiness I experienced for so long. Now it does not seem important or even desirable to be 'right' and in place... Better to wander out of place ... and not ever to feel too much at home anywhere" (294). Jin and his protagonist, as transpacific and linguistic migrants, have also learned to inhabit the limen, to live with the simultaneity of geography.

Both *Migrant* and *AFL* can be read in different registers. *Migrant* is at once a scholarly exegesis of writers from diverse shores; a literary manifesto or a set of criteria applicable to Jin's work specifically and to migrant literature in general; an indirect autobiography reflecting Jin's own beliefs, travails, and aspirations; and a circuitous remonstration against Chinese censorship. Jin's defense of Conrad and Nabokov in "The Language of Betrayal" doubles as an apologia—by an author vulnerable to the slings and arrows from both East and West—against charges of betrayal and linguistic deficiency. His shifting definitions of "homeland" signal his effort to inure himself against a native country that has banned most of his books and to anchor his creativity elsewhere. Yet Jin cannot help looking homeward. For all his misgivings about nostalgia, he persists in unearthing the history of his native land and entertaining a figurative return. The wistful note remains perceptible in his resounding credo: "Only literature can penetrate historical, political, and linguistic barriers and reach the readership that includes the people of the writer's native country" (*Migrant* 22).

In an interview J. M. Coetzee has told David Attwell, in so many words, that "all writing is autobiography: everything that you write, including criticism and fiction, writes you as you write it" (Coetzee 17). Nowhere is this truer than in Jin's *Migrant* and *AFL*. Infusing personal experience into critical and artistic works does not make them any less inventive. As I argue in Chapter 6, the sensibility peculiar to a hyphenated writer can contribute to literary innovation. Instead of asking whether an author using English as a second language can measure up to standard English and canonical authors, we can attend to what he or she has brought to the English language and to the American heritage. In "The Language of Betrayal," Jin sides with Nabokov against Wilson by touting Nabokov's literary pyrotechnics as "unique to a non-native speaker who has an alien perspective on English." "His word games are of a different order, more exciting and more original," Jin continues. "After Nabokov, who can say non-native writers cannot crack jokes in English?" (51).

Jin's unique experience similarly has enabled him to cultivate a style peculiar to a bilingual intellectual migrant. The shuffling of Chinese and American tropes deliberately detaches the expressions from their national moorings, a figurative move in keeping with the notion of freedom in the novel, which is as much about writing in an open climate as breathing clean air, transmigrating ontologically as migrating geographically, and transitioning to a second tongue as finding a new home. After Ha Jin, must anyone still ask a non-native English writer: "Can you imagine your work becoming part of *our* language?"

Notes

1. Recent ecocriticism has highlighted the relationship between landscape and power, exposing how both colonialism and the attendant economic exploitation of indigenous people have devastated their native lands (see DeLoughrey and Handley; W. J. T. Mitchell). As Ursula K. Heise warns, however, "neither environmentalism nor ecocriticism should be thought of as nouns in the singular, and that the assumptions that frame environmentalist and ecocritical thought in the United States cannot simply be presumed to shape ecological orientations elsewhere" (Heise 9). In Chinese literature, local authorities pose environmental threats similar to those associated with colonialism.
2. Tao, a renowned poet and a provincial governor himself, resigned from the Jin court at around age 40 to become a farmer.
3. As a student at Brandeis University in 1989, Nan was unfairly implicated in a scheme to kidnap Chinese delegates' children, resulting in the revocation of his passport (and implicitly termination of funding) by the Chinese regime.
4. Jin self-consciously models his text after Pasternak's *Doctor Zhivago*, which also includes poems by the protagonist at the end of the novel proper. Nan's penchant for drawing lessons from quotidian events in *AFL* is also in keeping with Emerson's instruction to take a numinous lesson from each event.
5. See Hang Zhang on the various ways Jin uses English to reflect Chinese culture.
6. What the Chinese historian fails to notice is that Emerson, who had read many Confucian classics, delivered a speech in which he deems China "old, not in time only, but in wisdom." See Emerson, "Speech at Reception of Chinese Embassy" (*works* 523).

7. The relegation of people of Asian descent, American-born included, as perpetually foreign has been an enduring legacy. Timothy Yu writes in response to Calvin Trillin's poem "Have They Run Out of Provinces Yet?" about the invidious distinction of "we" and "they": "Who are 'they' in the poem? It was this word, in the poem's very first line, that made me realize that I, as a Chinese-American reader, was excluded from it. Because the 'they' can only be the Chinese themselves... And the 'we,' by implication, can only be white American diners ... and 'they,' the Chinese, hover ominously just out of frame" (Yu). The editor's question to Nan suggests that Chinese American writers are likewise outside the cognitive frame of American letters.
8. I thank Robert Kyriakos Smith for alerting me to the Freudian implication.
9. Jin attended Heilongjiang University in Harbin (hence the "Ha" in his choice of pseudonym). He told Te-hsing Shan in a 2008 interview that the banning of all but one of his books in China had deterred him from visiting mainland China, and that he didn't so much as receive an acknowledgment when he applied for a teaching position at Peking University in 2004 (Shan 41).
10. In this piece, Jin also distinguishes between "native language" and "first language": "Chinese is not only my native language but also my first language. For a migrant, especially a young one, after a prolonged settlement in a foreign land, the mother tongue may gradually become a second tongue, even a third tongue. In terms of creative writing, the most ideal condition is creating in one's first tongue" (Jin, "Afterword" 137; my translation).
11. Chinese original: "用汉语写这些诗给我带来了多年来从未有过的平静和欢悦,只能在汉语中才能产生回声,才能有诗意…这本诗集的创作过程是一次愉快的旅行,像是一个美好的假期给自己带来安静的喜悦。… 从令一个角度来看,这种喜悦是短暂的,只是一个假期,因为我最终还得回到艰难的工作中去,就是继续用英语写作,把自己的路走下去,走到底。这样说当然也不无遗憾…. 我们必须接受自己的境遇和损失,在有限的空间里做些有意义的工作,并建立自己的家园" ("Afterword" 139–140).

Works Cited

Bradatan, Costica. "Born Again in a Second Language." 4 August 2013. *New York Times.* 4 August 2013 <http://opinionator.blogs.nytimes.com/2013/08/04/born-again-in-a-second-language/?emc=eta1&_r=0 (Accessed August 4 2013)>.

Cavell, Stanley. "Aversive Thinking: Emersonian Representation in Heidegger and Nietzsche." *New Literary History* 22.1 (1991): 129–160.
Chen, Guangchen. "Personal Landscape: Shen Congwen and Gao Xingjiang's Autobiographical Writings." *Ecology and Life Writing*. Ed. Alfred Hornung and Zhao Baisheng. Heidelberg: Universitätsverlag. Winter 2013. 177–197.
Cheng, Anne Anlin. "The Melancholy of Race." *Kenyon Review* 19.1 (1997): 49–61.
Cheung, King-Kok. "Affinity of Mindscape and Landscape in Tao Qian and Emerson." *US-China Foreign Language* 13.4 (2015): 272–291.
——. "The Chinese American Writer as Migrant: Ha Jin's Restive Manifesto." *Amerasia* 38.2 (2012): 2–12.
Coetzee, J. M. *Doubling the Point: Essays and Interviews*. Ed. David Attwell. Cambridge: Harvard University Press, 1992.
DeLoughrey, Elizabeth, and George B. Handley, *Postcolonial Ecologies: Literatures of the Environment*. New York: Oxford University Press, 2011.
Emerson, Ralph Waldo. "Literary Ethics." *Essays and Lectures*. New York: Library of America, 1983. 52–62.
——. "Nature (1836)." *The Portable Emerson*. Ed. Carl Bode and Malcolm Cowley. New York: Penguin, 1979a. 7–50.
——. "Self-Reliance (1841)." *The Portable Emerson*. Ed. Carl Bode and Malcolm Cowley. New York: Penguin, 1979b. 138–164.
——. *Society and Solitude: Twelve Chapters*. Fields, Osgood & Co, 1870.
——. "Speech at Reception of Chinese Embassy (1868)." *The Works of Ralph Waldo Emerson*. Vol. 3. New York: Hearst's International Library Co. Publishers, 1914. 523–525.
Fan Zhongyan 范仲淹. *Yueyang Lou Ji*《岳阳楼记》. http://hn.rednet.cn/c/2012/07/26/2692358.htm (Accessed 30 September 2015).
Freud, Sigmund. "Mourning and Melancholia (1917)." In *The Standard Edition of the Complete Psychological Works of Sigmund Freud*. Ed. and trans. James Strachey. London: Hogarth Press, 1956–1974. 24 vols. 14: 239–260.
Gao, Xingjian 高行健. "The Necessity of Loneliness." *The Case for Literature*. Trans. Mabel Lee. New Haven: Yale University Press, 2007. 164–166.
——. "Without Isms." *The Case for Literature*. Trans. Mabel Lee. New Haven: Yale University Press, 2007b. 64–77.
Guo, Yingjian. "*A Good Fall*: Surviving the Internationalized Net." *Amerasia Journal* 38.2 (2012): 13–18.
Heise, Ursula K. *Sense of Place and Sense of Planet*. New York: Oxford University Press, 2008.
Hofmann, Bettina. "Ha Jin's *A Free Life*: Revisiting the Künstlerroman." *Moving Migration: Narrative Transformations in Asian American Literature*. Ed. Johanna C. Kardux and Doris Einsiedel. Münster: LIT Verlag, 2010. 199–212.

Jin, Ha 哈金. "后记 [Afterword]." 《另一个空间: 哈金诗集 [*Another Space: Ha Jin's Poetry*]》]. Taipei: Linking Books 聯經出版事業制司, 2015. 137–140.
———. "The Censor in the Mirror." *American Scholar* 77.4 (2008): 26–32.
———. "Exiled to English." *Sinophone Studies: A Critical Reader*. Ed. Shu-mei Shih, Chien-hsin Tsai, and Brian Bernards. New York: Columbia University Press, 2013. 117–124.
———. *A Free Life*. New York: Pantheon, 2007.
———. "In Defence of Foreignness." *The Routledge Handbook of World Englishness*. Ed. Andy Kirkpatrick. New York: Routledge, 2010. 461–470.
———. "Op-Ed Contributor: Exiled to English." *New York Times*, 31 May 2009: WK9.
———. "序 [Preface]." 《落地 [*A Good Fall*]》. Taipei: China Times Publishing Company, 2010. 5–7.
———. "曾有人说我是卖国贼 [Someone Has Accused Me of Being a Traitor]." 《时代人物周报: *People in Focus Weekly*》, 30 June 2005: np.
———. "A Stonemason." *Amerasia* 38.2 (2012): 1.
———. *The Writer as Migrant*. Chicago: University of Chicago Press, 2008b.
Jin, Ha et al. "Ha Jin: Commentaries." *Amerasia Journal* 38.2 (2012): 1–42.
Karlinsky, Simon, ed. *Dear Bunny, Dear Volodya: The Nabokov-Wilson Letters, 1940–1971*. Revised and Expanded Edition. Berkeley: University of California Press, 1979; 2001.
Katrak, Ketu H. "South Asian American Literature." *An Interethnic Companion to Asian American Literature*. Ed. King-Kok Cheung. New York: Cambridge University Press, 1997. 192–218.
Kellman, Steven G. "Interview with Ha Jin." *Switching Languages: Translingual Writers Reflect on Their Craft*. Lincoln: University of Nebraska Press, 2003. 81–84.
Kong, Belinda. "Theorizing the Hyphen's Afterlife in Post-Tiananmen Asian America." *MFS Modern Fiction Studies* (2010): 136–159.
———. *Tiananmen Fictions Outside the Square*. Philadelphia: Temple University Press, 2012.
Kundera, Milan. *Ignorance: A Novel*. Trans. Linda Asher. New York: Harper Perennial, 2003.
Levenson, Joseph R., and Franz Schurmann. *China: An Interpretive History*. Berkeley: University of California Press, 1969.
Li Chi 李祁. "The Changing Concept of the Recluse in Chinese Literature." *Harvard Journal of Asiatic Studies* 24 (1962–1963): 234–247.
Lin Yutang, 林语堂. *Moment in Peking*. New York: John Day, 1939.
Liu, Xiaobo. "On Solitude." ["论孤独" 《百家》 2 (1988): 5–6]. *New Ghosts, Old Dreams: Chinese Rebel Voices*. Ed. Geremie Barmé and Linda Jaivin. New York: Random House, 1992. 207–209.

Liu Yiqing 刘意青. "拿诚实作交易:哈金和他的小说《等待》[Trade Upon Integrity: Ha Jin and His Novel Waiting]." 《中华读书报》 [Zhonghua Dushubao], 14 June 2000: BF26.
Mao Zedong 毛泽东. "Talks at the Yan'an Forum on Literature and Art 在延安文艺座谈会上的讲话." *Modern Chinese Literary Thought: Writings on Literature, 1893–1945*. Ed. Kirk A. Denton. Stanford: Stanford University Press, 1942, 1996. 458–484.
Marx, Leo. "Pastoralism in America." *Ideology and Classic American Literature*. Ed. Sacvan Bercovitch and Myra Jehlen. New York: Cambridge University Press, 1986. 36–67.
Mitchell, W. J. T. *Landscape and Power*. 2nd Ed. Chicago: University of Chicago Press, 2002.
Mo Yan 莫言. "Bull." *New Yorker*, 20 November 2012: 67–73.
Mullen, Harryette. *Muse & Drudge*. San Diego: Singing Horse Press, 1995.
Nabokov, Vladimir. "[Letter to Edmund Wilson dated November 18 1950]." *Dear Bunny, Dear Volodya: The Nabokov-Wilson Letters, 1940–1971*. Ed. Simon Karlinsky. Revised and Expanded Edition. Berkeley: University of California Press, 1979; 2001. 282.
Ninh, erin Khuê. *Ingratitude: The Debt-bound Daughter in Asian American Literature*. New York: New York University Press, 2011.
Pan, Arnold. "Belonging Across Cultures: Immigration and Citizenship in *A Free Life*." *Amerasia Journal* 38.2 (2012): 19–24.
Rushdie, Salman. *Imaginary Homelands: Essays and Criticism 1981–1991*. New York: Penguin, 1992.
Said, Edward W. *Out of Place: A Memoir*. New York: Norton, 2000.
——. *Reflections on Exile and Other Essays*. Cambridge: Harvard University Press, 2002.
Shan, Te-hsing 单德興. "Poetry, Freedom, and the Other: Reading Ha Jin's *A Free Life*." 《他者與亞美文學: *The Other and Asian American Literature*》. Ed. Te-hsing Shan. Taipei: Institute of European and American Studies, Academia Sinica, 2015. 40–74.
——. "辞海中的好兵:哈金访谈录 [The Good Soldier in Cihai: An Interview with Ha Jin.]." *In the Company of the Wise: Conversations with Asian American Writers and Critics*. Ed. Te-hsing Shan. Taipei: 允晨文化 [Yunchen Wenhua], 2009. 20.
T'ao Ch'ien 陶潜. "Peach Blossom Spring." *Anthology of Chinese Literature: From Early Times to the Fourteenth Century*. Ed. Cyril Birch. Trans. Cyril Birch. Vol. 1. New York: Grove Press, 1965. 167–168.
Trillin, Calvin. "Have They Run Out of Provinces Yet?" *New Yorker*, 4 April 2016.
Updike, John. "Nan, American Man: A New Novel by a Chinese Émigré." *New Yorker*, 3 December 2007: 100–102.

Whitman, Walt. *Leaves of Grass.* Ed. Malcolm Cowley. First 1855 Edition. New York: Penguin, 1976.

Wilson, Edmund. "[Letter to Nabokov dated 12 November 1940]." *Dear Bunny, Dear Volodya: The Nabokov-Wilson Letters, 1940–1971.* Ed. Simon Karlinsky. Revised and Expanded Edition. Berkeley: University of California Press, 1979; 2001. 34.

Yu, Timothy. "White Poets Want Chinese Culture Without Chinese People." *New Republic,* 9 April 2016.

Zhang, Hang. "Bilingual Creativity in Chinese English: Ha Jin's In the Pond." *World Englishes* 21 (2002): 305–315.

CHAPTER 9

Slanted Allusions: Marilyn Chin and Russell C. Leong

My second chapter demonstrates how Maxine Hong Kingston and Frank Chin "claim America" by combing through the Chinese heroic tradition to forge a usable past that can empower them as Asian Americans. This last chapter shows how Marilyn Chin and Russell C. Leong "reclaim the hyphen"—assert their dual heritage—not only by drawing literary inspiration from both Chinese and multicultural American sources but also by lunging at transpacific gender and class inequalities. Like Kingston and Frank Chin, Marilyn Chin and Leong enact anew the *wen-wu* ideal—writing and fighting. Furthermore, the two poets challenge the societal norms of *two* national cultures: they pull no punches in attacking both sides of the hyphen.

Within Asian American literary discourse, the use of Chinese material has been a fraught and controversial topic from the start. Critical misgivings about the evocation of the Orient in Chinese American literature are so pervasive that Chinese scholar Zhao Wenshu urges critics to turn their attention to "works that do not address China or Chinese culture" (256). On the contrary, Frank Chin advocated a thorough reclaiming of an authentic Asian heroic tradition. His wholesale endorsement of traditional classics, as I noted in Chapter 2, risked reinstalling patriarchal mores and even smacked of ancestral worship. This critical debate and Asian American literary studies in general have by and large focused on content, often overlooking the formal techniques of writers who engage in multilingual wordplay. The lack of stylistic research has led to an eclipse of poetry by prose, a stress on ethnographic rather than literary value, and a foreshortening of some distinctive bicultural works of art.[1] Trafficking in two languages can generate a host of dialogic possibilities. As M.M. Bakhtin observes, "The life of the word is contained in its transfer from one mouth to another, from one context to another context, from one social collective to another, from one generation to another" (202). This chapter advances an analytical strategy that foregrounds intercultural exchanges and encourages reciprocal scrutiny between Anglophone and Sinophone worlds. A similar strategy can be applied to texts by writers from other ethnic backgrounds who have dual linguistic expertise and transnational concerns.

Through the poetry of Marilyn Chin and Russell C. Leong, I demonstrate that it is possible to invoke ethnic heritage without either pandering to the desire for exotica or kowtowing to patriarchal authority. Looking askance at cultural legacies to unleash a two-pronged critique is, in fact, one of the distinctive features of Chinese American literature. My analysis of "Song of the Sad Guitar" and "Get Rid of the X" by M. Chin, and "Your *Tongzhi* Body" and "*Bie You Dong Tian*: Another World Lies Beyond" by Leong highlights the coordination of poetics and politics by the two writers, their ability to discern transnational affiliations produced by globalization, and their reshuffling of ethnic signifiers. The two poets steer clear of the Scylla of Orientalism and the Charybdis of ancestral worship.

Before discussing the four poems, I would like to use an expression from Maxine Hong Kingston's *The Woman Warrior*, already cited in Chapter 2, to illustrate my concept of "slanted allusions": "The [Chinese] idioms for revenge are 'report a crime'... The reporting is the vengeance—not the beheading, not the gutting, but the words" (Kingston, *WW* 53). Most China-born people would not associate the Chinese term for revenge *baochou* 报仇 with a verbal act, any more than native English speakers seeing the word *breakfast* would think of its etymological origin—breaking a fast. If her English translation is judged according to how accurately it brings over the indigenous Chinese expression, it is admittedly a poor rendition. In the context of *The Woman Warrior*, however, Kingston's intentional parsing of the idiom resonates with the major themes of her memoir, allowing the narrator to defy the silence imposed on her and to tailor the legend of the Chinese swordswoman to her own needs. The dorsal inscription Kingston invokes reminds Chinese readers not of the warrior in the Chinese "Ballad of Mulan" but of Yue Fei, a general in the Sung Dynasty whose mother carved four words on his back. By conflating Mulan and Yue Fei, Kingston claims literary privilege for Chinese women, who traditionally were denied education. This conflation also allows the author, an avowed pacifist, to redefine heroism by transferring the focus from martial prowess to discursive power. Instead of faulting Kingston for "distorting" the idiom *baochou* or the myth of Mulan, she should be credited for ingenious self-refashioning.

As my example of *baochou* illustrates, a slanted allusion may refer either to a novel interpretation of an autochthonous idiom or to a conscious repurposing of primary sources. More than merely a nod to Emily Dickinson's poem "Tell all the Truth but tell it slant—," my coinage—like the recuperated term *negritude*—carries a subversive edge, since "slant" (as in "slant-eyed") is a racial slur that often has been hurled at "heathen Chinee." I use the adjective to amplify how Asian American writers use literary allusions cheekily or defiantly. Paying attention to the myriad ways in which these authors draw from their transpacific roots may open up a discursive space for scholars interested in decentering the Western heritage, debunking essentialist notions of Chinese and American literary traditions, exploring the distinction between Asian and Asian American discourse, or teasing out the mesh of art and politics.

Marilyn Chin and Russell Leong, though they belong to a slightly younger generation, share with Kingston a bilingual ability and a hyphenated sensibility, a Buddhist bent, a predilection for progressive politics informed by the feminist and civil rights movements, and a penchant for polyglot interplay that implicates the dominant Chinese and US cultures. Both M. Chin and Leong are winners of the PEN Oakland Josephine Miles Literature Award, Leong in 1994 for *The Country of Dreams and Dust* and Chin in 1995 for *The Phoenix Gone, The Terrace Empty*; Chin also won the 2015 Anisfield-Wolf National Award for *Hard Love Province*. Both poets invested considerable time in their youth to learning Chinese. Chin earned a BA in Chinese from the University of Massachusetts, Amherst in 1977; Leong studied Chinese and Comparative Literature at National Taiwan University for over a year during 1974–1975. Both have acknowledged the impact of their Chinese educations on their writing. "How exciting to have this great opportunity to make a 'political' statement about my bicultural identity by exacting my ideas with hybridized forms… I often put a drop of yellow blood in conventional form to assert my bicultural identity… To disrupt the canonical order. To piss on that establishment tree" (M. Chin, "Interview" 113). Leong puts it more mildly: "I probably played around with words and double meaning when I was learning Chinese. It helped me appreciate the sense of pun in Chinese… Studying

Chinese helps me to be aware of the resonance of the language, and I will consciously choose names, titles, that I know make sense even in Chinese, such as *Phoenix Eyes*" (278). In fact, the phoenix—the bird that spreads its wings over both Eastern and Western mythologies—appears in Chin's *The Phoenix Gone, The Terrace Empty* (1994), as well as in Leong's *Phoenix Eyes* (2000).

Unlike early Asian American writers intent on "claiming America," these two reclaim both China and the United States—but on their own terms via rhetorical turns. They tilt their Chinese allusions so that the indigenous expressions acquire another shade of meaning. M. Chin, in "Song of the Sad Guitar," overhauls Chinese and multicultural literary references to female confinement to make room for a creative space; in "Get Rid of the X" she turns a Tang poem into a feminist declaration of independence. Leong, in "Your *Tongzhi* Body," transmutes a homophobic slur into a term of compassion and solidarity; in *Bie You Dong Tian*: Another World Lies Beyond" he invokes a proverb that promises an exotic vista only to reveal racial and social stratification and to remember migrant laborers on both sides of the Pacific. M. Chin's and Leong's cultural references resist—rather than reinforce—patriarchal authority and Orientalism.

M. Chin is an admirer of Kingston, to whom she dedicates "Song of the Sad Guitar," a prose poem:

> In the bitter year of 1988 I was banished to San Diego, California, to become a wife there. It was summer. I was buying groceries under the Yin and Yang sign of Safeway. In the parking lot, the puppies were howling to a familiar tune on a guitar plucked with the zest and angst of the sixties. I asked the player her name.
> She answered:
> "Stone Orchid, but if you call me that, I'll kill you."
> I said:
> "Yes, perhaps stone is too harsh for one with a voice so pure."
> She said:
> "It's the 'orchid' I detest; it's prissy, cliché and forever pink."
> From my shopping bag I handed her a Tsing Tao and urged her to play on.
>   She sang about hitchhiking around the country, moons and lakes, home-ward-honking geese, scholars who failed the examination. Men leaving for war; women climbing the watchtower. There were courts, more courts and inner-most courts, and scions who pillaged the country.

Suddenly, I began to feel deeply about my own banishment. The singer I could have been, what the world looked like in spring, that Motown collection I lost. I urged her to play on:

Trickle, trickle, the falling rain.
Ming, ming, a deer lost in the forest
Surru, surru, a secret conversation
Hung, hung, a dog in the yard.

Then, she changed her mood, to a slower lament, trilled a song macabre, about death, about a guitar case that opened like a coffin. Each string vibrant, each note a thought. Tell me, Orchid, where are we going? "The book of changes does not signify change. The laws are immutable. Our fates are sealed." Said Orchid—the song is a dirge and an awakening.

Two years after our meeting, I became deranged. I couldn't cook, couldn't clean. My house turned into a pigsty. My children became delinquents. My husband began a long lusty affair with another woman. The house burned during a feverish Santa Ana as I sat in a pink cranny above the garage singing, "At twenty, I marry you. At thirty, I begin hating everything that you do."

One day while I was driving down Mulberry Lane, a voice came over the radio. It was Stone Orchid. She said, "This is a song for an old friend of mine. Her name is Mei Ling. She's a warm and sensitive housewife now living in Hell's Creek, California. I've dedicated this special song for her, 'The Song of the Sad Guitar.'"

I am now beginning to understand the song within the song, the weeping within the willow. And you, out there, walking, talking, seemingly alive—may truly be dead and waiting to be summoned by the sound of the sad guitar.

for Maxine Hong Kingston (M. Chin, *Phoenix Gone* 25)

M. Chin's allusions to *The Woman Warrior* in this piece are readily apparent, even without the explicit dedication at the end. Kingston's memoir features five kindred and fabled women: a no-name aunt; Mulan, the legendary warrior; Brave Orchid, the narrator's mother; Moon Orchid, Brave Orchid's sister; and T'sai Yen, a Chinese poet.[2] Chin's narrator, Mei Ling (Chin's Chinese name), reminds the reader of Moon Orchid, who likewise becomes deranged after her husband's love affair; Mei Ling also takes after T'sai Yen, the poet in exile who creates lyrics to the measures of "barbarian" music. Stone Orchid, for her part, is reminiscent of Mulan, the androgynous warrior; of Brave Orchid, the champion storyteller; and of T'sai Yen, the lyricist.

The Woman Warrior is merely one of several literary texts embedded in Chin's poem. "Song of the Sad Guitar" clearly echoes "Ode to Pipa"《琵琶行》(which also can be translated as "Song of the Sad Pipa") by Bai Juyi (白居易, 772–846), a narrative poem about the Tang poet's postprandial encounter with a pipa player by the river. Just when the poet—the host—yearns for music to accompany his parting drink with his guests, the company suddenly hears pipa music afloat. The pipa player later recounts her sad life story: she had been a popular musician courted by many a youth, but when her beauty faded, she married a merchant from another town who often leaves her by herself (all translations of Chinese verses into English are mine unless otherwise stated):

> 去来江口守空船,绕船月明江水寒
> "In his absence I tend an empty boat surrounded by a chilly moonlit lake.
> 夜深忽梦少年事,梦啼妆泪红阑干
> Last night I dreamt of my lost youth and tears stained my rouged cheeks."

Bai Juyi, himself banished to a distant land, empathizes with the musician and asks her to play another song:

> 我闻琵琶已叹息,又闻此语重唧唧
> I sighed while listening to her pipa; hearing her story, I broke into sobs.
> 同是天涯沦落人,相逢何必曾相识
> "As fellow wayfarers on earth we need not have met to cherish this encounter.
> 我从去年辞帝京,谪居卧病浔阳城
> Dismissed from the capital last year, I was bedridden at Xunyang.
> 浔阳地僻无音乐,终岁不闻丝竹声
> Deprived of music in this hinterland, I heard no lutes or flutes all year long.
> ....
> 今夜闻君琵琶语,如听仙乐耳暂明
> Your exquisite pipa tonight is like ethereal music to my ears.
> 莫辞更坐弹一曲,为君翻作琵琶行
> Do not begrudge me another song; I'll render an ode for your pipa."
> 感我此言良久立,却坐促弦弦转急
> Touched by my words, she stands transfixed, then sits and strums fervently.
> 凄凄不似向前声,满座重闻皆掩泣

The plaintive tune strays from preceding strains; on listening all our eyes tear.
座中泣下谁最多?江州司马青衫湿
Whose eyes tear the most? The host's black robe is drenched.

Bai Juyi, the pipa player, and Mei Ling are all displaced artists. But while the Tang poet never asks the pipa player her name, M. Chin devotes a dialogue to the guitarist's first name. This naming bears an indirect tribute to *The Woman Warrior*. Given the common Chinese character *lan* 兰 (orchid), which appears in both Moon Orchid's and Brave Orchid's names, a symbolic sisterhood exists between them and Mulan in Kingston's text. To this trio, Chin has added "Stone Orchid." In bestowing an allusive name on her guitarist so she would not remain nameless like the musician in "Ode to Pipa" or the no-name aunt in *The Woman Warrior*, Chin implicitly claims lineage to a Chinese American feminist heritage.

Stone Orchid, however, abhors her floral name because it is "prissy, cliché, and forever pink." Presumably, she does not wish to follow the beaten track of a delicate Oriental maiden. (Perhaps that's also why M. Chin braces the flower with "Stone.") As if responding to her maverick disposition, Mei Ling offers her a Tsing Tao beer in lieu of coins for her music. Whereas only the male host and his fellow guests in "Ode to Pipa" indulge in wine, Chin gives her female musician the freedom to relish alcoholic beverages—which purportedly inspired many a Tang and Song verse, a notable example of which will be discussed shortly in connection with "Get Rid of the X." Furthermore, unlike the pipa player marooned in an "empty boat," the guitarist "sang about hitchhiking around the country." Chin thus tweaks her references to "Ode to Pipa" by giving her female musician a name and the traditionally masculine perks to imbibe alcohol and to travel.

Chin also inverts the meaning of the lines in Ezra Pound's "The River-Merchant's Wife," an English rendition of Li Bai's "Ballad of a Trader's Wife" 《长干行》: "At fourteen I married My Lord you... / At fifteen... I desired my dust to be mingled with yours ... forever and forever. / Why should I climb the lookout? / At sixteen you departed... The leaves fall early this autumn / They hurt me. I grow older." Li Bai's poem and Pound's rendition trace the deepening of connubial felicity into eternal love, followed by separation and solitary waiting. Mei Ling, conversely, sings of matrimonial disenchantment: "At twenty, I marry you. At thirty, I begin hating everything that you do."[3]

In addition to signifying on Bai Juyi and Li Bai, Chin also alludes to Li Qingzhao (李清照, 1084–c1151), the preeminent female poet of the Song Dynasty.[4] Like Bai Juyi, who commiserates with the pipa player as a fellow exile, Mei Ling feels "deeply about [her] own banishment" upon hearing the guitarist's lyrics: "There were courts, more courts and innermost courts." The line glances at the refrain that opens "An Immortal by the Lake" 《临江仙》 by Li Qingzhao who, in turn, borrows the line from Ouyang Xiu (欧阳修, 1007–1072): "庭院深深深几许"—literally, "how deep is the deep court(yard) that deepens into another."

Li Qingzhao is known especially for her lyrics about the sorrowful isolation caused by widowhood, as in these lines from "An Immortal by the Lake":

庭院深深深几许,云窗雾阁常扃
    How deep is the court that deepens into another, casements shrouded in mist
    ....
如今老去无成,谁怜憔悴更雕零,
    Aging and living in vain; who would pity a withered petal adrift?
试灯无意思,踏雪没心情
    Loath to light new lanterns; or to tread the snow.

The refrain about the deep courtyard calls forth the architecture peculiar to some old Chinese mansions, with a section consisting of a courtyard and a residential unit leading to another courtyard and residence. But the word *court* in M. Chin's poem holds dual meanings—referring at once to the imperial court and to the extension of a Chinese compound, in which the innermost court is often designated as the women's quarters. This pun couples ousted court functionaries with sequestered women, since "scholars who failed the examination" and officials (such as Bai Juyi and Li Bai) who fell out of favor with the ruling power were barred from the royal court and forced to lead an exilic life. Such an existence, Chin suggests, is comparable to the lonesome life in an innermost domestic "court" inhabited by royal concubines, forsaken or out-of-favor wives, and forlorn widows. The pun thus aligns the narrator of "Ode to Pipa," an official banished from the imperial court, with Moon Orchid, a jilted wife who locks herself in a dark room; the speaker in "An Immortal by the Lake," a widow who pines away in a boudoir; and Mei Ling, a woman "banished to San Diego … to become a wife" who, two years later, "sat in a pink cranny above the garage singing" a heartbreak song.

Like the various pockets of confinement mentioned in these texts, M. Chin's "pink cranny above the garage" similarly takes on a twofold meaning, brushing against a double entendre. It recalls the "lookout," the "empty boat," the "inner-most court," and perhaps also Harriet Jacobs's attic space in *Incidents in the Life of a Slave Girl*, the attic in Charlotte Brontë's *Jane Eyre*, and the "cage" in Maya Angelou's "I Know Why the Caged Bird Sings"—all places associated with female incarceration.[5] But "pink cranny" also conjures up a womb—or, more figuratively, a Woolfian "room of one's own" that incubates ideas. Instead of wallowing in loneliness and regret about "the singer [they] could have been," bereft women, Chin intimates, can transform captivity into creativity, parlay sobs into songs.

Bai Juyi's musician, Li Bai's river-merchant's wife, Li Qingzhao's widow, Kingston's Moon Orchid, and M. Chin's Mei Ling all share desolation (and loss of beauty or sanity) on account of a husband's absence or desertion. By referencing these women and placing Mei Ling next to them, M. Chin suggests that the havoc wrought by spousal abandonment is timeless: "The book of changes does not signify change... Our fates are sealed." But her simultaneous reincarnation of Mulan, Brave Orchid, and T'sai Yen (as well as Kingston, whose house burned down in 1991) in Stone Orchid and Mei Ling recasts "Song of the Sad Guitar" from a dirge bemoaning the loss of one's prime into a call for feminist awakening, urging women who lead lives of quiet desperation—"you, out there"—to rise from their living death and emulate the sassy guitarist who goes against the cliché of the lovelorn lady whose raison d'être depends on her lord. By having Stone Orchid, whose ability to create lyrics does not rest on male patronage, dedicate a song to Mei Ling, Chin broaches the possibility of female bonding and mutual support, of women succoring each other.

This prose poem's richness emanates from dense layers of allusions, structural as well as incidental. Just as there is a "song within the song" in the guitarist's performance, a Chinese-box structure scaffolds M. Chin's intertextual composition: Bai Juyi's dedication to the pipa player within Stone Orchid's dedication to Mei Ling within Chin's dedication to Kingston; Li Bai's merchant wife's letter within Ezra Pound's merchant wife's letter within Bai Juyi's merchant wife's song within Mei Ling's song; Li Bai's "*wangfutai* 望夫台 (descry husband tower)" within Pound's "lookout" within the guitarist's "watchtower" within Mei Ling's "pink cranny"; Ouyang Xiu's line within Li Qingzhao's line within Stone Orchid's lyric; the pipa player's song and T'sai Yen's song within "song of the sad guitar"; and Mulan's "Orchid" within Kingston's "Orchid(s)" within M. Chin's "Orchid."

The array of allusions to "Ode to Pipa," "The River-Merchant Wife," and "An Immortal by the Lake" is, however, askew. The three Chinese poems have in common a mournful feminine voice heard in the poetic subgenre known as Boudoir Complaint 闺怨诗, of which Li Qingzhao's "Immortal by the Lake" is a classic exemplar. But Chin harkens back to this subgenre less to lament the lot of abandoned wives than to inspire women to pull themselves together through their own gumption and mutual sustenance. Bai Juyi's pipa player, Li Bai's river-merchant's wife, and Li Qingzhao's widow bemoan their bleak seclusion, yet they are resigned to their lot. Chin's guitarist is a feisty singer who rouses dejected wives from their dolor, who reaches out to Mei Ling with her song and solicitude.

Like "Song of the Sad Guitar," M. Chin's "Get Rid of the X" (about a speaker in San Diego who also finds herself unhappily wed) pivots on gender trouble:

> My shadow followed me to San Diego
>   silently she never complained.
> No green card, no identity pass,
>   she is wedded to my fate.
> The Moon is drunk and anorectic,
>   constantly reeling, changing weight.
> My shadow dances grotesquely
>   resentful she can't leave me.
> The moon mourns his unwritten novels,
>   cries naked into the trees and fades.
> Tomorrow, he'll return to beat me
>   blue—again, again and again.
> Goodbye Moon, goodbye Shadow.
>   my husband, my lover, I'm late.
> The sun will plunge through the window.
>   I must make my leap of faith.
>
> (M. Chin, *Rhapsody* 45)

"Get Rid of the X" parodies "Drinking Alone under the Moon" 《月下独酌》 by Li Bai (李白, 701–762), known honorifically as Poet Immortal 诗仙:

花间一壶酒 A jug of wine amid flowers
独酌无相亲 Alone, I drink without companions;
举杯邀明月 I lift my goblet to toast Bright Moon
对影成三人 Along with Shadow we make three.
月既不解饮 But Moon knows not how to drink
影徒随我身 Shadow dogs my body in vain;
暂伴月将影 I'll stay with Moon and Shadow
行乐须及春 To cavort while spring lasts.
我歌月徘徊 As I sing, Moon lingers
我舞影零乱 As I dance, Shadow tangles;
醒时同交欢 Sober, we keep merry company
醉后各分散 Drunk, we part ways.
永结无情游 Tying an eternal knot with no strings attached
相期邈云汉 We shall meet beyond the stars.

(My translation)

The difference in agency between Li Bai's speaker and Marilyn Chin's speaker is pronounced. The male interlocutor, rhapsodic in his sublime solitude, is transfigured in Chin's poem into a miserable modern wife, who projects her emotions onto the moon and her shadow. Like her shadow, she seems to be a self-effacing and acquiescent illegal immigrant ("No green card, no identity pass") yoked to her spouse. Although both Li Bai and M. Chin personify the moon and the shadow, the male speaker in "Drinking Alone" always calls the shots, literally and figuratively: he takes the lead in drinking, singing, and dancing, disparaging the moon for being an inept drinking companion and the shadow for being an impersonator. The female speaker in "Get Rid of the X," conversely, seems diffident and obliging. While Li Bai's speaker belittles the moon and the shadow, Chin's speaker is the one who is being deprecated, resented, and disciplined.

This contrast mostly stems from gender difference. On one level the "drunk and anorectic" moon in M. Chin's second stanza is a clever anthropomorphic metaphor that captures the waxing and waning of the moon. But anorexia nervosa is an eating disorder mostly afflicting young women under pressure to live up to the Barbie Doll image, to stay willowy to please their boyfriends and lovers. By merging the changing images of the moon during its monthly cycles, a recurrent object correlative in Chinese poetry, with the conceit of a female body besieged by gendered standards of physical beauty and conveyed through the use of a modern clinical adjective, the Chinese American speaker reveals her own negative self-image, depression, eating disorder, and alcoholism. Similarly, the shadow's annoyance at being a hanger-on amplifies the self-loathing of the speaker, betokening her ambivalence toward her spouse and toward their enmeshment.

The third stanza sheds light on the marital problem. The husband seems to be a novelist manqué who takes out his frustrations on his wife.[6] The speaker, still projecting her own emotions onto inanimate objects (in this instance, the moon), mourns her spouse's writer's block, either because she measures her own worth by his success or because she dreads the violence he will mete out to her after his literary ambition is thwarted: "Tomorrow, he'll return to beat me / Blue—again, again and again." This rhythmic description of repetitive battering is a far cry from the self-actualizing, carpe diem motif in Li Bai's verse. In its stead is the prospect of endless pain and endless blue—in both its senses of bruising and melancholy.

In the last stanza, however, the "lunatic" influence of the moon is replaced by solar enlightenment. Unlike the Tang speaker, who hankers after a reunion in the galaxy with the moon and his shadow, Chin's female speaker is bidding a long farewell to her husband and her shadowy lover after discovering her pregnancy ("I am late"). Passive throughout the first three stanzas, she initiates her first—and perhaps also final—move in the last line of the poem: "I must make my leap of faith."

This ambiguous clincher is open to at least four interpretations. First, M. Chin may be toying with another analogue. Legend has it that the drunken Poet Immortal drowned when he fell from a boat while trying to embrace the moon reflected in a lake. This allusion to his besotted leap hints at a suicide attempt: Chin's speaker may have determined to leave her conjugal prison (which recalls the assorted metaphors for domestic confines in "Song of the Sad Guitar") by jumping out of the window. "Faith," in this instance, could refer to the Buddhist belief in reincarnation. A second possibility is that the speaker may be trying to induce an abortion by a fall. Alternatively, she may have resolved to take charge of her own life, to have "faith" in herself—to up and leave her overbearing husband and her self-denigrating alter ego. Finally, in a sense closely related to the previous scenario, she may be making her leap of imagination as a poet. In this interpretation, the speaker (unlike her unproductive husband and her mute shadow) has at last found her voice through the written word; she has "reported a crime" (to borrow Kingston's idiosyncratic paraphrase of the Chinese idiom for "revenge") and composed a vengeful poem, appropriately entitled "Get Rid of the X."

This enigmatic title is likewise open to multiple conjectures. "X" most likely refers to an *ex*-husband or an *ex*-lover: the speaker is quitting both her violent spouse and the maudlin moon. But X is also an unknown variable in algebra as well as a symbol often used by the illiterate in lieu of a personalized signature, and hence a mark of anonymity and illiteracy. In light of the weight M. Chin places in names and female literacy to contest the invisibility and illiteracy of traditional Chinese women in "Song of the Sad Guitar," ridding the "X" may suggest leaving behind her subordinate role as muse to the callous spouse and giving herself the literary imprimatur.

In the context of the speaker's pregnancy, "X" also figures in the genetics of sex: a female has two X chromosomes while a male has one X and one Y chromosome. Depending upon whether we opt for a suicidal or a pro-choice interpretation, the speaker either is getting rid of herself (a female made up of two X chromosomes) or getting rid of a presumably female embryo; she either wishes to be reborn as a male herself or wishes her embryo to be male. Since the speaker never asks to be given a "Y," however, it is possible that she merely wants to dispose of the second X: to be a unisex or to give birth to a child who does not carry any gender baggage. Lest this interpretation seem too much of a stretch, I enlist the authority of the author, whose protagonist in "Parable of the Guitar" imagines a novel populated by denizens who are "highly efficient creatures, each equipped with both a vagina and a penis for self-procreation" (M. Chin, "Parable" 193).

Both "Drinking Alone under the Moon" and "Get Rid of the X" celebrate some kind of self-sufficiency. However, "Get Rid of the X," in exposing domestic violence, implicitly cautioning against female dependence, and gesturing toward gender emancipation (through tinkering with sex chromosomes and adumbrating a lesbian ménage à trois with Moon and Shadow), plays fast and loose with the Tang poet's romantic reverie, much as Stone Orchid's dissident song tweaks the trope about an ineluctable female condition in "Ode to Pipa," "The River-Merchant Wife," and "An Immortal by the Lake." Chin's last line can thus be read as the poet's brash attempt to turn up her nose at ancestral worship: to free herself from the anxiety of the Chinese classical influence in general and specifically from the grip of the Poet Immortal. With her canted allusions and neologistic puns, Chin is crowing her own autonomy from Li Bai—to whose inebriating imagery she has issued a sobering riposte.

Chin's "Song of the Sad Guitar" and "Get Rid of the X" quarrel not only with the Chinese Boudoir Complaint but also with the American dream. Both poems frame the speakers' unhappy marriages within the context of Chinese immigration. This context presents the nuptial discord of the two poems in yet another register—allegorically, as an unfulfilled American dream reflecting the collective experience of Chinese Americans historically. In a long poem pointedly entitled "A Portrait of the Self as Nation, 1990–1991," Chin uses the conceit of marriage to explicitly set forth a parallel between sexual and racial subordination: "This is the way you want me— / asleep, quiescent, almost dead, / sedated by lush immigrant dreams / of global bliss, connubial harmony" (M. Chin, *Phoenix Gone* 95; see also Yao 209–216). Here the stereotype of the Asian woman as a docile wife morphs into the stereotype of the Asian American as model minority—accepted and even touted by the dominant culture as long as the subject refrains from protesting against institutionalized racism and sexism.

It is beyond the scope of this essay to elaborate on Chin's unabashed embrace of the personal as the political throughout her extensive repertoire. Suffice it to note that she invokes "Drinking Alone under the Moon" out of neither nostalgia for the Orient nor enchantment with the Occident, but rather to underscore the contrast between the Tang speaker's masculine prerogative, which allows him to indulge in a solipsistic ecstasy, and her female persona's embodied contingencies—including gender, citizenship, class, sexuality, and heteroglossia.

Russell C. Leong also manifests these contingencies in his lyrics, which employ marginalized groups—sexual minorities and migrant workers—to spur social awareness and promote communal support. If M. Chin deploys hybrid poetics to contest two patriarchal traditions, Leong uses it to dispute two homophobic and classist cultures. Dorothy J. Wang explicates how M. Chin wields Chinese and English poetic forms with cutting irony "to express the politicized and multiple perspectives of a twenty-first-century Chinese American female poet who belongs in the American body, political and poetic, as much as anyone else" (161). Even so Leong inserts sexual minorities and working-class people into the body politic, to show that they too belong as much as anyone else. In "Your *Tongzhi* Body," Leong redefines homosexuality as fluid and universal, breaking down the binary opposition of gay and straight, us and them, women and men, body and soul:

I see a brown *tongzhi* body—
Neither Female nor Male
Eyes from Beijing
Lips from Hong Kong
Spleen from Guizhou
Belly from Guangzhou
Feet from Singapore.

I touch a smooth *tongzhi* body—
Without day, month, or year of birth
Whose fingertips
Reach to Canada and America
Whose thighs and calves stretch to Malaysia
Whose toes touch Thailand and Vietnam
Whose body travels from Italy to Australia.

I hear a *tongzhi* body
Speak out—
A Voice sings, cries, and prays
As she/he tells stories
Of love and lust
Of homelessness and loneliness.

I know a *tongzhi* body like yours
Who is HIV positive
And HIV negative
But I will kiss you on the lips anyway
And on every part of your body
For everyone's love
And nobody's fault.

For I possess this brown *tongzhi* body—
And so do you and you and you.
For we are one, or are we not?

(Leong, "Tongzhi" 234–235)[7]

On the surface, "Your *Tongzhi* Body" is a transparent occasional poem in the *blazon* tradition commemorating the Second Chinese *Tongzhi* Conference—a forum for gays, lesbians, bisexuals, transsexuals, and transgenders—held in February 1998 in Hong Kong. The conference attracted 200 participants from 17 countries, including people from the places referenced in Leong's first two stanzas (A.D. Wong 764). Besides listing the disparate areas from which the conference participants hail, the specific enumeration of nine Asian Pacific sites undercuts the Chinese official line that homosexuality is a "Western disease." The mainland media has for a long time presented same-sex relationships as a foreign import, as blight from the West.

In the context of the conference in Hong Kong, Leong's title ostensibly uses a term of common address under Mao to refer to sexual minorities, as gay activists have done, flouting the nationalist and heteronormative practices of mainland China, Taiwan, Singapore, Hong Kong, and Malaysia. But the title does more: Leong "fleshes out" the epithet—through reiterative and multiplicitous embodiment—so that it pertains to all humankind, or at least to all peoples of color. A gloss at the end of the poem indicates that "*Tongzhi* is Hong Kong slang for gay or queer; it also means comrade in the Chinese language." The poem has given these two meanings a remix, nudging it from the queer margin to the human center. The *tongzhi* signifier in "Your *Tongzhi* Body" is a perfect example of a multiply slanted allusion. A brief review about the etymological development of this nomenclature is needed for us to appreciate how it has been turned and counterturned, shifted right and left politically, pushed to the fringes by homophobic journalists and reappropriated by gay activists, before Leong gives it yet another spin, at once centrifugal and centripetal, working it into a universal signifier and converting it from a derogatory and exclusionary slur into an endearing term of solidarity.

The etymology of "*tongzhi*" has been assiduously documented by Andrew D. Wong to illustrate M.M. Bakhtin's contention that, although the life of the word evolves from one context to another, "the word does not forget its own path and cannot completely free itself from the power of these concrete contexts into which it has entered" (Bakhtin 202; A.D. Wong 763). The association of the Chinese label with political discourse "began to strengthen when it was used in the will of Dr. Sun Yat-sen," which enjoins: "*Geming shangwei chenggong, tongzhi rengxu nuli!* 革命尚未成功,同志仍须努力 [The revolution is not yet over; comrades must continue to work strenuously]" (A.D. Wong 768; my English translation). The appellation acquired even stronger revolutionist flavor during the Communist Revolution (1921–1949), when it became an honorific "reserved for Chinese Communist Party members" signifying "solidarity, equality, respect, and intimacy among the revolutionaries." After the founding of the People's Republic in 1949, the Party promoted *tongzhi* as a common term of address among the masses so as to replace nomenclature that signals "differences in social status and class." In the 1980s, anti-gay journalists in Hong Kong hurled the epithet at gay rights activists to ridicule them and to "increase the entertainment value of news stories"; it was mostly used in lurid news stories about "murder, fist fights, gay sex clubs, and domestic disputes of gay and lesbian couples" (A.D. Wong 768, 769, 763, 766). Shortly after, the pejorative designation was reappropriated by gay rights activists in Hong Kong as a "superordinate term that refers to members of sexual minority groups (lesbians, gay men, bisexuals, transgenders, and transsexuals)" (A.D. Wong 790n1), accentuating its "positive connotations of respect, equality, and resistance" (Wong and Zhang 248–278; A.D. Wong 765). Before long, the expression also appeared in mainstream media as a neutral tag for sexual minorities. To this day this highly contested label is still widely used—derisively, subversively, or neutrally.

Leong harnesses the positive connotations of the term and extends it to an imagined international community, discerning beauty in variety and speaking to the need for tolerance, inclusion, and acceptance. By conjoining "a brown *Tongzhi* body" to various reaches of the globe, he not only charts the prevalence of sexual minorities in Greater Asia but also erodes the boundaries between people of different nationalities, between male and female, between heterosexuals and homosexuals (and all the variants), between people of different ages, between those with and without AIDS, and between the profane and the sacred. In troping the diverse geographical regions as distinct components of the human anatomy, Leong stresses how multifarious and yet inalienably human this sprawling population is, that there can be as many gradients of sexual difference as there are variances in human constitution, but they all belong to the same corpus, *E Pluribus Unum*.

In addition to refuting the official pronouncement that non-heteronormative preferences are Western imports and underscoring the common humanity of sexual minorities and majorities, the bio-sexual imagery militates against conventional denigration of the body (especially the female body) and undermines the widespread assumption that homosexuality is purely driven by lust, devoid of affection, and in flagrant violation of orthodox religions. As Rachel C. Lee observes, Asian females are frequently anatomized as body parts, as a "divisible corporeality" (Lee 2). Leong, however, transmutes what Lee calls "the logic of fragmentation" (Lee 3) into the logic of cohesion, linking the corporeal image to all humankind, even to divinity.

The almost religious cohesiveness and expansiveness is at once Whitmanesque and Buddhist. Like the prairie imagery in *A Free Life*, "Your *Tongzhi* Body" in its all-embracing tenor resounds with Whitman's "Song of Myself," especially the opening lines: "I celebrate myself, and sing myself... For every atom belonging to me as good belongs to you"; as well as, "Welcome is every organ and attribute of me, and of any man hearty and clean, / Not an inch nor a particle of an inch is vile, and none shall be less familiar than the rest" (Whitman). Like Whitman, Leong breaks down the barriers between people and cherishes every human organ. But like Ha Jin (Chapter 8), Leong pointedly highlights brown bodies occulted by Whitman's black and white folks.

Buddhist echoes are even more pronounced in "Your *Tongzhi* Body." Three images in particular align the *tongzhi* body with Buddhism. First is the gender-bending figure: "Neither female nor male" conjures forth the image of the androgynous Guanyin 观音, the goddess of mercy; and of Buddha, represented as female or genderless in some parts of the world. Second is the indefinite time: "Without day, month, and year of birth" recalls the Buddhist calendar, according to which people can be born and reincarnated in different epochs. Third are the burgeoning limbs: the "fingertips [that] reach to Canada and America," the "thighs and calves [that] stretch to Malaysia," and the "toes [that] touch Thailand and Vietnam" bring to mind the thousand-armed bodhisattva, portrayed variously as either female or male and often amalgamated with Guanyin in Chinese Buddhism. Although these extremities reach out to every corner of the earth, they reside within the same corporeal contours. By fusing this physique with a divinity sporting myriad helping arms, Leong implies that the many branches of the human conglomeration are constitutive "members" that must coordinate and cooperate for the visceral well-being of the family of humankind, or risk dismemberment.

Instead of bifurcating sexuality and spirituality, and denouncing homosexuality or transsexuality as sinful in the name of religion, Leong invokes Buddhism to foster expansive empathy and affiliative kinship. In softpedaling gender and age difference, Leong links the prejudice against sexual minorities with other forms of intolerance, including gender and age discrimination, all of which abets isolation, "homelessness and loneliness." AIDS victims, as depicted in Leong's "Phoenix Eyes," suffer perhaps the cruelest ostracism, quarantined even by their own families (see Chapter 5). Often confined to the closets (much like the aging women, abandoned wives, and waiting widows in Chin's "Song of the Sad Guitar"), sexual minorities, particularly AIDS victims, are the most silenced and repressed segments of a divisive society. Leong's poem, like the *Tongzhi* conference in Hong Kong, breaks this silence by allowing the hushed to be heard: "I hear a *Tongzhi* body / Speak out— / A Voice sings, cries, and prays / As she/he tells stories / Of love and lust."

Leong uses the pariah groups as the very founding "members" of a borderless community. What Cynthia Liu says of Leong's fiction is literalized in this poem: "Kinship and connection exist, for Leong, in extrafamilial bonds and political alliances rippling outward from the re-conceptualization of community begun by Asian American gays, lesbians and bisexuals" (Liu 1). The poet has transformed the microcosm of sexual minorities into a cosmic microcosm that in*corp*orates even the spiritual sphere. Implicitly, the mortal "songs, cries, and prayers" are heard by the immortal and multidextrous Goddess of Mercy, known for embracing the afflicted. Much as Guanyin lavishes mercy on all living beings, the speaker in "Your *Tongzhi* Body" makes a point to caress the "HIV positive / And HIV negative… For everyone's love / And nobody's fault," turning abject bodies into objects of affection. As in "Phoenix Eyes," Leong reconciles in "Your *Tongzhi* Body" the profane and the sacred, and acknowledges those in sickness and in health.

Since its usage as a common address under Communism, "*tongzhi*"—literally "same aspiration"—has been thrice tilted, by homophobic Hong Kongers who use the epithet as a slur, by the gay activists who reclaim it as a badge of pride, and finally by Leong, who stretches the queer self-reference to include every *body*, creating a global imagined community with a common aspiration. He does so by reinvesting the term with the positive connotations of "solidarity, equality, respect, and intimacy" (A.D. Wong 763) that have accrued through Sun Yat-sen's exhortation to work together, Chinese Communists' goal of an egalitarian society, and gay activists' quest for acceptance and inclusion. He further fortifies these connotations by parsing the moniker, by homing in on *zhi* 志 (aspiration) and crossing the two meanings of *tong* 同: "same" and "together." Throughout the poem Leong stresses the common traits of *tongzhi*, a plural entity inhabiting a human body. Being the *same*, the poet implies, they should share a common *aspiration*—working *together* toward tolerance, mutual acceptance, and harmony rather than splintering into cliques. The word *tong* readily recalls the phrase *tongxin heli* 同心合力, literally, *same* heart and united effort; lexically, the strength of teamwork.

Linking the different geographical regions with the topography of the body in the first two stanzas brings out both the prevalence of people with different sexual orientations and the interdependence of this "body" of constituents. But this incremental configuration of a united front culminating in the final line—"for we are one"—ends in a question: "or are we not?" Perhaps the speaker is allowing for variation among those members who prefer to underscore their irreducible differences within each disfranchised community as well as from the mainstream (and vice versa), instead of being homogenized. That each person is different from another, however, only turns difference into the *same* human condition. Given the poem's stress on humanity as one family that transcends all contrived groupings, those who refuse to acknowledge and accept difference may be placing themselves outside the human fold. Ontologically, either as *tongzhi* or humans in general, we are either as one or we are not at all— "we" don't exist.[8]

Leong envisages yet another global fellowship—that of migrant laborers—in "*Bie You Dong Tian*: Another World Lies Beyond," his poem about the Chinese garden at the Huntington Library. The wherewithal for building this garden—timber, rock, steel, water—is used by Leong as key imagery to call up the workers who have contributed to Chinese and US architectural grandeur. Just as the artisans turn the raw materials into intricate structures, Leong deftly works these concrete images into a sedimentary verse:

> I.
> *Through*
> This gate you enter the Garden.
> *Dawn*
> The garden is not finished, but the feeling is already here.
> Each step damp with dew descended from the Arroyo Seco.
> *Steel*
> Girders peep from under the wood columns of the tea pavilion.
> An orange tractor rigs its taciturn arm, waiting.
> A Latino security guard leans against the carved railing.
> Chinese workmen from Suzhou have not yet arrived.
> *Miles*
> Away, in the Lincoln Plaza Hotel cafe
> The workmen drink down their rice soup & steamed bread
> (Wu, Ding, Yi—their family
> Names—printed on orange work vests
> And helmets they will don again today.)

Heron
Dips its beak into the green lake water.
Air moistens with rain, gray roof tiles
Blacken, incised petal patterns blur.
Rain
Gathers to the curved dip of 10,000 tiles. Silver
Rain threads onto 600 tons of Taihu rocks
Rivulets down the hillside to *Di Lü Ting* –
Small hut—named by a scholar for washing away thoughts.

II.
Thought
Always returns. From below
The hut's thatched roof you can see
The San Gabriel peaks, this garden
Wholly formed in China, yet forming another America.
Beyond
Carved windows, among boulders
Of the Arroyo Seco, a man
Same heft as the workmen from Suzhou
Holds an abalone shell in his right hand.
Black
Eyes, sunburnt skin. Plain-clothed, blue and gray
Same colors as the men from Suzhou.
He places sage into the shell, what the Tongva do.
Nachochan
He whispers, then lifts the shell skyward.
*"You are new here. We have always been here.
Yet now we share this place. Know
How many worlds live in this garden."*
Suzhou
Workmen arrive. They sense a far-off mountain
Yet do not recognize the foreign scent.
Vagrant herb or voracious dynamite left
On the cotton trousers of 10,000 Chinese workers
Who dug tunnels for Huntington's Central Pacific?
Movement
By movement, through centuries
Ancient feelings converge here, carried
By Tongva, Chinese, Mexicans, Spanish
And Chinese again, who, in their labor
Become elemental with the Earth.
Bie You Dong Tian

Another world lies beyond.

(Leong, "*Bie You Dong Tian*" 41–42)

Leong's "*Bie You Dong Tian*" was written at the request of KUSC, a Los Angeles classical music station, to commemorate the opening on February 23, 2008, of the Suzhou-style Chinese garden—known as Liu Fang Yuan 流芳园 or the Garden of Flowing Fragrance—on the grounds of the Huntington Library of Southern California. This Library is famous not only for its collections of rare books and art but also for its spectacular botanical gardens, including the Desert Garden, the Rose Garden, the Shakespeare Garden, the Japanese Garden and, now, the Chinese Garden (Fig. 9.1).

According to the Huntington brochure, Liu Fang Yuan, "where nature's artistry and the spirit of poetry bloom in harmony," is one of the biggest Chinese gardens outside China and is designed to capture the grace and grandeur of that country's ancient civilization. The construction of the garden took some ten years and cost over $18 million. To approximate

Fig. 9.1 Liu Fang Yuan 流芳园, the Chinese Garden at the Huntington Library (Photo by Mary Kao)

the authentic Suzhou style, the Huntington Library contacted the Suzhou Garden Development Co. in China, which supplied 50 craftsmen, 11 stone artisans, and much of the material for construction, including 850 tons of Taihu rocks (Skindrud). The Chinese proverb *bieyou-dongtian* 別有洞天, along with its English translation, "Another world lies beyond," appears on a carved lintel at the garden's entrance. The proverb promises a transition from a workaday milieu to an entrancing landscape or, perhaps, a transcendent Taoist heaven.

Leong uses the inscription on the placard as his title, but his poem deviates considerably from the indigenous significance of the proverb and likely also from the expectations of his radio hosts, who might have expected a paean about the picturesque Chinese garden. Leong's poem reverses the proverb's trajectory: instead of going from a quotidian to a rarefied domain, it moves from the magnificent exterior of the garden to less privileged habitats. Part I is infused with water imagery—dew, tea, soup, lake, rain, rivulets. This garden still is under construction: "Girders peep from under the wood columns of the tea pavilion. / An orange tractor rigs its taciturn arm, waiting." The steel girders anticipate the railroad imagery in Part II, and the personified orange tractor heralds the arrival of the Suzhou craftsmen, clad in "orange work vests." Leong intentionally homes in on the unfinished garden so as to foreground the alien artisans rather than the product of their alienated labor.

Liu Fang Yuan, erected in part on account of "the rise of China as an industrial and technological power" (Skindrud), opened in 2008 to coincide with that country's hosting of the Olympic Games. Leong's determination to blazon the work of migrant laborers thus has transpacific reverberations. As with most people who admired the Bird's Nest or the Water Cube in Beijing during the 2008 Olympics, who usually did not give thought to the invisible migrant hands that built those grand edifices, visitors to the Huntington's Chinese garden in California are unlikely to think of the Suzhou artisans who came all the way from China to complete the landmark project.

To counter such oblivion, Leong insistently zooms in on these workers, on their simple diet and work uniform: "The workmen drink down their rice soup & steamed bread / (Wu, Ding, Yi–their family / Names–printed on orange work vests / And helmets they will don again today)."[9] These details decidedly shift the focus from the stately garden to the humble craftsmen. As in M. Chin's "Song of the Sad Guitar," naming confers identities. Moreover, the description of the workers' plain fare familiarizes the artisans to the readers, while resisting what Frank Chin calls "food pornography"—the exploitation of the "exotic" aspects of Chinese food to gain popular appeal (F. Chin 86; see also S.-l.C. Wong 58–65).

The last two stanzas of Part I limn idyllic scenes of a heron drinking from a green lake and rain seeping into Taihu rocks. The last two lines of this section inform us that the lake and the hut in the garden are meant to provide a respite from mental activity: "Rivulets down the hillside to *Di Lü Ting* – / Small hut–named by a scholar for washing away thoughts." But even in the midst of this lyrical evocation, the speaker hammers home the realities of the garden's painstaking construction by trotting out such figures as "600 tons of Taihu rocks" and "10,000 tiles"—the latter number connecting these imported materials to the "10,000 Chinese workers," also imported from China, of Part II.

The emphasis on physical labor in Part I thus provides a fitting overture to Part II, in which the speaker links the Suzhou artisans with the Tongva people, Native Americans of the Los Angeles Basin whose lands were commandeered by Euro-American colonizers, with the Mexicans who now supply the bulk of the labor force in Southern California and whose lands were similarly annexed by Anglo-American colonizers, as well as with the early Chinese emigrants who built the transcontinental railroad and who ended up dead or expelled (the last theme is discussed in Chapter 2). Earth imagery in this section replaces the water motifs of Part I. The various ethnic groups here are linked not by the highbrow culture of the literati emblematized by the Chinese garden, but rather by having "*black* / Eyes, sunburnt skin" and being "plain-clothed, blue and gray" folks "who, in their labor / Become elemental with the Earth."

Just as the brown *tongzhi* body integrates people of various sexual orientations, the "earthy" skin tone here links workers of different ethnicities synchronically and diachronically. The linkage is reinforced linguistically and imagistically, as in the oxymoronic "damp" and "seco" in "Each step damp with dew descended from the Arroyo Seco" and in the Tongva holding "an abalone shell," both of which bridging geologic time, pointing back to the era wherein the Arroyo Seco ("dry stream" in Spanish) was underwater (under the Pacific), and anticipating the line "You are new here. We have always been here."[10] Becoming "elemental with the Earth" also evokes what Julia A. Stern describes as the premature entombment of those on which the American Republic was built: "These invisible Americans, prematurely interred beneath the great national edifice whose erection they actually enable, provide an unquiet platform for the construction of republican privilege, disturbing the Federalist monolith in powerful ways" (Stern 2). While Stern is referring primarily to Native Americans and African Americans, the displaced Mexicans and Chinese railroad builders were the West Coast counterparts, though their bodies were buried under another vaunted necropolis.

There are counterparts around the world as well. Establishing a working brotherhood across temporal, ethnic, national, and geographical divides, "*Bie You Dong Tian*" recalls Bertolt Brecht's "Questions From a Worker Who Reads," which begins: "Who built Thebes of the 7 gates? / In the books you will read the names of kings. / Did the kings haul up the lumps of rock?" (Brecht 1935).[11] Brecht observes that world heritage sites such as the gates of Thebes, the triumphal arches of Rome, and the Great Wall of China glorify potentates who did not lift a finger in the construction of these monuments. Leong takes Brecht's irony one step further in suggesting that many of the actual builders actually "went under" these constructions for good. (The most literal examples of such live burial were the Chinese imperial tomb builders, buried along with the royal harems and retinues after the completion of the mausoleums.)

Leong's poem repurposes Chinese expressions such as *Bie you dong tian*, *Di lü ting* 涤虑亭, and *Liu fang yuan* 流芳园 to drill into the readers such a dissonant awareness. The Chinese proverb that beckons visitors to an Oriental Eden is instead used to bring into focus the daily drudgery behind the splendid artifact. *Dong tian* 洞天, literally "tunnel sky," also alludes to the course of a railway, summoning images of laborers digging tunnels and the movement of a train from a dark tunnel back out under the open sky. Instead of referring to the Taoist paradise for immortals, *dong tian* here encodes a haunting ground for the wandering apparitions of Chinese railroad workers, many of whom died while producing one of the engineering marvels of their time, having routinely been given the dangerous task of handling explosives during the construction of the Central Pacific Railroad.

Di lü ting (literally, "mind-cleansing pavilion"), "named by a scholar" as a "[pavilion] for washing away thoughts," actually is used in the poem to percolate them, inviting reflections about subjugated civilizations and the confluence of past and present, East and the West: "From below / The hut's thatched roof you can see / The San Gabriel peaks, this garden / Wholly formed in China, yet forming another America." We are reminded—"Movement / By movement, through centuries"—of the less glorious chapters of US and Chinese history, from the nineteenth-century's displacement of Native Americans and maltreatment of Chinese railroad builders to the current exploitation of migrant laborers in both the United States and China. Rather than offering a retreat from mundane affairs, the shelter triggers in the speaker an epiphany about accountability and solidarity across time, delivered in the voice of a member of the Tongva people: "*You are new here. We have always been here. / Yet now we share this place*" (Fig. 9.2).

In presenting the ground of the Chinese garden as a contact zone of the colonizers and the colonized, business tycoons and migrant laborers, wealthy tourists and displaced workers, Leong disrupts celebratory nationalist and biographical narratives, and exhumes its vexed and violent history. The name "Liu Fang Yuan" (literally, "Garden of Flowing Fragrance") is purposely redolent of the Chinese garden's many trees and flowers. Instead of capturing such an aroma, however, Leong's poem invites the reader and the Suzhou workmen to sniff the

Fig. 9.2 *Di lü ting* 涤虑亭 Pavilion for Washing Away Thoughts, Liu Fang Yuan, the Huntington Library

"foreign scent. / Vagrant herb or voracious dynamite left / On the cotton trousers of 10,000 Chinese workers / Who dug tunnels for Huntington's Central Pacific." This olfactory slippage steers us from the pleasant scenery of the present to a harrowing past. *Vagrant* is a zeugma referring at once to a herb transplanted from China and to the nomadic existence of the minority groups that have set foot on or been dislodged from the land on which the Huntington Library's ornate structures now stand. Similarly, *voracious* connotes the destructive power of dynamite that at once made the Central Pacific possible and devoured countless Chinese lives. The rocks in the garden are indeed conducive to creativity, but they do not elicit placid images of nature at rest, instead recalling the cascades of rocks and stones touched off by explosives that left many workers buried in the garden's vicinity. One is reminded of the incalculable workers buried under the Great Wall during its construction, and of the immured women alluded to in M. Chin's "Song of the Sad Guitar."

Leong's pungent wordplay also brings to mind another association with the garden's name, since *liu fang* 流芳 (flowing fragrance) also can mean "to leave an honorable name," as in the proverb *liufang-baishi* 流芳百世 ("Leave a good name for a hundred generations"). The Huntington Library, founded in 1919, is named after Henry Edwards Huntington (1850–1927), whose eponymous legacy includes a beach, a park, a hotel, a hospital, a middle school, and at least two cities. Huntington seems, at first glance, to have succeeded in leaving his good name behind. But a somewhat shady association lurks in Leong's poem, for Henry was the nephew of Collis P. Huntington, a railroad magnate and one of the Big Four who participated in the creation of the transcontinental railway. Henry himself held several key positions working alongside his uncle with the Central Pacific. It was in the course of toiling for the Huntingtons under treacherous conditions that many Chinese railroad builders perished. Often juxtaposed with *liufang-baishi* is the antonymous proverb *yichou-wannian* 遗臭万年—"leaving a stench for ten thousand years." In evoking the scent of explosives and conjuring up casualties, Leong's poem—under the guise of a tribute—emits an unpleasant whiff of dynamite and death, standing as a memorial to the many Chinese, Latino, and Native American workers who labored anonymously in the San Gabriel Valley. This shadowy history of exploitation, exclusion, and colonization runs diametrically opposed to the American ethos of life, liberty, and pursuit of happiness, and to the

Huntington enterprises created in the name of progress. But that, too, is part of the Huntington legacy.

While the radio hosts probably expected Leong to write an occasional poem transporting listeners to fabled Cathay, the poet resists the opportunity at every turn, though he admits enough lyrical tidbits and exotic references to tantalize his audience. His Sinophone allusions are grounded in historical sedimentation, imbricating and implicating both China and the United States in the exploitation of migrant laborers; his Liu Fang Yuan is a "garden / Wholly formed in China, yet forming another America." The Chinese-box structure I detect in M. Chin's "Song of the Sad Guitar" also enfolds this poem. Just as "there were courts, more courts and inner-most courts" in Chin's verse, beyond Leong's seductive title *"Bie You Dong Tian"* lies an ornamental garden that contains the workaday world of the Latino security guard, the sorrows of displaced people such as the Tongva and Mexicans, and the labors of the Suzhou migrants and their Chinese forefathers—not those who loitered in a sixteenth-century Chinese garden in Suzhou, but rather those who sacrificed the most but benefited least in building America. Contradicting the scholar who fancies the *Di lü ting* to be the perfect niche for cleansing the mind, Leong points out the garden's associative fecundity, jostling our memories of the unsung earthly laborers of diverse worlds.

The policing of Orientalism and the demand for fidelity to the Chinese original in Chinese American writing have been so intense on both sides of the Pacific that any references to China are scrutinized with suspicion. What such critics often leave unscanned is the aesthetic and oppositional marshaling of Chinese tropes. While Zhao rightly deplored the market forces that have predisposed some writers to include superficially "exotic" content in their works, his injunction to counter Orientalism by focusing on the "American world" and confining critical attention to "non-Chinese subject matter" is counterproductive (Zhao 256). Such a solution implies that Chinese and American inheritance can always be neatly divided for American citizens of Chinese descent and that the influence of traditional Chinese culture has no place in the United States. But there never has been a pure "American world." In Edward Said's words, "As an immigrant-settler society superimposed on the ruins of considerable native presence, American identity is too varied to be a unitary and homogeneous thing" (Said xxix). Leong's polyglot poem exemplifies this point.

Because the ancestral cultures of immigrants are very much a part of North America, for Chinese American writers and critics to quarantine

Chinese topics borders on self-denial, a form of censorship that can only impoverish (Asian) American literary studies. Not only is recognition of this influence important to an accurate understanding of history, but transnational resonances should be amplified rather than repressed in today's rapidly globalizing world. Critics can best combat Orientalism not by declaring a moratorium on Chinese tropes but rather by uncovering the inventive and subversive uses of Chinese sources—uses that may, in fact, challenge the supremacy of the Western heritage in the New World, as well as the cultural dominant in both Sinophone and Anglophone nations.

In the works of hyphenated US writers who have at their disposal two mother tongues, the interweaving of those languages can tell us much about the authors' reservations and hopes regarding both their ancestral and adopted countries.[12] The linguistic legerdemains of both Chin and Leong take on a double edge, chipping away at transpacific inequalities. In "Song of the Sad Guitar," Chin orchestrates multiple allusions—to "Ode to Pipa," "An Immortal by the Lake," "The River-Merchant's Wife," and *The Woman Warrior*—to syncretize a prose poem that urges women to break out of the domestic prisons punctuating Chinese classical literature (especially in the poetic subgenre of Boudoir Complaint) and resurfacing in American suburbia. In "Get Rid of the X," she uses intercultural juxtaposition, parody, and puns to depict an abject female alien yoked to an abusive husband as well as cabined, cribbed, and confined by US immigration laws. In creating a female speaker who differs markedly from the insouciant patriarch in Li Bai's drinking poem, Chin departs from the lyricism of the Tang verse to pitch a piquant utterance of her own.

In "Your *Tongzhi* Body" Leong turns a figure that has been stigmatized and even criminalized as deviant and disease-ridden into a composite subject of beauty. Blending Whitmanesque and Buddhist spirits, he envisions a self without borders. By reiterating and parsing the term *tongzhi*, the poet lifts it from its marginal position as a pejorative signifier to the center—the very core of humanity, and spirituality. In "*Bie You Dong Tian*," Leong skews the lexical meanings of Chinese tropes to extract semantic elements that reverberate with the migrant experience, digging beneath the resplendent Chinese garden in Southern California to ferret out buried chapters of transnational history. The slanted allusions of Chin and Leong insinuate against both Chinese and American national cultures. Unpacking their hybrid rhetorical strategies enhances our appreciation of their artistry and oblique political critique. Their provocative manipulations of bilingual discourse amount to formal insurrection.

Notes

1. The lack of scholarly attention to Asian American poetry has been addressed in the last decade with the publications of Xiaojing Zhou's *The Ethics and Poetics of Alterity in Asian American Poetry* (2006); Timothy Yu's *Race and the Avant-Garde: Experimental and Asian American Poetry since 1965* (2009); Steven G. Yao's *Foreign Accents: Chinese American Verse from Exclusion to Postethnicity* (2010); and Dorothy Wang's *Thinking Its Presence: Form, Race, and Subjectivity in Contemporary Asian American Poetry* (2013).
2. T'sai Yen is also the subject of M. Chin's "Bold Beauty" in *Rhapsody in Plain Yellow* (M. Chin, *Rhapsody* 52).
3. Another allusion to Li Bai and Pound is found in Stone Orchid's song: "women climbing watchtower" echoes "Why should I climb the lookout?"
4. Bing Xin, the Chinese author featured in Chapter 6, wrote her MA thesis on Li Qingzhao, directed by Professor Laura Hibbard Loomis at Wellesley. When Wu Bing, her eldest daughter, visited Wellesley in 1980, she photocopied the thesis, which has since been published as Vol. 8 of *The Complete Works of Bing Xin*《冰心全集》(Chen 114, 117); her thesis is also cited in Laura Hibbard Loomis's article on Li Qingzhao, entitled "A Chinese Sappho" (Loomis 132–139).
5. I thank Robert Kyriakos Smith for alerting me to M. Chin's wink at Harriet Jacobs, noting that the literary tradition of immured women is long and global.
6. M. Chin discloses that she is also "slyly commenting on the dominance of the novel over poetry" in the contemporary Western world (email correspondence, March 14, 2009).
7. The line breaks in my text differ somewhat from the printed version, in which Leong had to shorten the lines to fit the marginal design of *Asian Americans: The Movement and Moment*. I replicate the original format of the poem per Leong's request.
8. I thank David Martinez for this ontological suggestion.
9. Leong discloses that Wu Ding Yi actually is the Chinese name of Bill Wu, to whom the poem is dedicated (email correspondence, April 20, 2010).
10. I am most grateful to David Martinez and Robert Kyriakos Smith for their linguistic and geologic tips, respectively.
11. I thank Leong for alerting me to Brecht's poem (personal communication April 20, 2016). The poem resonates most eerily against America's founding myths. In Anne Anlin Cheng's words, "While all nations have their repressed histories and traumatic atrocities, American melancholia is particularly acute because America is founded on the very ideals of freedom and liberty whose betrayals have been repeatedly covered over" (Cheng 10).

12. Ha Jin has observed (feelingly I believe, on account of his own circumstances as an expatriate) that for many migrant writers, "homeland is actually their mother tongues" (*Migrant* 78).

WORKS CITED

Bakhtin, Mikhail. *Problems of Dostoevsky's Poetics*. Ed. Caryl Emerson. Trans. Caryl Emerson. Minneapolis: University of Minnesota Press, 1984.
Bing Xin, 冰心. 《冰心全集 [*The Complete Works of Bing Xin*]》. 9 Volumes. Ed. 卓如 Zhuo Ru. Fuzhou: 海峡文艺出版社 [haixia wenyi chubanshe], 1979, 2012.
Brecht, Bertolt. "Questions From a Worker Who Reads." https://www.marxists.org/subject/art/literature/brecht/ (accessed 10 April 2016).
Chen Shu, 陈恕. 《冰心全传 [Complete Biography and Works of Bing Xin]》. Beijing: 中国青年出版社 Zhongguo Qingnian Chuban She, 2011.
Cheng, Anne Anlin. *The Melancholy of Race: Psychoanalysis, Assimilation, and Hidden Grief*. New York: Oxford University Press, 2001.
Chin, Frank. *The Chickencoop Chinaman and The Year of the Dragon: Two Plays*. Seattle: University of Washington Press, 1981.
Chin, Marilyn. "An Interview with Marilyn Chin." *Indian Review* 26.1 (2004): 112–120.
——. "Parable of the Guitar." *The Revenge of Mooncake Vixen: A Manifesto in 41 Tales*. New York: Norton, 2009. 189–194.
——. *The Phoenix Gone, the Terrace Empty*. Minneapolis: Milkweed Editions, 1994.
——. *Rhapsody in Plain Yellow: Poems*. New York: Norton, 2002.
Jin, Ha. *The Writer as Migrant*. Chicago: University of Chicago Press, 2008.
Kingston, Maxine Hong. *The Woman Warrior: Memoirs of a Girlhood among Ghosts*. New York: Vintage, 1976.
Lee, Rachel C. *The Exquisite Corpse of Asian America: Biopolitics, Biosociality, and Posthuman Ecologies*. New York: New York University Press, 2014.
Leong, Russell C. "*Bie You Dong Tian*: Another World Lies Beyond." *Amerasia Journal* 37.1 (2011): 41–42.
——. "Your *Tongzhi* Body." *Asian Americans: The Movement and the Moment*. Ed. Steven G. Louie and Glenn K. Omatsu. Los Angeles: UCLA Asian American Studies Center Press, 2001. 234–235.
Liu, Cynthia. "'Phoenix Eyes and Other Stories' by Russell Charles Leong." *Tricycle* (Spring 2001): 1–2.
Loomis, Laura Hibbard. "A Chinese Sappho, with Translations by Wan Ying Hsieh." *Poet Lore* 41 (1930): 132–139.
Shan, Te-hsing. "Phoenix in Transit: An Interview with Russell Leong." *Exploration and Expansion of the Frontiers of Chinese American Literature and*

Culture: A Collection of Interviews and Research Papers. Ed. Te-hsing Shan. Tianjin: Nankai University Press, 2006. 273–287.

Said, Edward. *Culture and Imperialism*. New York: Knopf, 1993.

Skindrud, Erik. *Liu Fang Yuan–Garden of Flowing Fragrance, A Chinese Gem: An Ancient Landscape Art Comes to Southern California*. 20 April 2013. http://www.landscapeonline.com/research/article/10862

Stern, Julia A. *The Plight of Feeling: Sympathy and Dissent in the Early American Novel*. Chicago: University of Chicago Press, 1997.

Wang, Dorothy. *Thinking Its Presence: Form, Race, and Subjectivity in Contemporary Asian American Poetry*. Stanford: Stanford University Press, 2013.

Whitman, Walt. *Song of Myself (1892 Version)*. Ed. David McKay. Poetry Foundation. http://www.poetryfoundation.org/poem/174745 (accessed 15 January 2016).

Wong, Andrew, and Qing Zhang. "The Linguistic Construction of the Tongzhi Community." *Journal of Linguistic Anthropology* 10 (2000): 248–278.

Wong, Andrew D. "The Reappropriation of Tongzhi." *Language in Society* (2005): 763–791.

Wong, Sau-ling Cynthia. *Reading Asian American Literature: From Necessity to Extravagance*. Princeton: Princeton University Press, 1993.

Yao, Steven G. *Foreign Accents: Chinese American Verse from Exclusion to Postethnicity*. New York: Oxford University Press, 2010.

Yu, Timothy. *Race and the Avant-Garde: Experimental and Asian American Poetry since 1965*. Stanford: Stanford University Press, 2009.

Zhao, Wenshu. "Why Is There Orientalism in Chinese American Literature?" *Global Perspectives on Asian American Literature*. Ed. Guiyou Huang and Wu Bing. Beijing: Foreign Language Teaching and Research Press, 2008. 239–258.

Zhou, Xiaojing. *The Ethics and Poetics of Alterity in Asian American Poetry*. Iowa City: University of Iowa Press, 2006.

Coda

This book reflects a changing world and my own vicissitudes as an intellectual migrant. While a graduate student of English specializing in Renaissance British literature at Berkeley in the late 1970s and early 1980s, I was unable to use Chinese (my mother tongue) to fulfill the second language requirement of the doctoral program: only Indo-European languages qualified. (I took an intensive Latin workshop.) As the first Asian faculty member at the University of California, Los Angeles (UCLA) English department, I struck my colleagues then as the ideal candidate to tackle emerging Asian American literary studies, an interloper though I might have been in a field that considered American nativity as requisite credential. Because of the Anglophone emphasis in this field (and American studies generally) at the time and due to my institutional affiliation, none of the books I edited (*Asian American Literature: An Annotated Bibliography*, *An Interethnic Companion to Asian American Literature*, *Words Matter: Conversations with Asian American Writers*) lingered on the crossroads between Asia and Asian America, let alone included works penned in other tongues. But I have never veered from the inclusive principle adopted while compiling the book-length bibliography.

The transnational turn in American studies, the diasporic expansion in Asian American studies (and in Sinophone studies particularly), and the increasing mutual engagement of the United States and China have brought about significant curricular changes. This turn has allowed me to bring together many loves: Cantonese opera, Chinese poetry and novels, Homer, Shakespeare, Milton, Romantic poetry, and translation.

It has also brought to full circle my academic odysseys (including two appointments as faculty director of UC Education Abroad Programs in China). My understanding of the writers covered in this book has been enriched by the research of scholars in Hong Kong, Taiwan, and mainland China. Just as linking transpacific writers can generate new insights into Asian American literary studies, so greater intellectual exchanges between (Asian) Americanists across oceans can be mutually invigorating.

While this book focuses on the intersection between Chinese and Chinese American literature and cultures, this does not imply that such a locus is the most important area of inquiry in Asian American literary studies. It is, however, an index of my personal engagement with some of the seminal formulations about the field over the last few decades, as briefly outlined in the introduction: (1) the *Aiiieeeee!* editors' insistence on a radical separation between Chinese (or Americanized Chinese) and Chinese American culture; (2) the same editors' attempt, 17 years later, to reclaim a so-called Asian American heroic tradition as the most resonant inspiration (and by implication also the guiding principle) of Asian American literature; (3) the debate over whether it is more important for the field to go diasporic or remain US-centered; and (4) the crystallization of a "Third" literature that calls for alternative hermeneutics and that incorporates immigrant and Americas-born writers using different linguistic mediums and expressing geopolitical concerns a world away.

The radical division of Asian and Asian American literature at the outset has led to a certain skepticism against the incorporation of Asian material in Asian American writing, thereby giving short shrift to inventive bicultural poetics. I have tried to make up for this neglect by illuminating the artful deployment of Chinese sources by Frank Chin, Marilyn Chin, Ha Jin, Maxine Hong Kingston, and Russell C. Leong. At the same time, I caution against indiscriminate ancestral boosterism. My ambivalence toward F. Chin's unequivocal endorsement of the Asian heroic tradition grows out of his association of heroism and masculinity with belligerence and domination. I use works by Kingston, Bing Xin, Pang-Mei Natasha Chang, M. Chin, and Ruthanne Lum McCunn to shuffle feminine codes; works by Younghill Kang, Gus Lee, David Wong Louie, Li-Young Lee, William Poy Lee, Leong, Anchee Min, and Shawn Wong to discourage replicating machismo and to present viable alternatives.

With regard to the seemingly divergent routes taken by Asian Americanists who adhere to the original mission by working toward social justice in North America, or chart heterogeneous concerns in the diaspora, or brave a polyglot "Third" trail—my readings of McCunn, Bing Xin, Jin, M. Chin, Leong, Min, and Xu suggest that a transnational purview can trigger a reflexive social critique, glancing both homeward and across the shore. "The Photograph" by Bing Xin is set primarily in China, but it anticipates many key theoretical insights in Asian American studies vis-à-vis Orientalism, "racist love," and the model minority. M. Chin alludes to Tang and Song poetry to lay bare the gender and racial inequalities in both China and the United States; Leong addresses homophobia and exploitation of migrant laborers across the Pacific Rim. McCunn uses Chinese, white, and black narrators to implicate Sinocentrism, Eurocentrism, and bilateral xenophobia.

Finally, I bring out the contrapuntal sensibilities of Chinese native speakers such as Xu, Shen, Bing Xin, and Jin, reflecting the confluences of Chinese literature and Third literature. Xu was a precursor of today's diasporic Chinese intellectuals who feel at home in disparate worlds. As a cultural mediator, he was the counterpart of Pearl Buck: both viewed their native countries critically as a result of their sojourns abroad. Shen, a Chinese author of partial Miao/Hmong descent, evinces an ethnic consciousness not unlike that of hyphenated Americans. Both Bing Xin's "The Photograph" and Jin's *A Free Life* take on both China and the United States. Bing Xin's story about a white woman in China mirrors the isolation felt coevally by Asians stateside; Jin's metafiction draws on both Chinese and American pastoral to envision an ideal environment for a writer. Though it can be readily classified as an American immigrant novel, it contains pointed critiques of the Chinese political climate. This book thus stretches the contours of Asian American literary studies by introducing Sinophone and "Third" writers, along with interpretive strategies that unravel multiple geopolitical engagements.

There have been and will be myriad fruitful ways for Asian American literary studies to traverse borders. Compelling studies abound that cut across race and ethnicities, range over disciplines, and span continents, nations, and oceans.[1] From its inception as perhaps one of the most exclusive Anglophone niches, Asian American literary studies has evolved into one of the most inclusive hubs, with archival, linguistic, disciplinary, temporal, religious, continental, and oceanic crossings. We sail in weather foul and fair. Welcome aboard!

Note

1. Studies that cut across race and ethnicities include those by Leslie Bow, Jeannie Yu-Mei Chiu, Daniel Y. Kim, Stephen Knadler, Julia H. Lee, Colleen Lye, Christina Nagao, Crystal Parikh, Vijay Prashad, Chandan Reddy, Caroline Rody, Cathy Schlund-Vials, Min Song, Elda E. Tsou, and Caroline H. Yang. Works that range over disciplines include the imbricating of literary studies and food studies by Allison Carruth, Robert Ji-Song Ku, Anita Mannur, and Wenying Xu; explorations of cultural legacies and colonial histories of the Pacific Islands by Keith Camacho, Elizabeth DeLoughrey, and Erin Suzuki; the braiding of history, legal studies, and cultural studies by Joshua Takano Chambers-Letson, Monica Chiu, Kandice Chuh, Grace Kyungwon Hong, Lisa Lowe, David Palumbo-Liu, and Richard Jean So; the interfacing of biopolitics, psychoanalysis, and disabilities studies by Juliana Chang, Ann Anlin Cheng, James Kyung-Jin Lee, and Rachel C. Lee; and the interlocking of ethnic studies and postcolonial studies by Victor Bascara, Alan Punzalan Isaac, Jodi Kim, Susan Koshy, Malini Johar-Schueller, and Stephen Hong Sohn. Other works that span continents, nations, and oceans include Wen Jin's comparison of US and Chinese multiculturalisms, Belinda Kong's examination of Chinese emigrant writers in the USA and the UK, Viet Thanh Nguyen's chronicle of how the so-called Vietnam War is remembered multifariously by different countries, and Rajini Srikanth's exploration of South Asian American global connections; the extension of Asian American studies to the Americas by Donald Goellnict, Jennifer Ann Ho, Evelyn Hu-DeHart, Jinqi Ling, Eleanor Ty, and Lisa Yun; and the scrutiny of transpacific femininities and sexualities by Denise Cruz, David L. Eng, Tamara Ho, Laura Hyun Yi Kang, Sean Metzger, and Tan Hoang Nguyen.

INDEX[1]

A
Abe, Frank, 43
Achebe, Chinua, 252
Achilles, 45, 54, 57
adoption. *See* transracial adoption
aesthetics
   and politics, 2–5, 38, 189, 238, 264, 265, 291
aesthetics, bicultural or intercultural, 1, 14, 15, 17, 48, 53–60, 112, 122, 229, 234, 244, 246, 263–65, 291
affective labor, 203–8
affiliation *vs.* filiation, 17, 161–62, 177, 179, 264, 280, 295
African Americans, 32, 43, 47, 72, 75, 78, 80, 93–95, 96n10, 204, 216–18, 287
   in *China Boy*, 72, 75, 77
Ah Bing/阿炳/Hua Yanjun 华彦钧, 128, 131

AIDS. *See* HIV/AIDS
Aiiieeeee!, 6, 34, 43, 44, 50, 80, 81, 141, 152, 157, 211, 217, 229. *See also The Big Aiiieeeee!*
Althusser, Louis, 48
American Dream, 90, 235, 237, 239–41, 243, 247, 276
Americanese (film), 167n2
American Federation of Labor (AFL) brochure
   "The American Gulliver and Chinese Lilliputians," 69
   "Meat vs. Rice," 69, 84
American Knees (Shawn Wong), 14, 143–51, 152, 154, 158, 165
   alternative masculinity in, 144–48, 165, 166
   father-son relationship in, 145–46, 151, 152, 165
   stereotypes in, 149–50
   verbal art in, 146–47, 166

---

[1] Note: Page numbers followed by "n" denote notes.

American studies, 1, 2, 5–7, 9, 14, 156–57, 192, 229, 295, 297, 298n1
American Studies Association, 5
An, Qi, 196n8
ancestral worship, 211, 263, 264, 275
Angelou, Maya, 271
anonymity, 181, 275
Anti-Rightist Movement, 232, 253
April Rhapsody《人间四月天》, 114
Arroyo Seco, 282–83, 286
"Art and Life" (Xu Zhimo), 21n8, 112, 118
Articulate Silences (K. Cheung), 3, 167n3
Asian American literature
 diasporic analysis of, 8
 as ethnography, 3, 30, 35, 179, 187, 189, 201, 209, 217, 232, 263
 as history, 51, 59, 232, 256
 as social text, 8, 9
 transnational approach to, 14, 192, 201, 291
Asian Americans/Asian-Americans
 and assimilation, 41, 74, 79, 80, 82, 87, 88, 90–95, 187
 in Hollywood films, 12, 32–33, 69–72, 166
 hyphen, politics of, 6, 8–10, 229–30, 263, 291
 and hypochondria, 79
 and masculinity, 29–60, 67–95, 141–67
 as perpetual foreigners, 6
 stereotyping of, 30–35, 69–72, 161, 164, 201–25
Asian American sensibilities, 6, 16, 18, 19, 21n9, 229, 249, 256, 265
Asian American studies
 and gender, 70, 224
 and Orientalism, 18–20, 43–46, 187, 202–5, 207–9, 210–15, 217–18, 220–24, 263–64, 290–91, 297
 and racism, 32–33, 36, 39, 42–43, 49, 55, 59, 201–25
Asian Exclusion Act, 5
Asian Global, 10
Asian heroic tradition, 7, 30, 34, 43–50, 52, 59, 68, 71, 141, 150, 263, 296
 as usable past, 13, 31, 263
 See also Chin, Frank; Kingston, Maxine Hong
Attwell, David, 256
Auden, W. H., 122, 135n12
"An Autobiographical Account at Forty"《四十自述》(S. Hu), 174, 177, 182, 188, 193
autobiography, 15, 35–38, 173–96, 256–57.
 See also autobiography, Asian American; biography
autobiography, Asian American, 18, 35–38, 173–96
 and assimilation, 41
 and biography, 177–82, 194
 and Christianity, 35, 38, 173–74, 177–78, 180, 193, 195n1
 Coetzee on, 256
 and counternarratives, 181
 family in, 82, 179
 and feminism, 36, 187
 and fiction, 108, 188, 194, 195, 256
 interdependence in, 173–79, 181–84, 194–95
 literary, 176, 188–189
 and masculinity, 35
 and maternal legacy, 52, 177–82, 194, 195
 and memoir, 177, 189
 and polyphony, 15, 16, 175, 195, 267
 and self-fashioning, 35, 37, 40, 189
 Western, 35, 173, 180, 193
 See also Chin, Frank
Autobiography《从文自传》(C. Shen), 35, 38, 173–74, 177–78, 180, 193, 195n1, 196n5

auto-ethnography, 37, 187
autonomy, artistic, 237, 241, 246, 249, 251, 252.
  See also Jin, Ha
"aversive thinking," 237

B

Ba Jin 巴金, 223
Bacho, Peter, 152
Bai Juyi 白居易
  "Bidding Farewell on an Ancient Grassland"《賦得古原草送別》, 244
  "Ode to Pipa"《琵琶行》, 268–72, 275, 291
Bai Xianyong Kenneth 白先勇. See Pai Hsien-yung, Kenneth
Bai Xuexian 白雪仙.
  See Pak Suet Sin
Bakhtin, M. M., 264, 278
Baldwin, James, 46
"Ballad of a Trader's Wife" (Li Bai), 269, 292n3
"Ballad of Mulan," 39, 40, 47, 264
Bambara, Toni Cade, 47
baochou 报仇 ("report a crime"), 38, 76, 264–65, 274
Bascara, Victor, 211, 298n1
Bates, Lillieth (Sara Burton), 134n7
Behdad, Ali, 1, 18, 202, 205, 214
Bell, Julian, 111, 130
Benstock, Shari, 36
Bertolucci, Bernardo, 89–90
betrayal, 41, 48, 158, 231–33, 252, 256, 292n11
  writing in second language as, 231
  See also "The Language of Betrayal"
Bhabha, Homi, 79, 80, 91
"Bidding Farewell on an Ancient Grassland"《賦得古原草送別》 (Bai Juyi), 244

"*Bie You Dong Tian*" 別有洞天 (R. C. Leong), 16, 264, 266, 282–91
  allusion to Wu, Ding Yi, 282, 285, 292n9
  and Brecht's "Questions from a Worker who Reads," 287
  Chinese box structure of, 290
  Chinese expressions in, 287
  Di Lü Ting 涤滤亭 in, 287, 290
  displacement in, 16, 289
  Liu Fang Yuan in, 284, 285, 287, 290
  naming in, 285
  Suzhou workers in, 282, 283, 285, 286, 288, 290
  transcontinental railroad workers in, 286, 289
The Big Aiiieeeee!, 7, 34, 39, 40, 43–46, 50, 95, 141, 156, 195n1.
  See also *Aiiieeeee!*
bilateral hermeneutics, 2, 9, 14, 17
bilingualism, 1, 9, 16, 19, 31, 121–22, 230, 234, 254–55, 257, 264–65, 291
Bing Xin/Xie Wangying 冰心/謝婉瑩
  and Ba Jin 巴金, 223
  gendered reception of, 15, 201, 222–24
  and Li Qingzhao, 292n4
  and Ling Shuhua, 222, 223
  as "Male [男士]" (pseudonym), 223
  On Women《关于女人》, 223
  and Pearl Buck, 201, 203, 208, 210, 212, 223
  "The Photograph"《相片》15, 17, 201–25
  and Postcolonialist theory, 15, 201, 202, 211, 212, 214, 217, 224
  as representative of Boudoir Lady School, 222, 223
  as Sinophone writer, 17

biographical novel, 124, 174, 176–77, 180, 181, 187, 191, 195, 218
biography, 177–82, 193, 194
 and autobiography, 177–82, 194
 and fiction, 188, 194
 and history, 181, 189
 See also autobiography; autobiography, Asian American
The Bitter Tea of General Yen, 223
Blazon, 277, 285.
 See also "Your Tongzhi Body"
Bloomsbury Group, 111, 122.
 See also Xu Zhimo
body, 2, 5–6, 11, 51, 54–56, 74, 89, 112, 120, 130, 153, 157–60, 165, 186, 236–40, 249, 273, 276, 277, 279–82, 286
Bonetti, Kay, 43, 48
Boudoir Complaint (poems) 闺怨诗, 270, 272, 276, 291.
 See also "Get Rid of the X"; Li Qingzhao; "Song of the Sad Guitar"
Boudoir Lady School /guixiu pai 闺秀派, 222, 223.
 See also Bing Xin
Boudoir literature 闺秀文学, 222, 223, 272
Bound Feet and Western Dress (P. N. Chang), 14, 107, 119–24, 126, 134n3
Bow, Leslie, 298n1
Boxer Uprising, 122
Bradatan, Costica, 234, 243, 255
Brecht, Bertolt, 105, 287, 292n11
 "Questions from a Worker Who Reads," 287
Brontë, Charlotte, 271
Brooks, David, 11
Browning, Robert, 117
Bryer, Eric (*Americanese*), 167n2
Buck, John Lossing, 125, 126, 210

Buck, Pearl S. 赛珍珠
 and Agnes Smedley, 134n6
 All Men Are Brothers, 34, 127
 and Bing Xin 冰心, 201, 203, 208, 210, 212, 223
 A Chinese Woman Speaks, 125, 134-5n7
 East Wind: West Wind, 125
 Fighting Angel, 154, 155
 gendered reception of, 223
 The Good Earth, 124–26, 128–29, 132, 135n13, 203, 206, 209, 210
 "Is There a Case for Foreign Missions?," 127, 208–9, 210
 "Is There a Place for the Foreign Missionary?" 208
 and John Lossing Buck, 125
 as John Sedges (pseudonym), 223
 Letter from Peking, 125, 135n7, 136n15
 missionaries, critique of, 114, 127, 203, 208–11
 My Several Worlds, 125
 in *Pearl of China*, 14, 107, 112, 114, 124–33, 136n17, 203
 as postcolonialist pioneer, 209
 Welcome House, founding of, 212
 and "women's literature," 223
 and Xu Zhimo 徐志摩, 13, 107, 112–14, 121, 124–27, 129, 132–33, 134nn6–7, 135n13, 136n15, 136n17, 203
Buell, Frederick, 5, 6, 78
Buddha, 280
Buddhism, 14, 46, 154, 162–65, 196n9, 265, 274, 277–82, 286, 290–91
Butler, Judith
 on performativity 69–70
The Butterfly Lovers 《梁祝》, 104, 128
Byron, Lord, 108, 112, 127

C

cainu 才女 (female talent), 103, 133.
  See also women of letters
cainü–caizi 才女才子 (female and male talents), 103
Cai Yen 蔡琰/蔡文姬. See Ts'ai Yen
caizi 才子, 53, 101, 104, 108, 112, 133, 142, 146.
  See also poet-scholar
caizi-jiaren 才子佳人.
  See Scholar-Beauty
Callahan, Cynthia, 220, 221
calligraphy, 13, 73, 74, 95n4, 106.
  See also masculinity, Asian American
Cambridge University, 109, 122, 123, 132.
  See also Xu Zhimo
Campomanes, Oscar, 8
Cantonese opera, 105
Cao Cao. See Cho Cho 曹操
Cao Xueqin 曹雪芹
  Dreams of the Red Chamber 《红楼梦》, 46, 114, 117
Capra, Frank
  The Bitter Tea of General Yen (1933), 223
care, ethics of, 77–78, 142–43, 155, 162, 166.
  See also *ren/jen* (caring)
Carruth, Allison, 93, 298n1
Catholicism, 119, 165
Cavafy, C.P., 230, 231, 250, 251
  "Ithaka," 231, 250, 251
Cavell, Stanley, 237
censorship, 9, 187, 251, 253, 256, 291
Central Pacific (railroad), 59, 283, 287, 289
Chambers-Letson, Joshua Takano, 298n1
Chan, Jachinson, 70
Chan, Jackie, 71
Chan, Jeffery Paul, 6, 32, 34, 36
  "Racist Love," 32, 33, 203, 204, 208–12, 218, 297

Chan, Justin, 71
Chang, Aileen, 225n3
Chang, Pang-Mei Natasha 张邦梅, 14, 17, 36, 101, 124
  Bound Feet and Western Dress, 14, 107, 119–24, 107, 126
Chang Yu-i/Zhang Youyi 张幼仪, 107, 108, 113, 119.
  See also *Bound Feet and Western Dress*; Xu Zhimo
Chaplin, Charlie, 105
Chen Guangchen 陈广琛, 236
Chen, Joan 陈冲, 167n2
Chen Shu 陈恕, 210, 225n1, 292n4
Chen Xiying 陈西滢. See Chen Yuan
Chen Yuan/Chen Xiying 陈源/陈西滢, 130, 131, 133n2, 136n18.
  See also Ling Xuhua; Xu Zhimo
Cheng, Anne Anlin, 7, 79, 179, 189, 250, 292n11
Cheng, Vincent John, 202, 221
Cheung, Floyd, 35, 195n1
Chiang Yee 蒋彝, 218
Chin, Frank 赵健秀
  Aiiieeeee!, 6, 7, 34, 35
  and Asian heroic tradition, 7, 13, 30, 34, 44–46, 50–52, 57–60, 94, 263
  The Big Aiiieeeee!, 7, 34, 38, 43, 44, 46, 49, 50, 150
  bicultural aesthetics in, 29–30, 53, 59
  on bicultural literacy, 44, 174, 192, 194–95
  The Chickencoop Chinaman, 29, 56
  "Come All Ye Asian American Writers of the Real and the Fake," 34, 38–41, 46, 54, 56, 144, 190
  "Confessions of a Chinatown Cowboy," 32, 45
  Donald Duk, 50–53, 59, 73, 152

Chin, Frank (*cont.*)
  Eurocentrism, critique of, 43, 191–92
  on "food pornography," 286
  "Kung fu," 33, 54
  on Kwan Kung, 51, 54–56, 58
  on Lee Kuey, 50, 51
  on Maxine Hong Kingston,
    17, 29–60, 263, 296
  "The Most Popular Book
    in China," 39
  on the real and the fake, 7, 38,
    44–46, 54
  "Racist Love," 32, 33, 203, 204,
    208–12, 218, 297
  "This Is Not an Autobiography,"
    15, 35, 38, 44, 173, 178, 187,
    192–95, 195n1
  and Wittman Ah Sing, 49
  Year of the Dragon, 29, 56
Chin, Marilyn 陈美玲, 3, 17, 20n2,
    93, 96n9, 263–93
  and the American Dream, 276
  "Bold Beauty," 292n2
  "Get Rid of the X," 16, 264, 269,
    272–76, 291, 292n6
  Hard Love Province, 20n2, 265
  hybrid poetics of, 265, 276, 291
  and Maxine Hong Kingston,
    265–67, 271
  "Parable of the Guitar," 275
  *The Phoenix Gone, The Terrace
    Empty*, 265–67, 276
  《一抹黄色: Plain Yellow》, 20n2
  "A Portrait of the Self as Nation,
    1990–1991," 276
  "Song of the Sad Guitar," 16, 264,
    266–72, 274, 276, 280, 285,
    289–91
China Boy (G. Lee)
  as autobiography, 72
  father-son relationship in, 152
  pacifism in, 76
  violence in, 72, 76

Chinaman/Chinamen, 29, 31, 42, 44,
    50, 56, 58, 84, 87, 122, 132,
    135n13, 173, 248
China Men (M. H. Kingston), 6,
    41–43, 48, 51, 60n1, 68
  feminism in, 42, 48
  gender in, 6
  gender-bending in, 41–43, 68
  See also Kingston, Maxine Hong
Chinatowns, 30, 31, 45, 50,
    52, 57, 180
Chinese American literature, 2, 10–19,
    21n3, 31, 68, 218, 219, 263,
    264, 296
  Chinese allusions in, 14–17,
    263–66, 273–74, 290
  Chinese sources in, 29, 30, 36–39,
    41–42, 44, 48, 49, 53, 107,
    129, 263–66, 273–74, 278
  class in, 263, 266, 276
Chinese drama, 13, 104,
    106–7, 128, 142.
  See also Cantonese opera;
    scholar-beauty
Chinese Exclusion Act, 50
Chinnery, Ying, 130, 136n18
Chiu, Monica, 298n1
Cho Cho/Cao Cao 曹操, 49, 60.
  See also Chin, Frank; Kingston,
    Maxine Hong; *Romance of the
    Three Kingdoms*
Chow, Keith, 71
Chow, Rey, 202, 214
Chow, Stephen 周星驰, 106
Choy, Curtis, 43
Christian, Barbara, 15, 203
Christianity, 46, 47, 152–56, 163,
    165, 177, 185, 193, 195n1, 209,
    211, 218, 219, 224
  and assimilation, 221
  and autobiography, 35, 38,
    173–74, 177–78, 180,
    193, 195n1

Christian missionaries
  Chinese, condescension toward, 210, 217
  critique of, 114, 122, 127, 208–10, 221
  in "The Photograph," 202, 208–10
Chu, Patricia, 36, 49, 60n1
chün-tzu. See *junzi/chün-tzu* 君子 (Superior Man)
Chushingura, 34
civil rights movement, 4, 71, 142, 148, 176, 183–84, 265
claiming America, 2, 6, 9, 17, 19, 21n4, 30, 36, 53, 229, 263, 266
claiming diaspora, 2, 6, 10, 17, 21n4, 229
clan sisterhood, 184, 186
Clifford, James, 38, 187
Coetzee, J. M., 256
colonialism, 5, 257n1
color-blind racism, 79, 87
communism, 107, 176, 183, 237, 281
comparative literature, 1, 2, 15, 19, 265
  transpacific, 2
Confucianism, 12, 46, 158, 236, 246
Confucius/Kongzi 孔子, 74, 77, 78, 115, 142–43, 162
  on *ren* 仁, 142–43, 162
  as *wen* icon, 74, 115
  on women, 104
  on Superior Man 君子, 142
Conn, Peter, 125, 132, 134n7, 135n13
Conrad, Joseph, 230, 231, 233–34, 239, 248, 252–53, 256
  Heart of Darkness, 252
Constantino, Renato, 31
Crenshaw, Kimberlé, 29, 144
Crescent Moon Society 新月社, 109, 112
Crescent Monthly 《新月》月刊, 109, 112.
  See also Xu Zhimo
cross-dressing. See gender-bending
Crouching Tiger, Hidden Dragon, 71

Cruz, Denise, 298n1
cultural hybridity, 1, 7, 14, 107, 109, 111, 114, 116, 117, 123, 128, 133, 249, 265, 276
cultural nationalism, 6, 7, 18, 30, 36, 68, 141, 156
Cultural Revolution, 107, 117, 124, 184, 237

D
Dabashi, Hamid, 18
de Beauvoir, Simone, 102
de Certeau, Michel, 3
de Lauretis, Teresa, 53
DeLoughrey, Elizabeth, 257n
Dewey, John, 175
Di lü ting 涤滤亭, 283, 286–8, 290
  in "Bie You Dong Tian," 287
Diao, Keli, 101
Dickinson, Emily, 82, 244, 265
Dickinson, Goldsworthy Lowes
  Letters from a Chinese Official, 122, 135n12
  Letters from John Chinaman, 122
  and Pearl Buck, 114
  and Xu Zhimo, 107, 109, 111
Dimock, Wai-Chee, 5, 19
Ding Ling 丁玲, 112, 113, 225n3.
  See also Xu Zhimo
Dirlik, Arif, 202, 204–5, 208, 224
disinheritance, 181
Doctor Zhivago, 238, 257n4
Donald Duk (F. Chin), 50, 52–53, 59, 73, 152
  alternative masculinity in, 51–53
  Asian heroic tradition in, 7, 13, 50–53, 71, 263
  Chinese sources in, 50–52
  father-son relationship in, 50–53, 152
  naming in, 50
  redefinition of heroism in, 52
  See also Chin, Frank
dual memoir, 119, 124, 177

dual personality, 19, 229
Duara, Prasenjit, 57
Dragon, 71
Dream of the Red Chamber 《红楼梦》, 46, 114, 117
"Drinking Alone under the Moon" 《月下独酌》 (Li Bai), 272, 275, 276, 291. *See also* "Get Rid of the X"
Du Liniang 杜丽娘, 106. *See also The Peony Pavilion*

E
Eakin, Paul John, 35, 36, 180, 196n7
East Goes West (Y. Kang) 14, 21n9, 107, 116–19, 123–24, 132, 135n13, 136n15, 218. *See also* Kang, Younghill
Eaton, Edith Maud (Sui Sin Far)
 "Leaves from the Mental Portfolio of an Eurasian," 218
 "Pat and Pan," 221
 "The Story of a White Woman Who Married a Chinese," 126
Eaton, Winnifred (Onoto Wantanna)
 "The Loves of Sakura Jiro and the Three Headed Maid," 218
ecocriticism, 17, 257n1
The Eighth Promise (W. P. Lee), 174, 176, 177, 180–82, 186–88, 193–95
Eliot, T. S., 55, 82, 83
Ellison, Ralph
 Invisible Man, 7
Elmhirst, Leonard K., 109, 111
"emasculation," 6, 11, 14, 31–34, 42–44, 141, 144, 156, 159, 163
Emerson, Ralph Waldo
 "History," 193
 "Literary Ethics," 249
 "Nature," 236
 on nature, 236
 "Self-Reliance," 236, 237, 247
 Society and Solitude, 247
 on solitude, 235, 236, 246
 "Speech at Reception of Chinese Embassy," 257n6
Empress Dowager, 175
Eng, David L., 69, 78–79, 87, 91–92, 157, 202, 206, 211, 298n1
environmentalism, 239, 257n1
 and ethics 16, 239
 and politics, 16
epistemologies, contesting, 212–17
Espiritu, Yen Le, 31
essentialism, 56, 112, 150, 180, 215, 217, 222, 265
ethics of care, 141–43, 68
ethnic studies, 5, 17, 69, 183, 298n1
ethnocentrism, 3
ethnographic fallacy, 37, 187
ethnography, 3, 35, 38, 176, 187, 209, 217, 223
"A Eulogy," 246
Eurocentrism, 191–92, 224
exile, 17, 218, 232, 250, 270
exilic consciousness, 231, 250, 270

F
Fairbank, Wilma, 112, 134n3
familism, 15, 219, 220
family
 in autobiography, 177
 constructions of, 45
Fa Muk Lan/Hua Mulan 花木兰. *See* Mulan
Fang Hong 方红, 60n1
fansiwenxue 反思文学. *See* introspection literature
Fan Zhongyan 范仲淹
 Yueyang Lou Ji 《岳阳楼记》, 246
"Farewell Again, Cambridge" 《再别康桥》 (Xu Zhimo), 109, 111
Fargo, 93

father-son relationship
    in *American Knees*, 145–46, 151, 152
    in *China Boy*, 152
    in *Donald Duk*, 50–53, 152
    in *The Winged Seed*, 152–56, 166
Faulkner, William, 191, 202, 235, 241, 242, 246, 247
    Nobel Prize acceptance speech, 241
    "A Rose for Emily," 191
feminine ideals, Chinese
    of Old China and New China, 219, 220, 222, 225n3
    of submissiveness and passivity, 218, 220
    See also femininity and feminism
feminine mystique, 102, 120
femininity, 30, 31, 47, 70, 143, 203, 218, 225n3
feminism, 33–37, 42, 49, 141, 156, 165, 179, 187, 194
    and cultural nationalism, 6, 7, 18, 68, 141
    diversification of, 20
    and Kingston, 31, 42, 59
    mainstream, 30, 36
    and Marilyn Chin
Feng Huang 凤凰, 176
Feng, Pin-chia 冯品佳, 9
fengliu-caizi/flirting scholar 风流才子, 146
feng yen 凤眼 (phoenix eyes). *See* "Phoenix Eyes"
Ferens, Dominika, 202, 211, 217
filial obligation, 15, 47, 120, 144–45, 156, 158, 165, 167n7, 216, 217, 224
filiation. *See* affiliation *vs.* filiation
Filipino American, 5, 77, 95n2, 152, 218
Fish, Stanley, 3
Fishkin, Shelley Fisher, 5
Flirting Scholar《唐伯虎點秋香》, 104, 106, 146, 165

Flowers in the Mirror《镜花缘》, 41, 42
Fong, Katheryn M., 36, 191
Foote, Lorien, 11
Ford, Stacilee, 208
Forster, E. M., 107, 121–23, 133
France, Peter, 189
A Free Life (H. Jin).), 229–57
    American Dream in, 235, 237, 242, 243, 247
    artistic autonomy in, 237, 246, 249
    "Belated Love," 254
    Bai Juyi in, 244
    as Chinese American pastoral, 235–37, 244–46
    commodification in, 240
    double-voice in, 15, 230, 252–53
    Dr. Zhivago in, 238, 257n4
    ecology in, 239
    Emerson in, 237, 246–49, 257n4
    "A Eulogy," 246
    Fan Zhongyan 范仲淹 in, 246
    Faulkner in, 246–47
    Frost in, 235, 246–49
    homeland in, 19, 229, 234, 238–39, 249, 251, 254–58
    and Keats, 108
    melancholy (melancholia) in, 250, 254
    as metafiction 16, 230
    "My Pity," 242
    nation-state in, 229, 235, 237–39, 240, 251
    nomadic sensibility, 107
    parental sacrifice in, 235, 241, 244
    politics in, 15, 235, 236, 252, 253
    Mao Zedong in, 73
    solitude in, 16, 235, 244–49, 254
    Tao Qian/Tao Yuanming in, 235
    transpacific materialism in, 239–43
    Whitman in, 235, 244, 246
    See also Jin, Ha
Fresh Off the Boat (E. Huang), 72, 141

Freud, Sigmund, 250
  "Mourning and Melancholia," 250
Friedan, Betty, 102, 120
  The Feminine Mystique, 102
Friedman, Susan Stanford, 20, 37, 144, 156
Frost, Robert, 235, 246–8
Fry, Roger, 107, 111, 122, 133
Fu Manchu, 32
furen zhiren [womanly *ren*] 妇人之仁, 143, 154, 167n1.
  See also *ren*

G

ga bo (clan register), 181
Gabriel, Teshome, 9
Gao Xingjian 高行健, 237, 255
  Soul Mountain, 196n5
Garden of Flowing Fragrance. See Liu Fang Yuan
Garnett, David, 111
gender asymmetry, 42, 273–75
gender-bending
  in *China Men*, 39, 41–43, 48
  in Chinese literature, 104, 128
  in "Get Rid of the X," 17, 275
  in *The Woman Warrior*, 38–43, 54–55, 267
  in "Your *Tongzhi* Body," 17, 163, 280–81
gender norms, 30–31, 34, 46, 47, 141, 158.
  See also heteronormativity
gender studies, 2, 68, 70, 101, 104, 224.
  See also performativity of gender
genealogy, 183, 213
"Get Rid of the X" 16, 266, 272–76, 291
  algebra in, 275
  and the American dream, 276
  and Boudoir Complaint, 270, 272, 276, 291

and "Drinking Alone under the Moon" 《月下独酌》, 269, 272, 275, 276
  gender asymmetry in, 273–75
  gender-bending in, 275
  and "Parable of the Guitar," 275
  sex chromosomes in, 275
  See also Chin, Marilyn
Gilligan, Carol, 34, 77, 142
globalization, 5, 10, 107, 264
Goddess of Mercy. See Guanyin
The Good Earth (P. Buck), 124, 128–29, 132, 135n13, 203, 206, 209–10
  Orientalism in, 203, 206
  See also Buck, Pearl S.
Goellnicht, Donald C., 10, 42
Great Leap Forward, 253
Guan Gong/ Kwan Kung/Guang Yu/ 关公/关羽, 44, 56–58.
  See also Chin, Frank; *Donald Duk*; *Romance of The Three Kingdoms*
Guanyin 观音/Goddess of Mercy, 280, 281
Guan Yu 关羽. See Guan Gong 关公
Gubar, Susan, 40
Guixiu pai 闺秀派. See Boudoir Lady School
Guo Yingjian 郭英剑, 209

H

Hamlet, 79.
  See also *Pangs of Love*
Han, Chungpa (narrator of East Goes West), 116, 117, 121, 135n8, 135n13, 185, 190, 193, 218.
  See also Kang, Younghill
Happy Together, 71
Harding, Jason, 122
Hardy, Thomas, 112, 202
Heath Anthology of American Literature, 4

Heise, Ursula K., 257n1
Hernandez, Javier C., 11
heroic tradition, Asian. *See* Asian heroic tradition
heroism, redefinition of, 48–53, 265
Hessler, Peter, 184
  River Town: Two Years on the Yangtze, 184
heteronormativity, 12, 31–35, 43–48, 53, 67, 87–90, 94, 144, 152, 156–57, 162, 165–66, 276, 278, 279
historical amnesia, 232
HIV/AIDS
  in "Phoenix Eyes" (R. C. Leong), 14, 144, 156, 162–65, 167, 280, 281
  and silence, 162–63, 281
  in "Your *Tongzhi* Body" (R. C. Leong), 16, 163, 266, 276, 278–81, 291
Hmong. *See Miao* 苗
Ho, Jennifer Ann, 298n1
Ho, Tamara, 298n1
Hoffman, Bettina, 246
Hollywood films, 6, 32–33, 69–72, 166
Hom, Alice, 157
home, 12, 18, 47, 56, 73–77, 88–92, 111, 119, 122, 125, 128, 146, 151, 158, 178, 185, 204, 207, 211, 215, 225n3, 234, 239, 245, 249–51, 254–57, 286, 297
  and language, 16, 19, 230
  See also homeland
homeland, 16, 19, 118, 229, 234, 249, 251,–58, 293n12
  and native language, 234, 251, 252, 258n10
Homer
  The Iliad, 34, 45, 47, 57, 95n1
  The Odyssey, 45, 57, 95n1, 231, 250, 251

homophobia, 11, 16, 29, 32, 33, 58, 107, 156, 162, 276, 278, 297
  and patrilineage, 12, 162
  See also HIV/AIDS; queerness
homosexuality. *See* queerness
Hong, Grace Kyungwon, 298n1
hooks, bell, 47
House of Cards, 93
Hsu Chih-mo. *See* Xu Zhimo 徐志摩
Hsu Tsimou. *See* Xu Zhimo 徐志摩
Hua Mulan/Fa Muk Lan 花木兰. *See* Mulan
Hua Yanjun 华彦钧. *See* Ah Bing
Huang, Eddie, 72, 141
  Fresh off the Boat, 72
Hu Luping 胡路苹, 20n2
Hu Shi/Hu Shih 胡适, 17, 175
  "An Autobiographical Account at Forty" 《四十自述》, 174, 176–78, 182, 188, 193, 196n9
  Hundred Days' Reform 百日维新, 183
  "Mourning Zhimo" 《追悼志摩》, 111, 116
  "Prelude: My Mother's Betrothal," 188
  as Sinophone writer, 17
  and Xu Zhimo, 114, 118, 121
Hu-DeHart, Evelyn, 9, 298n1
Huntington, Collis P., 289, 290
Huntington, Henry Edwards, 289
Huntington Library, 281, 284, 288, 289
  Chinese Garden, 16, 282, 284, 285
  See also Liu Fang Yuan
Hurston, Zora Neale, 216
Hwang, David Henry, 12, 30, 54, 106, 168n8
  M. Butterfly, 7, 12, 30, 106
hybridity. *See* cultural hybridity
hyphen. *See* Asian Americans/Asian-Americans

I

Icarus syndrome, 115
identity politics, 2, 7, 184
Ignorance (M. Kundera), 252
immigration
 and antimiscegenation laws, 31
 Asian Exclusion Act, 5
 in *Donald Duk*, 50, 52, 59
 1965 Immigration and Nationality Act, 8
"Immortal by the Lake" (Li Qingzhao), 270, 272, 275, 291
imperialism, cultural, 9, 48, 201, 220, 224
imperialist nostalgia, 221, 222
Inada, Lawson Fusao, 6, 19, 34
"In Defence of Foreignness," 234.
 See also Jin, Ha
independence, 45, 146, 174, 193, 195, 210, 224, 237, 244–46, 249
 Gish Jen on, 173, 182
 vs. interdependence, 45, 173, 195
individualism, 34–35, 45, 56, 57, 77, 133, 142, 162, 224, 237–38, 248, 249
"An Individual's Homeland" (H. Jin), 231, 234, 249–51, 254, 293n12
In Search of Our Mothers' Gardens (A. Walker), 181
In the Mood for Love, 71
interdependence, 15, 18, 133, 142, 173, 182, 249
 Gish Jen on, 173–74, 182–83
 vs. independence, 45, 173, 195
 vs. individualism, 45, 133, 142
 and *ren* 仁/ethics of care, 12, 14, 57, 142–43
international adoption. *See* transnational adoption
intersectionality, 29, 53, 144
intertextual hermeneutics, 14
introspection literature/*fansiwenxue* 反思文学, 18, 219

Isherwood, Christopher, 122, 135n12
"Ithaka" (C. P. Cavafy), 231, 250, 251.
 See also Jin, Ha
Iwamura, Jane Naomi, 60

J

Jacobs, Harriet, 271, 292n5
Japanese Americans, 3, 5, 44
 internment of, 3, 5
Japanese epics, 34, 43–44, 141
Jardine, Alice, 43
jen/仁. *See ren*
Jen, Gish 任碧莲
 on interdependence versus independence, 173–74, 182–83, 184, 194, 195, 196n2
 Tiger Writing, 60n3, 173, 181–83, 184, 194, 196n2
Jiang Qing 江青, 124
Jin, Ha 哈金/Jin Xuefei 金雪飞, 9, 10, 17, 19, 229–57
 A Free Life, 15, 229–57, 280, 297
 "Afterword 后记" to 《另一个空间 [*Another Space*]》, 255
 Between Silences, 231
 on Cavafy, 231
 "The Censor in the Mirror," 253
 on Conrad, 231, 233, 239, 252, 253
 The Crazed, 253
 "In Defence of Foreignness," 234
 "Exiled to English" (op-ed), 232
 A Good Fall, 251, 255
 history in, 232
 "An Individual's Homeland," 231, 234, 249–51, 254, 293n12
 on Kundera, 252, 253
 "The Language of Betrayal," 231–3, 256
 on Lin Yutang, 230, 231
 A Map of Betrayal, 232
 Nanjing Requiem, 232

Jin, Ha (*cont.*)
   on Nabokov, 230, 231, 233, 234, 248, 253, 256
   Ocean of Words, 82, 253
   op-ed, *NYT*, 11, 71, 232, 238
   "Preface 序" to 《落地 [*A Good Fall*]》, 251
   "The Spokesman and the Tribe," 231
   "A Stonemason," 245
   War Trash, 232, 253
   Waiting, 233
   The Writer as Migrant, 15, 229–34, 249, 293n12
   on writer's role, 230
   See also *A Free Life*; *The Writer as Migrant*
Jin, Wen 金雯, 298n1
Jin, Xuefei 金雪飞. *See* Jin, Ha 哈金
Joan of Arc, 39
Johnson, Diane, 36, 193
Johnson, Samuel
   on biography, 193
   Rambler, 193
Journey to the West/Monkey 《西游记》, 34, 49, 57, 122
Joyce, James, 112
Juhasz, Suzanne, 36, 38
junzi/chün-tzu 君子 (Superior Man), 13, 73, 74, 142

K
Kang, Laura, 63
Kang, Lucy Lynn, 135n10
Kang, Younghill
   "China Is Different" [review of *The Good Earth*], 135n13
   East Goes West, 14, 17, 21n9, 107, 116–19, 123, 124, 132, 135n13, 136n15, 218
   Grass Roof, 119, 135n8, 218
   and Xu Zhimo, 118, 121, 132
Kang Youwei/K'ang Yu-wei 康有为, 175, 196n13

Karlinsky, Simon, 234
Katrak, Ketu H.
   "simultaneity of geography," 249, 250, 256
Keats, John, 108, 117
Keely, Frances, 119
Kellman, Steven G., 249
Kim, Daniel, 298n1
Kim, Elaine H., 6, 33, 36, 48
King, Katherine Callen, 34
King's College (Cambridge), 109–11, 123, 124
Kingston, Maxine Hong 汤亭亭
   and Asian heroic tradition, 7, 13, 30, 34, 43–45, 48, 263, 296
   Bill Moyers on, 196n6
   bicultural aesthetics in, 29–30, 53, 59
   China Men, 6, 41–3, 48, 51, 60n1, 68
   and Marilyn Chin, 266, 271
   Tripmaster Monkey, 49, 55, 60, 60n1, 68, 93
   The Woman Warrior, 7, 29–31, 39, 52, 54, 55, 173–96, 196n7, 264–65, 267, 269–72
   See also *China Men*; *The Woman Warrior*
Kinkley, Jeffery C., 113, 191
Klein, Christina, 202, 212, 220
Kong, Belinda, 9, 21n4, 225n3, 229, 298n1
Korean Americans, 5, 17, 21n9, 116–19, 132, 135n13, 152
Korean War, 183
Koshy, Susan, 8, 298n1
Künstlerroman, 246
Ku, Robert Ji-Song, 92–93, 298n1
Kundera, Milan, 230, 231, 252, 253
   Ignorance, 255
Kung fu, 4, 33, 54, 71, 102, 107
Kwan Gong. *See* Guan Gong 关公

L

labor
Chinese American, 34, 282, 283, 285–90
and Chinese exclusion, 50, 69
immigrant, 42, 59, 238
migrant, 16, 51, 59, 238, 266, 276, 282, 285, 287–91, 297
transpacific, 218, 291
See also affective labor; "*Bie You Dong Tian*"
Lahiri, Jhumpa, 10, 218
Lai, Paul, 10
lan 兰 (orchid), 269, 272
language
and betrayal, 231–33
code-switching, 4
and counternarrative, 4, 181
deterritorilization of, 243–49
and home, 250
and manhood, 79–82, 155–56
"The Language of Betrayal" (H. Jin), 231–34, 256
Lao She 老舍, 111, 223
Lao Zi, 46
The Last Emperor, 90
Lau, D.C., 72
Laurence, Patricia, 111–13, 121–23, 130, 133–34n2, 136n18
Lauter, Paul, 4
Lee, Ang 李安
Crouching Tiger, Hidden Dragon, 71
The Wedding Banquet, 71
Lee, Bruce, 33, 60n2, 71, 95n3
Lee, C. Y., 81
Lee, Chang-rae, 82, 152
Lee, Gus, 13, 67–96, 144
China Boy, 67, 72–78, 106
Honor and Duty, 75
Lee, James Kyung-Jin, 153, 298n1
Lee, Josephine, 20n2
Lee, Julia H., 298n1
Lee Kuey/Li Kui 李逵, 50, 51.
See also Chin, Frank; *Donald Duk*

Lee, Leo Ou-fan/L. O. Lee 李欧梵, 13, 108, 109, 112, 114–15, 120, 134n3, 134n4, 134n5
Lee, Li-young 李立杨, 14, 17, 141–68
The Winged Seed, 14, 143, 152–6, 159, 165, 166
Lee, Rachel C., 8, 279, 298n1
Lee, Robert G., 36, 57, 58
Lee, Sunyoung, 118, 119
Lee, William Poy 李培湛, 17, 173–96
The Eighth Promise, 174, 176, 177, 180–82, 186–88, 193–95
Lee, Yu-cheng 李有成, 73
"The Legend of Miss Sasagawara" (Yamamoto), 3, 20n1, 154, 196n11
Leong, Russell C. 梁志英, 9, 14, 16, 17
"Bie You Dong Tian 别有洞天," 282–91
The Country of Dreams and Dust, 165, 265
"Memories of Stone Places," 168n9
Phoenix Eyes, 266
"Phoenix Eyes," 14, 144, 156–67, 168n10, 168n11, 280, 281
"Rough Notes for Mantos," 157
"Toward a Third Literature," 9, 229
"Writing Sexuality," 157, 168n11
"Your *Tongzhi* Body," 16, 163, 264, 266–82, 286, 290–91
lesbians. See homosexuality; sexual minorities
"A Lesson from the Xinhai Revolution" 《辛亥革命的一课》 (C. Shen), 185–86
Letters from a Chinese Official (G. L. Dickinson), 122
Letters from John Chinaman (G. L. Dickinson), 122
Letter from Peking (P. Buck), 125, 134-35n7, 136n15
Leung, Gaylord, 11, 114
Levenson, Joseph R., 4, 13, 142
Li 礼 (decorum), 12

Li Bai/Li Po 李白
  "Ballad of a Trader's Wife" 《长干行》, 269, 272
  carpe diem motif (Li Bai), 274
  "Drinking Alone under the Moon" 《月下独酌》, 272
  "Farewell to Shuyun" 《宣城谢朓楼饯别校叔云》, 129
  as Poet Immortal 诗仙, 272, 274, 275
  See also Chin, Marilyn; Min, Anchee
Li Baiqing 李柏青, 207, 219
Li Chi 李祁, 260
Li, David Leiwei 李磊伟, 8, 21n6, 36
Li Guicang 李贵苍, 218
  Trans. 《一抹黄色》[yimo huangse], 20n2
Li Ju-Chen/Li Ruzhen/李汝珍, 64
  Flowers in the Mirror 《镜花缘》, 41
Li Kui. See Lee Kuey 李逵
Li Po. See Li Bai 李白
Li Qingzhao 李清照
  "An Immortal by the Lake" 《临江仙》, 270, 272
  and Boudoir Complaint, 272
  See also Bing Xin; Chin, Marilyn
Li, Yiyun 李翊云, 9
Li, Yu-ning, 177, 178, 183, 195
Liang Qichao 梁启超, 17, 113, 133, 174, 175, 177, 178, 182, 183, 188, 193, 196n3
  on literature as history, 188, 196n10
  "My Autobiographical Account at Thirty" 《三十自述》, 174, 177–78, 182, 183, 188, 193, 196n3, 196n9, 196n13
  as Sinophone writer, 17
  and Xu Zhimo, 134n3
  Yinbingshi heji 《饮冰室合集》, 188, 196n10
Liang Shan 梁山, 51, 104, 128.
  See also Water Margin
Liang Shanbo 梁山伯, 104, 128.
  See also Butterfly Lovers

Liang Sicheng 梁思成, 113, 133n2, 134n2
"The Life of the Sire of Five Willows" 《五柳先生传》(Tao Yuanming), 174
life-writing. 15, 16, 18, 35, 173–95.
  See also autobiography
Lim, Shirley Geok-lin 林玉玲, 8
Lin Changmin 林长民, 107
Lin, Ed, 141
Lin Huiyin (Phyllis) 林徽因, 107, 109, 116, 133, 222, 225n3.
  See also Xu Zhimo
  《悼志摩 [Mourning Zhimo]》, 116
Lin, Maya, 134n3
Lin Yutang 林语堂, 30, 218, 230, 231, 253
  Moment in Peking 《京华烟云》, 231
Ling, Jinqi 凌津奇, 298
Ling Shuhua 凌淑华
  Ancient Melodies, 269
  and Bing Xin, 222, 223, 225n3
  as Chen Yuan's wife, 130, 131, 136n18
  as Julian Bell's lover, 130
  and Lin Huiyin, 133, 222, 225n3
  parallels with Willow in Pearl of China, 130–32
  as representative of New Boudoir Lady School, 223
  and Virginia Woolf, 130
  and Xu Zhimo, 107, 109, 111–13, 116, 121, 130, 131, 133, 133n2, 136n18
  See also Bing Xin; Chinnery, Ying; Min, Anchee; Xu Zhimo
linguistic deterritorialization, 243–9
Literati School. See Rujia 儒家
literacy, bicultural or intercultural, 15, 19, 37, 44, 48, 54, 55, 112, 117–18, 122, 124, 126, 127, 132–33, 174, 175, 187–95, 222, 265

Liu Bang 刘邦
  and *furen zhiren* [womanly *ren*] 妇
    人之仁, 143, 167n1
Liu, Cynthia, 162, 164, 281
Liu Fang Yuan 流芳园 (Garden of
  Flowing Fragrance), 282–91
Liu, James, 68
Liu Mengmei 柳梦梅, 104, 106.
  See also The Peony Pavilion
Liu Xiaobo 刘晓波, 237
Liu Yiqing 刘意青 attack on Ha Jin,
  233
liufang-baishi 流芳百世 ["Leave a
  good name for a hundred
  generations"], 289
Loomis, Laura Hibbard, 292n4
Lord Guan. *See Guan Gong* 关公
Louie, David Wong 雷祖威, 13, 17,
  67–96, 106, 144
  The Barbarians are Coming,
    93, 96n9
  on ghettoization of Asian American
    writers, 50
  "Movers," 79, 85–87, 90, 91
  "One Man's Hysteria--real and
    imagined--in the twentieth
    century," 79, 81–85
  Pangs of Love (collection), 13, 67,
    78–81
  "Pangs of Love" (story), 88–95
Louie, Kam, 12, 53–55, 58, 67, 68,
  72, 73, 101–5, 107, 133, 142,
  167n1
"The Loves of Sakura Jiro and the
  Three Headed Maid" (W. Eaton),
  218
Lowe, Lisa, 5, 7, 31, 211, 298n1
Lowe, Pardee, 180
Lu Xiaoman 陆小曼, 107, 113, 121,
  128, 130, 131, 134n4, 134n5.
  See also Xu Zhimo

Lu Xun/Lu Hsün 鲁迅, 107, 111,
  118, 132, 135n9, 223
Lue Gim Gong 刘锦浓 (*Wooden Fish
  Songs*), 176, 181, 185, 193–94
Lye, Colleen, 18, 298n1, 41
Lyotard, Jean-François, 189

M
Ma, Sheng-mei 马胜美, 37, 190
machismo., 45, 49, 72, 94, 107, 296.
  See also masculinity
MacKinnon, Janice, 114, 134n6
MacKinnon, Stephen, 114, 134n6
Madame Butterfly, 95n1
Malcolm, Cheryl Alexander, 74
Malcolm X, 181
manhood, Asian American. *See*
  masculinity, Asian American
masculinity, Asian American, 6, 12, 29,
  31, 50, 60, 67–95, 141–67
  alternative, 12, 14, 17, 33, 35–38,
    51–53, 58, 59, 76–77, 95, 101,
    103–7, 117, 123, 142, 145–46,
    156–58, 166
  and artistry, 73–74, 152, 166
  and autobiography, 35
  and calligraphy, 73–74, 95n4
  Chinese vs. Japanese, 88–89, 96n8
  desexualization of, 69
  double bind in, 94
  and economic power, 87, 89, 90,
    107, 144
  and "emasculation," 7, 12, 30,
    33, 41–44, 94, 101, 132,
    156, 163
  and fatherhood, 50, 52, 87,
    145–46, 151–54
  and geographic location, 14, 144,
    152, 165–66
  and historical legacy, 87

and interracial romance, 87, 89, 106, 119, 125, 127–30
and language, 52, 81, 88, 103, 155–56
and matrimony, 87, 90
and nationality, 74
and physical power, 106, 107, 144
and political power, 69, 107
and race, 11–12, 14, 43, 46, 70, 152, 155
and *ren* (caring), 14, 77, 142–43, 166
and remasculinization, 1, 34, 44, 50, 52, 54, 59
and spirituality, 151, 152, 159
and violence, 32, 34, 46, 51, 71–73, 77, 84, 94, 95
See also wen; wen-wu; wenren; wu
masculinity, hegemonic/heteronormative, 12, 31–35, 43–48, 67, 87–90, 94, 101, 123, 132, 141, 144, 152, 156, 166, 278
Mannur, Anita, 298n1
Mansfield, Katherine, 112, 113, 121
Mao Zedong 毛泽东, 73–74, 238
Marchetti, Gina, 32, 70
Marco Polo, 18, 32
Marx, Leo, 236
masculinity studies, 2, 12, 30–34, 67
May Fourth Movement, 15, 201, 222
McBride, James, 177, 181
  The Color of Water, 177, 181
McCunn, Ruthanne Lum 林露德
  A Chinese Yankee, 31
  Wooden Fish Songs《木鱼歌》, 17, 173–95, 218
McDonald, Dorothy Ritsuko, 55
McMahon, Keith, 103, 128
"Meat vs. Rice," 69
media, popular. *See* popular culture, American
Mei Lanfang 梅兰芳, 12, 105, 106

melancholy/melancholia, 80, 250.
  See also Freud, Sigmund; Jin, Ha
memoir, 37, 38, 41, 48, 49, 72, 107, 119, 124–25, 129, 152, 159, 175–81, 183–87, 189, 194, 195, 255, 264, 267
metafiction, 83, 230, 249.
  See also A Free Life
Metzger, Sean, 298n1
Mexican Americans, 11, 32, 77, 286–89
Miao/Hmong 苗, 175, 179, 189, 193, 297
migrant aesthetics/migrant poetics, 230, 246, 255–57.
  See also Jin, Ha; nomadic identity
"The Milieu of My Upbringing"《我所生长的地方》(C.Shen), 190
Milton, John, 54
  Paradise Lost, 54
mimicry, 79, 91
Min, Anchee 闵安琪, 9, 14, 101–3
  "Author's Note," 135-36n14
  Pearl of China, 14, 107, 112, 114, 124–33, 135n14, 203
misreading, cultural, 175
missionaries. *See* Christian missionaries
Miss Saigon, 95n1
Mitchell, W. J. T., 257n1
Mo Yan 莫言181
  "Nobel Lecture: Storytellers," 175
model minority stereotype, 2, 15, 78, 94, 115, 118, 146, 201, 211, 218–20, 225, 276
  and filial piety, 2, 219–20
Mody, Perveez, 111
Monkey《西游记》. *See Journey to the West*
Morrison, Toni, 43
mother tongue, 17, 19, 76, 81, 248, 251–52, 255, 258n10, 291, 293n12, 295
  as home, 251
  See also Jin, Ha

"The Movers" (D. W. Louie), 85–87
  homosexuality in, 87, 88, 91
  impersonation in, 79, 85
  See also Louie, David Wong
Moy, James, 150
Moyers, Bill, 196n6
Mudan Ting《牡丹亭》. See *Peony Pavilion*
Mulan/Hua Mulan/Fa Muk Lan 花木兰, 38–40, 42, 47, 49, 54–55, 188, 189, 192, 264–67, 269, 271–72
Mullen, Harryette, 47
  Muse & Drudge, 245
Murray, Henry A.
  ascensionist personality, 115
  Icarus syndrome, 115
Murray, John Middleton, 121
"My Autobiographical Account at Thirty"《三十自述》(Q. Liang), 174, 188, 196n3
"My Family"《我的家庭》(C. Shen), 179
My Life in China and America (W. Yung), 195n1, 218
"My Pity" (H. Jin), 242

N

Nabokov, Vladimir, 230, 248, 253, 256
The Nabokov-Wilson Letters, 234
Naipaul, V. S., 230
naming, 2, 5, 30, 50–51, 59, 84, 104, 108, 116, 121, 135n12, 145, 163, 178–82, 185, 186, 189, 201, 229, 266–67, 269, 280–82, 285, 287, 289–90, 292n9
Nanking, University of 金陵大学, 125
Nanking Daily, 126
Nanking Incident, 135n14
The Narrative of Frederick Douglass, 176
nationalism, 6, 7, 18, 68, 238

Native Americans, 32, 283, 286–90.
  See also Tongva
nature
  in Chinese poetry, 244
  in Emerson, 236
  in *A Free Life*, 235, 254
  in Tao Qian/Tao Yuanming, 235
Nee, Victor G., and Brett De Bary Nee, 31
New Boudoir Lady School/*xin guixi pai* 新闺秀派, 223.
  See also Ling Shuhua
Ng, Fae Myenne 伍慧明
  Bone, 184
Ng, Lai-Sze, 111
Nguyen, Tan Hoang, 70, 95
Nguyen, Viet Thanh, 1, 34, 73, 76, 84, 96n5, 298n1
Nibelle, Paul, 214
Ninh, erin Khuê, 184, 219, 241
Nixon, Richard, 124
Noddings, Nel
  Caring, 77, 142, 143
nomadic identity, 111, 156.
  See also migrant aesthetics
nostalgia, 111, 204, 221, 249–51, 254, 276
nuan'nan [warm male] 暖男, 167

O

"Ode to Pipa"《琵琶行》, 268–72, 275, 291.
  See also Bai Juyi
"One Man's Hysteria—real and imagined—in the twentieth century" (D. W. Louie), 79, 81–86, 88
Ono, Kent A., 7, 60n2, 95n3
Orientalism
  aesthetic, 203–7, 157, 159, 221
  Asian complicity in, 15, 159, 202, 204, 205

and Asian American literature, 16–19,
30–33, 35–37, 46, 70–71,
93–94, 159, 175, 186–92,
201–24, 233, 263, 266, 290–93
and Asian inferiority, 95n3, 117
and the body, 157, 159, 282
internalization of, 202, 204–5, 208,
214–15, 218
and "The Photograph," 202–4,
207–9, 210–15, 217–18,
220–24
and white sympathy, 212
three strands of, 15, 218
Orientalist gaze, 15, 35, 157–59, 191,
211, 214–15, 217, 223
reversing of, 15, 158, 159
Orientalist melancholia, 214, 224
Orzeszkowa, Eliza, 233
Outlaws of the Marsh. See *Water Margin*
Ouyang Xiu 欧阳修, 270, 271

P
Pai, Hsien-yung Kenneth/Bai
Xianyong 白先勇, 9, 10, 168n10
Pak Suet Sin/Bai Xuexian 白雪仙,
105, 106
Palumbo-Liu, David, 7, 80, 211, 224
Pan, Arnold, 247
Pangs of Love (Louie collection),
78–95
allusion to *Hamlet*, 79
"Birthday," 79
displacement in, 78–79, 90, 237
extinction in, 78–80, 84, 85
hysteria in, 79, 83
interracial romances in, 78–95
masculinity in, 67–70, 74, 76–95
model minorities in, 78–81
"passing" in, 78–95
title, 79
trespassing in, 78–80

See also Louie, David Wong;
"Movers"; "One Man's
Hysteria"; "Pangs of Love"
"Pangs of Love" (Louie short story),
88–95
American Dream in, 90
assimilation in, 88
homosexuality in, 88–89, 276
intergenerational tension in, 88
masculinity in, 89
passing in, 91, 92
See also Louie, David Wong
Parikh, Crystal, 298n1
Partridge, Jeffrey F. L., 21n4
passing, 38, 50, 78–95, 163, 185, 249
Pasternak, Boris, 238, 257n4
pastoral tradition, 235
and ethics, 16
in *A Free Life*, 16, 235–37, 245
and politics, 16
two strands of, 244
patriarchy
American, 34, 38, 48, 59, 143, 166
Chinese, 31, 34, 38, 41–42, 46, 48,
68, 90, 143–45, 157–58,
161–62, 165–66
"Peach Blossom Spring" 《桃花源
记》 (Tao Yuanming), 192, 236
Peach Orchard Oath 桃园结义,
57–58, 60.
See also *Romance of the Three
Kingdoms*
peach-pink, 190–92.
See also Shen Congwen
Pearl of China (A. Min), 14, 107, 112,
114, 124–33, 135n14, 203
Peony Pavilion/Mudan Ting 《牡丹
亭》, 104, 106
People's Republic of China (PRC),
104, 107
performativity of gender, 12, 69, 70,
105, 106, 166

Pham, Vincent N., 60n2, 95n3
Phoenix, 57, 158, 163, 265, 266
"Phoenix Eyes" (R. C. Leong), 14, 144, 156–67, 265–66, 276, 280–81.
  alternative masculinity in, 156, 158–60, 165
  artistry in, 159–60, 166
  Buddhism in, 162–65
  caring in, 162, 165, 166
  filial obligation in, 158, 165
  geographical impact on masculinity in, 158, 164, 166
  naming in, 163
  reversing Orientalist gaze in, 157–59, 164
  queerness in, 14, 144, 156, 163–67, 280, 281
"The Photograph" 《相片》 (Bing Xin), 201–24
  Christian missionaries, critique of, 202, 208–10, 212–13, 220, 224
  co-dependence in, 207
  commodification in, 203–8, 214, 222
  Confucian culture, critique of, 219–20, 222, 224
  feminine ideals of Old and New China in, 219, 220, 222, 225n3
  filial obligation in, 216, 217, 224
  maternal love in, 207, 208, 224
  Orientalism, critique of, 202–4, 207–9, 210–15, 217–18, 220–24
  and postcolonialist theories, 201, 202, 211–12, 214, 217, 224
  racist love in, 203, 204, 208–12
  silence as virtue in, 203–5, 208, 214, 216, 218, 220, 224
《一抹黄色: Plain Yellow》 (M. Chin), 20n2
Plato, 192
Plutarch, 188
  "The Life of Alexander the Great," 188

Poet Immortal. *See* Li Bai
Poetry
  as masculine and feminine yardstick, 102, 103
  slanted allusions in, 17, 263, 266, 272, 275, 278, 291
  Song poetry, 297
  Tang poetry, 297
  wine as inspiration for, 269
  See also poet-scholars
poet-scholars, 104–5, 106, 142.
  See also *caizi*; *shusheng*; *wenren*
popular culture, American, 6, 32–33, 69–72, 166
postcolonial theories, 16, 122, 201–2, 211–12, 214, 217, 224
Pound, Ezra, 269, 271, 292n3
  "The River-Merchant's Wife," 269, 271, 275, 291
Prashad, Vijay, 298n1
Pu Songling 蒲松龄, 46
  Strange Tales from a Chinese Studio 《聊斋志异》, 46, 186

Q
Qiu, Xiaolong 裘小龙, 9
Qiu Yanping 邱艳萍, 207, 219
Qiuxiang 秋香, 146.
  See also Flirting Scholar
queerness, 32–34, 39, 70, 95, 105, 156–58, 165–66
  in Chinese culture, 12, 278
  in "Get Rid of the X" (M. Chin), 16, 264, 272–73, 276, 291
  in "The Movers" (D. W. Louie), 79, 85–87, 90, 91
  in "Pangs of Love" (D. W. Louie), 13, 67, 78–81
  in "Phoenix Eyes" (R. C. Leong), 14, 144, 156–67, 280, 281
  as "Western disease," 278

in "Your *Tongzhi* Body" (R. C. Leong), 16, 163, 266, 276, 278–81, 291
  See also HIV/AIDS; sexuality
queer studies, 157
Qu Yuan 屈原, 46

R
Rabb, Jane M., 202
Rabine, Leslie W., 36
racism. See color-blind racism; racist hate; racist love
racist hate, 32, 211, 212.
  See also Chan, Jeffery Paul; Chin, Frank
racist love, 32, 33, 203, 204, 211, 212, 297
  and silence, 204
  See also Chan, Jeffery Paul; Chin, Frank
Radhakrishnan, R., 8
railroad workers, 287
  in "*Bie You Dong Tian*," 286, 289
  in *China Me*n, 51
  in *Donald Duk*, 50–52, 59
reclaiming the hyphen, 6, 9, 10, 17, 229–30, 263, 291
reclusive ideal, 235–36, 249
reclusive poets, 235, 236, 240, 245.
  See also Tao Yuanming
Records of the Grand Historian/Shiji 《史记》 (Q. Sima), 174, 177
Records of the Worthies 《史记·淮阴侯列传》, 167n1
Reddy, Chandan, 298n1
Reiner, Andrew, 278
remasculinization, 1, 34
ren/jen 仁, (caring), 4, 13, 14, 57, 77, 142, 143
Ren Bai Lou 任白楼. See Yam Pak Building

Ren Jianhui 任剑辉. See Yam Kim Fai
"report a crime" (*baochou* 报仇), 38, 76, 264–65, 274
Revoyr, Nina, 43
Richards, I. A., 121, 122
"The River-Merchant's Wife" (E. Pound), 269, 271, 275, 291
Rody, Caroline, 298n1
Roediger, David, 223
Romance of the Three Kingdoms 《三国演义》, 34, 57–60.
  See also Chin, Frank; Kingston, Maxine Hong
Romanticism, 108, 112, 117
Romeo and Juliet, 128, 190
Romero, Dennis, 60
Rong Hong 容闳. See Yung Wing
Roosevelt, Theodore, 35
  "The Strenuous Life," 255
Rosaldo, Renato, 221
Rowe, Sharon, 142
Rujia [Confucian/Literati School] 儒家, 143
Rushdie, Salman, 231
Russell, Bertrand, 111, 113, 114
Rylands, Dadie, 111

S
sacrifice, 209, 233, 235, 241–44, 290
Said, Edward W.
  on contrapuntal awareness, 19, 114, 127
  Culture and Imperialism, 202, 290
  Humanism and Democratic Criticism, 21
  Orientalism, 19, 32, 164, 202, 209, 217
  "Orientalism Reconsidered," 217
  Out of Place, 255
  "Reflections on Exile," 19, 114, 191, 231

St. Augustine, 174
St. Clair, William, 189
Samarth, Manini, 52
Sand, George, 108
Santos, Bienvenido N., 218
Sartre, Jean-Paul, 189, 196n7
Schlund-Vials, Cathy, 298n1
Scholar-Beauty/Beauty-Scholar/*Caizi Jiaren* 才子佳人, 102–4, 108, 113, 128, 146
Schorer, Mark, 188
Schurmann, Franz, 13, 142
Sebald, W. G., 231
Sellmann, James D., 142
sexism, 29, 31, 36, 37, 39, 41–43, 45, 48, 53, 55, 59, 145
sexuality, 16, 17, 33, 58, 105–6, 123, 157, 276.
   See also queerness, sexual minorities
sexual minoritics, 30, 276–82.
   See also queerness
Shakespeare, William, 79, 95n1, 128
Shan, Te-hsing 单德兴, 233, 239, 258n9
Sharpe, Jenny
   on literary archeology, 180
Shelley, Percy Bysshe, 108, 117
Shen Congwen 沈从文, 17, 173–95
   Autobiography《从文自传》, 35, 38, 173–74, 177–78, 180, 193, 195n1, 196n5
   "A Lesson from the Xinhai Revolution"《辛亥革命的一课》, 185–86
   "The Milieu of My Upbringing"《我所生长的地方》, 190
   "My Family"《我的家庭》, 179
   as Sinophone writer, 17
   "What I Saw during *Qingxiang* [Purging of the Village]"《清乡所见》, 186, 190–91
   and Xu Zhimo, 17, 107, 112, 113, 121

Shen Fu 沈复
   Six Records of a Floating Life《浮生六记》, 174
Shigeta, James, 71
Shih, Shu-mei 史书美, 9, 60n1, 135n11, 201, 222
Shiji《史记》. See *Records of the Grand Historian*
shusheng 书生, 104.
   See also poet-scholars
silence
   and HIV/AIDS, 164
   and racist love, 204
Sima Qian/Suu-ma Ch'ien 司马迁
   Records of the Grand Historian/Shiji《史记》, 174, 177
"simultaneity of geography," 249, 250, 256
Sinophone Asian American literature, 15, 218–20
Sinophone studies, 10
Sixiang 思乡 (nostalgia), 111
slanted allusions, 3, 17, 263–66, 278, 291
   in "*Bie You Dong Tian*,"
   in "Get Rid of the X," 266, 273–76
   in "Song of the Sad Guitar," 266, 269–72, 276
   in *The Woman Warrior*, 264–65
   in "Your *Tongzhi* Body," 264, 266, 278–81, 291
Slotkin, Richard, 46
Smedley, Agnes, 107, 114, 121
Smith, Paul, 43
Snukal, Robert, 193
Sohn, Stephen Hong, 10, 157, 298n1
solitude
   and displacement, 254
   Emerson on, 236, 247
   in *A Free Life*, 235–37, 244–49, 254
   Gao Xingjian on, 237
   Jin on, 244–9, 254

Liu Xiaobo on, 237
   and loneliness, 249
   in pastoral literature, 244
   three strains of, 244
Solzhenitsyn, Alexander, 231
Song, Geng, 68
Song Jiang 宋江. *See* Soong Gong
Song, Min, 298n1
"Song of the Sad Guitar" (M. Chin), 16, 264, 266–72, 274, 276, 280, 285, 289–91
   and "Ballad of a Trader's Wife," 269
   Chinese-box structure of, 271, 290
   court(yard) in, 270
   female confinement in, 266, 269–72, 289
   and *I Know why the Caged Bird Sings*, 271
   and"An Immortal by the Lake," 270, 272, 275
   and *Incidents in the Life of a Slave Girl*, 271
   and *Jane Eyre*, 271
   naming in, 29, 285
   and "Ode to Pipa," 268–72, 275, 291
   and "Parable of the Guitar," 275
   and "The River-Merchant's Wife," 269, 271, 275, 291
   and *A Room of One's Own*, 271
   and *The Woman Warrior*, 266, 267, 269–72, 291
Sontag, Susan, 15, 202, 214, 215, 223
Soong Gong/Song Jiang 宋江 (*Water Margin*), 52
soul mates, 102, 104, 108, 126, 128–29, 130, 133
Spence, Jonathan, 112
spirituality, 14, 112, 129, 160, 196n9, 239, 276, 280, 291.
   See also Buddhism, Christianity
"The Spokesman and the Tribe" (H. Jin), 231–32

Spurling, Hilary, 112, 135n7, 208, 225n2
Stanislavski, Constantin, 105
Steele, Claude, 93–94
Stern, Julia A., 286
stereotypes
   "acceptable" and "unacceptable," 32
   model minority, 2, 15, 32, 78, 94, 115, 118, 146, 164, 201, 204, 218–19, 225, 276
   and racist love, 32
   and racist hate, 32
   Chinese culture as sexist, 36, 38, 39
   of tough-guys, 21n7
   See also stereotypes, Asian
stereotypes, Asian, 2, 4, 12, 15, 21n7, 30–36, 38–39, 44, 45, 58, 68–70, 73, 93–95, 95n2, 102, 106, 109, 123, 141, 144, 146, 149–50, 164, 187, 205–6, 212, 217, 221, 276
   as asexual nerds, 33, 102, 106, 107, 111, 146, 149–50, 166
   of Asian men, 44–45, 56, 58, 158
   as China dolls, 12, 206, 224, 276
   as coolies, 123
   as dragon ladies and vamps, 12, 32, 33
   of gay Asians, 58, 156–58, 161, 168n8
   as heathens, 15, 123, 153, 166, 185, 202, 208, 211, 212
   as kung fu fighters, 4, 33, 102, 107
   as model minorities, 2, 15, 32, 78, 94, 115, 118, 146, 164, 201, 204, 218–19, 225, 276
   as sexist, 36, 38, 39
   as submissive, 33, 51, 202–4, 212, 214, 225n3, 276
   as yellow peril, 32
   See also stereotypes
Stirling, Nora, 111, 112, 125, 132, 134n5, 134n7

Strange Tales from a Chinese Studio 《聊斋志异》(Pu Songlin), 46, 186
subject formation, 16, 173, 175, 183, 219
subjectivity
　colonial, 80
　ethnic, 175, 179, 182–87
Sui Sin Far. *See* Eaton, Edith Maud
Sun Tzu
　The Art of War, 3
Sun Yat-Sen 孙逸仙/孙中山, 278, 281
Superior Man. *See junzi/chün-tzu* 君子
Suu-ma, Ch'ien. *See* Sima Qian
Sydenstricker, Absalom, 126, 135n14, 154, 155
Sydenstricker, Carie, 126
Sydenstricker, Grace, 74, 93, 136n15, 284
Sydenstricker, Pearl. *See* Buck, Pearl S. 赛珍珠

T

Tagore, Rabindranath, 107, 109, 111, 113, 121, 134n4, 134n7
　The Crescent Moon, 109
Taiping Rebellion, 183
Takagi, Dana, 158
Takaki, Ronald, 31
Tan, Amy 谭恩美
　The Joy Luck Club, 7, 190, 192
　The Kitchen God's Wife, 192
　The Valley of Amazement, 192
Tan, Chee-Lay, 111
Tang Bohu 唐伯虎, 104, 146.
　See also Flirting Scholar
Tang Disheng/Tang Ti-sheng 唐涤生, 105
Tang Xianzu 汤显祖, 104
　Peony Pavilion 《牡丹亭》, 104, 106
Tang Yin 唐寅. *See* Tang Bohu

Tao Qian 陶潜. *See* Tao Yuanming 陶渊明
Tao Yuanming 陶渊明
　"The Life of the Sire of Five Willows"《五柳先生传》, 174
　"Peach Blossom Spring"《桃花源记》, 192, 235, 236
Taoism, 46, 236–37, 246
Tashima, Chris (in *Americanese*), 167n2
Third Cinema, 9
Third literature, 2, 9, 10, 229, 296, 297
Three Kingdoms. See *Romance of the Three Kingdoms*《三国演义》
Tiananmen Incident, 253
Tong, Benjamin R., 36, 46
Tongva, 283, 286, 288, 290
tongxin heli 同心合力, 281
tongzhi 同志
　as common term of address, 278
　as homophobic slur, 16, 266, 278–79
　as honorific reserved for Communist Party members, 278
　as neutral term for sexual minorities, 276, 278–81
　as used by Sun Yat-sen, 278, 281
　See also "Your *Tongzhi* Body" (R. C. Leong)
Tongzhi Conference, 277–78
transcendentalism, 118
translation, 16, 17, 47, 109, 115–16, 133, 159, 167n7, 186, 188, 190, 207, 233, 246, 251, 255, 258n10, 264, 268, 273, 278, 285, 295
transnationalism, 53, 218, 222, 229, 253, 264
transracial adoption
　in "The Photograph," 15, 201, 203, 208–10, 212, 220–22, 223
Trillin, Calvin, 258n7

Tripmaster Monkey (M. H. Kingston), 49, 55, 60n1, 68, 93
  Chinese sources in, 49
  pacifism in, 49, 59
  See also Kingston, Maxine Hong
Trump, Donald, 11
T'sai Yen/Cai Yan/Cai Wenji 蔡琰／蔡文姬, 49, 179, 267, 271, 292n2
Tsing Tao (beer), 266, 269
Tucher, Andie, 196n6
Ty, Eleanor, 9, 10, 298n1

U
Updike, John, 234

V
Vietnam War, 5, 184

W
Waley, Arthur, 111
Walker, Alice
  In Search of Our Mothers' Gardens, 181
  Third Life of Grange Copeland, 43
Wallace, Michele, 77, 94
Walsh, Richard, 134n6
Wang, Dorothy J., 3, 93, 276, 292n1
Wang Ning 王宁
  cultural China (*Wenhua Zhongguo* 文化中国), 9
  "Toward a Third Literature," 9
Wang, Xiaoxue, 51
Wantanna, Onoto. *See* Eaton, Winnifred
"Wanting to Fly" 《想飞》 (Xu Zhimo), 115
Water Margin/Outlaws of the Marsh 《水浒传》, 34, 127
The Wedding Banquet, 71
Welcome House, 212.
  See also Buck, Pearl
Welland, Natasha Su-ling, 113, 114, 116, 130, 131

Wells, H.G., 111, 119
wen 文, 4, 12, 54, 67, 71–74, 76–78, 95, 101–7, 112, 115, 119, 123, 132–33, 136, 142
  and calligraphy, 73–74, 95n4
  four treasures of the *wen* chamber, 74
  as masculine yardstick, 101–3, 133
  and music, 72
  and *ren*, 4
  and women, 103–6, 133
  See also women of letters
wen-jen. *See* wenren
wenren/wenjen 文人, 12, 13, 74, 80, 82, 95, 96n10, 101–8, 119, 132, 136, 142
  and moral character/integrity, 12, 74
  in *Pangs of Love*, 80, 82
  and self-cultivation, 12, 74
  See also poet-scholars
wen-wu 文武 [literary arts and martial arts], 1, 12, 13, 16, 53–55, 67–95, 96n10, 102, 103, 107, 263
  as male prerogatives, 53
  as masculine yardstick, 54
Wen wu shuang quan 文武双全, 96n10
Wenyizaidao 文以载道, 12–13
West Point, 75
West, Cornel, 167n5
West, Rebecca, 119
"What I Saw during *Qingxiang* [Purging of the Village]" 《清乡所见》 (C. Shen), 186, 190–91
What's Wrong with Frank Chin? (C. Choy), 43
White, Hayden, 189
white gaze. *See* Orientalist gaze
whiteness, 75, 79, 80, 84, 219
white supremacy, 39, 204, 211
Whitman, Walt
  Leaves of Grass, 244, 280
  "Song of Myself," 244, 280, 291
  See also *A Free Life*; "Your *Tongzhi* Body"
Williams, Juliet, 18

Wilson, Edmund, 231, 234, 256
The Winged Seed (L. Lee), 14, 143, 152–67
  artistry in, 152, 156, 166
  caring in, 152–55, 166
  Christianity in, 152, 154–56, 165
  father-son relationship in, 152–56, 165, 166
  geographical impact on masculinity in, 155–56, 166
Wittman Ah Sing, 49
wo 我 [I], 178.
  See also *The Woman Warrior*
Wolf, Christa, 34, 54, 192
Wolfe, Thomas, 119
The Woman Warrior (M. H. Kingston), 7, 29, 36–40, 60, 173–96, 225n3, 264–65, 267, 269–72
  as anthropology, 37
  as auto-ethnography, 37
  baochou 报仇 ("report a crime"), 76, 264–65, 274
  as biography, 36
  Chinese sources in, 36–43, 49, 54–55, 188, 189, 264–65
  critical reception of, 7, 29, 36, 37, 48
  feminism in, 36, 37, 41, 48, 59, 187
  gender asymmetry, 33, 273–75
  gender-bending in, 2, 38–43, 48
  "I" in, 178
  Mulan story in, 38–40, 42, 47, 49, 54–55, 188, 189, 192, 264–67, 269, 271–72
  myth in, 38, 90, 189
  pacifism in, 31, 48–49, 59, 189
  self-fashioning in, 35, 37, 40, 49, 180, 187, 189
  Yue Fei story in, 39, 40, 49, 54–55, 188, 189, 264
  See also Kingston, Maxine Hong; "Song of the Sad Guitar"
women, Asian (American)
  as *cainu* 才女 (literary or artistic talents), 14, 102–4, 133

  as China dolls, 12, 102, 206, 224
  as docile, 146, 276
  as dragon ladies, 12, 70, 102
  as literary and artistic talents, 14, 102–4, 105
  sexualization of, 69–72
  subjugation of, 13, 42, 146
  women of letters, 14, 102–5, 108, 121, 127–28, 130–33, 264.
    See also *cainu*
"women's literature," 223
"women's work," 32
Wong, Andrew D., 277–79, 281
Wong, Jade Snow, 30, 180
Wong, Kar-wai
  Happy Together, 71
  In the Mood for Love, 71
Wong, Sau-ling Cynthia 黄秀玲, 8, 35–36, 39, 55, 79, 96n10, 167n6, 192, 286
Wong, Shawn (Hsu) 黄忠雄/徐忠雄
  Aiiieeeee and *The Big Aiiieeeee*, 34, 150
  Americanese (film 2006), 167n2
  American Knees, 14, 17, 143–52, 154, 165
Wong, Sunn Shelley, 36
Woo, Deborah, 36
Woo, John, 71
Wood, Frances, 111, 113, 122
Wooden Fish Songs, 17, 173–95, 218
Woolf, Virginia
  and Ling Shuhua, 130
  A Room of One's Own, 271
The Writer as Migrant (H. Jin), 15, 229–34
  double-voice in, 15, 230–34
  on function of literature, 232, 256
  on historical amnesia, 232
  homeland in, 16, 231–32, 234, 249, 251, 254
  melancholy (melancholia) in, 250, 254
  on nostalgia, 249, 250, 256

See also "An Individual's Homeland"; "The Language of Betrayal"; "The Spokesman and the Tribe"
wu 武, 4, 54, 67, 71–72, 76, 96n6, 101–2, 106–7
and boxing, 76
See also Asian heroic tradition
Wu Bing 吴冰, 18, 219, 292n4
introspection literature/*fansiwenxue* 反思文学, 18
Wu, Ding Yi (Bill Wu), 292n9
Wu, Ting Fang, 218

X
Xiang Yu 项羽, 167n1
and *furen zhiren* [womanly *ren*] 妇人之仁, 167n1
xiaoren 小人, 13
Xie Wanying 谢婉莹. *See* Bing Xin
Xin guixiu pai 新闺秀派. *See* New Boudoir Lady School
Xu, Wenying, 298n1
Xu, Xinjian, 13, 196n4, 196n10
Xu Zhimo/Hsu Tsimou/Hsü Chi-mo/Hsu Chih-mo 徐志摩, 12, 13, 101–33, 175
and Agnes Smedley, 107, 114, 121
in *April Rhapsody* 《人间四月天》, 114
"Art and Life," 21n8, 112, 115, 118
and ascensionist personality, 115
and avant-garde poetry, 108
and Bloomsbury Group, 107, 111, 115, 122
in *Bound Feet and Western Dress*, 107, 119–24, 132
as "Boy Wonder," 108
and Cambridge, 109, 123, 132
"The Cambridge I Know," 111
and Chen Yuan, 130, 131, 133, 133n2
as "Chinese Byron," 112
as "Chinese Shelley," 14, 112, 125, 129
Confucian culture, critique of, 115
and *Crescent Monthly* 《新月》, 109, 112
and Ding Ling, 112, 113, 225n3
in *East Goes West*, 14, 21n9, 107, 116–19
in *East Wind: West Wind*, 125
and E.M. Forster, 107, 121–23, 133
"Farewell Again, Cambridge" 《再别康桥》, 109–11
and G.L. Dickinson, 107, 109, 111, 114, 121–22, 123, 127, 133
and Hu Shi, 17, 107, 111, 116, 121
and Icarus syndrome, 115
and Katherine Mansfield, 112, 113, 116, 121
and Keats, 108, 117
in *Letter from Peking*, 125, 135n7, 136n15
and Liang Qichao, 17, 107, 133, 134n3
and Liang Sicheng, 113, 133n2
and Lin Huiyin, 107, 109, 113, 116, 121, 133, 133–34nn2–4, 136n18
and Ling Shuhua, 107, 109, 111–13, 116, 121, 130, 131, 133, 133n2, 136n18
and Lu Xiaoman, 107, 113, 121, 134nn5
and Lu Xun, 118, 132
as modernist *wenren*, 108–16, 117, 123, 132, 142
and Pearl Buck, 13, 114, 121
"A Second Farewell to Cambridge," 《再别康桥》, 109–11
and Shen Congwen, 17, 107, 112, 113, 121

Xu Zhimo/Hsu Tsimou/Hsü Chi-mo/ Hsu Chih-mo 徐志摩 (*cont.*)
  as Sinophone writer, 17
  and Tagore, 109, 121, 134n4
  and Younghill Kang, 118, 121, 132
  in Pearl Buck's writing, 13
  in *Pearl of China*, 107, 124–33
  "Wanting to Fly" 《想飞》, 115

Y

Yalom, Marilyn, 36
Yam Kim Fai/Ren Jianhui 任剑辉, 105, 106
Yam Pak Building/Ren Bai Lou 任白楼, 105
Yamamoto, Hisaye
  "The Legend of Miss Sasagawara," 3, 154, 155, 196n11
Yamamoto, Traise, 35
Yan Geling 严歌苓, 9, 10
Yang, Bojun, 104
Yang, Caroline H., 298n1
Yang Quan, 114
Yao, Steven G., 276
Yeats, William Butler, 82, 193, 248
YMCA, 74, 77
Yogi, Stan, 219, 295
Yoshihara, Mari, 134n6, 202, 203, 205, 209, 223
"Your *Tongzhi* Body" (R. C. Leong), 16, 163, 264, 266–82, 286, 290–91
  as *blazon*, 277
  Buddhism in, 163, 164, 280
  gender-bending in, 280–81
  Guanyin in, 280–81
  1998 conference in Hong Kong, 277
  slanted allusion in, 264, 278, 291
  Sun Yat-sen in, 278, 281
  thousand-armed bodhisattva in, 280
  Whitman in, 280
  See also *tongzhi*
Yu, Timothy, 258n7, 292n1
Yue Cheng 岳诚, 124
Yue Fei 岳飞, 39–40, 49, 55, 188–89, 192, 264
Yueyang Lou Ji 《岳阳楼记》 (Fan Zhongyan 范仲淹), 246
Yichou-wannian 遗臭万年 [leaving a stench for ten thousand years], 289
Yun, Lisa, 298n1
Yung, Bell, 133n1
Yung Wing/Rong Hong 容闳, 30, 35, 195n1, 196n3, 218
  My Life in China and America, 195n1, 218

Z

Zhang Fei 张飞, 45, 57, 58.
  See also *Romance of the Three Kingdoms*
Zhang, Hang, 257n5
Zhang, Qing, 279
Zhang, Ya-Jie, 36–37
Zhang Youyi 张幼仪. See Chang Yu-i
Zhao Baisheng 赵白生, 188, 190, 196n12
Zhao Jibin 赵纪彬, 167n1
Zhao Wenshu 赵文书, 37, 43, 55, 56, 190, 263, 290
zhiji 知己 (intimate companion), 103
Zhong, Xueping, 68
Zhou, Xiaojing, 292n1
Zhu Yingtai 祝英台, 128.
  See also *Butterfly Lovers*
Zhuang Zi 庄子, 46

The manufacturer's authorised representative in the EU is Springer Nature Customer Service Centre GmbH, Europaplatz 3, 69115 Heidelberg, Germany. If you have any concerns regarding our products, please contact ProductSafety@springernature.com

Printed and bound by CPI Group (UK) Ltd, Croydon, CR0 4YY
23/03/2026
02076458-0005